Communications
in Computer and Information Science

1719

Rationale

The CCIS series is devoted to the publication of proceedings of computer science conferences. Its aim is to efficiently disseminate original research results in informatics in printed and electronic form. While the focus is on publication of peer-reviewed full papers presenting mature work, inclusion of reviewed short papers reporting on work in progress is welcome, too. Besides globally relevant meetings with internationally representative program committees guaranteeing a strict peer-reviewing and paper selection process, conferences run by societies or of high regional or national relevance are also considered for publication.

Topics

The topical scope of CCIS spans the entire spectrum of informatics ranging from foundational topics in the theory of computing to information and communications science and technology and a broad variety of interdisciplinary application fields.

Information for Volume Editors and Authors

Publication in CCIS is free of charge. No royalties are paid, however, we offer registered conference participants temporary free access to the online version of the conference proceedings on SpringerLink (http://link.springer.com) by means of an http referrer from the conference website and/or a number of complimentary printed copies, as specified in the official acceptance email of the event.

CCIS proceedings can be published in time for distribution at conferences or as post-proceedings, and delivered in the form of printed books and/or electronically as USBs and/or e-content licenses for accessing proceedings at SpringerLink. Furthermore, CCIS proceedings are included in the CCIS electronic book series hosted in the SpringerLink digital library at http://link.springer.com/bookseries/7899. Conferences publishing in CCIS are allowed to use Online Conference Service (OCS) for managing the whole proceedings lifecycle (from submission and reviewing to preparing for publication) free of charge.

Publication process

The language of publication is exclusively English. Authors publishing in CCIS have to sign the Springer CCIS copyright transfer form, however, they are free to use their material published in CCIS for substantially changed, more elaborate subsequent publications elsewhere. For the preparation of the camera-ready papers/files, authors have to strictly adhere to the Springer CCIS Authors' Instructions and are strongly encouraged to use the CCIS LaTeX style files or templates.

Abstracting/Indexing

CCIS is abstracted/indexed in DBLP, Google Scholar, EI-Compendex, Mathematical Reviews, SCImago, Scopus. CCIS volumes are also submitted for the inclusion in ISI Proceedings.

How to start

To start the evaluation of your proposal for inclusion in the CCIS series, please send an e-mail to ccis@springer.com.

Kottilingam Kottursamy · Ali Kashif Bashir ·
Utku Kose · Annie Uthra
Editors

Deep Sciences for Computing and Communications

First International Conference, IconDeepCom 2022
Chennai, India, March 17–18, 2022
Revised Selected Papers

 Springer

Editors
Kottilingam Kottursamy [iD]
SRM Institute of Science and Technology
Chennai, India

Ali Kashif Bashir [iD]
Manchester Metropolitan University
Manchester, UK

Utku Kose [iD]
Süleyman Demirel University
Isparta, Türkiye

Annie Uthra [iD]
SRM Institute of Science and Technology
Chennai, India

ISSN 1865-0929   ISSN 1865-0937 (electronic)
Communications in Computer and Information Science
ISBN 978-3-031-27621-7   ISBN 978-3-031-27622-4 (eBook)
https://doi.org/10.1007/978-3-031-27622-4

This Springer imprint is published by the registered company Springer Nature Switzerland AG
The registered company address is: Gewerbestrasse 11, 6330 Cham, Switzerland

Preface

This volume contains the refereed, selected, and presented papers at the First International Conference on Deep Sciences for Computing and Communications (IconDeepCom-2022) held on March 17th and 18th 2022. The conference only took place online, via Zoom, at SRM Institute of Science and Technology (formerly known as SRM University), India.

About the Institution

SRM Institute of Science and Technology (formerly known as SRM University) was established in 1985 and is one of the top-ranking Universities and premier engineering destinations in India. It is located on four campuses located in Tamil Nadu, at Kattankulathur, Ramapuram, Vadapalani, and Thiruchrapalli, and Delhi NCR Campus, Modinagar, Ghaziabad, Uttar Pradesh, with over 55,000 students and 3,000 faculty members. It offers a wide range of programs to students applying for undergraduate, post-graduate, and doctoral programs in Engineering, Management, Medicine & Health Sciences, Law, Science & Humanities, and Agricultural Sciences. SRMIST is engaged in nurturing minds through a rich heritage of academic excellence. Essentially a hub of bustling student activities, the green and beautiful Kattankulathur campus has been a second home to thousands of students in their journey to pursue higher education. With 165 MoUs and 60-plus international collaborations, SRMIST offers a Semester Abroad Program (SAP) for students. Over 150 students are sponsored by 35 foreign universities such as MIT, Carnegie Mellon, UC Davis, Warwick, and Western Australia.

Scope of the Conference

The 27 full papers included in these proceedings were selected among 97 submissions in a double-blind review process. The conference invited various articles involving cutting-edge techniques and innovative fields. The conference displayed various articles on Deep Convolution Neural Networks, Generative Adversarial Networks, Deep Belief Networks, Extreme Learning Methods, Transfer Learning, and much more.
The contributions were organized in topical sections as follows:

1. Deep Learning and Vision Computing
2. Deep Recurrent Neural networks (RNNs) for Industrial Informatics
3. Classification and Regression Problems for Communication Paradigms
4. Extended AI for Heterogeneous Edge Computing

The conference invited three major keynote addresses on

1. Internet of Things A Paradigm Shift, by Ali Kashif Bashir MMU, UK
2. Digital Twin and Internet of Health Things, by Utku Kose, SDU, Turkey
3. AI for Healthcare Informatics, by Nancy Jane, Anna University, India

We thank the authors for their submissions, members of the PC, and external reviewers for their efforts in providing exhaustive reviews. We thank our sponsors and partners: Career Labs, Byjus, and various participating institutes in and around the globe. We thank the honorable external session chairs, Veningston K, NIT, J&K, India, Sudhakar, VIT-AP, India, Sudha, VIT, Tamil Nadu, India and N. Prakash, B. S. Abdur Rahman Crescent Institute of Science and Technology, India. We are grateful to Amin Mobasheri, Alla Freund, and colleagues from Springer LNCS and CCIS editorial boards for their kind and helpful support.

January 2023

Kottilingam Kottursamy
Ali Kashif Bashir
Utku Kose
Annie Uthra

Organization

Program Chairs

Ali Kashif Bashir	Manchester Metropolitan University, UK
Revathi Venkataraman	SRM Institute of Science and Technology, India
Vijayan Sugumaran	Oakland University, USA
Vijayakumar Varadarajan	The University of New South Wales, Sydney, Australia
Kottilingam Kottursamy	SRM Institute of Science and Technology, India
Jun Wu	Shanghai Jiao Tong University, China
Amir Hussain	Edinburgh Napier University, UK
Raheel Nawaz	Manchester Metropolitan University, UK
Gunasekaran Raja	Anna University, India
P. D. D. Dominic	Universiti Teknologi PETRONAS, Malaysia

Industry Forum Chairs

Sheeba Backia Mary	Lenovo, Motorola Mobility, Germany
Keping Yu	Hosei University, Japan

International Advisory Committee

Atta ur Rehman Khan	Ajman University, UAE
Ultu Kose	Süleyman Demirel University, Turkey
Nirmala Shenoy	Rochester Institute of Technology, USA
Gunasekaran Manahoran	Howard University, USA
Satheesh	Sunchon National University, South Korea
Mehdi Shadaram	The University of Texas at San Antonio, USA
Zing-Ming Zhong	Tsinghua University, China
Korhan Cengiz	Trakya University, Turkey
Xavier Fernando	Ryerson University, Canada
A. S. M. Kayes	La Trobe University, Australia
Melvin Johnson	Google Inc., USA

National Advisory Committee

Jayashree P	Anna University, India
Janakiraman	Pondicherry University, India
Ponsy R. K. Sathia Bhama	Anna University, India
Kishore Kumar	NIT Warangal, India
Aravamudhan	PEC, India
Vinayak Shukla	CMC, Vellore, India
Yamin Khan	Microsoft, India
Purusothaman	GCT Coimbatore, India
Preethi	Anna University Coimbatore, India
Sudhakar T	VIT, India
Murugan K	VIT, India
Nandhakumar R	VIT, India
Muthurajkumar	Anna University, MIT, India

Additional Reviewers

R. Palson Kennedy
R. Kaladevi
A. Gayathri
Sreedevi
Lakshmi Narayanan
P. R. Jasmine Jenni
Rajaganapathy Dhanajayan
Priya
P. Solainayaki
Paul Rodrigues
Shanthi Bala
Zayaraz Godandapani
Yasir Ahmed

T. Sheela
Vaiyapuri Govindasamy
S. Surendran
A. Manju
P. V. Pramila
M. Thirumaran
Manoharan R
Selvaradjou Ka
Hung Bui
Sankar Ganesh
Prakash
Revathi
Suburam

Chief Patrons

T. R. Paarivendhar (Chancellor)	SRMIST
Ravi Pachamoothoo (Pro-chancellor (Administration))	SRMIST

P. Sathyanarayanan   SRMIST
   (Pro-chancellor (Academics))
R. Shivakumar (Vice President)   SRMIST
C. Muthamizhchelvan   SRMIST
   (Vice-chancellor)

Advisory Council

S. Ponnusamy (Registrar)   SRMIST
T. V. Gopal (Dean (CET))   SRMIST
Bernaurdshaw Neppolian (Dean   SRMIST
   (Research))
D. John Thiruvadigal (Chair)   School of Applied Sciences, SRMIST
C. Lakshmi   SRMIST

Organizing Committee

M. S. Abirami   C. Amuthadevi
M. Uma   E. Poongothai
G. Senthil Kumar   S. Amudha
A. Alice Nithya   A. Jackulin Mahariba
M. Ferni Ukrit   M. Maheswari
Shiny Angel   S Aruna
Selvakumarasamy   Sasi Rekha Sankar
Siva   S. Sadagopan
Hariharan   Vimaladevi

Organizers

Kottilingam K   CINTEL, SRMIST, KTR, Tamil Nadu, India
N. Arivazhgan   CINTEL, SRMIST, KTR, Tamil Nadu, India
S. Karthick   CINTEL, SRMIST, KTR, Tamil Nadu, India

Sponsors

Career Labs, Byjus

Contents

Extended AI for Heterogeneous Edge

Classification and Regression Problems for Communication Paradigms

Comparative Analysis of Book Recommendation System Based on User Reviews Using Hybrid Methods

Mounika Addanki[1](✉)[iD] and Saraswathi Selvarajan[2]

[1] Department of Computer Science and Engineering, Puducherry Technological University,
Puducherry, India
`mounikaaddanki1704@pec.edu`
[2] Department of Information Technology, Puducherry Technological University, Puducherry,
India
`swathi@pec.edu`

Abstract. In recent times, Recommendation System (RS) performs a main position in assisting clients to discover the best books of their interest. A novel solution for recommending accurate books to the user was proposed by applying an integration of the Collaborative Filtering (CF) and Content-Based Filtering (CBF) with Popularity Index (PI) methods. It recommends books to the registered users in the system and also to the new users. Firstly, the input data which is document level reviews transferred from analysis stage to analyzes the sentiment of the user and removes noisy data. Now, grouping of reviewers is done dependent on the kind of review they are given and their personal details such as age, region and sex by utilizing MySQL. CBF system and CF system are used to filter reviews. In additional, PI technique is also used to retrieve data from popular books by ranking in the database. Finally, after filtering, Recommender suggests the books to the users based on their interests accurately which satisfies the customer with an average accuracy of 85%.

Keywords: Popularity Index · Recommender system · User interest · Filtering methods · Grouping · Accuracy

1 Introduction

Sentiment Analysis (SA) is the zone which oversees choices, responses similarly as feelings, which is created from messages, being extensively used in domains like web mining, information mining and web-based broadcasting investigation. Opinions can be positive, negative, or impartial [1, 2].

Recommender frameworks are a derived class of data selecting structure that attempt to anticipate 'rating' or 'inclination' that a customer would accommodate for an item (like films, music or books) or web-based component (e.g., individuals or gathering) they had not yet thought of, utilizing a method worked from the attributes of an item (CBF techniques) or the client's web-based background (CF techniques). RS is a framework which gives proposals to a client. The RS is to create significant proposals to an assortment of clients for objects or items that may activity them. RS are described as the techniques utilized to expect the rating single person will accommodate for an object or web-based component. These objects can be cafes, motion pictures, books, and items on which single client have several inclinations. These inclinations are being expected to use dual procedures: CBF method which includes qualities of an object and CF method which reflects consumer's past direct to decide. In CF, companions are selected who will make proposals since they share similar assessments history with the objective client. One companion who have similar assessments to the main client may not be a trustworthy marker for a particular object. Along with these, the earlier file of the companion of producing a trustworthy idea likewise should be think about which is coordinated by dependability of a companion. To screen previous files of a recommender recognition framework comes into single client who really allocate popularity rankings to the companions. Applications: films, books, reports, song CDs, administrations and different items, for example, programming games.

The proposed recommendation system which uses different approaches to give best accuracy rate to recommend books to the already registered users and the new users with their interests. Either the user can search for their interested books by logging or without registering their details. The recommendation system can be used which is an integration of one technique namely Popularity index and two filtering approaches namely Collaborative and Content based recommended systems.

2   Literature Review

We studied various research papers related to different filtering methods in RS also their disadvantages.

Avi Rana et al. [3] developed a recommendation framework which used CF to provide high recommendation accuracy. JS index is calculated on few books. It is a proportion of normal clients who appraised saw books separated by the amount of clients who have evaluated seen the books exclusively. Higher the no. of normal clients larger will be the Jaccard Similarity thus best suggestions are given. Jaccard Similarity will show up first of the suggested books list is ranked.

Ricardo Mitollo Bertani et al. [4] proposed to work on the method involved with creating proposals to be specific a collaborative, diffusion-based hybrid algorithm has been developed in the writing to tackle the issue of sparse information, which influences the nature of proposals. This method depends on sparse information issue. This group of methods will not variate clients as indicated by their pre-owned forms. In this article, another method is developed for getting to know the client profile and furthermore producing customized suggestions through diffusion, joining oddity with the fame of objects outperformed than existing algorithm in the same settings.

Jing Zhang et al. [5] proposed to represent client inclinations to make it extra appropriate for customized suggestion that uses object concern components to build client inclination systems and joins these systems with CF that incorporates concern attributes into a customized suggestion and furthermore helps to recognizing the implied connections among clients, which are ignored by the traditional CF technique performed best comparatively.

Yen-Liang Chen et al. [6] proposed to analyze clients' inclinations for motion pictures by utilizing a CF technique to anticipate the clients' film appraisals. Then made 2 film records for every client, where one is the motion pictures, the client enjoys that is more or genuine rating and another is the films the client would rather avoid that is less or genuine rating. Depends on these two film records, a client positive form and a client negative form was taken. This proposed method will suggest to clients' films that are generally like their positive and negative forms.

M. Sridevi et al. [7] proposed to produce result for the previously mentioned issue which works dependent on CF which at first classifies the clients dependent on demographic elements, then at that point, utilizing k-means grouping technique groups the divided clients dependent on client rating lattice. It sorts the motion pictures in the enhancing form of client's inclinations estimated by MAE (Mean Absolute Error) demonstrated best thought about against customary techniques.

Prem Melville et al. [8] are developed an approach namely CB to upgrade existing client information, and give customized ideas through CF. This substance supported CF; they initially make a pseudo client evaluations vector for each client in the data set. Books will be suggested to the clients from the data set.

M.S. Pooja Malhotra et al. [9] are addressed another methodology for suggesting books to the purchasers by thought to be numerous boundaries like substance of the book and nature of the book. They considered CF and evaluations of different purchasers. Giving more grounded suggestions, it likewise utilizes associative model.

Lalita Sharma et al. [10] clarified the different difficulties with respect to the methods that are utilized for producing the suggestion. The primary recommendation methods they have developed are CF, CBF and Hybrid systems.

Nirav M. Khetra et al. [11] are developed a method: CF for social adapted RS which consists of a client is addressed by a client ordinariness vector which can show the clients inclination on every sort of products and it chooses neighbors of clients by estimating client's comparability.

Cach N. Darn et al. [12] introduced and assessed a proposal approach that coordinates SA into CF techniques. It depends on a versatile design, which incorporates further developed methods for feature extraction and DL techniques in SA to enhance the RS work.

Dhiman Sarma et al. [13] proposed a framework utilized the K-means Cosine Distance method to gauge distance and Cosine Similarity method to discover Similarity between the book groups. The outcome infers those proposals, in light of a specific book, are more precisely compelling than a client-based RS.

Praveena Mathew et al. [14] introduced Book Recommendation System (BRS) in view of joined highlights of CF, CBF and ECLAT to deliver proficient and successful recommendation. So, they proposed a hybrid technique which combines above mentioned methods to help the RS to suggest the book in view of the purchaser's interest.

Ramakrishnan et al. [15] proposed and contrasted different methods with include implicit data into RS. It considers explicit ratings to clients contingent upon the implicit data given by clients to explicit books utilizing different methods.

The greater part of the researcher selects CF to the create recommendation framework. CF needs an immense measure of continuous client information that isn't practical for most recommender frameworks. The significant disadvantages of a CF recommender framework are sparsity and cold-start problems. These problems can be taken out utilizing a kernel-based fuzzy method that scored a 95% precision rate.

The CBF technique was utilized to suggest products in light of the Similarity among articles. The significant disadvantage of this technique is that it overlooks present clients' ratings while proposing new products. In any case, client rating is relevant for suggesting new books or diaries. As the client rating data is absent in the reports, the CBF has low exactness in the present book or diary proposal. So, RS utilized an integration of PI with two filtering approaches namely Collaborative and Content based recommended systems.

3 Proposed System

RS are programming devices that provide ideas of products to be suggested to clients. The ideas intend to work with clients in numerous decision-making methods, for example, what products to buy, what movies to watch, for sure books to peruse. RS are utilized to create great proposals to a gathering of clients for books that match to their interest. This recommendation processes in two phases. First grouping of reviewers and the recommendation system is done secondly using various approaches and integration of different methods.

3.1 Grouping of Reviewers

The readers are combined dependent on the kind of review they are specified from the outset and afterward dependent on the readers age, region and sex they are combined utilizing MySql. The inquiries and the groups might be of multiple groups (Fig. 1).

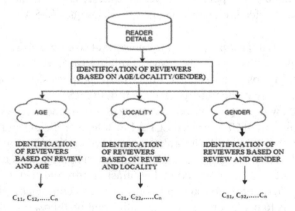

Fig. 1. Identification of reviewers (based on age/locality/gender)

3.2   Recommendation of Books

The development of the web has given the accessible admittance to various objects. In the course of recent years, RS have been increasingly more viable in assisting individuals with recognizing their favored assets from an enormous quantity of applicant objects. The Recommendation System evaluates the inclinations of clients who have recently exposed an interest in specific books, to suggest books which higher suit the objective client's inclinations. It assists individuals with saving a lot of shopping time. The fundamental benefit of CF methodology is that they need no data about clients or books and, in this way, they can be utilized as a rule. Also, the more clients connect with books the more current suggestions become exact: for a proper arrangement of clients and books, new connections documented after some time deliver new data and make the framework increasingly powerful.

RS provide a rundown of suggestions in various methods - through different techniques like CBF, CF, PI and hybrid approach. On account of CF technique, construct the method from different perspectives like clients' previous conduct, which incorporates books bought by the client earlier just as the rating given by the clients for a specific book. This methodology assists with anticipate the fascinating book that the client might have. CBF works dependent on the depiction or content of a specific book. Popularity Index (PI) works based on Ranking model and it may suggest book to the user who just signed up. Hybrid approach will give better results based on the input data type and user expected output (Fig. 2).

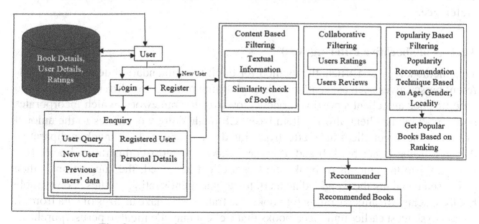

Fig. 2. Architecture for proposed recommendation system

The above flow diagram explains about the book recommendation system. New user should first register and login to the system where already the member of the system can login directly into the system as the details are already existing with the system while registering. Next the flows continue to the enquiry level based in the query given by the user and the database checks for two different data namely new user and registered user. According to the data of the user, the reply is moved to the next level for the reply to the request. Next level is filtering method which contains various filtering techniques like content based, collaborative based and popularity index. In CBF, based on textual information and checking of similarity of books filtering is made. In CF, based on user ratings and user reviews filtering is made. In PI, based on popularity of books and its rankings filtering is made. After the filtering by above mentioned methods or integration of methods the user query moves to the recommender and the recommender suggests the user interested and suitable books which should be satisfied. In this way recommendation of books are made depends on the client's preferences. Finally, integration of these three recommendation systems with popularity index is used and compared to check the best accuracy to recommend books through recommender.

3.2.1   Content Based Filtering (CBF)

CBF framework chooses and decides books dependent on the connection and interrelation among the substance of the books in the database. For our situation, article portrays the substance of the book and bought history of a specific book by the client. It involves a progression of attributes from the book to suggest extra books with comparative substance. Substance of the book will be given as an outline to the client. So, client can undoubtedly discover the book they need to utilize or purchase. CBF sift the whole quantity of books from the database dependent on the substance of the book, where client is intrigued to peruse. RS utilizes CBF for performing the partition and filtering of books from different books which is having comparable sort of substance. Additionally, this assists with finding the substance of bought history from the perusing information. These prompts bring about a best suggestion of books to the client dependent on their preference.

3.2.2   Collaborative Filtering (CF)

This methodology constructs the method for book recommendation dependent on different perspectives such as, sentiment through rating provided by different clients for a specific book and client's previous conduct towards the framework, which incorporates books read by the client already. Item based CF methodology examines to the amount of books, the target client have effectively rated and evaluates how much comparative they are to the target book b and afterward chooses k-most comparative books $\{b_1, b_2,....,b_k\}$ to the amount of books the target client has rated, the suggestion is then processed by taking the weighted mean of the target client's rating on these comparable books. Clients will allocate rating for books; the framework make utilizes of data from all clients to suggest earlier unnoticed books that a client may identical to peruse/purchase. CF method assists with anticipating and suggest the fascinating books as indicated by client necessities.

3.2.3   Popularity Based Filtering

Popularity based recommendation system works basically by using the books which are in trend right now. The methodology used to this recommendation system is calculating popularity model, identification is done by generating score and the rank based on the top ranked books are recommended for the users. One basic method y computes the unidentified accesses in the lattice z is to utilize the benchmark method. The fundamental thought is that an unidentified rating of client m on the substance n, z_{mn}, could be processed dependent on the mean rating the client m provides for all substance rated by the client, the mean rating the substance n has collected and the mean of all rating shown in formula (1).

Baseline estimate for z_{mn} is;

$$z_{mn} = x + y_m + y_n \qquad (1)$$

where,

x = average rating of all client's total books

y_m = rating bias of client m = average of all ratings by client m − x

y_n = rating bias of book n = average of all ratings on book n − x

In the concluding recommendation, the request for the book is taken into account dependent on the book which consists best rating evaluate to rest of books and organize in decreasing direction.

4 Result and Analysis

4.1 Dataset Description

The Book information have been accumulated from the kaggle site. Insights concerning almost 1097 books were gathered and put away in the data set. The reader information was gathered from the fake name generator, to keep away from the repetition of the names; the user's name, user id, password, email, phone number, age, gender and locality is generated for each reader. The readers are generated with different countries. All these details about the reader are then stored into the database. The reviews gathered are in the document level. These reviews are gathered from the amazon site. The reviews constitute a 5 GB dataset. Total number of Reviews = 307.

The following Table 1 consists of reader related attributes such as attribute name and its description.

The following Table 2 consists of categories and count in which the books are present in the dataset.

The following Table 3 consists of the total number of review count and the count of reviews used for training and testing.

The accuracy is determined dependent on precision, f-measure & recall.

Precision: It provides the precision of the classifier. It is the proportion of quantity of efficiently anticipated positive reviews to the entire quantity of reviews anticipated as positive.

$$\text{Precision} = \frac{TP}{TP + FP} \qquad (2)$$

Recall: It estimates the fulfillment of the classifier. It is the proportion of quantity of efficiently anticipated positive reviews to the real quantity of positive reviews existing in the corpus.

$$\text{Recall} = \frac{TP}{TP + FN} \qquad (3)$$

Table 1. Reader related attributes

S.No.	Attribute Name	Description
1.	User id	Id of registered user
2.	User name	Name of registered user
3.	Password	Password of registered user
4.	Email	Mail id of registered user
5.	Phone number	Phone number of registered user
6.	Age	Age of registered user
7.	Gender	Gender of registered user
8.	Locality	Location of registered user

Table 2. Book categories

CATEGORY	COUNT	CATEGORY	COUNT	CATEGORY	COUNT
action	87	Crime	51	musical	45
adventure	25	Document	160	mystery	79
animation	44	Drama	94	romance	65
children	71	Fantasy	91	Sci-fi	56
Comedy	57	Horror	59	Thriller	68
war	51	modern	70	literature	109

Table 3. Total number of reviews

Sentiment	Training	Testing	Total Count
Positive	140	38	178
Negative	105	24	129

F-measure: It is the harmonic average of precision & recall. F-measure will have high-quality worth as 1 and most noticeably terrible worth as 0.

$$\text{F-measure} = \frac{2 * Precision * Recall}{Precision + Recall} \qquad (4)$$

Accuracy: It is one of the maximum frequent overall work assessment parameters and it is determined as the proportion of quantity of efficiently anticipated reviews to the quantity of general quantity of reviews existing in the corpus.

$$\text{Accuracy} = \frac{TP + TN}{TP + TN + FP + FN} \tag{5}$$

Confusion Matrix (CM) is produced to tabularize the overall work of any classifier. This lattice displays the connection among accurately and incorrectly anticipated reviews. In CM, TP (True Positive) addresses the quantity of positive book reviews that are accurately anticipated though FP (False Positive) provides the incentive for quantity of positive book reviews which can be anticipated as negative. Also, TN (True Negative) is quantity of negative reviews accurately anticipated and FN (False Negative) is quantity of negative reviews anticipated as positive.

From Table 4, it is evident that the performance of the proposed hybrid approach (Collaborative Filtering with Popularity Index) is better compared to others in terms of accuracy, precision, recall, and F-measure. This is because the model combines the advantages of Collaborative filtering and popularity index which helps to recommend users the most appropriate books based on their age, gender and region in lesser memory and time. The updates during this technique are sparsed in the process, and so, a large range of datasets can also be computed efficiently.

Table 4. Accuracy calculation

Method	Polarity of reviews	Precision	Recall	F-Measure	Accuracy
Popularity	Positive	0.78	0.62	0.58	78.81%
Index (PI)	Negative	0.68	0.61	0.71	
Content based	Positive	0.86	0.69	0.79	78.48%
Filtering (CBF)	Negative	0.76	0.81	0.69	
Collaborative	Positive	0.81	0.86	0.85	89.19%
filtering (CF)	Negative	0.75	0.72	0.86	
Content based	Positive	0.81	0.74	0.72	87%
Filtering +	Negative	0.72	0.69	0.68	
Popularity					
Index					
(CBF+PI)					
Collaborative	Positive	0.86	0.72	0.79	92%
filtering +	Negative	0.76	0.61	0.62	
Popularity					
Index (CF+PI)					

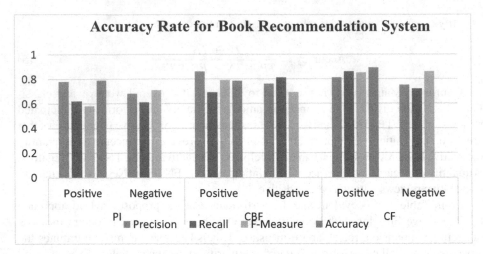

Fig. 3. Graphical representation of accuracy calculation

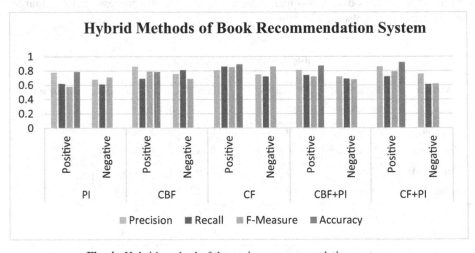

Fig. 4. Hybrid method of the various recommendation systems

The Fig. 3 depicts that the collaborative filtering approach shows better result, when compared to other filtering methods for the given input data.

The Fig. 4 depicts that the integration of collaborative filtering with popularity index shows better results, when compared to other filtering approaches.

5   Conclusion

RS is generally utilized from the past many years. Book RS is suggesting books to the clients that match to their preferences. This framework will save the information of the books which clients have purchased previous and observe the kind of book from clients purchasing history. After grouping, books are recommended to the users based on filtering methods such as content based, collaborative filtering and popularity recommendation algorithms which helps to recommend users the most appropriate books based on their age, gender and region. This also includes a comparative study of filtering methods like collaborative and content-based hybrid with popularity Index which obtained an average accuracy of 85%. This framework may supportive for many individuals just as understudies who requires the better books accessible from the data set for both general and scholarly reason. In addition, we would like to implement on a large dataset and compare the results with various traditional methods.

References

1. Srujan, K.S., Nikhil, S.S., Raghav Rao, H., Karthik, K., Harish, B.S., Keerthi Kumar, H.M.: Classification of Amazon book reviews based on sentiment analysis. In: Bhateja, V., Nguyen, B.L., Nguyen, N.G., Satapathy, S.C., Le, D.-N. (eds.) Information Systems Design and Intelligent Applications. Advances in Intelligent Systems and Computing, vol. 672, pp. 401–411. Springer, Singapore (2018). https://doi.org/10.1007/978-981-10-7512-4_40
2. Scheicher, R.B., Sinoara, R.A., Felinto, J.C., Rezende, S.O.: Sentiment classification improvement using semantically enriched information. In: Proceedings of the ACM Symposium on Document Engineering 2019, pp. 1–4 (2019). https://doi.org/10.1145/3342558.3345410
3. Rana, A., Deeba, K.: Online book recommendation system using collaborative filtering (with Jaccard similarity). J. Phys. Conf. Ser. **1362**(1), 012130 (2019). https://doi.org/10.1088/1742-6596/1362/1/012130
4. Bertani, R.M., Bianchi, R.A., Costa, A.H.R.: Combining novelty and popularity on personalised recommendations via user profile learning. Expert Syst. Appl. **146**, 113149 (2020). https://doi.org/10.1016/j.eswa.2019.113149
5. Zhang, J., Peng, Q., Sun, S., Liu, C.: Collaborative filtering recommendation algorithm based on user preference derived from item domain features. Phys. A Stat. Mech. Appl. **396**, 66–76 (2014). https://doi.org/10.1016/j.physa.2013.11.013
6. Chen, Y.L., Yeh, Y.H., Ma, M.R.: A movie recommendation method based on users' positive and negative profiles. Inf. Process. Manag. **58**(3), 102531 (2021). https://doi.org/10.1016/j.ipm.2021.102531
7. Sridevi, M., Rao, R.R.: Decors: a simple and efficient demographic collaborative recommender system for movie recommendation. Adv. Comput. Sci. Technol. **10**(7), 1969–1979 (2017)
8. Melville, P., Mooney, R.J., Nagarajan, R.: Content-boosted collaborative filtering for improved recommendations. In: Proceedings of the Eighteenth National Conference on Artificial Intelligence (AAAI 2002), pp. 187–192 (2002)
9. Rajpurkar, S., Bhatt, D., Malhotra, P., Rajpurkar, M.S.S., Bhatt, M.D.R.: Book recommendation system. Int. J. Innov. Res. Sci. Technol. **1**(11), 314–316 (2015)
10. Sharma, L., Gera, A.: A survey of recommendation system: research challenges. Int. J. Eng. Trends Technol. **4**(5), 1989–1992 (2013)
11. Khetra, N.M., Yagnik, S.B.: A collaborative approach for web personalized recommendation system. Int. J. Eng. Dev. Res. **2**(4) (2014). ISSN: 2321-9939
12. Dang, C.N., Moreno-García, M.N., Prieta, F.D.L.: An approach to integrating sentiment analysis into recommender systems. Sensors **21**(16), 5666 (2021). https://doi.org/10.3390/s21165666

13. Sarma, D., Mittra, T., Hossain, M.S.: Personalized book recommendation system using machine learning algorithm. Int. J. Adv. Comput. Sci. Appl. **12**(1) (2021). https://doi.org/10.14569/IJACSA.2021.0120126
14. Mathew, P., Kuriakose, B., Hegde, V.: Book recommendation system through content based and collaborative filtering method. In: 2016 International Conference on Data Mining and Advanced Computing (SAPIENCE), pp. 47–52. IEEE (2016). https://doi.org/10.1109/SAPIENCE.2016.7684166
15. Ramakrishnan, G., Saicharan, V., Chandrasekaran, K., Rathnamma, M.V., Ramana, V.V.: Collaborative filtering for book recommendation system. In: Das, K.N., Bansal, J.C., Deep, K., Nagar, A.K., Pathipooranam, P., Naidu, R.C. (eds.) Soft Computing for Problem Solving. AISC, vol. 1057, pp. 325–338. Springer, Singapore (2020). https://doi.org/10.1007/978-981-15-0184-5_29
16. Pan, Y., Wu, D., Luo, C., Dolgui, A.: User activity measurement in rating-based online-to-offline (O2O) service recommendation. Inf. Sci. **479**, 180–196 (2019). https://doi.org/10.1016/j.ins.2018.11.009
17. Shirude, S.B., Kolhe, S.R.: Improved hybrid approach of filtering using classified library resources in recommender system. In: Mandal, J.K., Sinha, D. (eds.) Intelligent Computing Paradigm: Recent Trends. SCI, vol. 784, pp. 1–10. Springer, Singapore (2020). https://doi.org/10.1007/978-981-13-7334-3_1
18. Kanetkar, S., Nayak, A., Swamy, S., Bhatia, G.: Web-based personalized hybrid book recommendation system. In: 2014 International Conference on Advances in Engineering & Technology Research (ICAETR-2014), pp. 1–5. IEEE (2014)
19. Wen, G., Li, C.: Research on hybrid recommendation model based on PersonRank algorithm and TensorFlow platform. J. Phys. Conf. Ser. **1187**(4), 042086 (2019). IOP Publishing
20. Al-Otaibi, S., et al.: Customer satisfaction measurement using sentiment analysis. Int. J. Adv. Comput. Sci. Appl. **9**(2), 106–117 (2018). https://doi.org/10.14569/IJACSA.2018.090216
21. Bakshi, R.K., Kaur, N., Kaur, R., Kaur, G.: Opinion mining and sentiment analysis. In: 3rd International Conference on Computing for Sustainable Global Development (INDIACom), IEEE, pp. 452–455 (2016)
22. Bandana, R.: Sentiment analysis of movie reviews using heterogeneous features. In: Proceedings of the 2nd International Conference on Electronics, Materials Engineering & Nano-Technology (IEMENTech), Kolkata, India (2018). https://doi.org/10.1109/IEMENTECH.2018.8465346
23. Cambria, E., Schuller, B., Xia, Y., Havasi, C.: New avenues in opinion mining and sentiment analysis. IEEE Intell. Syst. **28**(2), 15–21 (2013). https://doi.org/10.1109/MIS.2013.30
24. Can, E.F., Ezen-Can, A., Can, F.: Multilingual sentiment analysis: an RNN-based framework for limited data. In: Proceedings of ACM SIGIR 2018 Workshop on Learning from Limited or Noisy Data (LND4IR 2018), Ann Arbor, Michigan, USA (2018)
25. Chakravathy, A., Deshmukh, S., Desai, P., Gawande, S., Saha, I.: Hybrid architecture for sentiment analysis using deep learning. Int. J. Adv. Res. Comput. Sci. **9**(1), 735–738 (2018). https://doi.org/10.26483/ijarcs.v9i1.5388
26. Chen, T., Xu, R., He, Y., Wang, X.: Improving sentiment analysis via sentence type classification using BiLSTM-CRF and CNN. Expert Syst. Appl. **72**, 221–230 (2017). https://doi.org/10.1016/j.eswa.2016.10.065
27. Guerreiro, J., Rita, P.: How to predict explicit recommendations in online reviews using text mining and sentiment analysis. J. Hosp. Tour. Manag. **43**, 269–272 (2020). https://doi.org/10.1016/j.jhtm.2019.07.001
28. Sánchez-Moreno, D., Batista, V.F.L., Vicente, M.D.M., González, A.B.G., Moreno-García, M.N.: A session-based song recommendation approach involving user characterization along the play power-law distribution. Complexity **2020**, 1–13 (2020)

29. Revankar, O.S., Haribhakta, Y.: Survey on collaborative filtering technique in recommendation system. Int. J. Appl. Innov. Eng. Manag. **4**(3), 85–91 (2015)
30. Färber, M., Jatowt, A.: Citation recommendation: approaches and datasets. Int. J. Digit. Libr. **21**(4), 375–405 (2020). https://doi.org/10.1007/s00799-020-00288-2

Health Care Support for Elderly People in Resource Poor Areas

R. Kaladevi[1] ⓘ, A. Revathi[2(✉)] ⓘ, and A. Gayathri[3]

[1] Department of Computer Science and Engineering, Saveetha Engineering College, Chennai 602105, Tamilnadu, India
[2] Department of Computational Intelligence, SRM Institute of Science and Technology, Kattankulathur 603 203, Tamilnadu, India
revathia1@srmist.edu.in
[3] Department of Computer Science and Engineering, Saveetha School of Engineering, Saveetha Institute of Medical and Technical Sciences (SIMATS), Chennai, India

Abstract. Healthcare is an essential service as a well as high revenue yielding sector. There has been increasing demand for chronic care in rural area. On the other hand, the Healthcare industry is combating against workforce crisis due to inadequate infrastructure, shortage of doctors, specialists, and medical assistants. The phenomenal growth of computing and connectivity has redefined the Health-care environment with the help of Information and Communication Technologies (ICT). Life span of people has increased with technological support and statistics reveals that by 2030 the population of elderly people (above 65 years) will become double. This automatically increases chronic diseases and aging related ailments in the society. After doing careful analysis this chapter aims to suggest better algorithm for which considers people above 50 years of age who need continuous medical support due to the increase of chronic diseases and insufficient medical assistance. The Linear classifier SVM and parallel ensemble Random Forest Algorithm are applied appropriately to predict the disease. The patient who suffer from more than one ailment may take multiple and repetitive pills which results in adverse side effects. The proposed system coordinates these issues through decision support system and reduces unnecessary medications and side effects. The proposed system classifies diseases and their severity and suggests medications without any conflict. This will reduce human effort, time, cost, unnecessary medication and side effects.

Keywords: Healthcare · Support vector machine · Random forest algorithm · Elderly people

1 Introduction

The population census conducted in the year 2011 reports that there are nearly 104 million elderly persons (aged 60 years and above) i.e. 51 million males and 53 million females in India. Among two-third of the elderly population are in villages and almost half of them are in lower social economic conditions [1]. The additional years of elderly

K. Kottursamy et al. (Eds.): IconDeepCom 2022, CCIS 1719, pp. 16–24, 2023.
https://doi.org/10.1007/978-3-031-27622-4_2

people are not always healthy and it automatically leads to chronic diseases and aging related ailments. It is due to less availability of medical personnel, equipment, physical location, economic status and so on. Apart from the above reasons, pandemic virus like COVID-19 made the entire world into pathetic situation via lockdown, self-quarantine and isolation. We need a multisector approach to address the underlying causes of gender and socio-economic inequalities. Ultimately, it will increase the mode of providing health care services to remote areas using online via laptops and smart phones. Subsequent paragraphs, however, are indented.

World Health Organization (WHO) report states that the overall need of healthcare workforce were 60.4 million in the year 2013 whereas the factual amount is 43 million. AI, machine learning and big data plays a vital role in health care services [2, 3]. It facilitates disease prediction, diagnosis, treatment, self-management, and support through care takers or robots. Machine intelligence eases the above tasks and reduces the burden of a physician in diagnosing the disease of a patient [4].

Though voluminous work has been reported on the health care services for the remote areas, only discrete references are available on the development of proficient techniques which includes many aspects such as optimizing medications, avoiding side effects and supreme care. Diabetes is a common chronic disease and its severity damages tissues in heart, eyes, kidney and nerves [5]. Heart diseases are highly prone among elders. Kidney related diseases are life threatening and cost consuming diseases. The proposed work identifies suitable machine leaning algorithm such as Support Vector Machine and Random Forest algorithm for classification and prediction of diseases.

This chapter is organized as follows. Section 2 investigates the existing Machine learning based Healthcare system to assess the recent improvements. In Sect. 3, proposed work is elaborated with the help of different data sets. The Result section shows the experimental environment and examines the performance of the proposed method. Finally, the Conclusion section concludes the progress of our proposed work and suggests directions for future enhancement.

2 Related Work

The traditional theoretical hypothesis based statistical methods are replaced by machine learning algorithms which recognizes pattern present in the data and reveals the association that exists among them. The existence of multiple diseases like prolonged sugar, Hypertension, heart problem, kidney disease, impaired metabolism in elderly people increases the possibility of adverse effects due to multiple medication interactions. The appropriate machine learning algorithm helps in proper classification and diagnosis of diseases [6]. Some of the recent machines learning approaches in healthcare systems are discussed in this section.

David and Zaki suggested that the understanding of AI technologies related to medical domain is essential for all healthcare professionals [7]. Machine learning, natural language processing, robotic process automation and deep learning becomes indispensable for all healthcare professionals. Guoguang Rong et al. (2020) have made a comprehensive survey to recognize the incredible potential of Artificial Intelligence in biomedicine and to keep track of novel scientific undertakings [8]. They concluded that the application of Artificial Intelligence is still in its early stage and the application and its scope will continue to evolve exponentially.

Vijayaprasad and Satish Kumar (2015) aim to define the extents and elements of trust in health care services in resource deprived locations [9]. Assured treatment regardless of payment and time, perceived competence, readiness to admit the downsides of healthcare, loyalty and respect to physician are considered as the primary influences of trust in healthcare. In addition, health consciousness, attitude of the physician, personal care of the patients, is identified as the key elements which determine the level of trust in health care sector.

Rapid growth of computational power, data storage and parallelism contributed to optimized high level feature generation and semantic interpretation of input data [10]. The detailed analysis of relative merit and probable hazards of Deep Learning (DL) in health informatics and the primary applications of DL in medical imaging and informatics, bioinformatics and public health are explored evidently in the article.

Mahsa Madani et al. (2020) proposed a novel algorithm using Markov Blankets (MB) in Bayesian Networks (BN) [11]. The case study was conducted on diabetic patients having different characteristics, patients who suffer from numerous comorbidities and patients who take multiple pills in parallel. The proposal aims to optimize the medications intake by doing careful analysis of medication intake of similar patients. However, the comparative effectiveness of medications is not examined accurately in a big data environment.

The investigation on predicting medication adherence and non-adherence in Korean patients with heart failure by applying Support Vector Machine was conducted by Youn-Jung Son et al. [12]. The selective power of SVM is compared with Bayesian Network, neural network and logistic regression. Accuracy of 77.6% is achieved with the help of simulated SVM model for the HF (Heart Failure) data set. However the multivariate analysis to study medication adherence is not supported by the application of SVM model.

Zahangior Alam et al. (2019) proposed a generalized methodology which emphasizes selection of highly ranked features [4]. The authors applied Random forest algorithm, Bayes Network and Support Vector Machine algorithm on the subset of selected models to explore the performance of machine learning algorithms. The accuracy of Bayes network and SVM was reported as 0.975 and 0.99 on breast cancer data set. But the performance fall significantly with Bupa data set as 0.69 for both SVM and Random Forest Algorithm. They proposed a generalized methodology which outperforms with all medical data sets. The authors identified important features with the help of k-fold cross validation by applying various feature ranking selection algorithms which plays a key role in generalization.

The detailed review of literature on diverse machine learning algorithms and data sets forms the foundation and the background knowledge for identification of proper machine learning algorithm and other important factors to be considered.

3 Proposed Work

The proposed work aims to provide healthcare service to elderly people who reside in resource poor area. People of age fifty and above are considered as elderly people in this case study. As per the forecast of WHO India may have Ninety Eight million adults with type 2 diabetes by the year 2030. Jha et al. (2006) stated in his paper that cardiovascular disease is major cause of death in older people [5]. They are affected by various chronic diseases such as high blood pressure, digestive disorders, kidney problem, rheumatism, vision problem etc. [13, 14]. Hence the proposed work mainly considers heart disease, diabetes and kidney disease which are most common in elderly people. The appropriate dataset available in Kaggle data repository are taken and filtered with elder people constraints (age ≥ 50). The proper machine learning algorithm classifies the disease from the given data set and based on the size of training set and experience learnt, the classification algorithm fine tunes itself.

Application of ML is almost in all field like speech recognition, face recognition, natural language processing, automation, computer vision, E-commerce, medicine, information retrieval, marketing, manufacturing and so on. Generally, ML consists of supervised learning, unsupervised learning and reinforcement learning techniques [15]. The proposed work considers supervised learning algorithms for efficient classification of diseases by specifying classes with labels for learning. The most appropriate machine learning algorithms such as Support Vector Machine (SVM) and Random Forest are applied based on the data set to improve accuracy in disease prediction. The work flow of machine learning algorithm is shown in Fig. 1.

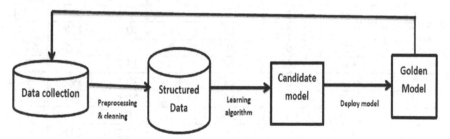

Fig. 1. Work flow of machine learning algorithm

Preliminary Data Processing to Apply Machine Learning
To build accurate machine learning models the data needs to be encoded so that the algorithm can interpret the data easily. The following steps show the process of preparing data for the machine learning algorithm.

Data Collection
The data set available in Kaggle data repository for heart disease, kidney disease and diabetes are considered for proposed process. To meet the problem requirements, datasets are filtered with age greater than or equal to 50. The data set for experimental purpose includes 1025 Heart disease patient record with 76 attributes, Diabetes dataset with

size 768 and 8 attributes and 400 records of Kidney disease patients with 25 attributes (Figs. 2, 3 and 4).

Snippet of Dataset

age	sex	Cp	trestbps	chol	fbs	restecg	thalach	exang	oldpeak	slope	ca	thal
52	1	0	125	212	0	1	168	0	1	2	2	3
53	1	0	140	203	1	0	155	1	3.1	0	0	3
70	1	0	145	174	0	1	125	1	2.6	0	0	3
61	1	0	148	203	0	1	161	0	0	2	1	3
62	0	0	138	294	1	1	106	0	1.9	1	3	2
58	0	0	100	248	0	0	122	0	1	1	0	2
58	1	0	114	318	0	2	140	0	4.4	0	3	1
55	1	0	160	289	0	0	145	1	0.8	1	1	3
54	1	0	122	286	0	0	116	1	3.2	1	2	2
71	0	0	112	149	0	1	125	0	1.6	1	0	2

Fig. 2. Snippet of heart disease dataset

No.of Pregnancies	Glucose	Blood Pressure	Skin Thickness	Insulin	BMI	Diabetes Pedigree Function	Age
6	148	72	35	0	33.6	0.627	50
2	197	70	45	543	30.5	0.158	53
8	125	96	0	0	0	0.232	54
10	139	80	0	0	27.1	1.441	57
1	189	60	23	846	30.1	0.398	59
5	166	72	19	175	25.8	0.587	51
11	143	94	33	146	36.6	0.254	51
13	145	82	19	110	22.2	0.245	57
5	109	75	26	0	36	0.546	60
4	111	72	47	207	37.1	1.39	56

Fig. 3. Snippet of diabetics dataset

age	bp	sg	al	su	rbc	pc	pcc	...	htn	dm	cad	appet	pe	ane
62	80	1.01	2	3	normal	normal	notpresent	...	no	yes	no	poor	no	yes
51	80	1.01	2	0	normal	normal	notpresent	...	no	no	no	good	no	no
60	90	1.015	3	0			notpresent	...	yes	yes	no	good	yes	no
68	70	1.01	0	0		normal	notpresent	...	no	no	no	good	no	no
52	100	1.015	3	0	normal	abnormal	present	...	yes	yes	no	good	no	yes
53	90	1.02	2	0	abnormal	abnormal	present	...	yes	yes	no	poor	no	yes
50	60	1.01	2	4		abnormal	present	...	yes	yes	no	good	no	yes
63	70	1.01	3	0	abnormal	abnormal	present	...	yes	yes	no	poor	yes	no
68	70	1.015	3	1		normal	present	...	yes	yes	yes	poor	yes	no
68	80	1.01	3	2	normal	abnormal	present	...	yes	yes	yes	poor	yes	no

Fig. 4. Snippet of kidney disease dataset

3.1 Classification Using Support Vector Machine (SVM)

SVM algorithm is one of the widely used supervised learning strategies which classify data points in the N-dimensional space using hyperplane. Hyperplane classifies training and testing data based on labels also called as support vectors [16]. In N-dimensional (ND) region, the hyperplane is a line separating data into two classes where each class lies in one side of hyperplane which is shown in Fig. 5. Hyperplanes act as decision boundaries to classify the data and number of features decides the dimension of the hyperplane. Margin is the perpendicular distance between the hyperplane and the training samples. Obviously SVM tries to find out the optimal hyperplane that gives minimum distance margin to the trained data set [17].

On the basis of careful review carried out, Support Vector Machine (SVM) has proven its performance in big data and healthcare applications which include various disease prediction, diagnosis, gene analysis etc. [18].

Hence the proposed work applies SVM algorithm for the different disease data sets. The classification performance achieved by SVM algorithm is analyzed using the correct prediction of disease from the given dataset. Accuracy is calculated using the following formula 1.

$$Classification\ Accuracy = \frac{Number\ of\ true\ predictions\ made\ by\ the\ classifier}{Total\ number\ of\ true\ predictions} \quad (1)$$

SVM shows 90.48% classification accuracy for the heart disease dataset. For the diabetes dataset it shows 65.21% classification accuracy and 92% for kidney disease dataset.

3.2 Classification Using Random Forest Algorithm

Random Forest is an ensemble algorithm as a combination of many decision trees used for both classification and regression. It constructs multitude of decision tree randomly and finalizes best solution among the decision trees through voting. Random Forest supports high dimensional data and faster in training the input data. It is robust to nonlinear data and outliers. On the average this algorithm has low bias and moderate variance.

This algorithm selects random data and constructs many decision trees. Most of the tree produces correct prediction of the class for majority of the data. Also many researches support the performance benefits of Random Forest Algorithm with medical data [4, 19]. For the heart disease dataset the classification accuracy of Random Forest is 92%. For diabetics dataset it predicts disease with 66.6% accuracy and accuracy for kidney disease dataset is 96%.

3.3 Results and Discussion

To address the objective of the proposed system, three datasets i.e. heart disease, diabetes and kidney disease have been taken into consideration in the age group of 50 and above. For classification of these datasets two supervised machine learning algorithm i.e. SVM and Random Forest Algorithm are considered to predict the classification accuracy of the given dataset. The performances of the classifiers are depicted in Fig. 5.

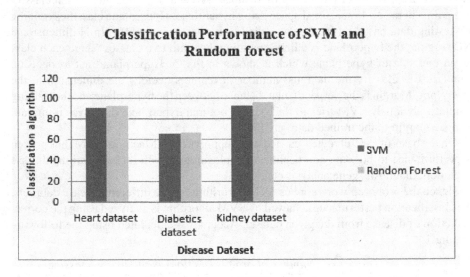

Fig. 5. Classification performance of SVM and random forest algorithm

The blood glucose level is the key component in diagnosing diabetes. The important organs such as eyes, heart, kidney, nerves and blood cells are affected by diabetes. The data set of the proposed work correlates with each other by including blood sugar level as the key attribute. Kidney disease dataset chosen for study contains sugar, random blood glucose, and diabetes mellitus attributes and heart disease dataset includes fasting blood sugar attribute.

The chronic kidney disease gradually leads to heart related issues and vice versa is also true. Reduced blood flow to the kidneys due to heart problem affects kidneys.

Angiotensin-converting enzyme (ACE) inhibitors are the suggested drug for heart disease, but it will act adversely when the person is dehydrated. This may lead to chronic kidney disease.

Standard protocol does not work for a person has chronic disease with various complications. Monitoring patients by expert team with individual care and attention will help them to avoid unwanted medicines and side effects of medications intake.

4 Conclusion

Life expectancy of people is increased with the help of technological and medical advancements. It ultimately leads to the necessity of increased healthcare facilities. Huge availability of medical data and technologies like AI and machine learning reduces and eases the tasks of healthcare professionals. Still the availability of correct data, relevant attributes, and selection of algorithm for processing those data are the tedious task. The proposed work considered the most critical chronic disease i.e. diabetes, heart and kidney diseases that exist commonly among elder population. SVM and Random Forest Algorithms are considered to classify the disease from the dataset. The classification performance of Random Forest is comparatively better than SVM due to its ensemble nature and size of the dataset. For the small sized diabetes dataset both algorithms produced less accuracy. People who are suffered from heart or kidney aliments along with diabetes need careful suggestion and treatment from expert team comprised of nephrologists, endocrinologists, nutritionists, and cardiologists. This kind of expert's treatment can reduce repeated pills and side effects of medications.

References

1. Alam, M., Karan, A.: Elderly health in India: dimensions, differentials, and over time changes. United Nations Population Fund, New Delhi (2010). Building knowledge base on ageing in India: a series of programmatic and research studies
2. Tran, B.X., et al.: Global evolution of research in artificial intelligence in health and medicine: a bibliometric study. J. Clin. Med. **8**(3), 360 (2019)
3. Witten, I.H., Frank, E.: Data Mining: Practical Machine Learning Tools and Techniques, 2nd edn. Morgan Kaufmann, San Fransisco (2005)
4. Alam, M.Z., Rahman, M.S., Rahman, M.S.: A random forest based predictor for medical data classification using feature ranking. Inform. Med. Unlocked **15**, 100180 (2019)
5. Jha, P., et al.: Prospective study of one million deaths in India: rationale, design, and validation results. PLoS Med. **3**(2), e18 (2006)
6. Raghupathi, W., Raghupathi, V.: An empirical study of chronic diseases in the United States: a visual analytics approach to public health. Int. J. Environ. Res. Public Health **15**(3), 431 (2018)
7. Wiljer, D., Hakim, Z.: Developing an artificial intelligence–enabled health care practice: rewiring health care professions for better care. J. Med. Imaging Radiat. Sci. **50**(4), S8–S14 (2019)
8. Rong, G., Mendez, A., Assi, E.B., Zhao, B., Sawan, M.: Artificial intelligence in healthcare: review and prediction case studies. Engineering **6**(3), 291–301 (2020)
9. Gopichandran, V., Chetlapalli, S.K.: Trust in healthcare: need for perspectives from developing healthcare settings. Asian Bioeth. Rev. **7**(1), 98–108 (2015)

10. Ravi, D., et al.: Deep learning for health informatics. IEEE J. Biomed. Health Inform. **21**(1), 4–21 (2016)
11. Hosseini, M.M., Zargoush, M., Alemi, F., Kheirbek, R.E.: Leveraging machine learning and big data for optimizing medication prescriptions in complex diseases: a case study in diabetes management. J. Big Data **7**(1), 1–24 (2020). https://doi.org/10.1186/s40537-020-00302-z
12. Son, Y.J., Kim, H.G., Kim, E.H., Choi, S., Lee, S.K.: Application of support vector machine for prediction of medication adherence in heart failure patients. Healthc. Inform. Res. **16**(4), 253–259 (2010)
13. Angra, S.K., Murthy, G.V., Gupta, S.K., Angra, V.: Cataract related blindness in India & its social implications. Indian J. Med. Res. **106**, 312–324 (1997)
14. Kumari, R.S.S.: Socio-economic conditions, morbidity pattern and social support among elderly women in a rural area. Medical College; Thiruvananthapuram, Kerala (2001)
15. Huddleston, S.H., Brown, G.G.: Machine learning. Informs analytics body of knowledge (2018). https://doi.org/10.1002/9781119505914.ch7
16. Wang, P.W., Lin, C.J.: Support vector machines. Data classification: algorithms and applications (2014). https://doi.org/10.1201/b17320
17. Gholami, R., Fakhari, N.: Learn more about support vector machine support vector machine: principles. Parameters, and applications quantitative structure-activity relationship (QSAR): modeling approaches to biological applications technical aspects of brain rhythms and sp. (2017)
18. Janardhanan, P., Sabika, F.: Effectiveness of support vector machines in medical data mining. J. Commun. Softw. Syst. **11**(1), 25–30 (2015)
19. Rallapalli, S., Suryakanthi, T.: Predicting the risk of diabetes in big data electronic health records by using scalable random forest classification algorithm. In: 2016 International Conference on Advances in Computing and Communication Engineering (ICACCE), pp. 281–284. IEEE (2016)

Finding Best Voting Classifier for Diabetic Disease Classification

S. Meganathan⬭, A. Sumathi(✉)⬭, V. Bharanika, P. Hemalakshmi, and M. Kamali

SRC, SASTRA Deemed to be University, Thanjavur, Tamil Nadu, India
{meganathan,sumathi}@src.sastra.edu

Abstract. Diabetes is a metabolic disorder that affects a large amount of people globally. Among diabetic disorders, diabetes mellitus is the most common ailment. Currently, while treating diabetes, hospitals gather required facts via suitable medical tests and appropriate treatment is administered primarily based on prognosis. Early detection of diabetes is important to prevent diabetes from progressing into a chronic illness. Machine learning helps to identify and predict diabetic even at beginning stage. An ensemble machine learning technique helps to get better classification and higher accuracy to predict from diabetic data set. Different voting classifier techniques are present for ensemble machine learning. The present paper proposes a suitable voting classifier for diabetic classification that can be used to predict diabetes with better accuracy. Analysis of the obtained results, show that hard-voting method provides greater accuracy than soft-voting method, the three diabetes data sets used for the study. Implementation is done by applying ML algorithms on three different diabetes data sets obtained from various repositories. ML-algorithms like Logistic Regression, Ada Boost, Decision Tree, Cat Boost, Naïve Bayes, SVM, XG Boost, RF, KNN, MLP, Bagging Classifier, and Gradient Boost Classifier are used.

Keywords: Ensemble voting classifier · Hard voting · Soft voting · Diabetic classification

1 Introduction

Diabetes is a metabolic disease that shoots up blood sugar. Many complications arising out of this can be prevented if early prediction is possible. Machine Learning (ML) techniques are very efficient in predicting diabetes datasets and present a reliable outcome from the existing data. Prediction uses traditional classification techniques. However, an ensemble machine learning technique yields higher classification accuracy in predicting datasets. Comparative approach is also carried out with ensemble technique to further improve accuracy of classification. The aim behind ensemble learning is to build multiple models instead of a single model to predict the target or future. An ensemble approach can help to provide better predictions and to achieve greater performance than any single model. In this paper, several combined learning approaches are used to reduce complexity and achieve higher accuracy.

K. Kottursamy et al. (Eds.): IconDeepCom 2022, CCIS 1719, pp. 25–33, 2023.
https://doi.org/10.1007/978-3-031-27622-4_3

This paper attempts to predict diabetes data set with finer accuracy by ensembling five ML algorithms [5, 10] Logistic Regression (LR), Ada Boost, and Random Forest, Naive Bayes and Decision Tree and implementing both soft-voting and hard-voting classifiers. For this purpose, along with the existing work, various diabetes data sets from repositories are chosen and different voting classifiers have been applied on the data sets in an attempt to predict diabetes [7] more accurately. When ensembling five algorithms with soft and hard-voting classifiers, it is found that accuracy is enhanced by the ensemble with a hard-voting classifier. Three distinctive diabetes [7, 9] data sets from diverse repositories help to confirm the performance of the suggested work.

2 Literature Survey

Rani and Jyothi (2016) [1] proposes an ensemble approach using J48, KNN, NB, ANN, NB, filtered classifier and parameter selection to improve the performance and reached 77.01% accuracy. Bashir et al. (2017) [2] proposed an ensemble of ID3, CART and C4.5 achieved 76.5%. Adil Husain and Muneeb H. Khan (2018) [3] proposed an ensemble model with Random Forest, Gradient Boosting, KNN, Logistic Regression and improved the overall performance using combined model and obtained an AUC of 0.75, which indicates higher performance. Cut Fiarni, Evasaria M. Sipayung and SitiMaemunah (2019) [4] proposed a novel methodology by ensembling of Decision Tree, Naïve Bayes, C4.5 and k-means achieved 68% accuracy.

3 Methodology

3.1 Data Description

This paper uses three diabetes datasets from varied (UCI, Kaggle) repositories. Pima Indian Diabetes Dataset (dataset 1) contains 768 rows, 9 feature columns, Dataset of diabetes-Frankfurt Hospital (dataset 2) contains 2000 rows, 9 feature columns and Diabetes Detection Dataset (dataset 3) contains 1500 rows and 9 feature columns. These nine feature columns of the data sets [11] contain data on glucose levels, pregnancy month, fold thickness of triceps, skin plasma, BP, age of patients, quantity of insulin, pedigree function, Body Mass Index (BMI) and a target (0 or 1).

3.2 Data Pre-processing

Data pre-processing is a critical process to arrange information into a useful and systematic layout, so that it can moved on to processing by ML algorithms. Checking for null values is one of the foremost methods used for information pre-processing. After which, a general scalar is used to standardize the pre-processed information. The numerous data sets considered may contain many values that lack numerous attributes. The lacking value or attribute is filled using a specific imply. Figure 1 below shows the various steps involved in data pre-processing.

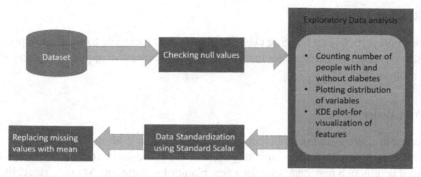

Fig. 1. Steps in data pre-processing

4 Model Architecture

4.1 Ensemble Learning

Ensemble models use ensemble learning to provide better results by combining the useful attributes of different algorithms. They are considered valuable as they help to increase the performance of an anticipating model significantly.

4.2 Voting Classifiers

The Voting classifier method is a combined classifier which takes input as multiple classifiers and classifies the disease based on majority voting. It is classified as Soft and hard-voting. Soft voting method takes the input data based on the probabilities of all the forecasts made by different classifiers and weighs them in relation to each classifier. In the latter, the output or results of all the single models alone are taken out, combined and average value of the combined output is shown as the final output value. Additionally, hard voting categorizes the data based on class labels and weighs them in relation to each classifier.

4.3 Logistic Regression

Logistic regression approach containing linear learning rules and used to invest dichotomous results (y = zero or 1). It predicts in phrases of possibilities and forecasts the likelihood of an occasion. This set of rules map every fact and factors the use of logistic features to offer an s-fashioned curve.

4.4 Naïve Bayes

Naive Bayes is a convenient and unique algorithm that allows to construct rapid ML-models to make brief predictions. As it makes predictions based on the probability of an object, it is called a stochastic classifier. In order to derive the likelihood of a particular category, the general probabilities and terms are used.

4.5 Random Forest

Random Forest [6, 8] is a bagging classifier that uses DT models to forecast improved results. It develops numerous trees in a bootstrapped manner and applies it to every tree in the training data set.

4.6 Ada Boost

At every stage, the Ada boost technique uses sampling to add up to n weights to the incorrect classified points. The weightage points are increased exponentially stage by stage that results in a new data set with a new plane of separation. At every stage, these planes are applied to the data set that handles all the errors.

4.7 Decision Tree

Decision tree is used for tackling classification, arrangement and relapse issues. It resembles a tree, wherein a terminal node represents the outcome, the intermediate node represents the features and the branches represent the decision rules. It has two hubs, the first one is decision node and the second one is leaf node. The decision hubs are used to resolve choices and various branches are the results of that decision tree. Highlighting of choices is performed using the given data set. It presents a graphical representation of all the possible or potential answers for an issue based on a given condition.

4.8 Workflow

The implementation follows an extended approach by ensembling five machine learning techniques—decision tree, ada boost, Naive Bayes, logistic regression and RF with a soft voting and hard voting classifier. It is observed through results that the accuracy of the hard-voting classifier is higher than that of the soft-voting classifier. Figure 2 below presents the sequence of tasks followed during the implementation.

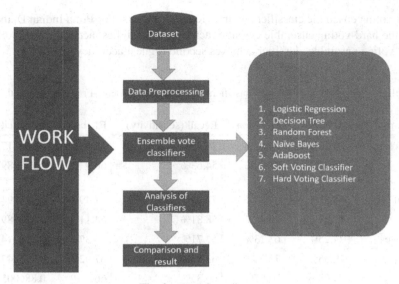

Fig. 2. Workflow diagram

5 Experimental Results

Table 1. Performance measures of various classifiers for Pima Indian diabetes dataset

Algorithms	Accuracy	Precision	Recall (sensitivity)	F1 score	Specificity
DecisionTree	74.89%	60.0%	64.86%	62.34%	0.796178
LogisticRegression	77.92%	70.91%	52.7%	60.47%	0.898089
RandomForest	78.79%	71.93%	55.41%	62.6%	0.898089
KNN	77.06%	65.67%	59.46%	62.41%	0.853503
NaiveBayes	76.19%	66.67%	51.35%	58.02%	0.878981
MLP	78.35%	68.18%	60.81%	64.29%	0.866242
SVM	75.32%	65.45%	48.65%	55.81%	0.878981
XG-Boost	78.35%	66.67%	64.86%	65.75%	0.847134
BaggingClassifier	76.62%	66.67%	54.05%	59.7%	0.872611
CatBoost	76.19%	66.1%	52.7%	58.65%	0.872611
Gradient BoostClassifier	77.06%	66.15%	58.11%	61.87%	0.859873
AdaBoost	72.73%	67.97%	54.05%	55.94%	0.815287
Classifier: Softvoting	79.22%	70.31%	60.81%	65.22%	0.878981
Hardvoting	**79.65%**	**72.88%**	**58.11%**	**64.66%**	**0.898089**

Dataset Link: https://www.kaggle.com/datasets/uciml/pima-indians-diabetes-database

Table 1 shows the performances of various classifiers for Pima Indian Diabetes Dataset from the analysis hard voting ensemble classifier achieves higher accuracy than soft voting ensemble classifier and individual classifiers. For Pima Indian Diabetes Dataset the hard-voting ensemble classifier achieves first highest accuracy i.e. 79.65%. The soft voting ensemble classifier achieves second highest accuracy (79.22%).

Table 2. Performance of various classifiers for dataset of diabetes-Frankfurt hospital

Algorithms	Accuracy	Precision	Recall (sensitivity)	F1 score	Specificity
DecisionTree	83.21%	74.62%	76.43%	75.52%	0.866817
Logistic Regression	76.27%	68.89%	54.63%	60.93%	0.873589
RandomForest	85.82%	83.85%	72.03%	77.49%	0.928894
KNN	77.69%	70.45%	58.81%	64.11%	0.873589
NaiveBayes	74.25%	63.13%	57.71%	60.3%	0.827314
MLP	79.55%	72.5%	63.88%	67.92%	0.875847
SVM	79.03%	73.07%	60.35%	66.1%	0.886005
XG-Boost	83.21%	78.99%	68.72%	73.5%	0.906321
Bagging Classifier	86.19%	85.12%	71.81%	77.9%	0.935666
CatBoost	75.37%	70.67%	46.7%	56.23%	0.900677
Gradient-Boost Classifier	84.1%	82.13%	67.84%	74.31%	0.924379
AdaBoost	84.78%	79.48%	74.23%	76.77%	0.901806
Classifier: Softvoting	86.34%	80.87%	78.19%	79.51%	0.905192
Hardvoting	**86.72%**	**85.38%**	**73.35%**	**78.91%**	**0.935666**

Dataset Link: https://www.kaggle.com/datasets/johndasilva/diabetes

Table 2 shows the performances of various classifiers for dataset of diabetes Frankfurt Hospital from the analysis hard voting ensemble classifier achieves higher accuracy than soft voting ensemble classifier and individual classifiers. For dataset of diabetes Frankfurt Hospital, the hard-voting ensemble classifier achieves first highest accuracy i.e. 86.72%. The soft voting ensemble classifier achieves second highest accuracy (86.34%).

Table 3 presents the performances of various classifiers for Diabetes Detection Dataset from the analysis hard voting ensemble classifier achieves higher accuracy than soft voting ensemble classifier and individual classifiers. For Diabetes Detection Dataset the hard-voting ensemble classifier achieves first highest accuracy i.e. 83.8%. The bagging classifier achieves second highest accuracy (83.6%).

Figure 3 represents accuracy, precision, recall, sensitivity, F1 score and specificity of Soft and Hard voting in for Pima Indian Diabetes Dataset respectively. Results show that the accuracy received when using the hard-voting classifier is almost greater than the results obtained from the soft voting.

Table 3. Performance measures of various classifiers of diabetes detection dataset

Algorithms	Accuracy	Precision	Recall (sensitivity)	F1 score	Specificity
DecisionTree	78.73%	71.2%	63.77%	67.28%	0.865356
LogisticRegression	77.24%	71.8%	55.36%	62.52%	0.886536
RandomForest	82.7%	78.6%	68.12%	72.98%	0.903177
KNN	75.05%	66.32%	55.36%	60.35%	0.853253
NaiveBayes	75.65%	65.72%	60.58%	63.05%	0.835098
MLP	78.53%	67.76%	65.8%	66.76%	0.836611
SVM	82.7%	70.48%	64.35%	67.27%	0.859304
XG-Boost	77.53%	77.95%	72.75%	75.26%	0.892587
BaggingClassifier	83.6%	69.07%	38.84%	49.72%	0.909228
CatBoost	73.06%	67.05%	51.3%	58.13%	0.868381
Gradient BoostClassifier	83.0%	77.53%	71.01%	74.13%	0.892587
AdaBoost	74.65%	75.07%	74.2%	74.64%	0.871407
Classifier: Softvoting	82.7%	77.32%	70.14%	73.56%	0.892587
Hardvoting	**83.8%**	**79.74%**	**70.72%**	**74.96%**	**0.906203**

Dataset Link: https://www.kaggle.com/competitions/rn-2019-diabetes/overview

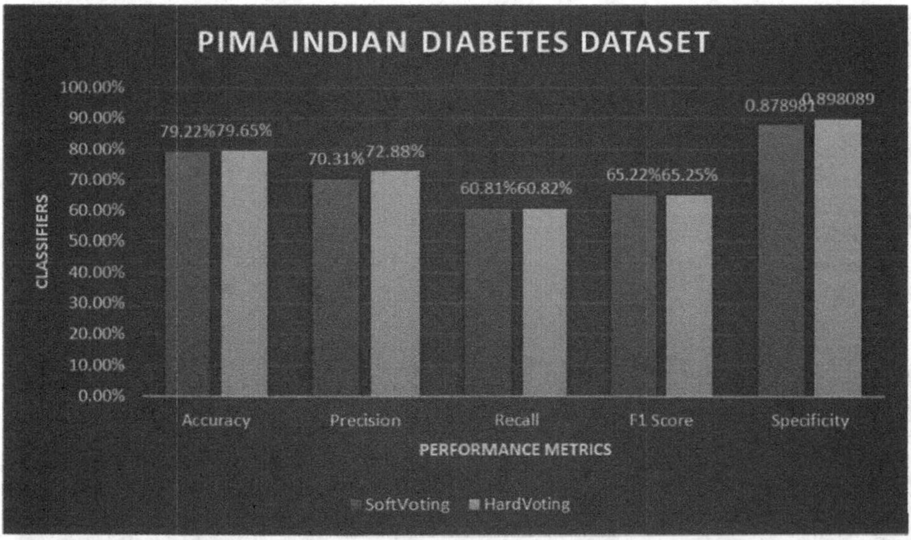

Fig. 3. Comparision of performance metrics of Pima Indian diabetes dataset

Figure 4 represents accuracy, precision, recall, sensitivity, F1 score and specificity of Soft and Hard voting in dataset of diabetes Frankfurt Hospital respectively. Results

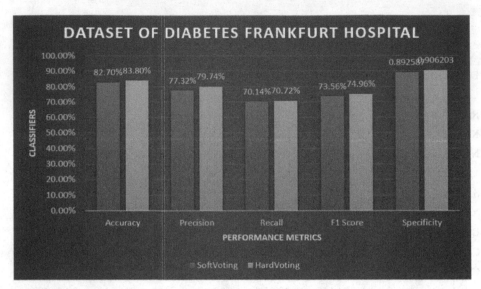

Fig. 4. Comparision of performance metrics dataset of diabetes-Frankfurt hospital

show that the accuracy received when using the hard-voting classifier is almost greater than the results obtained from the soft voting.

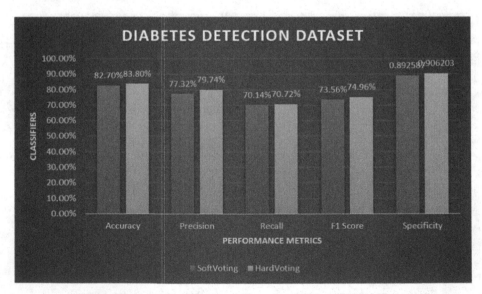

Fig. 5. Comparision of performance metrics diabetes detection dataset

Figure 5 represents accuracy, precision, recall, sensitivity, F1 score and specificity of Soft and Hard voting in Diabetes Detection Dataset respectively. Results show that the accuracy received when using the hard-voting classifier is almost greater than the results obtained from the soft voting.

6 Conclusion

Three diabetes data sets from different repositories are used to validate the efficiency of the base classifier methods. The soft-voting classifier and hard-voting classifier are used to analyse the performance of voting classifiers. It is inferred from the results, the hard-voting classifier offers better accuracy than the soft-voting classifier. The accuracy obtained by the hard-voting classifier for data sets 1, 2 and 3 are 79.65%, 86.72% and 83.8% respectively. This performance can be improved using diverse ML algorithms. The results obtained clearly show that hard-voting classifier provides high accuracy than the soft-voting classifier. Therefore, hard-voting classifiers can be used to develop diabetes prediction applications. Hyper-parameter tuning can be carried out in future studies to further improve performance accuracy.

References

1. Rani, A.S., Jyothi, S.: Performance analysis of classification algorithms under different datasets. In: 2016 3rd International Conference on Computing for Sustainable Global Development (INDIACom), pp. 1584–1589. IEEE (2016)
2. Bashir, S., Qamar, U., Khan, F.H., Javed, M.Y.: An efficient rule-based classification of Diabetes using ID3, C4. 5, & CART ensembles. In: 2014 12th International Conference on Frontiers of Information Technology, pp. 226–231. IEEE (2014)
3. Husain, A., Khan, M.H.: Early diabetes prediction using voting based ensemble learning. In: Singh, M., Gupta, P.K., Tyagi, V., Flusser, J., Ören, T. (eds.) ICACDS 2018. CCIS, vol. 905, pp. 95–103. Springer, Singapore (2018). https://doi.org/10.1007/978-981-13-1810-8_10
4. Fiarni, C., Sipayung, E.M., Maemunah, S.: Analysis and prediction of diabetes complication disease using data mining algorithm. Procedia Comput. Sci. **161**, 449–457 (2019)
5. Kavakiotis, I., Tsave, O., Salifoglou, A., Maglaveras, N., Vlahavas, I., Chouvarda, I.: Machine learning and data mining methods in diabetes research. Comput. Struct. Biotechnol. J. **15**, 104–116 (2017)
6. Nami, S., Shajari, M.: Cost-sensitive payment card fraud detection based on dynamic random forest and k-nearest neighbors. Expert Syst. Appl. **110**, 381–392 (2018)
7. Shu, T., Zhang, B., Tang, Y.Y.: An improved noninvasive method to detect diabetes mellitus using the probabilistic collaborative representation based classifier. Inf. Sci. **467**, 477–488 (2018)
8. Alam, M.Z., Rahman, M.S., Rahman, M.S.: A random forest based predictor for medical data classification using feature ranking. Inform. Med. Unlocked **15**, 100180 (2019)
9. Nagarajan, S., Chandrasekaran, R.M., Ramasubramanian, P.: Data mining techniques for performance evaluation of diagnosis in gestational diabetes. IJCRAR **2**, 91–98 (2014)
10. Gnanadass, I.: Prediction of gestational diabetes by machine learning algorithms. IEEE Potentials **39**(6), 32–37 (2020)
11. Kumari, S., Kumar, D., Mittal, M.: An ensemble approach for classification and prediction of diabetes mellitus using soft voting classifier. Int. J. Cogn. Comput. Eng. **2**, 40–46 (2021)

Convolutional Neural Networks for Traffic Sign Classification Using Enhanced Colours

V. E. Sathishkumar[1], C. Sharmila[2]([⊠]), S. Santhiya[2], M. Poongundran[2], S. Sanjeeth[2], and S. Pranesh[2]

[1] Department of Industrial Engineering, Hanyang University, Seoul, Republic of Korea
[2] Computer Science and Engineering, Kongu Engineering College, Erode, India
sharmiatexcel@gmail.com

Abstract. These days, traffic signs etched on the roadways improve traffic safety by notifying drivers of speed restrictions as well as other potential hazards such as deep curvy routes, upcoming road repairs, or pedestrian crossings. This study focuses on a three-stage real-time Traffic Sign Recognition and Classification system that includes image segmentation, traffic sign detection, and classification based on the input image. To extract red areas from an image, a colour enhancement approach is utilized. Convolutional Neural Networks (CNN) are used to determine the content of the traffic signals discovered during detection, classification, and identification. Results show that CNN model provides the highest accuracy of 99% in validation phase.

Keywords: Traffic sign · Deep learning · Image classification · Convolutional Neural Network

1 Introduction

In this theory, traffic and road signs are those that utilize a visual/symbolic language that drivers can comprehend to describe the route(s) ahead. The terms are interchangeable, but they may also occur together as "road system" elsewhere. They provide motorists with information and make driving safer and easier. The directional sign, which communicates the upcoming directions for travelling to the identified destinations or on numbered routes largely using text rather than symbols, is one sort of sign not explored in this work. Traffic and road signs must be installed appropriately in the proper locations, and an audit of them is required to ensure that they will be updated & maintained to ensure. By offering a quick way of detecting and categorizing indicators, an autonomous system for detecting and identifying traffic lights can make a substantial contribution to this aim. This method aids in the construction of accurate and consistent inventory. Human operators will be able to recognize distorted or obscured signals more easily after this is accomplished.

An Intelligent Transport System (ITS) that continually analyzes the operator, vehicle, and road might theoretically include a traffic and road sign recognition system. Figure 1 depicts the relationships between the three fields. The objective of intelligent transport system (ITS) is to integrate technology into transportation vehicles and infrastructure.

K. Kottursamy et al. (Eds.): IconDeepCom 2022, CCIS 1719, pp. 34–43, 2023.
https://doi.org/10.1007/978-3-031-27622-4_4

Intelligent transportation systems aim to increase traffic performance, road safety, and environmental effect by utilizing advanced communication technology [1, 2].

1.1 Problem Description

It is challenging to create an artificial intelligence based system that can help individuals in their daily lives. There are many factors that change over time, such as luminance and visibility that are easily handled by human identification systems but pose severe challenges for computer recognition.

Fig. 1. Images from the dataset

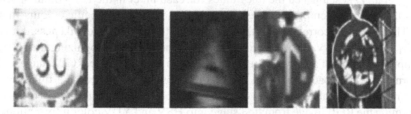

Fig. 2. Difficulties faced while capturing the images

When considering the difficulty of recognizing traffic signs, it is clear that the goal is properly stated and that the problem appears to be simple. Road signs are placed in conventional locations, have standard shapes, colors, and pictograms, and are well-known. Speed restrictions, prohibited entry, traffic signals, children crossing, no passing of big trucks, are few examples of traffic signs. Figure 1 shows the images from the dataset. Figure 2 shows some difficulties that were faced while capturing the images.

Deep learning is a form of neural networks. It is a vital component of data science, that incorporates statistics with predictive modelling. It will be vastly valuable to data scientists who really are responsible for obtaining, analyzing, and interpreting large amounts of data. The process is sped up and simplified. Learning may be regarded as a means to automated predictive analytics at its most fundamental level. Deep learning algorithms, unlike typical machine learning algorithms, are developed in a gradient of increasing complexity. Once the output is precise enough, every algorithm in the structure conducts a nonlinear adjustment on it and then utilizes just what is learned to construct a statistical model.

The purpose of current research is to create an approach for classifying road signs in order to build a library that will help transportation authorities update and maintain traffic signs. It works by capturing pictures with a webcam from the moving vehicle and looking for indications utilizing colour segmentation, shape recognition and categorization.

2 Literature Review

Ghica et al. [3] suggested the method that worked by computing the distance between a pixel color and a reference color in RGB space. If the unknown pixel is close enough to the reference color, it is deemed an object pixel. Estevez and Kehtarnavas [4] created a traffic sign recognition system that can detect Stop, Surrender, and Do-Not-Enter signals. Color segmentation, edge localization, RGB discretization, feature extraction, statistic extraction, and classification are among the six modules.

Yuille et al. [5] suggested the method to assist vision handicapped persons. The authors created a sign finder system. The signs have two colors and sign borders are standardized. Hypothesis regions are based on a series of experiments, a region expanding method was utilized. Yabuki et al. [6] devised a technique for recognizing road signs using the colour distribution of the sign in the XYZ colour space. The authors used the colour distribution to produce a colour similarity map, which was then used in the picture function. A traffic sign that has been entangled inside an active net can be untangled.

Fang et al. [7] established the hue values for each pixel in the HSI colour space, as well as the link between hue and the observed hue values for specific colours in road signs. The degree of correlation is then compared to the degree of likeness. Shadeed et al. [8] employed HSV and YUV color spaces, a method for recognizing traffic signs. The implementation of the system is split into two sections. The RGB image is first transformed to Yuv space, then a Y channel distribution is leveled, and finally a new Color image is generated. In the second phase, color segmentation is performed by transforming the RGB image from first stage into HSV and YUV color information, and then added an appropriate basis to the H and UV values.

In Bénallal and Meunier [9], many trials were conducted with a variety of traffic signs to investigate color stability under various lighting circumstances. The RGB color space is used to segment data. The disparities between red, green, and blue components were demonstrated to be significant and used for segmentation with an acceptable threshold. Priese et al. [10] built a real-time traffic surveillance system in which numerous modules of the recognizer detect traffic signs and analyze their ideograms. There are sections for arrow strength and orientation, numbers, restriction sign, speed limits, and obligatory sign arrows, as well as a restriction sign, speed restrictions, and mandatory sign arrows module.

Aoyagi and Asakura [11, 12] devised a system based simply on brightness for recognising traffic signs. The object was isolated from the background that use the Laplacian filter after eliminating noise with a smoothing filter. The binary picture was created using a certain threshold, and detection was done using genetic algorithms that can seek for the complete circle that was provided as gene information.

Adorni et al. [13] recognized roadway traffic lights and communication system was deployed. To extract the boundary pixel from the image, a gradient operator was employed, followed by a bad value cutoff to eliminate tiny gradients strength pixels, and lastly a 5×5 CNN just one filter to perform pixel which was before with respect to neighborhood pixels. In Gavril [14], Distance transforms and template matching were presented as a method for categorizing traffic signs. The method conveyed the difference between circular and triangle signals. Edge orientations were used as a feature to support the algorithm. For circles and triangles, many designs with radii ranging from 7 to 18 pixels were employed. Based on edge orientation, each template is divided into eight types. Perez and Javidi [15] carried out a scale and lighting invariant road sign detection system. The reference objective was chosen to be the stop sign. It was put to the test in a variety of lighting and backdrops. The composite filter and the filter bank are both put to the test.

In Perez and Javidi [16], a composite filter bank, a traffic sign identification system was proposed. The mechanism is designed to allow the road sign to rotate in-plane and out-plane. It identified road signs that were slightly inclined as well as out of plane rotations caused by the acquisition system's various angles. Sandoval et al. [17] devised a method for identifying traffic signals that was angle-dependent. The method works by creating a position-dependent convolution mask that takes into account the angular location of the pixels. This technology may be used to discover circular edges as a filtration method.

Azami et al. [18] utilized a threshold to distinguish character areas from Route Guidance Signs (RGS). The search was performed horizontally because the letters were from the same length and arranged horizontally. In comparison to characters, arrow candidates had a higher surface area. Topology characteristics such as reduction and template matching were used to identify them. There were seven different types of arrows. By matching this structure to an RGS database, the RGS as well as its contents may be recognized. The approach was used in the development of driving assistance systems.

3 Proposed System

3.1 Dataset Collection

Data collection is critical to the success of any project. The dataset of Traffic Sign photos is painstakingly collected here. The information contained in the dataset The GTSRB-German Traffic Sign Detection Benchmark was chosen as the data set for our study. This is a well-known traffic sign dataset on services like Kaggle. For train, validation, and testing, this data set comprises over 40 picture classes and 50000 photographs. We split the data into train, validation, and testing categories, allowed us to assess the effectiveness of our approach.

The split between the testing and training datasets is done by designating 25% of the dataset for testing and 75% of the dataset for training images. This is performed to ensure that there is as much data as possibly provided for training, leading to a model that is more accurate. The complete dataset must be randomized before the split can be performed.

3.2 Data-Preprocessing

One of CNN model's flaws is that it cannot be trained on photos of different sizes. As a result, the dataset must comprise photographs of the same dimension. To see if the images can be processed to be the same size, all of the images in the collection's dimensions were examined. Because the pictures in this dataset contain a broad number of different aspects, ranging between 16 * 16 * 3 to 128 * 128 * 3, they cannot be directly fed into the ConvNet model.

The images were compressed or interpolated to a single dimension. To compress a large amount of data while not stretching the image too much, we chose a dimension that was halfway between the two and maintained the image data mainly accurate. 64 * 64 * 3 was chosen as dimension. In this work, image changing techniques like rotation, colour distortion, and blurring was used to populate the dataset. The model was trained on the original dataset, and its accuracy was tested. After that, more data was added, balanced out each class, and tested the model's accuracy.

The RGB is an analogous color model that generates a broad range of colours by mixing red, green, and blues light in different ways. The model's name is composed of the initials R, G, & B, that stand again for three basic bright colors red, green, and blue. It's difficult to use these codes as features because they are made up of three values spanning from 0–255. Converting the RGB codes to "labels" and then looked for the closest colour name that exists. The web colours palette, which contains 140 different colours, was the largest colour space with well-known names. These are enough to ensure that the RGB value was appropriately described by the colour name.

3.3 Classification

Classification is a supervised learning technique in which a software system learns from data and creates new discoveries or categories. Classification is the process of categorizing a set of data. Both structured and unstructured data can be used with it. The technique's first step is to predict the type of data points. The classifications are described using the phrases "target," "label," and "category." The method of calculating the mapping function from discrete input variables to discrete output variables was known as predictive modelling. The main goal is to figure out which category or class the new data belongs to.

3.4 Algorithms

Artificial neural networks (ANNs) are often used to handle pattern recognition challenges. In that it comprises of neural units connected by artificial neurons. A neural net is considered as a mathematical model that is equivalent to biological neurons. Normally, neurons are grouped in pairs of two, with connections only developing between neurons in nearby layers. The input lowered vectors are placed in the top layer, and as it moves down the layers, it becomes a raised vector. The number of output layer neurons is equivalent to the number of classification classes. The outcome is a vector with chances that represents the likelihood that the input vector belongs to a particular class.

An artificial neuron implements the weighted adder, and this neuron's result is as follows:

$$a^i = a(\sum ka^{i-1}w^{ij}), \tag{1}$$

where ai represents the jth cell in the ith layer and wij shows the amount of a synapse connecting the jth cell in the ith layer to the kth cell in layer $i - 1$. The logistic function, which is widely used during regression, is applied as an input signal. It is worth mentioning that the binary logistic function is performed by a single artificial neuron.

The training methodology employs redion methods that are based on training algorithm, often refered as backpropagation, inorder to minimize the cost function. The most commonly used cost function in categorization difficulties is to determine efficiency:

$$H(e, q) = -\sum_i Y(i)\log y(i) \tag{2}$$

Due to the vanishing gradient problem, training deep cnns (networks with many layers) using gaussian activation is difficult. The ReLU functional is used as an input signal to solve this problem:

$$\begin{aligned} ReLU(x) = \{&0, \ x \le 0 \\ &x, \ else\} \end{aligned} \tag{3}$$

Each convolutional layer produces an activation map by combining a set of easy to train filters that calculate dot productions between both the filters as well as the layer input. These filters, usually referred to as kernels, enable the identification of the same characteristics in many locations. Figure 3 shows the result of an image performing convolution with four kernel, for example. The term kernel represents the filters.

Fig. 3. Input image convolution.

3.5 Results and Discussion

This work designed, tested, and assessed a system for recognizing road and traffic signs that may be used to create a traffic signs inventory. To use a mix of computer vision & pattern matching tasks, this system was capable of extracting traffic signals from still photographs in difficult circumstances with variable lighting. Algorithms were created in the computer vision section to divide using colors and also to classify the data using color combinations as prior information.

Color categorization in low-light environments was created specifically for this study to counteract the effects of fog & snow. The color stability is affected by certain lighting conditions. To counteract these effects, the color segmentation method is supplemented by each color treatment.

The RGB channels of the captured image are treated independently using the histogram equalization technique, and the resulting Color image then is filtered using color constancy algorithm. It shows how effectively the algorithm enhances the color segmentation of the image. When snowfall is detected, the user picks this strategy manually. As a result, if snow is detected in the future, an automated technique for swapping to this algorithm may be implemented.

The Fig. 4 depicts the accuracy percentage arrived at both training and testing process and Fig. 5 depicts the loss occurred during the training and validation process. Table 1 displays the accuracy and loss.

There have been several earlier implementations of traffic sign classification, as well as picture classification in general. Despite this, our CNN model has a substantially higher accuracy rate (99%) than the majority of the other models.

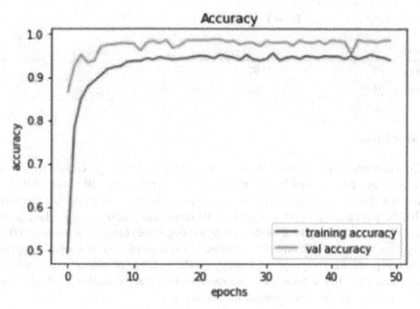

Fig. 4. Comparing the accuracy of training and testing

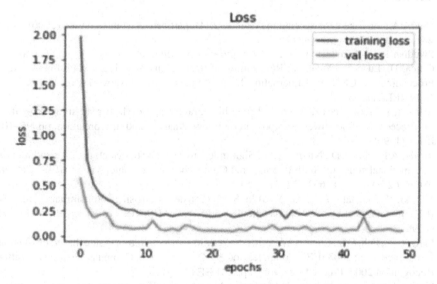

Fig. 5. Comparing the loss of training and testing

Table 1. Accuracy and loss details

Dataset	Accuracy	Loss
Training - 75%	97	0.45
Validation - 25%	99	0.22

4 Conclusion

The Convolutional Neural Network is a powerful tool for image categorization and recognition, as demonstrated by the results of our experiments. Because of its basic architecture, it is much easier for the researcher to work on it. A high performance classifier has been obtained for a difficult and sophisticated task like traffic sign classification and identification. Although the model was powerful, it does have certain inherent flaws, such as over-fitting. As a result, data augmentation is employed as a simple approach to solve this problem. The proposed strategy produces better results as evidenced by its classifier accuracy. In the future, the proposed method can be further applied to more transportation image data and enhance the accuracy.

References

1. David, A.: Intelligent transportation systems. US Department of Transportation (2006). http://www.its.dot.gov/its_overview.htm
2. Swedish-Road-Administration (2006). http://www.vv.se/templates/page3____15600.aspx
3. Ghica, D., Lu, S.W., Yuan, X.: Recognition of traffic signs by artificial neural network. In: Proceedings of ICNN 1995-International Conference on Neural Networks, vol. 3, pp. 1444–1449. IEEE (1995)
4. Estevez, L., Kehtarnavaz, N.: A real-time histographic approach to road sign recognition. In: Proceeding of Southwest Symposium on Image Analysis and Interpretation, pp. 95–100. IEEE (1996)
5. Yuille, A.L., Snow, D., Nitzberg, M.: Signfinder: using color to detect, localize and identify informational signs. In: Sixth International Conference on Computer Vision (IEEE Cat. No. 98CH36271), pp. 628–633. IEEE (1998)
6. Yabuki, N., Matsuda, Y., Fukui, Y., Miki, S.: Region detection using color similarity. In: 1999 IEEE International Symposium on Circuits and Systems (ISCAS), vol. 4, pp. 98–101. IEEE (1999)
7. Fang, C.Y., Fuh, C.S., Chen, S.W., Yen, P.S.: A road sign recognition system based on dynamic visual model. In: 2003 IEEE Computer Society Conference on Computer Vision and Pattern Recognition 2003. Proceedings, vol. 1, p. I. IEEE (2003)
8. Shadeed, W.G., Abu-Al-Nadi, D.I., Mismar, M.J.: Road traffic sign detection in color images. In: 10th IEEE International Conference on Electronics, Circuits and Systems (ICECS 2003). Proceedings of the 2003, vol. 2, pp. 890–893. IEEE (2003)
9. Benallal, M., Meunier, J.: Real-time color segmentation of road signs. In: CCECE 2003-Canadian Conference on Electrical and Computer Engineering. Toward a Caring and Humane Technology (Cat. No. 03CH37436), vol. 3, pp. 1823–1826. IEEE (2003)
10. Priese, L., Lakmann, R., Rehrmann, V.: Ideogram identification in a realtime traffic sign recognition system. In: Proceedings of the Intelligent Vehicles 1995. Symposium, pp. 310–314. IEEE (1995)

11. Aoyagi, Y., Asakura, T.: A study on traffic sign recognition in scene image using genetic algorithms and neural networks. In: Proceedings of the 1996 IEEE IECON. 22nd International Conference on Industrial Electronics, Control, and Instrumentation, vol. 3, pp. 1838–1843. IEEE (1996)
12. Aoyagi, Y., Asakura, T.: Detection and recognition of traffic sign in scene image using genetic'algorithms and neural networks. In: Proceedings of the 35th SICE Annual Conference. International Session Papers, pp. 1343–1348. IEEE (1996)
13. Adorni, G., D'Andrea, V., Destri, G., Mordonini, M.: Shape searching in real world images: a CNN-based approach. In: 1996 Fourth IEEE International Workshop on Cellular Neural Networks and their Applications Proceedings (CNNA 1996), pp. 213–218. IEEE (1996)
14. Gavrila, D.M.: Multi-feature hierarchical template matching using distance transforms. In: Proceedings Fourteenth International Conference on Pattern Recognition (Cat. No. 98EX170), vol. 1, pp. 439–444. IEEE (1998)
15. Perez, E., Javidi, B.: Scale and illumination-invariant road sign detection. In: LEOS 2000. 2000 IEEE Annual Meeting Conference Proceedings. 13th Annual Meeting. IEEE Lasers and Electro-Optics Society 2000 Annual Meeting (Cat. No. 00CH37080), vol. 2, pp. 748–749. IEEE (2000)
16. Perez, E., Javidi, B.: Composite filter bank for road sign recognition. In: LEOS 2000. 2000 IEEE Annual Meeting Conference Proceedings. 13th Annual Meeting. IEEE Lasers and Electro-Optics Society 2000 Annual Meeting (Cat. No. 00CH37080), vol. 2, pp. 754–755. IEEE (2000)
17. Sandoval, H., Hattori, T., Kitagawa, S., Chigusa, Y.: Angle-dependent edge detection for traffic signs recognition. In: Proceedings of the IEEE Intelligent Vehicles Symposium 2000 (Cat. No. 00TH8511), pp. 308–313. IEEE (2000)
18. Azami, S., Katahara, S., Aoki, M.: Route guidance sign identification using 2-D structural description. In: Proceedings of Conference on Intelligent Vehicles, pp. 153–158. IEEE (1996)

A Systematic Review on Fog Computing Security Algorithms on Current IoT Applications and Solutions

V. Balaji[ID] and P. Selvaraj[✉][ID]

Department of Computing Technologies, College of Engineering and Technology, Faculty of
Engineering and Technology, SRM Institute of Science and Technology, SRM Nagar,
Kattankulathur, Chengalpattu Dt, Chennai 603203, TN, India
`{bv0089,selvarap}@srmist.edu.in`

Abstract. Fog computing models consist of a cloud-like platform that possesses
different layers like application services, data, storage, and computation. Fog computing and cloud computing were considered similar in multiple aspects although
the cloud operates as a centralized infrastructure whereas Fog computing is a distributed decentralized system. With Fog systems a large amount of data can be
processed and operated through the on-premise equipment. Fog systems can be
installed on heterogeneous hardware. It is indispensable to have Internet of Things
(IoT) devices with rapid processing and transmitting capabilities. Several security
issues about monitoring, data, malware, segregation, virtualization, and network
are intensified by this broad range of functionality-driven applications. This survey focuses on the modern applications of Fog computing to identify the research
gaps in terms of security. Technologies such as Micro-data centers and Cloudlets
have also been analyzed in this work. Many of the applications of Fog computing
overlook the aspect of security and more attention is given only to the improved
functionality. This survey also discusses the consequences of the vulnerabilities
and possible solutions, as well as the improved level of security measures in Fog
systems.

Keywords: Internet of Things (IoT) · Fog computing · Fog applications ·
Security issues · 5G · Edge computing

1 Introduction

There have been several research works proposed in Cloud computing for the minimization of time intensive data transmission and data handling necessities to handle
the large superfluous data volumes in a more optimized way. There is a perpetual rise
in IoT devices that motivate the paradigm of Fog computing. With the ever-increasing
amount of data (in terms of velocity, volume, and variety) the need for sophisticated big
data computing architecture is ever increasing. The performance aspects of the virtual
connections for the evolving next generation applications are highly data-driven. The
computing resources needed by these devices for processing the attained data should

© The Author(s), under exclusive license to Springer Nature Switzerland AG 2023
K. Kottursamy et al. (Eds.): IconDeepCom 2022, CCIS 1719, pp. 44–59, 2023.
https://doi.org/10.1007/978-3-031-27622-4_5

work in a more reliable way. It is essential to employ faster decision making processes while maintaining and calculating the networking constraints in a higher-level. With the standard client-server architecture, reliability and scalability issues are very prevalent. In the event of web-server getting overloaded in client server based architecture several unusable networking devices could not able to render its services correctly. To combat this issue, the Fog paradigm provides improved scalability with decentralized data management. In Cisco [1] they have developed a new cloud-assisted hierarchically distributed system (Refer Fig. 1).

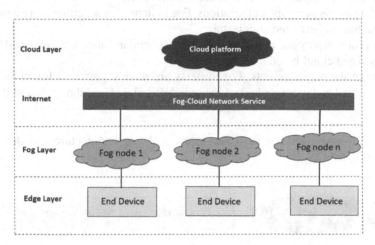

Fig. 1. Cloud assisted hierarchically distributed Fog architecture

In Tang B et al. [2] they have proposed the architecture to filter, aggregate, process, analyze, transmit the data in a time and resource-efficient manner. Marston S et al. [3] and Parkinson S et al. [4] proposed that, the enormous amount of end-user devices can be connected with Cloud assisted Fog system. Stojmenovic I, Wen S [5], Kim JY and Schulzrinne H [6] stated that the small, medium and bigger enterprises and government firms can be benefitted by Cloud computing by rendering extremely efficient and cost-effective resource handling and management. The Fog computing-based data processing model pioneered by Cisco has extended the architecture that compute considerable amount of computation at the client-side. According to the Bonomi F et al. [7] a Fog system possesses the following notable characteristics:

- The edge node provides the required support to the clients with heterogeneous device connectivity through rich end-user interfaces
- Instant response capability, support may be provided to a wider range of enterprise applications
- Fog based system can undertake a variety of services including networking, computation, and storage management
- The Fog node that operates locally can provide portable, inexpensive, and flexible deployment to realize multiple virtualized connections

Sareen P and Kumar P [8] recommended that apart from the above qualities, the Fog system differs from Cloud computing in several ways. According to Vaquero LM and Rodero-Merino L [9], Saharan K and Kumar A [10] the following are the few notable inconsistencies identified while comparing the Fog with Cloud computing paradigms:

- When comparing to Cloud systems, small computing resources such as storage, memory, and processing are required in a Fog based system.
- Irrespective of the increase in demand, the Fog systems can able to process the data generated from various devices in an ala-carte manner.
- Depending on the geographical locations, Fog systems can act either as a dense based or sparse based distributed architecture.
- Wireless connectivity and machine-to-machine communication are supported by both Fog based and cloud-based systems.
- Apart from the above aspects, Fog systems are mainly preferred for its improved portability and enhanced mobility Dastjerdi AV et al. [11], Mahmud R and Buyya R [12].

Cisco [13] have analyzed the Cisco's practical Fog architecture and the various layered functionalities.

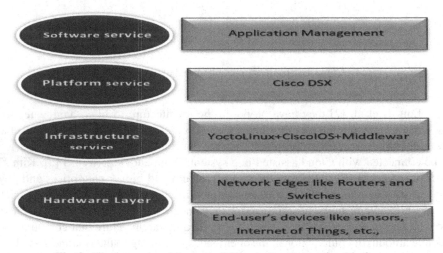

Fig. 2. The layered architecture of Cisco's Fog Computing Platform

The different layers from hardware to the layer of application are as shown in the above figure (Ref. Fig. 2). It is believed by commercial infrastructure developers and many researchers that, in future the innovative Fog based systems with reliable and enriched management may be highly demanded. In Fog based virtualized environment, the possibility of threats is more predominant and such threats may be frequently amplified by the desire of the designer for providing functional systems with all the distributed characteristics. Schumacher M et al. [14] proposed that, most of the distributed systems are designed in a way that more focus is given to the architectural design aspects and the strategy adopted rather than the security issues. The networking operating systems such as Cisco IOx and Linux can be integrated easily with the Fog Infrastructure as a Service (IaaS) platform. Furthermore, hardware such as cameras, switchers, servers, and routers can be used as Fog nodes to provide network connectivity, processing, and storage services. In this context, the Fog nodes can work together by forming a group of Clusters or by exploiting Master-Slave architecture or a Peer-to-Peer network. P.Selvaraj and Lakshmi Kanthan Narayanan [75] proposed that the Cisco's IOx Application Program Interface (APIs) may be used to develop fog applications that communicate with Cloud systems and IoT devices with any of the user-defined policies through the meta algorithm selection approach. Cisco DSX is used to connect a variety of IoT devices to realize Software as a Service (SaaS) and a Platform as a Service (PaaS) for the IoT based applications. The nature or the type of the services could volunteer in determining the appropriate node (fog/cloud) for data analysis. To provide a higher quality of service, the security concerns of anonymous data movements should be managed efficiently. Hence this survey focuses on providing a broad overview of current security solutions to highlight and identify security flaws. It also proposes some recommendations for possible security solutions to avoid the security issues found in the existing Fog systems. The survey is also extended to include several related subject areas, such as the Internet of Things, Edge computing, Microdata center, and cloudlets. The literature on the Fog system and its implementation with some of their similar systems are covered in the next section of this survey. Potential security vulnerabilities which have to be identified are also discussed in the sub sequent section. After that, a summary is discussed to classify some of the general issues and limitations while somehow emphasizing their significance. Mitigating circumstances factors are also highlighted in the next subsequent section. And finally in the conclusion, some of the motivating future research directions and its discussions are given. The survey ends with the acknowledged flaws and deficiencies.

2 Major Fog Computing Platforms

The phrase "fog computing" was originally coined by Cisco. In this field, there has been a lot of research done, and many researchers have studied and practically applied the same in the real time applications.

2.1 Edge Computing

Klas GI [20], Ahmed A and Ahmed E [21] presented a full comparison of edge computing. Edge computing deals with the processing capabilities of the local device with the support of Programmable Automation Controllers (PAC) Series Q et al. [22], in handling the communication, data processing, and data offloading issues. The edge computing provides an advantage over fog computing. However, fog and edge possess some identical qualities in organizing and aggregating the sensor data Pierson RM [23].

2.2 Cloudlet

Cloudlet is at the heart of a three-tier architecture that also encompasses mobile devices and the cloud server. They are based on standard Cloud technology, and provide sufficient compute capacity with self-configurability Ha K and Satyanarayanan M [24]. Cloudlet and Fog computing vary in the way of handling the virtualized applications and managing the required resources. According to Li Y and Wang W [25], Jaiswal A et al. [26] Cloudlets cannot be operated in offline mode, and it is not appropriate for non-virtualized environments.

2.3 Microdata Center

Microdata center has been considered as a small but highly functional data center with a larger number of servers and the ability to provide several virtual machines. Microdata centers improve performance by lowering latency and increasing dependability, and technologies like Fog Computing can help to maximize all of these benefits [27].

2.4 Network Level Virtualization and Fog Computing

By allowing network administrators to take control of the network by exploiting Network Level Virtualization (NLV) and real-time Fog Computing data services, one may easily control and manage the entire network from a remote location. For implementing NLV, Open Pipe [28] uses fog computing (for wireless communication). P.Selvaraj and V.Nagarajan [73] demonstrated that, the entire fog based system can be managed with an intelligent Software Defined Network (SDN) controller that can orient the solutions with respect to the real time event statistics of the network. The Extended OpenFlow (exOF) protocol is used to connect SDN and local controllers. With OF protocol the performance metrics of the long haul communication pipes like network overhead, load balancing, Quality of Service (QoS), latency, energy efficiency and handover events can be easily monitored and optimized on the fly with higher level abstractions. Hence with higher level network abstraction, the number of Fog nodes can also be restructured and reduced to trade with the maximum data transmission speed Clinch S et al. [29], Sindhu S and Mukherjee S [30], Satyanarayanan M et al. [31] and University CM [32]. Almorsy M et al. [33] discussed about the utilization of a highly virtualized environment and its security issues. With Targeted Advanced Persistent Threats (APT), illegal privilege escalation, and side-channel attacks the non-privileged users can easily gain access to resources and data storage systems and compromise the system. The virtualization vulnerabilities potentially allow an attacker or malicious user to compromise the account credentials and access systems Younis YA et al. [34]. The problems associated with shared virtual technology are susceptible to high vulnerabilities and even minor misconfigurations that would allow attackers to take advantage of the resources. To mitigate the virtualization-based attacks there have been several techniques proposed that mainly includes the process/data separation models, setting up private networks, enforcing multi-factor or mutual authentication, enabling user-based permissions model, deploying host and network intrusion detection system Shahid MA, Sharif M [35].

3 Various Application Domains of Fog Computing and Its Security Issues

Satyanarayanan M [15] Justified that Similar techniques to Fog Computing are currently being investigated for boosting the Cloud platform's potential and usability. Fog computing platforms, such as Micro-data centers, Edge computing, and Cloudlets, are vulnerable to any attack that compromises Confidentiality, Integrity, and Availability (CIA) Zissis D and Lekkas D [16]. Many other researchers Stojmenovic I et al. [18] Yi S et al. [19] have also witnessed these security flaws in their studies. Because of its on-demand, dispersed, and shared nature, most of the security problems can have a direct impact on cloud servers and storage systems. Even though Fog is a virtualized environment, it is vulnerable to the most of the security threats that Cloud computing architecture witnesses. According to Alliance CS [17], twelve critical security issues have been identified by Cloud Security Alliance (Refer Fig. 3).

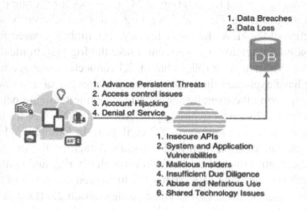

Fig. 3. Latent security problems of Fog computing

3.1 Web Optimization Using Fog Computing

Cisco has employed fog computing to improve the performance of their websites Zhu J et al. [36]. Instead of using HTTPS for to seek images, URL redirections, fog nodes were used for executing, fetching, and integrating the web contents. Additionally, fog nodes can identify users based on the identified local network status. Krishnan YN et al. [37], Abdullahi I and Arif S, Hassan S et al. [38], Su J, Lin F and Zhou X, Lu X [39] have explained the management of Fog nodes by embedding feedback scripts into the web pages for the effective monitoring and rendering of the contents in the browser. Sivasubramanian S et al. [40] demonstrated that storing, computing and processing at the network edges will result in added performance improvement while supporting heterogeneous devices. They also discussed about content-aware data caching to avoid edge servers storing a lot of duplicate data. Using the Fog platform to optimize the web services raises several challenges on maintaining security mandates. For example, code injection attacks such as SQL injection will make the program susceptible and vulnerable. It could also lead to the compromission of the database by tampering or spoofing the data and taking the full control to a central server Halfond WG et al. [41]. To enforce the security in a Fog platform drive-by attacks, malicious redirections, and cookies could be effectively used to proactively mitigate the attacks Egele M et al. [42]. Furthermore, web attacks can target other Fog platform applications by introducing potentially sensitive information and malicious code (cross-site scripting). In general, conducting periodic auditing, securing the application code, patching vulnerabilities, adding anti-malware protection, and hardening the firewall with strict egress and ingress traffic rules are the major tasks in risk mitigation systems.

3.2 Provisioning 5G Mobile Networks with Fog Computing

It is a universal fact that mobile applications have proven to be an integral component of modern living. Because of the widespread use, mobile data consumption has increased, necessitating the implementation of 5G networks for mobile devices Gao L et al. [43]. According to Luan TH et al. [44], Fog nodes are inherently scattered with localized connections to achieve the lower latency. The mobility based fog nodes and mesh topology based connection management, make the fog system ideal for the SDN and Network Level Virtualization (NLV) based 5G connection management. In Oueis J et al. [45] they have explained the load balancing challenges of a 5G network. They analyzed about improving the overall user experience while reducing network latency, and increasing service delivery by exploiting the APIs' of SDN, NLV for the active network monitoring and re-configuration Hu YC et al. [46]. In Desmedt Y [47] they have illustrated about the launching a Man in the Middle Attack by the malicious internal user and taking the control of the Fog platform through filtering and sniffing. The data communication of the underlying network may be hampered as a result of the aforementioned factors. To eliminate these issues, Open Authorization 2.0 (OAuth 2.0) protocol based encryption with mutual authentication and compromised node isolation through certificate pinning, was discussed by Nayak GN and Samaddar SG [48].

3.3 Amplifying Healthcare Systems Using Fog Computing

Prieto González L et al. [49], Stantchev V et al. [50] have researched about utilizing cloud and fog based architecture in health care systems. In Denmark, healthcare programs are provided in the context of optimal use of Smart Items Technologies (OpSIT). Smart devices are low-power devices that can mediate between a variety of distributed data processing systems and handle the provision of services at a local site Shi Y et al. [51]. Another Fog computing application in the healthcare sector is the extraction of electrocardiogram (ECG) features for the diagnosis of coronary heart disease Gia TN et al. [52]. Cao Yet al. [53], Cao Y et al. [54] Proposed a system that sends the data to the Fog layer, and stores information in a distributed database based on ECG features. With rapid detection and reporting of patients, transferring computational tasks to the Fog and the Cloud-based platform is vital for offering an efficient and scalable solution. While utilizing the system and exploiting a vulnerability to prevent unauthorized access to your data Li M et al. [55]. Data integrity, in-system availability, and patient's privacy may be threatened when sensors and the underlying communication network are compromised. Wireless sensors are commonly employed in unmanaged, potentially hazardous, and open places, posing a risk of denial-of-service, distortion, and selective-forwarding attacks Ren K et al. [56]. Furthermore, with the lacks in current access control techniques there is a risk of data leakage from unauthorized access, account hijacking in handling the sensitive data. To avoid such problems, a strict system, with selective coding technique must be established.

3.4 Video Surveillance with Fog Computing

Chen N et al. [57], Shi W and Dustdar S [58] proposed an Edge based surveillance system to monitor the activities of the infants and children. To handle the video feeds from each of the surveillance camera's a proximal approach was employed to solve the joint resource allocation problem Do CT et al. [59]. The camera's sensor generates a video data stream, and the same was sent to the cloud nodes. The flow rate must be maintained since it covers audio and video data that is delivered to a diverse group of users. The security is crucial not only for the Fog node, but also for the network and all devices linked to the end-user that are involved in the transfer, particularly against APTs (APTs). Due to a lack of attention, the captured video can be seen, modified, and destroyed during the course of fog platform or network outages. It's critical that the Fog node, should possess the ability to establish a secure connection between other devices through an encrypted secure channel. With the fine-grained access control techniques and the selective coding, the audio-visual content can be secured effectively Varalakshmi L et al. [60].

3.5 Vehicular Ad-Hoc Network and Fog Computing

The use of fog computing in the New-Vehicle Ad-Hoc Network(VANET) architecture, also known as Fog-based software-defined networking, is described by Truong NB et al. [61] (FSDN). The SDN Controller (SDNC) has complete control over the network, including Fog and Resource Management Orchestration (RMO). The SDNC will gather car information as well as public transportation information from the Base Stations (BSs). Fog-enabled Base Stations (BSs) and Road-Side-Units (RSUs), will allow the commands to be executed more quickly without having to contact the SDNC during every maneuvers. Stojmenovic I and Wen S [5], Datta SK et al. [62] have proposed other, equivalent solutions considering the shortage of devices connected to the primary SDNC and in the Cloud. They built a crime surveillance system in Roy S et al. [63] to reduce the number of accidents and fog by making intelligent decisions to improve swift data transfer and hence the road safety deliberations. There are three tiers in the suggested system: bottom, middle, and top. The bottom layer can recognize hand-held gadgets while driving, the automobile, and the problem are communicated to a nearby station using a camera and a sensor. The Fog server, located in the middle layer, is responsible for evaluating the driver's actions. Finally, the server, the top layer, marks the problem as a legal violation and alerts the proper authorities with the computation abilities of the cloud. As a result, the challenges of protecting fog platforms in vehicles and on highways are analogous to those encountered in 5G cellular networks. Furthermore, vehicles with networks do not have a predefined architecture, and nodes can be connected in a variety of ways. As described by Joshi B and Singh NK [64], Defta LC and Iacob NM [65], the lack of a central authority in such a network led to Denial of Service (DoS) and information leaking attacks.

3.6 Cyber-Physical Systems and Fog Computing

Fog Computing is commonly used in variety of commercial Cyber-Physical Systems (CPS) based applications Bingjun Wan et al. [74]. As stated by Chen RY [66] one of the applications of fog computing in CPS is food tracking. In fog based food tracking system, a decision based on a fog based Fuzzy protocol was used to identify the quality of food. The traceability of food will be sent into the fog network, in which the complete food chain has been traced, as well as the quality of the data.By exploiting the location and transport procedure of the system, the attackers would be able to isolate the food supply chain. If a fog node is negotiated through methods such as account hijacking, vulnerabilities and data can be replicated, leading to low-quality products and the selling of inferior goods. For a variety of reasons, Machine-to-Machine (M2M) links have been launched. The resonance assault, which causes the sensors to operate at a different frequency and/or transmits deceptive information to the fog node, is one of the most common attacks against the fog platform. This type of attack could affect the real-time availability of your network and data, as well as overall capacity Saqib A et al. [67].

3.7 Assortment and Pre-processing of Speech Data Using Fog Computing

In Monteiro A et al. [68] They have been proposed a new Fog Computing Interface (FIT) for smartwatches and Android devices that could be coupled with smart-tablets. Speech data from Parkinson's disease patients were captured, recorded, and analyzed. FIT is used to extract characteristics such as short-time energy, volume, the spectral centroid of the speaker, zero-crossing rate, and long-term cloud analysis, rather than transmitting audio data. They have also demonstrated with six patients were chosen to test the app, and fog computing allowed for the processing of large amounts of audio samples in a short length of time. Orsini G et al. [69] proposed the capabilities of Mobile Edge Computing (MEC) in the context of a new programming model and framework, which allows mobile app developers to create scalable, flexible, edge-based apps. The large choice of applications available on tablets and smartphones might add to the complexity in terms of safety and quality Heuser S et al. [70], Wei X et al. [71]. The malware-based attacks have the potential to contaminate and disrupt data connections that need Confidentiality, Integrity, and Availability (CIA). Singh P et al. [72] have conducted extensive research in these areas and have addressed several techniques to improve security (Table 1).

Table 1. Overall comparison of performance of algorithms in fog environment

S. no.	Algorithm	Metrics	Advantage	Inference
1	Resource Scheduling Algorithm based on FCAP RSAF and Fuzzy Clustering Algorithm with the Particle Swarm Optimization (FCAP) G. Li et al. [76]	Make-span, Reliability, and User Satisfaction	The RSAF method can more quickly match user requests with appropriate resource classifications, increasing service quality	Not taking into account the dynamic variations in resource availability
2	Max– Min Ant System (MMAS) H.R. Boveiri et al. [77]	Utilization of resources	When compared to Highest Level First with Estimated Times, the Max–Min Ant System (MMAS) is very flexible, allowing it to fully use the potential of an increase in the number of processors	Energy consumption is not addressed
3	Bee Life Algorithm (BLA) S. Bitam et al. [78]	Memory allotted	Give better results in terms of execution time	Task execution has a long response time
4	Fog-based Region and Cloud (FBRC) D. Hoang et al. [79]	Utilization of resources	When compared to region-based and cloud-based resource management, this provides an efficiency outcome in terms of latency response and resource consumption	Time complexity is high Processing time is long
5	Hybrid-EDF G.L. Stavrinides and H.D. Karatza [80]	Percentage of deadlines that are missed	On average, a hybrid strategy results in a 76.69 percent lower deadline miss ratio	Due to the use of cloud resources, there would be a rise in monetary costs

(continued)

Table 1. (*continued*)

S. no.	Algorithm	Metrics	Advantage	Inference
6	Non-dominated Sorting Genetic Algorithm II (NSGA-II) Y. Sun et al. [81]	Stability and Latency	Reduce the time it takes for a service to respond	Not recommended for topologies with a lot of complexity
7	HH (Hybrid Heuristic) J.Wang and D. Li [82]	Energy consumption	Good performance metrics relate to completion time, power consumption, and reliability	Task clustering and fog nod clustering are excluded from this method
8	Cost-Makespan aware Scheduling (CMaS) X.Q. Pham et al. [83]	Use of the cloud resource comes at a fee	When compared to other existing approaches, it is more cost-effective and produces superior results	Not appropriate for use on a wide basis
9	Time-Cost aware Scheduling (TCaS) B.M. Nguyen et al. [84]	Make-span	This algorithm strikes a balance between the amount of time it takes to complete a task and the amount of money it costs to run it	Costs of transmission, computation resources, and energy use are minimal
10	Laxity-based Priority and Ant Colony System (LBP-ACS) J. Xu et al. [85]	Failure rate and energy consumption	Reduces the amount of energy required to complete all tasks	Examine the arranging of activities that are simply associated with one another

4 Conclusion

Many of the suggested data protection solutions are insufficient to preserve the security of the Fog platform. As the fog networks do not fulfill modern safety requirements in their present state. To acquire access to policies and best practices this systematic literature survey has suggested the ways to enhance security measures against insider threat, unauthorized users, and poor administration. However, the most significant issues about shared technologies, such as a lack of access limitations, service outages, a lack of vulnerability patches, user account management, data loss and/or interruption, as well as a flawed monitoring and control system, must be addressed instantly. Any one of these threats can allow attackers to isolate the network, prohibit connectivity, and expose the network to fog-CIA. Other similar technologies and standardized security protocols can be used to overcome the obstacles and issues stated. The fog platform's components and interactions aren't completely new, as they've existed over far more than a fictional Cloud. The major challenge that needs to be addressed is integrating security measures to the evolving requirements of the Fog based applications.

References

1. Cisco: Fog Computing and the Internet of Things: Extend the Cloud to Where the Things are Online (2015). https://www.cisco.com/c/dam/en_us/solutions/trends/iot/docs/computing-sol utions.pdf
2. Tang, B., Chen, Z., Hefferman, G., Wei, T., He, H., Yang, Q.: A hierarchical distributed fog computing architecture for big data analysis in smart cities. In: Proceedings of the ASE Big Data and Social Informatics, vol. 28. ACM (2015)
3. Marston, S., Li, Z., Bandyopadhyay, S., Zhang, J., Ghalsasi, A.: Cloud computing-the business perspective. Decis. Support Syst. 51(1), 176–189 (2011)
4. Parkinson, S., Ward, P., Wilson, K., Miller, J.: Cyber threats facing autonomous and connected vehicles: future challenges. IEEE Trans. Intell. Transp. Syst. 18, 2898–2915 (2017)
5. Stojmenovic, I., Wen, S.: The fog computing paradigm: scenarios and security issues. In: 2014 Federated Conference on Computer Science and Information Systems (FedCSIS), pp. 1–8. IEEE (2014)
6. Kim, J.Y., Schulzrinne, H.: Cloud support for latency-sensitive telephony applications. In: 2013 IEEE 5th International Conference on Cloud Computing Technology and Science (CloudCom), vol. 1, pp. 421–426. IEEE (2013)
7. Bonomi, F., Milito, R., Zhu, J., Addepalli, S.: Fog computing and its role in the internet of things. In: Proceedings of the First Edition of the MCC Workshop on Mobile Cloud Computing, pp. 13–16. ACM (2012)
8. Sareen, P., Kumar, P.: The fog computing paradigm. Int. J. Emerg. Technol. Eng. Res. 4, 55–60 (2016)
9. Vaquero, L.M., Rodero-Merino, L.: Finding your way in the fog: towards a comprehensive definition of fog computing. ACM SIGCOMM Comput. Commun. Rev. 44(5), 27–32 (2014)
10. Saharan, K., Kumar, A.: Fog in comparison to cloud: a survey. Int. J. Comput. Appl. 122(3), 10–12 (2015)
11. Dastjerdi, A.V., Gupta, H., Calheiros, R.N., Ghosh, S.K., Buyya, R.: Fog computing: principals, architectures, and applications. arXiv preprint arXiv:1601.02752 (2016)
12. Mahmud, R., Buyya, R.: Fog computing: a taxonomy, survey and future directions. arXiv preprint arXiv:1611.05539 (2016)
13. Cisco: Cisco Fog Computing Solutions: Unleash the Power of the Internet of Things. (2015). https://www.cisco.com/c/dam/en_us/solutions/trends/iot/docs/computing-solutions.pdf
14. Schumacher, M., Fernandez-Buglioni, E., Hybertson, D., Buschmann, F., Sommerlad, P.: Security Patterns: Integrating Security and Systems Engineering. Wiley (2013)
15. Satyanarayanan, M.: A brief history of cloud offload: a personal journey from odyssey through cyber foraging to cloudlets. GetMobile: Mob. Comput. Commun. 18(4), 19–23 (2015)
16. Zissis, D., Lekkas, D.: Addressing cloud computing security issues. Future Gener. Comput. Syst. 28(3), 583–592 (2012)
17. Alliance, C.S.: The Treacherous 12 Cloud Computing Top Threats in 2016 (2016). https://downloads.cloudsecurityalliance.org/assets/research/topthreats/Treacherous-12_Cloud-Computing_Top-Threats.pdf
18. Stojmenovic, I., Wen, S., Huang, X., Luan, H.: An overview of fog computing and its security issues. Concurr. Comput. Pract. Exp. 28, 2991–3005 (2015)

19. Yi, S., Qin, Z., Li, Q.: Security and privacy issues of fog computing: a survey. In: Kuai, X., Zhu, H. (eds.) WASA 2015. LNCS, vol. 9204, pp. 685–695. Springer, Cham (2015). https://doi.org/10.1007/978-3-319-21837-3_67

20. Klas, G.I.: Fog computing and mobile edge cloud gain momentum open fog consortium, etsi mec and cloudlets (2015)

21. Ahmed, A., Ahmed, E.: A survey on mobile edge computing. In: 2016 10th International Conference on Intelligent Systems and Control (ISCO), pp. 1–8. IEEE (2016)

22. Series Q, Safety MQ.: Programmable automation controller

23. Pierson, R.M.: How Does Fog Computing Differ from Edge Computing? (2016). https://readwrite.com/2016/08/05/fog-computing-different-edge-computing-pl1/

24. Ha, K., Satyanarayanan, M.: Openstack++ for Cloudlet Deployment. School of Computer Science, Carnegie Mellon University, Pittsburgh (2015)

25. Li, Y., Wang, W.: The unheralded power of cloudlet computing in the vicinity of mobile devices. In: 2013 IEEE Globecom Workshops (GC Wkshps), pp. 4994–4999. IEEE (2013)

26. Jaiswal, A., Thakare, V., Sherekar, S.: Performance based analysis of cloudlet architectures in mobile cloud computing

27. Bahl, V.: Emergence of Micro Datacenter (cloudlets/edges) for Mobile Computing (2015). https://www.microsoft.com/en-us/research/wp-content/uploads/2016/11/Micro-Data-Centers-mDCs-for-Mobile-Computing-1.pdf

28. Liang, K., Zhao, L., Chu, X., Chen, H.-H.: An integrated architecture for software defined and virtualized radio access networks with fog computing. IEEE Netw. **31**(1), 80–87 (2017)

29. Clinch, S., Harkes, J., Friday, A., Davies, N., Satyanarayanan, M.: How close is close enough? Understanding the role of cloudlets in supporting display appropriation by mobile users. In: 2012 IEEE International Conference on Pervasive Computing and Communications (PerCom), pp. 122–127. IEEE (2012)

30. Sindhu, S., Mukherjee, S.: Efficient task scheduling algorithms for cloud computing environment. In: Mantri, A., Nandi, S., Kumar, G., Kumar, S. (eds.) HPAGC 2011. CCIS, vol. 169, pp. 79–83. Springer, Heidelberg (2011). https://doi.org/10.1007/978-3-642-22577-2_11

31. Satyanarayanan, M., Bahl, P., Caceres, R., Davies, N.: The case for VM-based cloudlets in mobile computing. IEEE Pervasive Comput. **8**(4), 14–23 (2009)

32. University CM: Elijah: Cloudlet Infrastructure for Mobile Computing. GitHub (2017)

33. Almorsy, M., Grundy, J., Müller, I.: An analysis of the cloud computing security problem. arXiv preprint arXiv:1609.01107 (2016)

34. Younis, Y.A., Kifayat, K., Shi, Q., Askwith, B.: A new prime and probe cache side-channel attack for cloud computing. In: 2015 IEEE International Conference on Computer and Information Technology; Ubiquitous Computing and Communications; Dependable, Autonomic and Secure Computing; Pervasive Intelligence and Computing (CIT/IUCC/DASC/PICOM), pp. 1718–1724. IEEE (2015)

35. Shahid, M.A., Sharif, M.: Cloud computing security models, architectures, issues and challenges: a survey. Smart Comput. Rev. **5**, 602–616 (2015)

36. Zhu, J., Chan, D.S., Prabhu, M.S., Natarajan, P., Hu, H., Bonomi, F.: Improving web sites performance using edge servers in fog computing architecture. In: 2013 IEEE 7th International Symposium on Service Oriented System Engineering (SOSE), pp. 320–323. IEEE (2013)

37. Krishnan, Y.N., Bhagwat, C.N., Utpat, A.P.: Fog computing-network based cloud computing. In: 2015 2nd International Conference on Electronics and Communication Systems (ICECS), pp. 250–251. IEEE (2015)

38. Abdullahi, I., Arif, S., Hassan, S.: Ubiquitous shift with information centric network caching using fog computing. In: Phon-Amnuaisuk, S., Au, T.W. (eds.) Computational Intelligence in Information Systems. AISC, vol. 331, pp. 327–335. Springer, Cham (2015). https://doi.org/10.1007/978-3-319-13153-5_32

39. Su, J., Lin, F., Zhou, X., Lu, X.: Steiner tree based optimal resource caching scheme in fog computing. China Commun. **12**(8), 161–168 (2015)
40. Sivasubramanian, S., Pierre, G., Van Steen, M., Alonso, G.: Analysis of caching and replication strategies for web applications. IEEE Internet Comput. **11**(1), 60–66 (2007)
41. Halfond, W.G., Viegas, J., Orso, A.: A classification of SQL-injection attacks and countermeasures. In: Proceedings of the IEEE International Symposium on Secure Software Engineering, vol. 1, pp. 13–15. IEEE (2006)
42. Egele, M., Kirda, E., Kruegel, C.: Mitigating drive-by download attacks: challenges and open problems. In: Camenisch, J., Kesdogan, D. (eds.) iNetSec 2009. IAICT, vol. 309, pp. 52–62. Springer, Heidelberg (2009). https://doi.org/10.1007/978-3-642-05437-2_5
43. Gao, L., Luan, T.H., Liu, B., Zhou, W., Yu, S.: Fog computing and its applications in 5G. In: Xiang, W., Zheng, K., Shen, X. (eds.) 5G Mobile Communications, pp. 571–593. Springer, Cham (2017). https://doi.org/10.1007/978-3-319-34208-5_21
44. Luan, T.H., Gao, L., Li, Z., Xiang, Y., Sun, L.: Fog computing: focusing on mobile users at the edge. arXiv preprint arXiv:1502.01815 (2015)
45. Oueis, J., Strinati, E.C., Barbarossa, S.: The fog balancing: load distribution for small cell cloud computing. In: 2015 IEEE 81st Vehicular Technology Conference (VTC Spring), pp. 1–6. IEEE (2015)
46. Hu, Y.C., Patel, M., Sabella, D., Sprecher, N., Young, V.: Mobile edge computing-a key technology towards 5G. ETSI White Pap. **11**, 1–16 (2015)
47. Desmedt, Y.: Man-in-the-middle attack. In: van Tilborg, H.C.A., Jajodia, S. (eds.) Encyclopedia of Cryptography and Security, pp. 759–759. Springer, Boston (2011). https://doi.org/10.1007/978-1-4419-5906-5_324
48. Nayak, G.N., Samaddar, S.G.: Different flavours of man-in-the-middle attack, consequences and feasible solutions. In: 2010 3rd IEEE International Conference on Computer Science and Information Technology (ICCSIT), vol. 5, pp. 491–495. IEEE (2010)
49. Prieto González, L., et al.: Fog computing architectures for healthcare: wireless performance and semantic opportunities. J. Inf. Commun. Ethics Soc. **14**(4), 334–349 (2016)
50. Stantchev, V., Barnawi, A., Ghulam, S., Schubert, J., Tamm, G.: Smart items, fog and cloud computing as enablers of servitization in healthcare. Sens. Transducers **185**(2), 121 (2015)
51. Shi, Y., Ding, G., Wang, H., Roman, H.E., Lu, S.: The fog computing service for healthcare. In: 2015 2nd International Symposium on Future Information and Communication Technologies for Ubiquitous HealthCare (Ubi-HealthTech), pp. 1–5. IEEE (2015)
52. Gia, T.N., Jiang, M., Rahmani, A.M., Westerlund, T., Liljeberg, P., Tenhunen, H.: Fog computing in healthcare internet of things: a case study on ECG feature extraction. In: 2015 IEEE International Conference on Computer and Information Technology; Ubiquitous Computing and Communications; Dependable, Autonomic and Secure Computing; Pervasive Intelligence and Computing (CIT/IUCC/DASC/PICOM), pp. 356–363. IEEE (2015)
53. Cao, Y., Hou, P., Brown, D., Wang, J., Chen, S.: Distributed analytics and edge intelligence: pervasive health monitoring at the era of fog computing. In: Proceedings of the 2015 Workshop on Mobile Big Data, pp. 43–48. ACM (2015)
54. Cao, Y., Chen, S., Hou, P., Brown, D.: Fast: a fog computing assisted distributed analytics system to monitor fall for stroke mitigation. In: 2015 IEEE International Conference on Networking, Architecture and Storage (NAS), pp. 2–11. IEEE (2015)
55. Li, M., Yu, S., Ren, K., Lou, W.: Securing personal health records in cloud computing: patient-centric and fine-grained data access control in multi-owner settings. In: Jajodia, S., Zhou, J. (eds.) SecureComm 2010. LNICSSITE, vol. 50, pp. 89–106. Springer, Heidelberg (2010). https://doi.org/10.1007/978-3-642-16161-2_6
56. Ren, K., Lou, W., Zhang, Y.: Leds: providing location-aware end-to-end data security in wireless sensor networks. IEEE Trans. Mob. Comput. **7**(5), 585–598 (2008)

57. Chen, N., Chen, Y., You, Y., Ling, H., Liang, P., Zimmermann, R.: Dynamic urban surveillance video stream processing using fog computing. In: 2016 IEEE Second International Conference on Multimedia Big Data (BigMM), pp. 105–112. IEEE (2016)
58. Shi, W., Dustdar, S.: The promise of edge computing. Computer **49**(5), 78–81 (2016)
59. Do, C.T., Tran, N.H., Pham, C., Alam, M.G.R., Son, J.H., Hong, C.S.: A proximal algorithm for joint resource allocation and minimizing carbon footprint in geo-distributed fog computing. In: 2015 International Conference on Information Networking (ICOIN), pp. 324–329. IEEE (2015)
60. Varalakshmi, L.M., Sudha, G.F., Jaikishan, G.: A selective encryption and energy efficient clustering scheme for video streaming in wireless sensor networks. Telecommun. Syst. **56**(3), 357–365 (2013). https://doi.org/10.1007/s11235-013-9849-0
61. Truong, N.B., Lee, G.M., Ghamri-Doudane, Y.: Software defined networking-based vehicular adhoc network with fog computing. In: 2015 IFIP/IEEE International Symposium on Integrated Network Management (IM), pp. 1202–1207. IEEE (2015)
62. Datta, S.K., Bonnet, C., Haerri, J.: Fog computing architecture to enable consumer centric internet of things services. In: 2015 International Symposium on Consumer Electronics (ISCE), pp. 1–2. IEEE (2015)
63. Roy, S., Bose, R., Sarddar, D.: A fog-based DSS model for driving rule violation monitoring framework on the internet of things. Int. J. Adv. Sci. Technol. **82**, 23–32 (2015)
64. Joshi, B., Singh, N.K.: Mitigating dynamic dos attacks in mobile ad hoc network. In: Symposium on IEEE Colossal Data Analysis and Networking (CDAN), pp. 1–7 (2016)
65. Defta, L.C., Iacob, N.M.: Aodv-authentication mechanism in manet. Calitatea **17**(S3), 59 (2016)
66. Chen, R.Y.: An intelligent value stream-based approach to collaboration of food traceability cyber physical system by fog computing. Food Control **71**, 124–136 (2017)
67. Saqib, A., et al.: Cyber security for cyber physcial systems: a trust-based approach. J. Theor. Appl. Inf. Technol. **71**(2), 144–152 (2015)
68. Monteiro, A., Dubey, H., Mahler, L., Yang, Q., Mankodiya, K.: Fit a fog computing device for speech teletreatments. arXiv preprint arXiv:1605.06236 (2016)
69. Orsini, G., Bade, D., Lamersdorf, W.: Computing at the mobile edge: Designing elastic Android applications for computation offloading. In: 2015 8th IFIP Wireless and Mobile Networking Conference (WMNC), pp. 112–119. IEEE (2015)
70. Heuser, S., Negro, M., Pendyala, P.K., Sadeghi, A.R.: Droidauditor: forensic analysis of application-layer privilege escalation attacks on Android. Technical report, TU Darmstadt (2016)
71. Wei, X., Gomez, L., Neamtiu, I., Faloutsos, M.: Malicious Android applications in the enterprise: what do they do and how do we fix it? In: 2012 IEEE 28th International Conference on Data Engineering Workshops (ICDEW), pp. 251–254. IEEE (2012)
72. Singh, P., Tiwari, P., Singh, S.: Analysis of malicious behavior of Android apps. Procedia Comput. Sci. **79**, 215–220 (2016)
73. Selvaraj, P., Nagarajan, V.: Migration from conventional networking to software defined networking. In: IEEE-International Conference on IoT and its Applications (ICIOT-2017). E.G.S Pillay Engineering College, Nagapattinam (2017). ISBN 978-93-84893-49-4
74. Wan, B., Xu, C., Mahapatra, R.P., Selvaraj, P.: Understanding the cyber-physical system in international stadiums for security in the network from cyber-attacks and adversaries using AI. Wirel. Pers. Commun. **127**, 1207–1224 (2021). https://doi.org/10.1007/s11277-021-085 73-2
75. Selvaraj, P., Narayanan, L.K.: IoT enhanced smart mirror for personal and commercial applications. Int. J. Adv. Trends Comput. Sci. Eng. (IJATCSE) **9**(4) (2020)
76. Li, G., Liu, Y., Wu, J., Lin, D., Zhao, S.: Methods of resource scheduling based on optimized fuzzy clustering in fog computing. Sensors (Basel) **19**, 2122 (2019)

77. Boveiri, H.R., Khayami, R., Elhoseny, M., Gunasekaran, M.: An efficient swarm-intelligence approach for task scheduling in cloud based internet of things applications. J. Ambient Intell. Hum. Comput. **10**, 3469–3479 (2019)
78. Bitam, S., Zeadally, S., Mellouk, A.: Fog computing job scheduling optimization based on bees swarm. Enterpr. Inform. Syst. **12**, 373–397 (2018)
79. Hoang, D., Dang, T.D.: FBRC: optimization of task scheduling in fog-based region and cloud. In: Proceedings of the 2017 IEEE Trustcom/BigDataSE/ICESS, Sydney, NSW, Australia, pp. 1109–1114. IEEE (2017)
80. Stavrinides, G.L., Karatza, H.D.: A hybrid approach to scheduling real-time IoT workflows in fog and cloud environments. Multimed. Tools Appl. **78**(17), 24639–24655 (2018). https://doi.org/10.1007/s11042-018-7051-9
81. Sun, Y., Lin, F., Xu, H.: Multi-objective optimization of resource scheduling in Fog computing using an improved NSGA-II. Wirel. Pers. Commun. **102**, 1369–1385 (2018)
82. Wang, J., Li, D.: Task scheduling based on a hybrid heuristic algorithm for smart production line with fog computing. Sensors (Basel) **19**, 1023 (2019)
83. Pham, X.Q., Man, N.D., Tri, N.D.T., Thai, N.Q., Huh, E.N.: A cost and performance-effective approach for task scheduling based on collaboration between cloud and fog computing. Int. J. Distrib. Sens. Netw. **13**, 1550147717742073 (2017)
84. Nguyen, B.M., Binh, H.T.T., Anh, T.T., Son, D.B.: Evolutionary algorithms to optimize task scheduling problem for the IoT based bag-of-tasks application in cloud–fog computing environment. Appl. Sci. **9**, 1730 (2019)
85. Xu, J., Hao, Z., Zhang, R., Sun, X.: A method based on the combination of laxity and ant colony system for cloud-fog task scheduling. IEEE Access **7**, 116218–116226 (2019)

Enhanced and Effective Ensemble Model for Breast Cancer Detection and Prediction in Modern Medical System in Machine Learning

T. R. Saravanan[1,2] (iD), A. Jackulin Mahariba[1,2] (iD), and S. Priya[1,2(✉)] (iD)

[1] Department of Computational Intelligence, SRM Institute of Science and Technology, Kattankulathur, India
{jackulia,priyas3}@srmist.edu.in
[2] Department of Computing Technologies, SRM Institute of Science and Technology, Kattankulathur, India

Abstract. Humanoid fitness, is the wide-ranging state-run of corporal, societal, and intellectual well-being and not just the absenteeism of infection, sickness, or disability, is as vibrant a source as H2O, foodstuff, or liveliness. Human has undergone phenomenal transformations during last six decades. This has affected health a very large extent. As technology has enhanced and cancer has increased in recent years. Cancer is most widely detected in both men and women. But the female are widely affected by cancer. In Existing system for breast cancer there are many repositories available with cancer data, many online sources, many hospital information etc. As all are separate entity predictions of cancer is very less. All the medical resources available are underutilized. There are many Artificial Intelligence and Machine Learning approaches Logistic Regression, KNeighbors, Random Forest and Decision Tree Classifier, are available for prediction and the effectiveness needs to be improved. In proposed work breast cancer dataset is taken as input and all the best possibilities of the predicted output using various classifications algorithms are combined and a ensemble model is generated. The proposed ensemble model achieves high accuracy, precision and recall for breast cancer detection and prediction, effectiveness outperforms all existing classifiers.

Keywords: Logistic Regression · Breast cancer · Ensemble model

1 Introduction

The utilization of clinical innovation apparatuses shields patient wellbeing. To start with, there are alarms taking drugs, banners and updates, counsel and analysis [9] reports, and the simpler accessibility of patient information. Especially, cautions can assist somebody with sticking to explicit therapies and timetables of treatment. Health was defined as the ability of the body to function well. However, the definition of health has also evolved over time. It cannot be fully emphasized that health is paramount and everything else follows. If you stay healthy, everything else falls into place. Cancer growth indicates to any of an enormous quantity of infections described by the enhancement of unusual

K. Kottursamy et al. (Eds.): IconDeepCom 2022, CCIS 1719, pp. 60–74, 2023.
https://doi.org/10.1007/978-3-031-27622-4_6

cells that dividing wall excitedly can infiltrate and obliterate distinctive body muscle. Cancer often habitually can spread all through your body. Cancer is the subsequent - lashing reason for bereavement on the planet. Cancer affects Skin, Lung, Prostate, Breast, Colorectal, Kidney, Bladder etc. The most widely predictable sympathetic of cancer on the incline is breast cancer, with massive new-fangled circumstances estimated in the United States in year 2021. Other furthermost communal cancers are prostate cancer [10] and lung cancer. Other common cancers are colon and rectal cancers.

Cancers that most frequently influence ladies are breast, colorectal, endometrial, lung, cervical, skin, and ovarian cancers. Being familiar with these diseases and how you might assist with forestalling them or think that they are early. There are 10 symptoms which gives early diagnosis of cancer. They are listed as follows. Uncharacteristic vaginal blood loss, Mysterious heaviness loss, vaginal emancipation stained by means of body fluid, Persistent weariness, Forfeiture of hungriness or sensitivity full all the period, Discomfort in the pelvis or abdominal extent, Fluctuations in your lavatory behaviors, Tenacious dyspepsia or queasiness. Ordinary mammograms can assist with observing cancer growth at a beginning phase, when treatment is probably going to be effective. A mammogram can frequently observe breast changes that could be disease years before actual side effects create. A mammogram is an X-beam of the breast. Mammograms are in general hand-me-down to estimate for breast cancer. Assuming a variance is predictable on a showing mammogram, then doctor might prescribe a symptomatic mammogram to additionally assess that irregularity using Breast ultrasound [16].

As we know there are more breast cancer information available in multiple sources such as medical repository, private hospital database, online sources and many reviews sourced information. Even though many information are available for in our repositories for more than 50 years. All the data remain underutilized for the want of application of the Artificial Intelligence and Machine learning as a supplement to major component of these operational system [14]. So these existing challenges needs to be addressed. As the information available be located less employed at hand is a prerequisite for a revolution for subsequently expending all manageable statistics viably to stopover away from the death toll and chattels. Even though we have many Artificial Intelligence classification and prediction techniques [12, 13] no hybrid model available to detect and predict breast cancer to have an efficient mechanism [17]. Even though large bases of evidence about breast cancer [3] obtainable we are incompetent to envisage as we are impotent to narrate all sources together. So in proposed work a hybrid model is developed to cater the needs of modern medical in the field of breast cancer.

2 Literature Review

Anji Reddy Vaka et al. [1] proposed machine learning method for breast cancer detection. It is informed that India has seen 30% of the instances of breast cancer growth during the most recent couple of years and it is probably going to increment. Breast cancer growth in India accounts that one lady is analyzed at regular intervals and like clockwork, one lady passes on. Early recognition and determination can save the existences of disease patients. a clever strategy to distinguish breast cancer growth is proposed by utilizing procedures of Machine Learning. An exploratory examination utilizing Deep Neural

Network with Support Value on a dataset to assess the exhibition. Proposed strategy has created exceptionally exact and effective outcomes when contrasted with the current technique.

Pei Liu et al. [5] demonstrated a Subsistence Investigation of XGBoost to envisage disease undertaking of Breast Cancer. Another gradient boosting calculation, termed EXSA, by streamlining continued existence investigation of XGBoost structure for connections to anticipate the illness movement of breast cancer growth to break down clinical and footpath up information of massive breast cancer patients. EXSA depends on the XGBoost system in AI and the Cox relative risks model in endurance examination. Hazard mark of sickness improvement is assessed by the model, in addition the gamble gathering and nonstop capacities sandwiched between hazard grooves and sickness improvement rate at 5-and 10- year be situated additionally illustrated. The proposed EXSA technique can be used as a viable strategy for endurance investigation. Proposed strategy in this method can give a significant means to follow-up information of bosom malignant growth or other illness research.

Kihan Park et al. [4] proposed an portable diagnostic tool and a micro electro mechanical systems which has Biomarker for Breast Tissue in Breast Cancer An electromechanical coupling element of bosom tissue is acquainted with approve a new bio marker. A versatile demonstrative device and a miniature electro mechanical frameworks established biochip, which is incorporated through a piezo resistive detecting coating for estimating the response power as well as a miniature radiator for temperature regulator. While the firmness of bosom tissues can be caught as an agent mechanical mark which permits single to discrete among tissue categories particularly in the higher strain locale, the electromechanical connecter influence shows more unmistakable contrasts between the ordinary and IDC bunches over the whole strain area than the mechanical mark. Portrayal of mechanical tissue belongings has been verified to be helpful for separating harmful tissue from typical tissue. Proposed technique is so productive than existing innovations.

Noreen Fatima et al. [11] has performed breast cancer assessment and analysis. Similar investigation of machine learning, data mining, deep learning strategies actuality utilized for the forecast of breast cancer. Numerous specialists partake placed their endeavors on breast cancer growth determinations in addition guesses, each procedure has different precision rate and it fluctuates for various circumstances, instruments and datasets being utilized. The fundamental center is to similarly break down various surviving Machine Learning and Data Mining dealings to discover the most fitting technique that will uphold the huge dataset with great exactness of forecast. The fundamental reason for this audit is to feature every one of the past investigations of AI calculations that are actuality utilized for breast cancer expectation and this thing gives the all essential data to the amateurs who need to dissect the machine education algorithms to achievement the basic of deep knowledge.

Saad Awadh Alanazi et al. [18] proposed a Boosting Breast Cancer Detection Using Convolutional Neural Network. A convolutional neural network technique is projected in this to sustenance the programmed ID of breast cancer growth by breaking down antagonistic ductal carcinoma tissue zones in entire slide pictures. The proposed framework that utilizes different convolutional neural organization models to consequently recognize breast cancer, contrasting the outcomes and those from AI (ML) calculations. All structures were directed by a major dataset of around 275,000, 50 × 50-pixel RGB picture patches. Approval tests were finished quantifiable outcomes utilizing the exhibition measures for each strategy. The proposed framework is viewed as effective, accomplishing results with 87% exactness, which could diminish human mix-ups in the determination cycle. In addition, our proposed framework accomplishes exactness greater than the 78% precision of AI (ML) calculations. The wished-for framework accordingly further develops exactness by 9% above outcomes from AI (ML) calculations.

Chuang Liu et al. [19] proposed a technique for Enhancing cancer driver gene prediction. A cancer specific genetic network is prepared in a network based classification Seven various cancer types are analyzed the proposed method has achieved a high range of prediction and accuracy which is best associating to all the methods available. The feature comparison achieved is very upright network grounded features are very imperative than the biological features, as well as the mutation frequency in addition genetic differential expression.

3 Proposed Work

3.1 Overview

As Breast cancer is widely available for women varying all ages. The information regarding breast cancer is available in many locations and most of the datas are underutilized. So an Ensemble model is prepared with the classification received from various classification algorithms [6]. Initially we start with breast cancer dataset. The data set is checked for missing data and unwanted columns are dropped. Malignant cases, benign cases are analyzed and analysis is performed. Analysis with kernel density estimation is performed for malignant cases, benign cases for distribution of various features. Testing and training are done for 20% and 80% accordingly. We use the concept of principal component analysis to obtain the number of features from large dataset, standard scalar is used instead of arbitrarily choosing dimensions. Classification and prediction is done using Logistic Regression, KNeighbors classifier, Support vector machine classifier, Decision Tree classifier, Random Forest classifier, we received accuracy, precision, Recall for all the classifiers and one algorithm provide best in one aspect and other algorithm provides best in other. So to make our breast cancer effective and efficient a hybrid model is proposed using ensemble model. By aggregating all the values received through all classifiers using soft voting approach.

3.2 Proposed System Architecture

The following Fig. 1 clearly illustrates hybrid model developed for breast cancer detection.

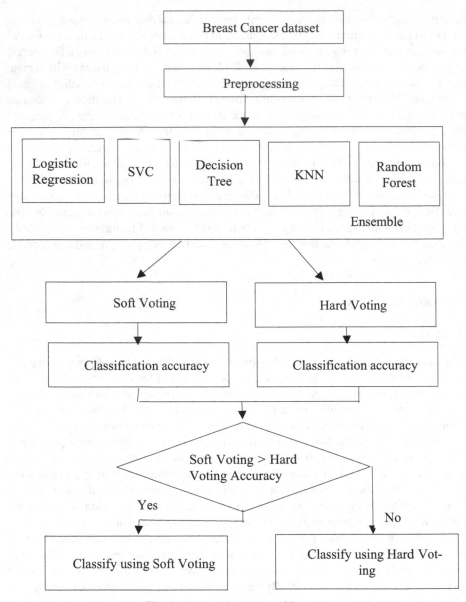

Fig. 1. Proposed system architecture

The above Fig. 1 clearly explains about the proposed system architecture. For breast cancer detection [2]. The detailed description is given in following section.

3.3 Data Pre-processing

The features and shapes are checked with the number of columns and if the there are any unwanted features the columns are dropped. In our data set we have 33 columns and we will be checking for any missing data. Data cleaning procedure is achieved all the categorical data's are transformed to numerical value. Substitute the missing value with its mean value of the corresponding attribute. In this proposed work we have dropped unwanted columns and we finalized as 22 columns.

3.4 Principal Component Analysis

It is a measurable system that utilizes a symmetrical change that changes a bunch of correlated variables over to a bunch of uncorrelated features. It is in general make use of investigative statistics examination and in machine erudition for predictive mockups. It is an unsubstantiated erudition process that is cast-off for the dimensionality lessening in machine learning. The new transformed features are called the Principal Components. It is a feature taking out system, so it comprehends the imperative variables and globules the minimum significant variable. The sequence of steps to be followed are Signifying data addicted to a structure, Regulating the data, Manipulative the Covariance, Scheming the Eigen Values in addition Eigen Vectors, Arranging the Eigen Vectors in order, Take away inconsequential features on or after the new dataset.

3.5 Classification and Prediction

After separating data frames for malignant and benign cases for plotting the details which we have created our dataset. Classification is performed by five different classifier and predictions [15] such as Logistic Regression, Decision Tree KNeighbors, Support vector machine, Random Forest. The values of Accuracy, precision and Recall are calculated.

3.5.1 Logistic Regression

It is a numerical procedure to understand the assembly amongst the needful variable and at minimum one self-sufficient features by measuring likelihoods utilizing a premeditated relapse situation. This sort of investigation can contribution you with get ahead the possibility of an occasion taking place or a decision being made. The steps used for logistic regression process are the step ladder to be surveyed are Data Pre- dispensation step, Fitting Logistic Regression to the Training set, guessing the test result, test exactness of the result. The dataset is fragmented into a training set and test set. Feature clambering since we need exact outcome of calculations. At this time we will solitary gauge the autonomous variable since dependent variable will have values as 0 and 1. Confusion matrix is generated to test the accuracy of the result. The precision and recall rate are given as result. It is a parametric model that supports only linear functions.

3.5.2 KNeighbours Classifier

It is a straightforward calculation that stores every one of the accessible cases and groups the new information or case in light of a closeness measure. It is generally used to arrange an information point in light of how its neighbors are characterized. It accepts the likeness flanked by the new statistics and easy to get to cases and put the new case into the organization that is in general like the accessible classes. It is only output the labels as it is a non-parametric model. The Accuracy, precision, recall values are calculated and the recall values received as output are lesser than logistic regression recall values.

3.5.3 Support Vector Machine

This is one of the most notable Supervised Learning estimations, which is used for Classification. The advantages of help vector machines are given as Effective in high layered spaces. Still strong in circumstances where number of perspectives is more unmistakable than the amount of tests. Objective is to become peaceful on the greatest line or verdict border that can seclude n-layered intergalactic into modules so we can short of a doubt domicile the new suitable element in the right prearrangement well along on. Direct SVM is hand-me-down for openly detachable facts, and that put forward if a dataset can be set up into double classes by using a lone straight line. Non-Linear SVM is used for non-straightforwardly disengaged data, and that suggests if a dataset can't be set up by utilizing a conservative line. In hyper plane can be different decision cutoff points to separate out the classes in n-layered interstellar, but we truly need to find the most ideal decision limit that helps with gathering the important things. This best breaking point is known as the hyper plane of SVM.

3.5.4 Decision Tree

A sort of Overseen Machine Erudition wherever the statistics is repetitively separated by a explicit borderline. The tree can be illuminated by two elements, to be explicit special hubs and leaves. The stages are itemized as shadows. Initiate the tree through the root hub, articulates S, which encompasses the complete dataset, Invention the superlative attribute in the dataset exploiting Characteristic Choice Quantity. Division of the S into subgroups that comprises probable abilities for the top attributes. Produce the optimal tree hub, which encompasses the preeminent eminence. Recursively become calm on new-fangled optimal trees applying the subsets of the dataset finished. Carry on with this cycle while waiting for a segment is here at where you can't added depict the hubs and termed the last hub as a leaf hub.

3.5.5 Random Forest Classifier

This classifier that holds a number of excellent trees on not the same subdivisions of the specified dataset and proceeds the customary to work on the discerning meticulousness of that dataset. This classifier is used in environments when it want selected venture when analogized with poles apart intentions. It have need of some speculation as soon as distinguished through, It envisages vintage with in height precision, in any event, for the gigantic dataset it runs. Professionally, It can the same possess up with correctness when an massive level of statistics is absent.

4   Results and Discussions

4.1 Dataset Description

Wisconsin Breast Cancer Diagnosis dataset from UCI repository is used to train and test and test our proposed architecture. There are 33 features in the dataset. The features are 'id', 'diagnosis', 'radius_mean', 'texture_se', 'perimeter_se', 'area_se', 'smoothness_se', 'compactness_se', 'texture_mean', 'perimeter_mean', 'area_mean', 'smoothness_mean', 'compactness_mean', 'concavity_mean', 'concave points_mean', 'symmetry_mean', 'texture_worst', 'smoothness_worst', 'compactness_worst', 'concavity_worst', 'concave points_worst', 'symmetry_worst', 'fractal_dimension_worst'. 'fractal_dimension_mean', 'radius_se', 'concavity_se', 'concave points_se', 'symmetry_se', 'fractal_dimension_se', 'radius_worst' 'perimeter_worst', 'area_worst',

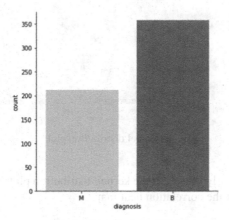

Fig. 2. Distribution of data

The dataset contain two class label namely Benign (B) and Malignant (M). The distribution of the dataset are shown in Fig. 2.

4.2 Kernel Distribution Plot

The kernel distribution plot for the spreading of malignant and benign hand baggage for various features is shown in Fig. 3. The highly correlated features are identified using the pearson coefficient and the heat map is shown is Fig. 4. Some of the features show high correlation such as texture_mean and texture_worst, concave points_mean and concavity_mean, radius_se, perimeter_se and area_se are very strongly correlated. The highly correlated features are dropped inorder to avoid high variance. For example, area_mean, perimeter_mean, radius_worst, area_worst and perimeter_worst are dropped.

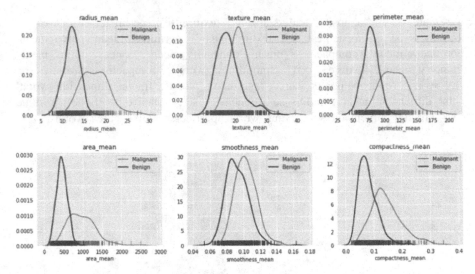

Fig. 3. Kernel distribution plot

The above Fig. 3 clearly illustrates the kernel distribution plot. The following figure. Clearly illustrates about the correlation heat map.

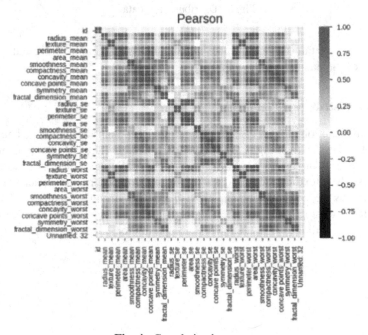

Fig. 4. Correlation heat map

The above Fig. 4 clearly depicts Correlation heat map and it shows high degree of correlation.

4.3 Elbow Plot

The 22 features which are not correlated to each other are selected. And then the Principal Component Analysis (PCA) is useful to diminish the sum of structures. PCA aids in dimensionality reduction and before applying PCA, it is important to standardize the predictors to confirm all structures are on the equal scale. Or else, landscapes that devour high variance will encouragement the consequence of PCA [8]. The data is normalized using the min-max normalization followed by PCA. Instead of arbitrarily choosing the number of dimension, the number of dimensions that can explain most of the variance are chosen (usually 95% of the variance). 95% of the variance was captured by the 10 components of PCA and the elbow plot for PCA is shown is in Fig. 5.

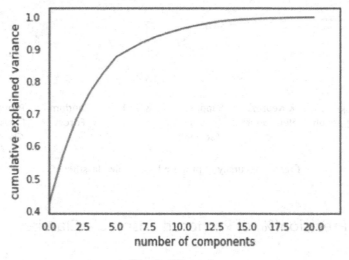

Fig. 5. Elbow plot

The above Fig. 5 clearly explains about the Elbow plot given with no of components in the x axis and cumulative explained variance in the y axis.

4.4 Proposed Ensemble Classifier

The individual classifiers are trained using the 80% of the dataset and the performance of the individual classifiers are plotted [7] in Table 1 and Fig. 6. Our proposed ensemble prototypical is accomplished through the dataset and the authentication is done for the challenging data. The classification accuracy of the ensemble is obtained using the hard voting and soft voting. The hard voting is based on the majority voting, and the final classification is given based on the majority of votes given by the individual classifier.

The performance of hard voting and soft voting are shown in Table 2.

Table 1. Comparison of Individual and proposed classifer

Classifier	Accuracy (%)	Precision (%)	Recall (%)
Logistic regression	97.49	97.89	95.21
K-Nearest neighbor	97.49	98.48	89.70
Support vector machine	96.23	91.88	93.94
Decision tree	90.5	87.14	87
Random forest	91.71	93.86	82.88
Proposed ensemble classifier	98.24	99.29	95.89

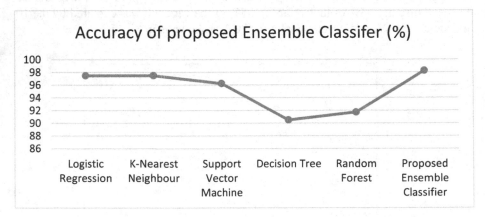

Fig. 6. Accuracy of proposed ensemble classifier

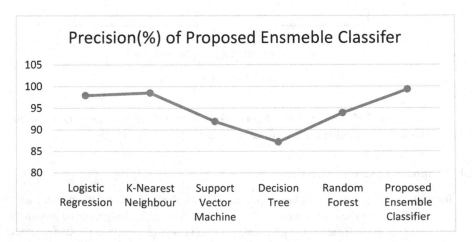

Fig. 7. Precision% of proposed ensemble classifier

The above Fig. 6 clearly illustrates the accuracy of proposed Ensemble classifier.
The above figure clearly explains about precision % of proposed ensemble classifer (Fig. 7).

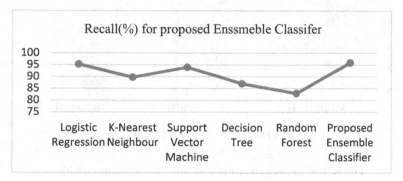

Fig. 8. Precision% of proposed ensemble classifier

The above Fig. 8 clearly depicts the precision % of proposed ensemble classifier. In the soft voting, the class markers are projected grounded on the expected prospects of the distinct classifier. The soft voting classifier gives the averaging of the probabilities of individual classifier.

Table 2. Performance of hard voting and soft voting

Voting classifier	Accuracy (%)	Precision (%)	Recall (%)
Hard voting	97.88	98.43	94.22
Soft voting	98.24	99.29	95.89

The performance of hard voting and soft voting classifier is shown in Fig. 9. The soft voting classifier has performed better than the hard voting classifier and the best classification output is chosen as the final classification result.

The accuracy of hard voting classifier is compared with the soft voting classifier and the best accuracy is chosen as the classification output. The presentation metrics such as accuracy, precision and recall is cast-off. Confusion Matrix is the technique to quota the presentation of a classification problem and the confusion matrix has Actual and Predicted class. Both the dimensions of the confusion matrix has True Positives (TP), True Negatives (TN), "False Positives (FP)", and "False Negatives (FN)". Exactness is most normal execution metric for grouping calculations. It de-fined as the quantity of right forecasts of specific class made as a proportion of all expectations made. Accuracy is the likelihood of patients thought by the classifier to have the illness that really had the infection. Recall is the ratio between the number of people classified as disease to the total number of people examined.

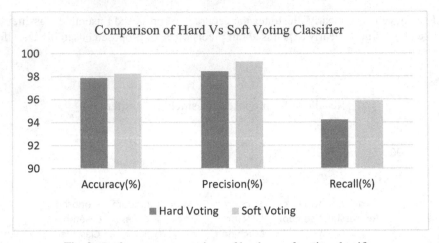

Fig. 9. Performance comparison of hard vs. soft voting classifier

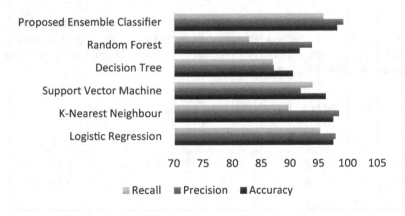

Fig. 10. Recital judgment of prevailing and projected system

The above Fig. 10 explains about the performance of existing and proposed system. The accuracy of proposed ensemble classifier is 98.24 better than the performance of the individual classifiers.

5 Conclusion

The research article clearly describes about various classification process and calculated accuracy, precision and recall percentages. After performing computations in five classification algorithms it is found some algorithms perform some algorithms are better in some calculated values. To improve the efficiency of classification we proposed an ensemble model with an accuracy 98.24%, precision 99.29% and recall 95.89%. So the class labels are anticipated founded on the hard voting and soft voting and the performance improvement is clearly illustrated in graph and tabular form. Based on the ensemble model created it clearly proved that the efficiency is improved comparing with existing methodologies.

References

1. Vakaa, A.R., Sonia, B., Reddy, S.: Breast cancer detection by leveraging Machine Learning. Korean Inst. Commun. Infor. Sci. (KICS), ICT Express **6**, 320–324 (2020)
2. Kathale. P.: Breast cancer detection and classification. In: 2020 International Conference on Emerging Trends in Information Technology and Engineering, pp.1–5 (2020)
3. Bhise, S., Gadekar, S., Gaur, A.S., Bepari, S., Deepmala Kale, D.S.A.: Breast Cancer Detection using Machine Learning Techniques. Int. J. Eng. Res. Technol. **10**(07), 98–103 (2021)
4. Park, K., Chen, W., Chekmareva, M.A., Foran, D.J., Desai, J.P.: Electromechanical coupling factor of breast tissue as a biomarker for breast cancer. IEEE Trans. Biomed. Eng. **65**(1), 96–103 (2018)
5. Liu, P., Fu, B., Yang, S.X., Deng, L., Zhong, X., Zheng, H.: Optimizing survival analysis of XGBoost for ties to predict disease progression of breast cancer. IEEE Trans. Biomed. Eng. **68**(1), 148–160 (2021)
6. Bergstra, J., Bengio, Y.: Algorithms for hyper-parameter optimization. In: Proceedings of the International Conference Neural Information Processing System, pp. 2546–2554 (2011)
7. Bergstra, J., et al.: Hyperopt: a python library for model selection and hyperparameter optimization. Comput. Sci. Discovery **8**(1), 014008 (2015)
8. Heagerty, P., et al.: Time-dependent ROC curves for censored survival data and a diagnostic marker. Biometrics **56**(2), 337–344 (2000)
9. Kalbfleisch, J.D., Prentice, R.L.: The Statistical Analysis of Failure Time Data, 2nd edn. John Wiley & Sons, Hoboken (2011)
10. Yan, L., et al.: Predicting prostate cancer recurrence via maximizing the concordance index. In: Proceedings of the KDD'04, 22–25 August (2004)
11. Fatima, N., Liu, L., Hong, S., Ahmed, H.: Prediction of breast cancer, comparative review of machine learning techniques, and their analysis. IEEE Access **8**, 150360–150376 (2020)
12. Williams, K., Idowu, P.A., Balogun, J.A., Oluwaranti, A.I.: Breast cancer risk prediction using data mining classification techniques. Trans. Netw. Commun. **3**(2), 1 (2015)
13. Bharati, S., Rahman, M.A., Podder, P.: Breast cancer prediction applying different classification algorithm with comparative analysis using WEKA. In: Proceedings of the 4th International Conference on Electrical Engineering and Information Communication Technology (iCEEiCT), pp. 581584 (2018)
14. Mekha, P., Teeyasuksaet, N.: Deep learning algorithms for predicting breast cancer based on tumor cells. In: Proceedings of the Joint International Conference Digital Arts, Media Technology with ECTI Northern Section Conference on Electrical, Electronics, Computer and Telecommunications Engineering (ECTI DAMT-NCON), pp. 343346 (2019)
15. Salma, M.U.: BAT-ELM: a bio inspired model for prediction of breast cancer data. In: Proceedings of the International Conference on Applied and Theoretical Computing and Communication Technology (iCATccT), pp. 501506 (2015)
16. Shen, L., Margolies, L.R., Rothstein, J.H., Fluder, E., McBride, R., Sieh, W.: Deep learning to improve breast cancer detection on screening mammography. Sci. Rep. **9**(1), 112 (2019)
17. Zheng, J., Lin, D., Gao, Z., Wang, S., He, M., Fan, J.: Deep learning assisted efficient AdaBoost algorithm for breast cancer detection and early diagnosis. IEEE Access **8**, 9694696954 (2020)

18. Alanazi, S.A., et al.: Boosting breast cancer detection using convolutional neural network. J. Healthc. Eng. (2021). https://doi.org/10.1155/2021/5528622
19. Liu, C., Yao, D., Yu, K., Zhang, Z.K.: Enhancing cancer driver gene prediction by protein-protein interaction network. IEEE/ACM Trans. Comput. Biol. Bioinf. **19**(4), 2231–2240 (2021)

Deep Learning and Vision Computing

Hand Gesture Recognition for Human-Computer Interaction Using Computer Vision

Kavin Chandar Arthanari Eswaran[1], Akshat Prakash Srivastava[1], and M. Gayathri[2(✉)]

[1] SRM Institute of Science and Technology, SRM Nagar, Kattankulathur 603203, India
{ka7290,as9075}@srmist.edu.in
[2] Department of Computing Technologies, SRM Institute of Science and Technology, SRM Nagar, Kattankulathur 603203, India
gayathrm2@srmist.edu.in

Abstract. We use gestures to communicate with friends, family, and colleagues every day. Gestures have always been a natural and intuitive form of interaction and communication, from waving our hands across the hallway to signal someone to keep the elevator doors open or greet friends from afar. Gestures are the universally understood extension of our body language and comprise a core part of everyday interaction. When we consider this idea for vision-based interaction with computers, we get hand gesture recognition for human-computer interaction using computer vision. We perform a predefined set of gestures in front of a camera and assign individual actions to them. Hence, a computer can recognize the said gestures and complete the appropriate actions. We use this exact method to develop a way to interact with computers with little to no contact. The advent of computer vision and machine learning data libraries makes this dream of contactless interactive technology possible. In light of the pandemic, We wish to create an AI virtual computer mouse. We recognize predefined gestures with a camera and assign appropriate actions that a mouse commonly performs to them. Since the limitations of a physical mouse no longer bind us, we can redefine the conventions of operating a computer with a new set of convenient and easy to grasp rules. We are starting this by developing a virtual gesture-based volume controller. We can perform these feats due to the marvelous works done by academics and researchers that have come before us. The main goal is to use the advantages of computer vision and machine learning to combat the pandemic's challenges and push forward the future of interactive technology. Thus, we get Human-computer interaction using hand recognition technology.

Keywords: Computer vision · Human-computer interaction · Hand gesture recognition · Contactless interactive technology · Vision-based techniques

1 Introduction

For the longest time, Contactless human-computer interaction has been at the forefront of making life more accessible and convenient for all. From voice-controlled automotive systems on cars and gesture-based entertainment systems in the living room. Video

K. Kottursamy et al. (Eds.): IconDeepCom 2022, CCIS 1719, pp. 77–90, 2023.
https://doi.org/10.1007/978-3-031-27622-4_7

Games, Virtual Reality Simulations, Voice assistants, etc. These are a few of the many applications built for comfort and entertainment. However, there are plenty of scenarios where contactless human-computer interaction can be the essential and more optimal approach relative to current methods, in the case of factory workers or medical professionals whose hands are preoccupied. Industry Professionals can immensely benefit from a system that can be purely operated with little to no contact. In light of the covid-19 pandemic and living in the post-pandemic world, It has become a necessity for contactless human-computer interaction systems to carry the burden of slowing transmission rates moving forward. Therefore, We aim to contribute to this cause of developing a low cost and highly accessible system that could be used for all. This deal that sounds too good to be true is now a reality due to the significant leaps in computer vision and machine learning fields.

1.1 Hand Tracking Module

The first step was to design a hand tracking module to recognize hand gestures accurately. This would be the foundation for other applications going forward. We can achieve this by using the computer vision and machine learning libraries in python to get optimal results. We also aim to learn and increase hand detection confidence to get even more accurate results.

1.2 AI Virtual Mouse

The best place to start was to develop a virtual mouse that was already a multifunctional device in terms of operating a computer system. Thus, we can create the bare minimum functionality needed to manage a computer system fully. Using the Hand tracking module mentioned above, we can accurately track the positions of the 21 points on an average human hand. We can then use this data to assign standard mouse functions such as cursor movement and click automation to our hand gestures. Thus, we can now fully simulate a physical working mouse using our hands and a camera to operate a computer system adeptly.

1.3 Gesture-Based Volume Controller

Now that we have a hand tracking module, the physical limitations of a mouse no longer bind us. We can simulate a volume slider using the index finger and thumb finger position data since this uses the same data already acquired for the virtual mouse. There is no extra cost in obtaining data. Furthermore, Since the physical limitations of a mouse no longer bind us. We can venture into the realm of discovering new rules to replace the old conventions of operating a mouse. We can look forward to many such innovations in the future.

1.4 Software Requirements

Python is the programming language we use for building our appliances. **OpenCV** is often used as a python library of methods primarily for real-time computer vision and an exquisite tool for image processing. It's an open-source library that may perform face detection, objection tracking, landmark detection, and much more. It supports multiple languages, including python, java, C++.

On the other hand, **Mediapipe** is popularly used as an ML solutions library for all major platforms developed by Google that provide out-of-the-box solutions for computer vision tasks, etc. **win32api** is employed for assigning cursor movement. It's a library of python extensions for windows that allows the user to use the Win32 application programming interface features.

PyAutoGui is employed primarily for click automation purposes. It's a Python automation library accustomed to clicking, dragging, scrolling, moving, etc. **Pycaw** is utilized for acquiring admin access to the quantity slider in windows. It's a python module developed by Stanford students used for Python Core Audio Windows Library.

We use those modules together to form a **computer-vision-based hand gesture recognition module** to simulate human-computer interaction at a coffee cost and in a highly accessible fashion.

2 Literature Survey

The literature in this field comprises three core aspects- Hand gesture recognition, Human-computer interaction, and computer vision.

[1, 4] - We see researchers use algorithms to identify particular gestures. To name a few, a novel finger skin pixel algorithm which they claim has a hand recognition rate of 94.3%. The K-nearest neighbor algorithm is also used for recognition based on Kanade's Pyramidal optical flow algorithm. There are also mentions of a full-fledged multi-participant visual environment (VE), Which is essentially a 3D environment to move objects with only our hands.

[5, 6] - We see references to multimodal human-computer interaction research for facial expression recognition(MMHCI). We also see methods to improve the precision of gestures by factoring user fatigue into account. There are even mentions of autonomous gesture commands.

[7, 8] - Here, we see advances in using perceptive user interfaces for head tracking, facial expression recognition, eye tracking, and other forms of gestures. There are also models and algorithms for detecting sign language at a recognition rate of 92% and in 2.76 s. They also claim that there is no need for training sample data for their algorithm to provide said results.

[9, 10] - These papers refer to using Microsoft's Kinect sensors to accurately recognize hand insensitive variations and other distortions using RGB and depth data.

[11, 16] - The researchers here look for methods to move on from standard mouse and keyboard setups to other forms of gesture-based systems to push forward means of human-computer interaction. Computer vision-based gesture recognition is done for Augmented reality Interfaces. They use algorithms for detection, tracking, and recognition to build 3D hand models for more accurate results. This particular survey examines 37 papers on depth-based gesture recognition and provides comparisons on optimal methods for optimal use cases. Thus, We have an overview of similar research work done in hand gesture recognition, human-computer interaction, and computer vision.

[17, 19] - Here, we discover fields such as Fuzzy systems towards human-centric computing which showcase user-friendly nature of systems with a tradeoff between accuracy and transparency. Next up, we see QA2MN, a question-aware memory network to update the attention on questions during the reasoning process. This helps in performing intelligent human–robot interactions. Finally, we observe an interesting study that aims to learn how colors affect a person's product preferences by using an eye-tracking device intended to identify the role of their eye movements.

3   System Architecture and Design

3.1   Architecture Block Diagram

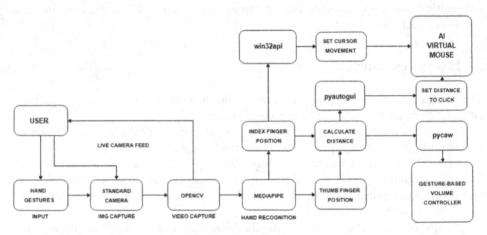

Fig. 1. Block diagram

The above block diagram clearly illustrates the workings of the modules in tandem to make the AI Virtual Mouse and Gesture-based volume controller a reality (Figs. 1 and 2).

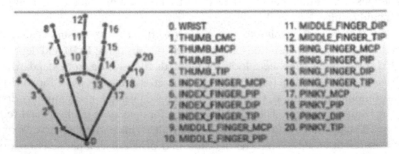

Fig. 2. Hand landmarks

The 21 Hand landmarks displayed above are crucial in deploying the aforementioned architecture diagram into a functioning prototype. They serve as the rope tying all these modules together to function as one.

3.2 Design of Modules

OpenCV module is a computer vision library that helps capture and display output. (pip install OpenCV). **Mediapipe** is an open library of ML solutions to recognize hand landmarks. **Win32api** is used for cursor movement. (pip install mediapipe). **PyAutoGUI** allows us to use python scripts to control the mouse and keyboard to automate interactions with other applications. (pip install pyautogui). We calculate the distance between the index and the thumb finger in real-time. This distance is used for click automation. **Pycaw** helps us access the windows volume slider and uses the same distance range as a volume slider. **For the Ai Virtual Mouse,** We use the OpenCV module and media pipes open dataset to recognize hands and display the same using OpenCV's custom methods. Win32api is used for cursor movement and click automation. PyAutoGUI allows us to use python scripts to control the mouse and keyboard to automate interactions with other applications. The API is designed to be simple. We use a hand tracking module for the Gesture-based volume controller to calculate the distance between the index and the thumb finger in real-time using OpenCV and mediapipe. Pycaw helps us access the windows volume slider.

4 Methodology

4.1 Hand Tracking Module

The Hand tracking module is developed to provide a foundation for all our upcoming vision-based human-computer interaction projects that rely on hand recognition. It helps us lay the bricks ahead of time since it's made reusable and versatile for various purposes in mind.We use the time module to calculate the full frames per second. On the other hand, cv2 is the OpenCV library. We use it to capture the live camera feed and feed the image output into the mediapipe. Mediapipe is an ML solutions module that allows users to recognize the hands of an image with its highly trained datasets. Next, we implement a class for hand detection recognition. It serves with necessary and respective methods needed for implementing future projects. The default constructor here takes mode, max_Hands, Detection confidence, Tracking confidence into account. These variables are initialized with values that help shape the overall project. For example, First, the max_Hands variable determines the total number of hands recognized on the camera. It allows us to restrict the number of recognized hands based on use-case. Secondly, The detection and tracking confidence help us determine the recognized object to be the intended object. This base constructor serves the critical purpose of setting the base conditions necessary for future endeavors. The first method we have defined is the Find hands method which returns the respective frame from a live camera feed if the module recognizes a hand. We first convert the input image from BGR to RGB. Since mediapipe doesn't directly recognize BGR images. Then the image is processed for the hand landmarks. The method draws connections to visualize the identified points if landmarks are present and the draw condition is set to True. We then return the updated image in real-time. The second method we have defined is the Find position method which returns a list of positions of all the 21 hand landmarks identified at any given moment. We iterate through the self.results gained from the previous method. The handNo parameter helps us choose a particular hand out of all recognized hands. The height and width of the image are then multiplied with the respective x and y coordinates of each hand landmark. Compiling this information into a list of positions indexed with their respective landmark indices. This constantly updating list of positional landmark coordinates helps us recognize the exact position of the recognized hand at any moment. This data is beneficial in identifying gestures and assigning actions to them in real-time.

4.2 AI Virtual Mouse

The AI virtual mouse we implement here is synonymous with a regular mouse commonly used to operate a computer. The goal is to create a version that works with little to no contact required from the user. To achieve the said goal above, we import the aforementioned modules. Noteworthily, we import the hand tracking module we developed beforehand to serve the function of hand recognition in this project. We introduce two new modules, win32api and pyautogui. These are vital for this model to simulate a working mouse on any windows machine fully. We use the object 'detector,' an instance of the hand_detector class. We can access the previously defined methods find_Hands and find_Position. These methods aid us in hand gesture recognition by detecting hand-like features from our camera feed and returning the positions of the 21 hand landmarks relative to the image shape. By checking if poslist exists, we can determine if our hand tracking module recognizes hands at any moment to attain the following data. We only require positional data of the index_tip, thumb_tip, middle_finger_pip, and middle_finger_dip. Using this, we can bring life to the AI virtual mouse and gesture-based volume controller going forward. We check if the x and y coordinates of the index_tip exist given the camera. If detected, we then use win32api's SetCursorPos to set the cursor position relative to the frame of the computer specifications. Since this condition is placed inside a while loop that runs until our camera footage dies, We can constantly update the cursor position in real-time by moving our index_tip part given the camera. Using this method, we can fully simulate the cursor moment of a regular mouse using only a camera and the tip of our index finger. Another neat feature is implementing inverted controls for our virtual mouse by flipping the camera orientation into its mirror counterpart. This will prove beneficial to people accustomed to inverted controls on their devices. Now that we can traverse the computer screen with the cursor freely. We set out to implement the other essential functions that define the standard computer mouse—starting with the most crucial button for interaction. We designed this by keeping in mind the needs and wants of the user. It is created comfortably for the user to left click without any obstructions. The user is meant to adopt a particular hand position to traverse the screen freely. We then use the positional data of the thumb_tip and middle_finger_pip to calculate the euclidean distance between them at any given moment. Now we can use the distance calculated to create a switch. So when we bring our thumb_tip closer to the middle_finger_pip landmark in front of the camera. The euclidean distance between them is being calculated at every passing moment. We check if the space drops below a certain threshold to detect a user's intent to click. Hence when we notice the user's intent, we use pyautogui.click() to automate the left click functionality at the user's beck and call. However, pyautogui.click() performs multiple clicks in the span of a short moment due to the nature of the video camera footage. Therefore, we employ a method to slow down the detection process by checking if the euclidean distance is a multiple of five under the threshold distance of 20. Hence only four out of twenty instances are noticed in a single moment. This gives the user more agency and control over this particular action. Now, To implement the other standard function of the mouse. It helps us access many options depending on the cursor's position and application. To go following the position the user adopts. We employ the same euclidean distance-based switch. We implement it between the thumb_tip and middle_finger_dip. Now by examining this distance relative to a threshold. We can use pyautogui.click (button = 'right') to provide the right-click functionality when the euclidean distance measure detects the user's intent to click. Same as before to reduce the rate of clicks and keep it similar in feel to the left click automation. We check the euclidean distance values that break the threshold to see if they are multiples of five. This action happens many times in the span of a single moment. Hence, This allows the user more agency and control over this right-click automation.

4.3 Gesture-Based Volume Controller

We have a functioning vision-based virtual mouse that performs the expected functionalities of a regular mouse. We move on to test the potential of vision-based systems. In doing so, we hope to establish new and improved conventions to overwrite the old and outdated ones. We start by developing a gesture-based volume controller. We chose this because it doesn't require any additional data and can perform well from the data we accumulated for the virtual mouse.The hand-tracking module we established is used here, proving its versatile and reusable nature. Numpy is used here to relate the distance measure with other ranges. We introduce an all-new module here called pycaw. Pycaw is a module developed by Stanford students to gain admin access to the window's audio libraries. By combining them with our code, we can realistically conceive the dream of operating a system without any physical contact. The volume controller function encompasses the whole process. First, we define all the necessary attributes, such as the width and height of the camera used. Then we use cv2.Videocapture(0) to acquire the live camera feed. We also set the image specifications. Prev_time is a variable defined here, which will aid us later in calculating the overall frames per second. We also call a detector, an object of the hand tracking module. This allows us to contact the default constructor of the hand_Detector() class. We initialize several member variables required for hand recognition later. Then we use GetSpeakers(), a method of AudioUtilities from the pycaw module. This method acquires all the active audio devices connected to the machine and stores that information in the variable devices. Interface and cast() methods check for the recognized devices' current audio levels and assign those values to the volume variable. We use GetVolumeRange() to get the volume range of an audio device. Then we define the minimum volume and maximum volume and align them to their respective variables and VolRange indices. These stored values gained from the pycaw module will be used to specify the parameters needed for feature-based volume control. We begin our live camera feed by using capture.read() we acquire the frame to be analyzed for one iteration. We pass this frame as input to the hand tracking module methods find_Hands and find_Position. They return an updated picture with visualized hand connections and a list of positions of all the 21 hand landmarks recorded by the module. We only require the positional coordinates of the thumb_tip and index_tip for this particular module. So we store those distinct values alone in variables such as thumb_x, thumb_y, index_x, and index_y. These values are crucial to determining the distance measure needed to detect the user's intent to change the volume. We then calculate the midpoint between the thumb_tip and index_tip. We visualize the distance measure between the thumb_tip and index_tip using cv2.line() and the midpoint using cv2.circle(). We calculate the euclidean distance between the thumb_tip and index_tip using math.hypot(). We can now use this length measure against a threshold of value 20 to detect the user's intent through the gesture of bringing the thumb and index finger closer together. When we notice such an intention, we use cv2.circle() again to change the midpoint color, visualizing the lower bound. Hence, This action loosely translates to the workings of a switch. We used this already for left click and right click automation in the last project. However, in this context, it acts as a mute switch to set the volume to 0. Now that we have established our lower bound, we use the NumPy module's interp() method to relate the length measure between the thumb_tip and index_tip to the volume range between the predefined minimum volume and maximum volume of a recognized audio device. We can then use the volume.SetMasterVolumeLevel() method from pycaw to update the master volume level concerning the changes in the length measure. VolBar and VolPer variables are calculated to simulate the audio changes. We then pass these to the volume bar() function to visualize the process in real-time. The volume bar utility function here displays the changes in volume and the live camera feed in real-time. By combining methods from openCV and values calculated using NumPy, we can show the correlation between the distance measured between the index and thumb and the volume slider in windows.

4.4 Utility Functions

We write a few functions ahead of time to maintain the readability and cleanliness of our code. These functions tend to require use more than once. So we establish these as utility functions to prevent redefining them from scratch every time. The fps function uses the time() method from the time python module to acquire the current time at any given moment. We then perform the above-shown fps calculation and visualize them using the putText() method from the cv2 module. We update the prev_Time variable at every function call instance to ensure the calculation remains up to date with the live camera feed. We use the display function above to view the recognized 21 hand landmarks and their connections. This function is essential as it showcases the individual working of our heavily customized hand recognition module. We use the fps() utility function here to calculate and display the total frames per second calculated at any given moment in the live camera feed. Here it serves to show the efficiency of the Hand Tracking module on a particular device. This method provided by OpenCV allows us to view our ever updating image in unison with the live camera feed. This allows us to observe the fruits of our labor instantly. This method exists within the while loop and constantly updates with every input. We use matplotlib.pyplot to plot the efficiency of our overall code in a devised graph format with time measured in seconds on the x-axis and fps on the y-axis. We also use it to test and plot the efficiency of our overall code in a colored bar graph format with time measured in minutes on the y -axis and fps on the x-axis. Then, the cv2.waitkey(10) and 0xFF = ord('x') commands use these as exit conditions to break the while loop thereby, breaking the whole live camera feed. So the user can press the key 'X' on his keyboard to terminate the program when it is running.

5 Output

5.1 Hand Tracking Module

(See Figs. 3, 4, 5 and 6).

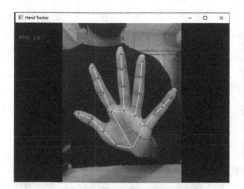

Fig. 3. Front view

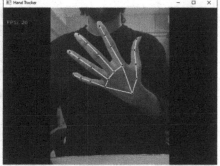

Fig. 4. Back view

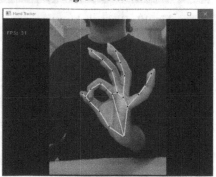

Fig. 5. Random gesture

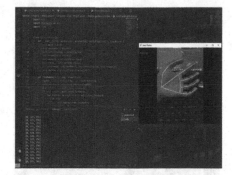

Fig. 6. Position data

5.2 AI Virtual Mouse

(See Figs. 7, 8, 9 and 10).

5.3 Gesture-Based Volume Controller

(See Figs. 11, 12 and 13).

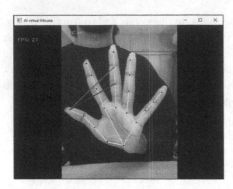

Fig. 7. Base virtual mouse

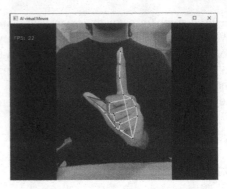

Fig. 8. Cursor gesture

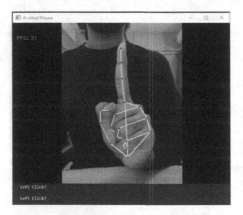

Fig. 9. Left-click gesture

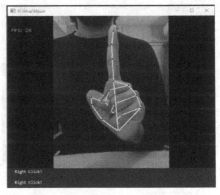

Fig. 10. Right-click gesture

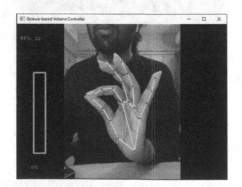

Fig. 11. Volume at 0%

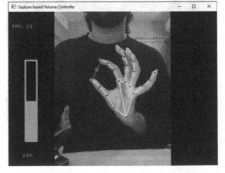

Fig. 12. Volume at 50%

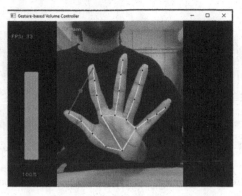

Fig. 13. Volume at 100%

6 Results and Discussions

Our algorithm amalgamates triumphs in computer vision, machine learning, hand-recognition technology, and human-computer interaction. It works with all the necessary advanced technological models developed in said fields. We measured the total frames per second to judge the efficiency of our applications.

Hand Tracker Module
(See Figs. 14 and 15).

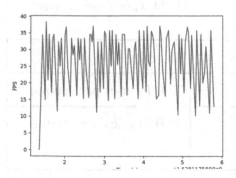

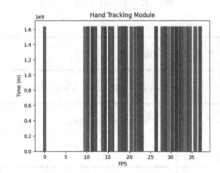

Fig. 14. Fps drop rate graph   **Fig. 15.** Fps consistency graph

AI Virtual Mouse
(See Figs. 16 and 17).

Gesture-Based Volume Controller
(See Figs. 18, 19 and 20).

The frames per second in each module were more or less identical due to using mediapipe advanced models. However, The frames per second were observed to drop depending on low lighting, distorted camera vision, too much movement, etc. These actions caused the frames per second to fluctuate instead of the expected steady 30

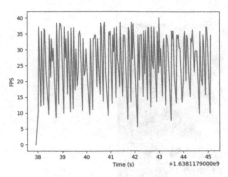

Fig. 16. Fps drop rate graph

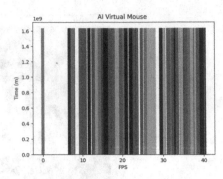

Fig. 17. Fps consistency graph

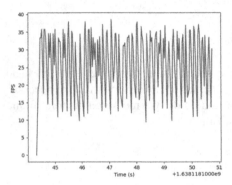

Fig. 18. Fps drop rate graph

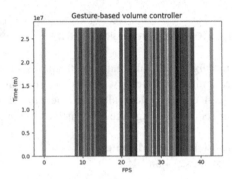

Fig. 19. Fps consistency graph

S.No	Modules	Average Fps
1.	Hand Tracking Module	26.0 Frames per second
2.	AI Virtual Mouse	25.0 Frames per second
3.	Gesture-based Volume Controller	26.0 Frames per second

Fig. 20. Synopsis of proposed models

frames per second. However, These flaws can be overcome by installing a better graphics processing unit (GPU) in the computer.

7 Challenges

We are raising Hand Recognition Confidence using any standard camera on any traditional system. To make this widely accessible, we aim to create a model that works best for all available current devices without needing much investment from the user in terms of camera specifications. We are looking for ways to improve consistency in the detection of gestures. Currently, there are inconsistencies due to low light settings and other distractions that occur in the camera frame. We are looking for methods to improve this as much as possible while keeping the cost as low as possible. We are assigning an action to gestures. Administrative access to certain functionalities is not readily available at a coffee cost. This has proven to be quite a challenge to overcome on our own. We wish to develop a dynamic Software system to work on any compatible system with a camera and computer. Currently, Our model only works on PC machines with windows operating systems. We aim to expand this forward to all sorts of devices. We are improving the user interface and experience. We only have working prototypes, but we hope to develop full-fledged applications convenient to use shortly. We are improving accuracy and quality while maintaining feasibility and accessibility. We aim to optimize as much as we can to keep costs low without compromising on the integrity of the application. Thus, We have successfully implemented a hand tracking module to create a functioning model of an AI virtual mouse and gesture-based volume controller using computer vision and machine learning solutions. This is the first of many steps yet to be taken to use hand recognition technology using computer vision commercially for human-computer interaction at a low cost and highly accessible fashion.

8 Conclusion and Future Enhancement

With the arrival of new and exciting technologies such as computer vision, interactive intelligence, and machine learning, We can create advanced human-computer interaction models due to the advances made in such fields. Our algorithm uses these advances to detect the needed positions, such as the index and the thumb finger. Using these positions, we can calculate the Manhattan distance between them. This relative distance is used for click automation and as a volume slider when appropriate. We also use the index finger position when in the frame and assign it to cursor movement. These two simple actions assigned to advanced miracle models in hand recognition and computer vision give an AI mouse with a gesture-based volume controller. In the future, This technology can be custom-tailored to be of use in a wide variety of areas such as healthcare solutions, consumer electronics, security and entertainment systems, etc. Models then gesture recognized through cameras can potentially control all devices sign or even give birth to fully virtually controlled environments. Predictions show that the market for gesture recognition technologies is growing, and the sky's the limit. We evolved from analog-controlled devices to touch-controlled devices. Eventually, the future points to contactless interactive technology through voice and gestures, to name a few. For example, Kinect, developed by Microsoft, was initially intended to track whole-body movements. KinTrans Hands Can Talk is a project that uses AI to learn and process sign the body movements of sign language. GestSure allows surgeons to navigate through MRI and CT scans without touching a screen. Audi and BMW have already implemented a system that will enable drivers to use gestures to control the infotainment system inside the car. There are also numerous open-source projects for hand gesture recognition, like Real-time GesRec based on PyTorch. The Future is immensely bright going forward with Gesture-based technology.

References

1. Rios-Soria, D.J., Schaeffer, S.E., Garza-Villarreal, S.E.: Hand-gesture recognition using computer-vision techniques (2013)
2. Lai, H.Y., Ke, H.Y., Hsu, Y.C.: Real-time hand gesture recognition system and application. Sens. Mater **30**, 869–884 (2018)
3. Garg, P., Aggarwal, N., Sofat, S.: Vision-based hand gesture recognition. World Acad. Sci. Eng. Technol. **49**(1), 972–977 (2009)
4. Rautaray, S.S., Agrawal, A.: Vision-based hand gesture recognition for human-computer interaction: a survey. Artif. Intell. Rev. **43**(1), 1–54 (2015)
5. Jaimes, A., Sebe, N.: Multimodal human-computer interaction: a survey. Comput. Vis. Image Underst. **108**(1–2), 116–134 (2007)
6. Lenman, S., Bretzner, L., Thuresson, B.: Computer vision-based hand gesture interfaces for human-computer interaction. Royal Institute of Technology, Sweden (2002)
7. Zabulis, X., Baltzakis, H., Argyros, A.A.: Vision-based hand gesture recognition for human-computer interaction. Univ. Access Handb. **34**, 30 (2009)
8. Panwar, M., Mehra, P.S.: Hand gesture recognition for human-computer interaction. In: 2011 International Conference on Image Information Processing, pp. 1–7. IEEE (2011)
9. Ren, Z., Yuan, J., Meng, J., Zhang, Z.: Robust part-based hand gesture recognition using Kinect sensor. IEEE Trans. Multimed. **15**(5), 1110–1120 (2013)
10. Tang, M.: Recognizing hand gestures with Microsoft's kinect. Department of Electrical Engineering of Stanford University, Palo Alto (2011)
11. Murthy, G.R.S., Jadon, R.S.: A review of vision-based hand gestures recognition. Int. J. Inf. Technol. Knowl. Manag. **2**(2), 405–410 (2009)
12. Störring, M., Moeslund, T.B., Liu, Y., Granum, E.: Computer vision-based gesture recognition for an augmented reality interface. In: The 4th IASTED International Conference on Visualization, imaging, and Image Processing, vol. 766, p. 771 (2004)
13. Pavlovic, V.I., Sharma, R., Huang, T.S.: Visual interpretation of hand gestures for human-computer interaction: a review. IEEE Trans. Pattern Anal. Mach. Intell. **19**(7), 677–695 (1997)
14. Davis, J., Shah, M.: Recognizing hand gestures. In: Eklundh, J.-O. (ed.) ECCV 1994. LNCS, vol. 800, pp. 331–340. Springer, Heidelberg (1994). https://doi.org/10.1007/3-540-57956-7_37
15. Rautaray, S.S., Agrawal, A.: A novel human-computer interface based on hand gesture recognition using computer vision techniques. In: Proceedings of the First International Conference on Intelligent Interactive Technologies and Multimedia, pp. 292–296 (2010)
16. Wu, Y., Lin, J.Y., Huang, T.S.: Capturing natural hand articulation. In: Proceedings Eighth IEEE International Conference on Computer Vision. ICCV 2001, vol. 2, pp. 426–432. IEEE (2001)
17. Pedrycz, W., Gomide, F.: Fuzzy Systems Engineering: Toward Human-Centric Computing. Wiley, Hoboken (2007)
18. Li, X., Alazab, M., Li, Q., Yu, K., Yin, Q.: Question-aware memory network for multi-hop question answering in human–robot interaction. Complex Intell. Syst. (2021)
19. Wu, B., Zhu, Y., Yu, K., Nishimura, S., Jin, Q.: The effect of eye movements and cultural factors on product color selection. Hum.-Cent. Comput. Inf. Sci. **10**(48), 1–14 (2020)

Deep Learning Taxonomy on Human Face Expression Recognition for Communication Applications

Raja Bhargava[1]([✉]), N. Arivazhagan[1], and K. Sureshbabu[2]

[1] Department of Computing Intelligence, SRM Institute of Technology, Kattankulathur, Chennai, India
rb8020@srmist.edu.in
[2] Department of Computing Science and Engineering, ISTS Women's Engineering College, Rajahmundry, Andhra Pradesh, India

Abstract. In social communication applications, the most challenging and power task is human face expression recognition system. Basically, communication with emotions and intentions in direct way is nothing but face expression. For the non-verbal communication one of the main characteristics in faces expressions. Face Expression Recognition (FER) techniques are introduced in this paper. This FER will divide into three stages mainly they are pre-processing, feature extraction and classification. Based on their major contributions techniques of FER are introduced. Performance is analyzed based on the complexity of algorithms of FER. From recent papers it reveals that classification techniques are more powerful and reliable with peculiar characteristics.

Keywords: Classification · Face Expression Recognition (FER) · Feature extraction · Preprocessing · First Section

1 Introduction

In social communications human facial expressions plays major role. This is the combination of both verbal and nonverbal communication. By using facial expressions nonverbal communication is expressed. For larger communication signals are delicate through facial expressions. Communication between animals and humans is nothing but non-verbal communication which is contacted through their facial expression, eye contact and body language. Basically, mixture of ideas is obtained to through the eye contact which is an important phase of communication. Links, contributions, discussions are controlled t = with the help of eye contact. There are different types of face expression they are anger, sad, surprise, smile and fear.

A smile on human face shows their happiness and it expresses eye with a curved shape. The sad expression is the feeling of looseness which is normally ex-pressed as rising skewed eyebrows and frown. The anger on human face is related to unpleasant and irritating conditions. The expression of anger is expressed with squeezed eyebrows,

K. Kottursamy et al. (Eds.): IconDeepCom 2022, CCIS 1719, pp. 91–102, 2023.
https://doi.org/10.1007/978-3-031-27622-4_8

slender and stretched eyelids. The disgust expressions are expressed with pull down eyebrows and creased nose. The surprise or shock expression is expressed when some unpredicted happens. This is expressed with eye-widening and mouth gaping and this expression is an easily identified one. The expression of fear is related with surprise expression which is expressed as growing skewed eyebrows.

Face Recognition has been one of the major areas of interest in the field of biometric and security for the past few decades. Humans have a very strong face recognition technique. Human brain is so sophisticated that it can recognize faces even with the vast changes in appearance. The scientists have always been amazed by the human brain capacity to recognize face under different varied condition. A lot of attempts were made to replicate this technique of our brain. Various algorithms were developed for face recognition based on this. The efficiency of recognition depends on feature extraction method adopted.

Evolutionary algorithms like neural networks, fuzzy logic etc. were also incorporated with the face recognition algorithms to increase the recognition rate. But there are a lot of constraints that has been implemented in applying these algorithms, like the poses should not vary, or there should not be any difference in the illumination, the expressions should not vary, there should not be many changes with age etc.

Overcoming even a single constraint is a great challenge. In this paper techniques that has overcome one of the constraints i.e., the face expression is considered. An algorithm which has a good recognition rate in normal face recognition may fail when used to recognize a face with expression. This is because a face with expression will be showing a lot of variations from the neutral face. In this paper different algorithms adopted for face expression recognition are reviewed. Both 2D methods and 3D methods are considered and compared.

The key factor in the Face Expression Recognition is the descriptor. FER's efficiency depends on how easily features can be extracted for the descriptor and also on the efficiency of the descriptor. Descriptors of different expression should show high variance while same expressions should show little or no variance. Geometric feature based and appearance-based methods are the two common approaches that are used for facial feature extraction. In Geometric feature-based method the image is represented with the help of geometric parameters like points, curves etc.

This representation is achieved by locating the distinct parts of the face such as eyes, nose, ears, mouth etc. and measuring their relative positions, width and constructing geometric shapes to represent these parameters. In Appearance based method importance is given to pixel values rather than relative distance or shape of feature components. In this method various parameters of the pixels to representation histogram and intensity are utilized. Templates are nothing but whereby using 2D array values are represented. To get good recognition rate two approaches are combined in some algorithms.

2 Stages in FER

Multistage process is nothing but face expression recognition system. It is processed mainly in five stages mainly they are preprocessing, face detection, facial component detection, feature extraction and classification.

2.1 Preprocessing

For any image processing technique preprocessing is the first step. For the purpose of processing image is taken from different conditions based on different equipment. But this will be not in standard form of images. Various disturbances like backgrounds, illumination variations and noise are affected by the using the input images. By varying different sizes images are obtained. There is resizing, enhancement, noise removal in the process of standardization of image for the first step of FER. Hence in preprocessing stage this is done. This stage will not use the color images, but they use the grey scale images in FER techniques. Therefore, in preprocessing stage conversion is done form color to gray scale. Therefore, in the pre-processing stage images are standardized.

2.2 Face Detection

The main intent is to remove the unwanted backgrounds in the image after obtained from the preprocessed stage. This will extract the dace alone in processing stages. This is nothing but face detection. Edge detection is most commonly used in the face detection techniques. In face recognition, edge detection techniques are soble. Kirsch, Laplacian, and peewit.

2.3 Facial Component Detection

Detection of various regions of interest is done in this stage. Based on nose, eyebrows, eyes, ear, forehead the ROIs face detection is done. Hence to detect ROIs face both global and local approaches are used.

2.4 Feature Extraction

In this FER is used which is most critical stage. This stage is determined based on the efficiency. The concept of most popular feature extraction technique is introduced by the Jyoti Kumari et al. This will extract the facial features in very effective way. Local Binary Patterns (LBP), Principal Component Analysis (PCA), Linear Discriminant Analysis (LDA) and Gabor filters re the most common feature extraction techniques.

2.5 Classification

Here features are extracted based on the classes of expressions from the face images. The most useful classifier is SVM. For classification most commonly used are Neural Networks and Nearest Neighbor.

3 Strategic Survey on FER

Expression invariant 3D Face Recognition using Patched Geodesic Texture Transform [1].

The Texture of the 3D face image is extracted for face recognition in this method. Local Feature vectors are extracted from the texture of the face by using Geodesic texture transform accompanied by Pseudo Zernike Moments. Fars hid et al. [1] has proposed a method of face recognition using Patched Geodesic Texture trans-form (PGTT) which is expression independent. The algorithm is as follows. The range and texture images of the 3D face model is created. One point on the face is chosen as the reference point. The Geodesic distance for all the face points is calculated with reference to this reference point. The texture image of the face is transformed into a new texture image based on the computed Geodesic distance. The new image is called transformed texture image. The transformed texture im-age is then partitioned to patches. The patches are of same size and also, they are non-overlapping. Feature vector is extracted for each patch by applying a patch descriptor. All the feature vectors that are extracted from the individual patches are concatenated to get the final feature vector. The input face feature vector is compared with the face feature vectors in the gallery and the similarity between the query image and the image in the database is taken to identify the face.

Curvelet Feature Extraction for Face Recognition and Facial Expression Recognition [2];

Xianxing and Jieyu Zhaohas proposed a new approach for facial expression recognition based on the Curvelet transform and PCA. This method is based on the fact that the face expression contains details like curves and lines. It is more accurate to use curvelet rather than wavelet in this condition because the wavelets can represent only point singularities. The algorithm follows a four-stage process for the expression recognition.

Face and Expression Recognition Based on Bag of Words Method Considering Holistic and Local Image Features [3].

Bag of Words method is a Local matching approach introduced by Zisheng et al. [3]. Here the image is represented as a collection of local features. The collection is order less. These patches of local features are the basic elements called "words". These patches are represented as numerical vectors by applying feature descriptors to these patches. These numerical vectors are converted to "code words" to produce a "codebook". The codebook is made using clustering methods. The code words are defined as the centers of the learned clusters. The image is represented by a code word histogram by mapping each patch in the image to a code word through clustering process. For facial expression recognition the face as a whole is not considered for partitioning. Instead of this the facial components are extracted first and clustered. This method can effectively classify the facial expressions.

Local Directional Number Pattern for Face Analysis: Face and Expression Recognition [4].

The local Directional Number pattern introduced by Adin Ramirez Rivera and Jorge Rojas Castillo encodes the structural information and intensity variations of the face's texture.

Directional information is analyses by using the LDN analysis in encoding structure. In the compass mask the calculation of eight neighborhoods is done based on the edge responses. The descriptor is produced based on all directions in the positive and negative.

This will assist with recognizing the force changes in the surface. Additionally in this strategy the descriptor is created considering the whole area and not the meager focuses like in LBP. Here significance is given for design of the texture and its force changes. These parts are addressed by utilizing a six-cycle paired code relegated to every pixel of the information picture.

FARO: Face Recognition Against Occlusions and Expression Variations [5].

Maria De Marsico et al. introduces the concept of face recognition which is based on the PIFS theory. (i) PIFS theory application. Both domains and ranges are de-fined in PIFS theory. (ii) centroid is computed. In this region are separated based on the PIFS face components. (iii) Feature Vector Structure. In this comparison of centroids are computed based on feature vector structure.

Gradient Feature Matching for Expression Invariant Face Recognition using Single Reference Image [6].

Filled by the consistent multiplying pace of processing power at regular intervals, face discovery and acknowledgment has risen above from an exclusive to a famous area of examination in PC vision and one of the better and effective utilizations of picture investigation and calculation-based understanding. As a result of the natural nature of the issue, PC vision isn't just a software engineering area of re-search, yet in addition the object of neuro-logical and mental investigations, for the most part due to the overall assessment that advances in PC picture handling and understanding examination will give experiences into how our cerebrum work as well as the other way around. Due to general interest and interest with regards to this issue, the creator has proposed to make an application that would permit client admittance to a specific machine in light of a top to bottom investigation of an individual's facial elements. This application will be created utilizing Intel's open-source PC vision project, OpenCV and Microsoft's .NET system.

A design for Integrated Face and Facial Expression Recognition [7].

Using convolutional networks includes highlight realizing, which sounds extremely encouraging for this task where characterizing highlights isn't insignificant. Addition-ally, the organization was assessed utilizing two distinct corpora: one was utilized dur-ing organization's preparation, and it was likewise useful for boundary tuning and for organization's design definition. This corpus comprised of facial acted feelings. The organization giving best order precision results was tried against the second dataset. Despite the fact that the organization was pre-pared utilizing just a single corpus; the organization announced propitious out-comes when tried on an alternate dataset, which showed facial nonacute feelings. While the results achieved were not state of-the-art; the evidence gathered points out deep learning might be suitable to classify facial emotion expressions. Thus, deep learning has the potential to improve human machine interac-tion because its ability to learn features will allow machines to develop perception. And by having perception, machines will potentially provide smoother responses, drastically im-proving the user experience.

Facial expression analysis [8].

Various machine learning algorithms have been developed for emotion detection in a multimedia element, such as an image or a video. These techniques can be measured by comparing their accuracy with a given dataset to determine which algorithm can be selected among others. This paper deals with the comparison of two implementations of emotion recognition in faces, each implemented with specific technology. Open CV is an open-source library of functions and packages mostly used for computer-vision analysis and applications.

Cognitive services are a set of APIs containing artificial intelligence algorithms for computer-vision, speech, knowledge, and language processing. Two Android mobile applications were developed to test the performance between an OpenCV algorithm for emotion recognition and an implementation of Emotion cognitive service. For this research, one thousand tests were carried out per experiment. Our findings show that the OpenCV implementation got a better performance than the Cognitive services application. In both cases, performance can be im-proved by increasing the sample size per emotion during the training step.

Comprehensive database for facial expression analysis [9].

Face recognition technology has widely attracted attention due to its enormous application value and market potential, such as real-time video surveillance system. It is widely acknowledged that the face recognition has played an important role in surveillance system as it doesn't need the object's co-operation. We design a real-time face recognition system based on IP camera and image set algorithm by way of OpenCV and Python programming development. The system includes three parts: Detection module, training module and recognition module.

The extended Cohn–Kanade dataset (CK+): A complete dataset for action unit and emotion-specified expression [10].

Taking a step forward, human emotion displayed by face and felt by brain, captured in either video, electric signal (EEG) or image form can be approximated. Human feeling recognition is the need of great importance so present-day counterfeit intelligent frameworks can copy and check responses from face. This can be useful to settle on educated choices be it with respect to recognizable proof regarding goal, advancement of offers or security related dangers. Perceiving feelings from pictures or video is a trifling errand for natural eye however ends up being extremely trying for machines and requires many picture handling procedures for highlight extraction. A few machine learning calculations are appropriate for this work. Any discovery or acknowledgment by AI requires preparing calculation and afterward testing them on a suit-capable dataset. This paper investigates a few AI calculations as well as element extraction strategies which would help us in exact ID of the human inclination.

Web-based database for facial expression analysis [11].

This framework contains three modules which are identification, preparing and acknowledgment. Essentially, the discovery module identifies the face which gets into the field of vision of the camera and recoveries the face as a picture in JPG design. LDA is a technique to observe a straight mix of highlights which portray or isolate at least two classes of items or occasions. Straight classifier can be acquired from the resultant. Enormous number of pixels are utilized to address face in modernized face acknowledgment. Before order Linear discriminant examination is utilized to diminish highlights and makes it more sensible. New aspects are a direct mix of pixel values which shapes a layout.

Web-based database for facial expression analysis [12].

The primary target of facial acknowledgment is to confirm and recognize the facial elements. Nonetheless, the facial highlights are caught continuously and handled utilizing haar course recognition. The consecutive course of the work is characterized in three distinct stages where in the principal stage human face is recognized from the camera and in the subsequent stage, the caught input is examined in view of the highlights and data set utilized with help of keras convolutional brain network model.

In the last stage human face is verified to group the feelings of human as blissful, nonpartisan, furious, pitiful, nausea and shock. The proposed work introduced is rearranged in three goals as face identification, acknowledgment and feeling or-der. On the side of this work Open CV library, dataset and python writing computer programs is utilized for PC vision methods included. To demonstrate continuous viability, a trial was directed for a very long time to distinguish their in-ward feelings and track down physiological changes for each face. The consequences of the investigations exhibit the consummations in face examination framework. At long last, the presentation of programmed face identification and acknowledgment is estimated with Accuracy.

Facial Emotion Detection using Deep Learning [13].

It is a challenging task for a computer vision to recognize as same as humans through AI. Face detection plays a vital role in emotion recognition. Emotions are classified as happy, sad, disgust, angry, neutral, fear, and surprise. Other aspects such as speech, eye contact, frequency of the voice, and heartbeat are considered. Nowadays face recognition is more efficient and used for many real-time applications due to security purposes. We detect emotion by scanning (static) images or with the (dynamic) recording. Features extracting can be done like eyes, nose, and mouth for face detection. The convolutional neural network (CNN) algorithm follows steps as max-pooling (maximum feature extraction) and flattening.

A Real Time Face Emotion Classification and Recognition using Deep Learning Model [14].

Though there are methods to identify expressions using machine learning and Artificial Intelligence techniques, this work attempts to use deep learning and image classification method to recognize expressions and classify the expressions according to the images. Various datasets are investigated and explored for training expression recognition model are explained in this paper. Inception Net is used for expression recognition with Kaggle (Facial Expression Recognition Challenge) and Karolinska Directed Emotional Faces datasets. Final accuracy of this expression recognition model using Inception Net v3 Model is 35% (~).

A performance comparison of two emotion-recognition implementations using OpenCV and Cognitive Services API [15].

With the recent advancement in computer vision and machine learning, it is possible to detect emotions from images. In this paper, we propose a novel technique called facial emotion recognition using convolutional neural networks (FERC). The FERC is based on two-part convolutional neural network (CNN): The first part removes the background from the picture, and the second part concentrates on the facial feature vector extraction. In FERC model, expressional vector (EV) is used to find the five different types of regular facial expression. Supervisory data were obtained from the stored database of

10,000 images (154 persons). It was possible to correctly highlight the emotion with 96% accuracy, using an EV of length 24 values.

The two-level CNN works in series, and the last layer of perceptron adjusts the weights and exponent values with each iteration. FERC differs from generally followed strategies with single-level CNN, hence improving the accuracy. Furthermore, a novel background removal procedure applied, before the generation of EV, avoids dealing with multiple problems that may occur (for example distance from the camera). FERC was extensively tested with more than 750K images using extended Cohn– Kanade expression, Caltech faces, CMU and NIST datasets. We expect the FERC emotion detection to be useful in many applications such as predictive learning of students, lie detectors, etc.

Real Time Facial Expression Recognition Based on Deep Convolutional Spatial Neural Networks [16].

The primary step of face detection is done with Viola Jones algorithm using haar features. This DCSNN is made up of three convolutions, two pooling, one fully connected and a SoftMax layer with Rectified Linear unit (ReLu) activation function to classify the expressions using the probability function. In this paper they have shown DCSNN as an alternative solution to the traditional FER methods.

Optimized Facial Emotion Recognition Technique for Asserting User Experience [17].

A novel optimized solution in image processing with two preprocessing filters i.e., brightness and contrast filter and edge extraction filter combined with CNN and Support Vector Machine (SVM) for emotion classification. The preprocessing filter parameters are automatically tuned after analyzing the outcomes from CNN. They have claimed an accuracy of 98.19% using CNN. With such high accuracy and efficiency, they have demonstrated that their system has great potential in embedded applications like asserting user experience in games etc.

Face Expression Recognition Based on Deep Convolution Network [18].

The experiments were carried out on CK+ and JAFFE dataset using a CNN with five continuous convolution, three max pooling, one fully connected and one out-put layer to recognize the expressions using SoftMax classifier. Based on the ac-curacy table provided, the algorithm used in this paper gives overall accuracy of 87.2% for both the datasets which is high compared to methods like HOG, LBP and traditional CNN.

Dynamic Facial Expression Recognition Based on Convolutional Neural Networks with Dense Connections [19].

The architecture consists of only four convolutional layers with dense connections, one SoftMax layer, no connected layers for efficient feature sharing with ReLu activation function. They proposed a dynamic FER system trained on the CK+ and Oulu-CASIA database with an accuracy of 97.25% and 83.33% respectively.

A Framework for Driver Emotion Recognition using Deep Learning and Grossmann Manifolds [20].

By using the haar cascades and DNNs region of interest is founded. Features are extracted based on the AlexNet and VGG16. This is mainly based on the Grossmann Graph embedding Discriminant Analysis (GGDA).

Deep Learning Models for Facial Expression Recognition [21].

The CNN built from scratch has two convolution, two max pooling and two dense layers. Training and testing are carried out on different types of appearance-based face images like raw images, difference images and LBP. The outcomes presented show that accuracy obtained on VGG Face is higher compared to the other mentioned pretrained models.

Multimodal 2D+3D Facial Expression Recognition with Deep Fusion Convolutional Neural Network [22].

The DNN consisted of three fully connected layers and a SoftMax output layer to categories expressions while there were three convolution, three max pooling, two fully connected and SoftMax layer with ReLu activation in CNN. They have obtained recognition rate of 72.78% and 86.54% for DNN and CNN respectively and hence concluded that CNN performs better compared to DNN.

3D Facial Expression Recognition using Orthogonal Tensor Marginal Fisher Analysis on Geometric Maps [23].

In this paper, a novel 3D facial expression recognition algorithm by Orthogonal Tensor Marginal Fisher Analysis (OTMFA) on geometric maps was proposed. In order to describe expressions properly in detail and simplify calculation, five kinds of geometric 2D maps including Depth Map (DM), three Normal Maps (NOMs) and Shape Index Map (SIM) are extracted. These maps are treated as second order tensors and they are used to learn low dimensional tensor subspaces by OTMFA, where preserves the manifold structure of expressions and reduces dimensions simultaneously. Next, features are further extracted by projecting these geometric maps into tensor subspaces. Finally, multi-class SVM classifiers are trained and tested respectively for each map and their contributions are combined using the sum rule for final recognition. The effectiveness of proposed method is verified on BU-3DFE database, and the performance achieves an average of 88.32% and 84.27%, which is comparable to the state-of-the-art ones.

Development of Deep Leaning-based Facial Expression Recognition System [24].

Face RoI was segmented using AAM normalized to 224 * 224 pixels. Since they had a small database, they fine-tuned ResNet10 on four macro expression datasets and later on micro expression dataset eventually concluded that their approach gives high weighted Average Recall (WAR) and Unweighted Average Recall (UAR) than the traditional (LBP-TOP, HOG3D) ones. The average accuracy of the model was 74.70% with F1 score of 0.64.

From Macro to Micro Expression Recognition: Deep Learning on Small Datasets Using Transfer Learning [25].

This hybrid model consists of two CNNs, spatial CNN to process static face images and another one called temporal CNN to process optical flow images. These CNNs are fine-tuned using pretrained model and the joint features obtained. For the purpose of classification DBN are used. The combination of two hidden layers and one visible layer is nothing but DBN. Based on the one SoftMax classification layer theses layers are fed together. 55. .85%, 73.73% and 71.43% are the BAUM-1S, RML and MMI accuracies.

A Deep Neural Network-Driven Feature Learning Method for Multi-view Facial Expression Recognition [26].

They have carried out data augmentation- rotation, shifting and scaling on FER 2013 dataset. Pretrained model VGG16 is retrained with augmented FER 2013 and transfer learning is done using VGG19 on Jaffe and CK+. This paper de-scribes the step-by-step procedure on how to use pretrained models for FER. Overall accuracy mentioned was 93%.

Learning Affective Video Features for Facial Expression Recognition via Hybrid Deep Learning [27].

An appearance-based network (first CNN) which separates the LBP highlights and a mathematical based network (second CNN) that removes the distinction be-tween the pinnacle and the impartial articulation picture in this way building a hearty component which is given for grouping task. Their calculation appears to have higher accuracy contrasted with the other best in class designs on CK+ and Jaffe datasets. For CK+ the exactness recorded was 96.46% and for Jaffe 91.27%.

Facial Expression Recognition using Transfer Learning [28].

It is notable that profound models could separate powerful and theoretical elements. We propose a productive look acknowledgment model in light of move highlights from profound convolutional networks (ConvNets). We train the pro-found ConvNets through the errand of 1580-class face ID on the MSRA-CFW data set and move undeniable level highlights from the prepared profound model to perceive appearance. To prepare and test the look acknowledgment model on an enormous extension, we assembled a look data set of seven fundamental inclination states and 2062 imbalanced examples relying upon four look information bases (CK+, JAFFE, KDEF, Pain articulation's structure PICS). Contrasted and 50.65% recognition rate in light of Gabor highlights with the seven-class SVM and 78.84% recognition rate in view of distance highlights with the seven-class SVM, we accomplish average 80.49% acknowledgment rate with the seven-class SVM classifier on oneself constructed look information base. Considering blocked face as a general rule, we test our model in the impeded condition and exhibit the model could keep its capacity of grouping in the little impediment case.

Efficient Facial Expression Recognition Algorithm Based on Hierarchical Deep Neural Network Structure [29].

With the continued development of artificial intelligence (AI) technology, re-search on interaction technology has become more popular. Facial expression recognition (FER) is an important type of visual information that can be used to understand a human's emotional situation. In particular, the importance of AI systems has recently increased due to advancements in research on AI systems ap-plied to AI robots. In this paper, we propose a new scheme for FER system based on hierarchical deep learning. The feature extracted from the appearance feature-based network is fused with the geometric feature in a hierarchical structure. The appearance feature-based network extracts holistic features of the face using the preprocessed LBP image, whereas the geometric feature-based network learns the coordinate change of action units (AUs) landmark, which is a muscle that moves mainly when making facial expressions. The proposed method combines the result of the SoftMax function of two features by considering the error associated with the second highest emotion (Top-2) prediction result. In addition, we propose a technique to generate facial images with neutral emotion using the autoencoder technique.

Spatial-Temporal Recurrent Neural Network for Emotion Recognition [30].

SJTU Emotion EEG Dataset (SEED) and CK+ were used with 7° clockwise and 12° anti-clockwise rotation. To have a good discriminant ability of emotions, sparse projection was introduced. Model accuracy was demonstrated as 95.4%.

4 Conclusion

In this paper some of the efficient methods for face and face expression recognition are reviewed. The paper also gives a brief idea of the algorithm used by these techniques. The expressions that are considered for recognition are Happy, Anger, Disgust, Fear, Sadness and Surprise. The techniques here are considered to give a very good recognition rate when applied to the most widely used databases available. These techniques are using a hybrid algorithm in which both holistic and local features are considered so as to increase the recognition rate and achieve greater performance. Among the Techniques used FARO and Bag of Words method can recognize face even in the presence of occlusions in the image.

References

1. Hajati, F., Raie, A.A., Gao, Y.: Expression invariant 3D face recognition using patched geodesic texture transform. In: 2010 Digital Image Computing: Techniques and Applications, pp. 249–254 (2010)
2. Wu, X., Zhao, J.: Curvelet feature extraction for face recognition and facial expression recognition. In: 2010 Sixth International Conference on Natural Computation (ICNC 2010), pp. 1212–1216 (2010)
3. Li, Z., Imai, J., Kaneko, M.: Face and expression recognition based on bag of words method considering holistic and local image features. In: 2010 International Symposium on Communications and Information Technologies (ISCIT) (2010)
4. Rivera, A.R., Castillo, J.R.: Local directional number pattern for face analysis: face and expression recognition. IEEE Trans. Image Process. 22(5), 1740–1752 (2013)
5. De Marsico, M., Nappi, M., Riccio, D.: FARO: face recognition against occlusions and expression variations. IEEE Trans. Syst. Man Cybern. - Part A: Syst. Hum. 40(1), 121–132 (2010)
6. Alex, A.T., Asari, V.K., Mathew, A.: Gradient feature matching for expression invariant face recognition using single reference image. In: 2012 IEEE International Conference on Systems, Man and Cybernetics, pp. 851–856 (2012)
7. Song, K.-T., Chen, Y.-W.: A design for integrated face and facial expression recognition, pp. 4306–4311 (2011)
8. Tian, Y.L., Kanade, T., Cohn, J.F.: Facial expression analysis. In: Li, S.Z., Jain, A.K. (eds.) Handbook of Face Recognition, pp. 247–275. Springer, New York (2005)
9. Kanade, T., Cohn, J., Tian, Y.L.: Comprehensive database for facial expression analysis. In: Proceedings of the 4th IEEE International Conference on Automatic Face and Gesture Recognition, pp. 46–53 (2000)
10. Lucey, P., Cohn, J., Kanade, T., Saragih, J., Ambadar, Z., Matthews, I.: The extended Cohn–Kanade dataset (CK+): a complete dataset for action unit and emotion-specified expression. In: Proceedings IEEE Computer Society Conference on Computer Vision and Pattern Recognition-Workshops, pp. 94–101 (2010)

11. Lyons, M., Akamatsu, S., Kamachi, M., Gyoba, J.: Coding facial expressions with gabor wavelets. In: Proceedings of the 3rd IEEE International Conference on Automatic Face and Gesture Recognition, pp. 200–205 (1998)
12. Pantic, M., Valstar, M., Rademaker, R., Maat, L.: Web-based database for facial expression analysis. In: Proceedings of the IEEE International Conference on Multimedia Expo, pp. 1–5 (2005)
13. Spiers, D.L.: Facial emotion detection using deep learning. IT 16 040 Examensarbete 30 hp (2016)
14. Hussain, S.A., Al Balushi, A.S.A.: A real time face emotion classification and recognition using deep learning model. In: ICE4CT 2019 Journal of Physics: Conference Series, vol.1432, p. 012087 (2020)
15. Prieto, L.A.B., Komínkova-Oplatkova, Z.: A performance comparison of two emotion-recognition implementations using OpenCV and cognitive services API. In: MATEC Web of Conferences, vol. 25 (2017). https://doi.org/10.1051/matecconf/201712502067
16. Subarna, B., Viswanathan, D.M.: Real time facial expression recognition based on deep convolutional spatial neural networks. In: International Conference on Emerging Trends and Innovations in Engineering and Technological Research (ICETIETR) (2018)
17. Lin, X., Lee, K.: Optimized facial emotion recognition technique for asserting user experience. In: IEEE Games, Entertainment, Media Conference (GEM) (2018)
18. Wang, M., et al.: Face expression recognition based on deep convolution network. In: 11th International Congress on Image and Signal Processing, BioMedical Engineering and Informatics (CISP-BMEI) (2018)
19. Dong, J., et al.: Dynamic facial expression recognition based on convolutional neural networks with dense connections. In: 24th International Conference on Pattern Recognition (ICPR) (2018)
20. Verma, B., Choudhary, A.: A framework for driver emotion recognition using deep learning and grassmann manifolds. In: 21st International Conference on Intelligent Transportation Systems (ITSC) (2018)
21. Sajjanhar, A., et al.: Deep learning models for facial expression recognition. In: Digital Image Computing: Techniques and Applications (DICTA) (2018)
22. Li, H., et al.: Multimodal 2D+3D facial expression recognition with deep fusion convolutional neural network. IEEE Trans. Multimed. 19(12), 2816–2831 (2017)
23. Li, Q., et al.: 3D facial expression recognition using orthogonal tensor marginal fisher analysis on geometric maps. In: International Conference on Wavelet Analysis and Pattern Recognition (2017)
24. Jung, H., et al.: Development of deep leaning-based facial expression recognition system. In: 21st Korea-Japan Joint Workshop on Frontiers of Computer Vision (FCV) (2015)
25. Peng, M., et al.: From macro to micro expression recognition: deep learning on small datasets using transfer learning. In: 13th IEEE International Conference on Automatic Face & Gesture Recognition (2018)
26. Zhang, T., et al.: A deep neural network-driven feature learning method for multi-view facial expression recognition. IEEE Trans. Multimed. 18(12), 2528–2536 (2016)
27. Zhang, S., et al.: Learning affective video features for facial expression recognition via hybrid deep learning. IEEE Access 7, 32297–32304 (2019)
28. Ramalingam, S., Garzia, F.: Facial expression recognition using transfer learning. In: International Carnahan Conference on Security Technology (ICCST) (2018)
29. Kim, J.-H., et al.: Efficient facial expression recognition algorithm based on hierarchical deep neural network structure. IEEE Access 7, 41273–41285 (2019)
30. Zhang, T., et al.: Spatial-temporal recurrent neural network for emotion recognition. IEEE Trans. Cybern. 49(3), 839–847 (2019)

An IoMT Based Prediction Model for Cardiac Monitoring Using Machine Learning Algorithms

K. Poomari Durga⬚ and M. S. Abirami(✉)⬚

Department of Computational Intelligence, SRM Institute of Science and Technology,
Kattankulathur, Chengalpattu, India
{pk5050,abiramim}@srmist.edu.in

Abstract. The complex health issues faced by the people are studied and different heart disease monitoring techniques are discussed to present complications. The observation of this monitoring is to enhance human fitness regardless of the situation. The Proposed Methodology is implemented on the benchmark University of California Irvine Dataset and various machine learning techniques are applied and the accuracy is calculated. The main objective of the research work is to improve the wellness of the people and to decrease the mortality rates. Internet of Medical Things (IoMT) is now a recent technology to monitor human health remotely without any human intervention. Further such implementation is developed into IOMT Based Cardiac Monitoring System which alerts the medical staff in case of any abnormality found. Data are collected through sensors to measure patient physical status and monitored and saved in the cloud which can be received by the medical specialists. With the help of a remote cardiac monitoring system, the patients have confidence to contact the doctors without visiting medical centres. The remote cardiac monitoring system is practiced in affluent countries but it is still not implemented in underdeveloped countries. The proposed cardiac Monitoring system plays a vital role in monitoring patients. In the proposed work the ML algorithms such as KNN, SVM, AD, DT, MLP, RF, NB, LR and XGBoost were done and the accuracy percentage of 87.5 was found from XGBoost. The Ultimate goal is to implement different machine learning methodologies for keeping track of the patient's health.

Keywords: Internet of Medical Things · Cardiovascular disease · Random Forest · XGBoost · Ensemble classification

1 Introduction

IoT-based healthcare applications are used to collect critical information, such as real-time variations in health attributes and updates on the severity of medical characteristics within a specific time, IoT devices constantly produces large quantities of health data [2]. The Internet of Things can be used in a variety of fields, including industry, medicine, and agriculture. Wearable devices have gained popularity, with health monitoring system applications, pushing the Internet of Medical Things forward. The emergence of a new concept known as the Internet of Medical Things (IoMT) has emerged from the

© The Author(s), under exclusive license to Springer Nature Switzerland AG 2023
K. Kottursamy et al. (Eds.): IconDeepCom 2022, CCIS 1719, pp. 103–118, 2023.
https://doi.org/10.1007/978-3-031-27622-4_9

widespread adoption and deployment of well-integrated hardware and sensors for personalised healthcare [6]. The IoMT plays a substantial role in dropping death rates by detecting diseases early.

IoMT is a collection of medical devices that are linked to a healthcare provider's computer system through the Internet. IoMT can generate, store, analyse, and disseminate health information. IoMT comprises remote patient monitoring, sensor-based beds, wearables, and health tracking gadgets. The objective of IoMT is to improve patient satisfaction as well as the quality of care provided by insurers and healthcare providers [3]. The Internet of Medical Things and artificial intelligence plays an important role in heart disease prediction. AI learning approaches processes IoMT data and offer good prediction and diagnosis. This model reduces financial as well as administrative difficulties in chronic disease treatment. The bottleneck is high accuracy and stability [11, 12].

Independent and healthy living is the ambition of each person despite their age, and gender. However, they have limitations because of age, sickness, medicines, epidemic and pandemic things. Moreover, advancement of knowledge technology, Internet of Things and remote health watching systems, time period, consulting time and the price paid for that area unit are greatly reduced. Most of the hospitals switched over to mobile phone applications to manage records. Staying in hospitals is mostly avoided. Health care professionals monitor necessary signs like pulse, blood pressure and temperature throughout the tests. Heart Disease is one of the diseases which results in the highest mortality rate [8, 9].

The WHO reports nearly 31% of worldwide people are suffering from cardiovascular disease. Nearly 15.2 million people lost their lives due to heart disease [1]. Fifty percent of people spotted with the CVD will die within 1–2 years. Medical field is spending 3% of the budget on treating heart disease. Several Tests should be taken to accurately predict heart disease. Even lack of expertise will lead to false predictions [10].

Prediction of HD plays a significant role in the medical field and serving society [4, 5]. The risk factors for increasing the chance of getting heart diseases are Diabetes, Alcoholism, Smoking, High cholesterol, High BP, Obesity. Monitoring heart rates might be difficult even for the patients who are admitted in the hospital. Periodic checking cannot protect against fast heart rate changes, and traditional equipment used in the hospital for cardiac monitoring requires patients tied to wired machines permanently, limiting their movement.

The contributions of the proposed work are follows:

- First, using the UCI dataset it is found that males are suffering more from heart disease than females and the comparative results are given.
- Second, pre-processing is done and duplicate values, redundancy and outliers are removed and the feature extraction and selection are done with the help of heat maps.
- Finally comparative study of various machine learning algorithms is done and the accuracy percentage was given.

The rest of the manuscript is subdivided into six sections. Section 2 reviews related work related to early prediction and health care for heart disease. Section 3 details about the different phases of the proposed work. Section 4 defines the datasets used and the problems that must be overwhelmed while dealing this type of data and the experimental results. Section 5 describes classification algorithms. Finally, Sect. 6 provides conclusions, Future Work, and references.

2 Literature Review

Sambit Satpathy et al. [17] proposed an internet-of-things based field-programmable gate array (FPGA) analysis system that sends out alerts when any of the health measures falls below or exceeds a specific threshold. A fuzzy classifier that predicts the pathological circumstances of heart disease with high accuracy is constructed in comparison to previous models developed using KNN, decision tree, SVM, and NB Classifiers.

Kaur et al. [18] suggested RF classifier and IOT which is applicable for HD's and provided good accuracy outcomes for UCI dataset. The main drawback is security is not concerned. **Mohan et al.** [14] proposed Hybrid Random Forest with Linear Model which has accuracy level 88.7% and the system will not have the capability to monitor patients in real time.

AKM Jahangir et al. [20] suggested a multisensory system utilizing a smart IOT which combines signal processing along with an ML algorithm that identifies sudden heart attack with high accuracy. The algorithm did not point to data security.

S. Nashif et al. [21] suggested SVM Technique with the highest accuracy and in this not work with the real time monitoring system. S.Satpathy [17] proposed FPGA technique with high accuracy and low execution time and did not cover data security. Zafer al et al. [14] suggested utmost recognition accuracy and lowest time complexity and this does not employ optimization algorithms and feature selection techniques.

Mehdi Hosseinzadeh et al. [22] proposed an Internet-of-Things based health monitoring system for assessing vital signs and detecting biological and behavioural anomalies. IoT monitoring objects collect the necessary data for detecting the risk factors in patients physiological and behavioural deviations, and data is analysed using different ML [7, 15] methods like J48, SMO, MLP, and NB classifiers. Future work will entail putting the system in a real time environment to learn more about the difficulties that exist in the real world, as well as verifying its resilience with a larger dataset.

Samira Akhbarifar et al. [23] developed a light-weight block chain encryption technique to keep medical data private. They are using data mining to analyze patient healthcare data, and they're encrypting patient data collected through IoT devices with a light-weight block encryption method. Experimental results show that low weight block encryption methodology produces good results when compared to RF [13], SVM, MLP, and J48 classifiers, while k-star produces the better results. To offer safe IOT information, this health-monitoring system employs IOT platforms based on clouds. The association between chronic conditions and infection COVID-19 in a real-world context, as well as its deployment in a IoT system based on cloud, will be the focus of future research.

Saiteja Prasad Chatrati et al. [25] suggested building a user-friendly GUI based programme that analyses diabetes and BP in patients and delivers notifications to the hospital after the information is submitted Support vector machine classification algorithms are the most accurate for training the model when compared to other classification techniques.

Jie et al. [25] presented a wearable health monitoring system based on a BASN. WISE transfers BASN data to the cloud, where it may be seen at any time, and a wearable LCD can be integrated for real-time data access.

Shashidhar R et al. [26] suggested a health-monitoring system that solves the problem that many hospitals only store hard copies of patient records rather than allowing them to be transmitted to the cloud. For the records to appropriately depict the patient's situation, the graphs/reports are based on prior and current health records. This will need to be made into a mobile application in the future so that patients may use it on their phones.

Kadhim Takleef Kadhim et al. [27] proposed an internet healthcare monitoring system (HCMS) that provides medications to patients based on their medical status without requiring physical interaction. The use of IoT in healthcare to deliver accurate diagnosis and high-quality service to patients is the subject of this study.

Munish et al. [28] proposed a smart, non-invasive wearable physiological parameter monitoring system that can detect human falls and monitor temperature and heart rate. When the device detects that the person needs medical attention, it sends a text message to the doctor. The heart rate sensors do not employ discrete components, and a digital filter filters the TCRT1000 signal that is processed inside the board to improve heart disease accuracy. In the future, mobile devices will be equipped with online monitoring capabilities based on graphs and machine learning.

Cuijuan et al. [29] suggested an Implicit Irregularity Detection mechanism that develops an unsupervised machine learning algorithm based on daily behaviour to accurately recognise regular and irregular daily behaviour. In the future, multidimensional aspects of daily behaviours will be examined, allowing for a more refined categorization of older behaviour.

S. Casaccia et al. [29] suggested a domotic sensor network that uses a Techniques developed on regular surveys to monitor the health of aged people. A sensor network is deployed, and two machine learning methods, RF algorithm and RT algorithm are compared [3]. The user's health data is compared to three reference indices derived from daily surveys: bodily, psychological, and overall health indexes. The ML algorithm is trained with the retrieved indices to estimate the health of solo or multi-residents. The concept is put to the test using a variety of environments. The results reveal that the RF algorithm performs better compared to RT.

3   Proposed Methodology

In this Section we collected University of California Irvine Dataset which contains 303 patient records, completed pre-processing operation and feature extraction is done with the help of heat maps and the features having highest values are selected. 80% of the overall datasets are used for training and 20% of the dataset is used for performance evaluation. Different ML techniques such as KNN [16], SVM, DT, RF, NB, LR and XG-Boost are implemented on training datasets and the accuracy of the model is evaluated. The IOMT Based Cardiac Monitoring System is given in Fig. 1.

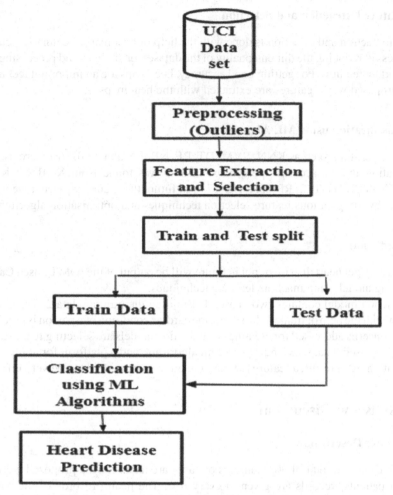

Fig. 1. Proposed IoMT based cardiac monitoring system

3.1 Data Acquisition

Sensors are used to collect data from the patients.

3.2 Pre-processing

It's a vital step and this should be done for good representation. This stage includes the steps such as replacing missing values, Removal of Redundancy, Normalization. The duplicate values, redundant values will affect the model and, in this step, duplicate values are eliminated.

3.3 Feature Extraction and Selection

Feature extraction and selection is done with the help of heat maps. Feature selection is the process of reducing the dimensionality of the dataset for analysis and processing with the important features. For getting good accuracy, heat maps are an important technique. In this proposed work features are extracted with the heat maps.

3.4 Classification using ML Algorithms

The ML algorithms such as KNN, SVM, DT, RF, NB, LR and XGBoost were used for classification and the accuracy percentage of 87.5 was found from XGBoost K-NN-83.6, SVM-80.2, DT-81.2, RF-85.4, NB-77.9. In future the accuracy percentage will be improved by using various feature selection techniques and optimisation algorithms.

3.5 Prediction

A person may get heart disease or not in future will be output of the IOMT based Cardiac Monitoring model using machine learning techniques.

Prediction model contains two phases 1. Building the training data 2. Training the classifier with the help of trained classifiers, the cardiac condition of a person is predicted. Critical concerns addressed for creating classification models are selecting features from the pre-processed data, selecting a proper ml algorithm, and a platform for applying the ml algorithm. As a result, a feature extraction method is considered to be very effective.

4 Results and Discussion

4.1 Dataset Description

From the dataset, a total of 303 numbers of cases are taken for the proposed work and different patients' records are given in every row. The health records of the patients contain some of the attributes for age, sex, cp, target, restecg, exang, slope, thalach, thal, fbs, chol, trestbps, ca, oldpeak and the description of the attributes are given in Table 1.

Table 1. University of California Irvine dataset description

Attribute	Description
Age	Age of the individual
Sex	Gender
Cp	Chest pain
Trestbps	Resting BP value

(continued)

Table 1. (*continued*)

Attribute	Description
Chol	Amount of Cholesterol in blood
Fbs	Sugar level in blood
Resting Ecg	ECG values at rest
Thal	Heart beat value increases to 10 beats per second
Exang	Exercise induced pain
Oldpeak	Exercise induced ST depression in rest
Slope	ST segment is abnormally below the baseline line
Ca	Several major vessels affected
Thal	Status of heart
Target	Heart disease diagnosis

4.2 Pre-processing

There is no missing values and the redundancy and the outliers are removed. The dataset is good, and Fig. 2 illustrates that the attributes age, sex, cp, target, restecg, exang and slope don't have outliers.

The attributes thalach, thal, fbs, chol, trestbps, ca, oldpeak are having outliers is shown in Fig. 3. The highest value and the lowest value is the max and min value of the data-set. Min to 50% is the median of the data which is the first quartile and 50% to max is the median of the data which is the third quartile. The values that are beyond (1.5 * interquartile range) are the outliers from the 25 or 75 percentiles and outliers are removed.

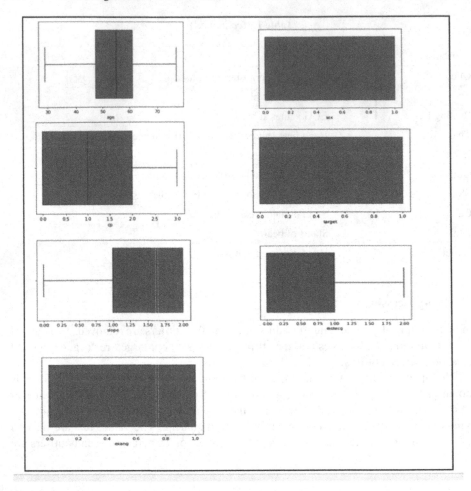

Fig. 2. Attributes without outliers

4.3 Feature Extraction and Selection

Feature extraction and selection is done with the heat maps. In the heat map there are many shades for each colour. The dark shades are assigned negative values. For entirely different values different colours will be used. Figure 4 illustrates the data visualisation of correlation of attributes.

From the results of the heat map the most obvious indication is chest pain. The chest pain is of three types, but only atypical angina is strongly related to the heart disease which is represented in Fig. 5.

From the results of the 303 cases target 0 is predicted as not having heart disease and target 1 is predicted as having heart disease. From the results of the pie chart sex_1, target _1 is male which is most affected by heart disease than female.

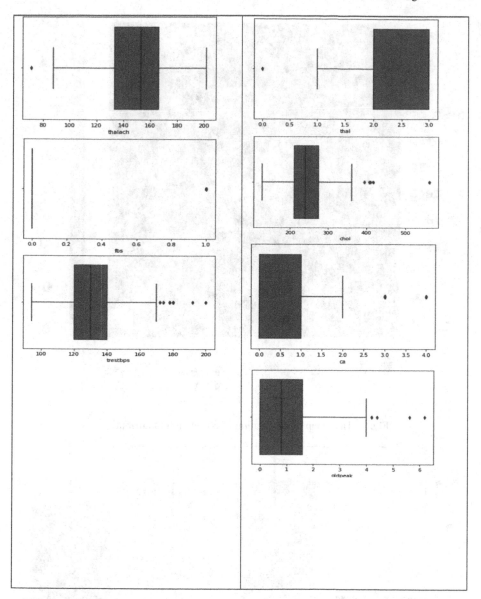

Fig. 3. Graph for the attribute thalach, thal, fbs, chol, trestbps, ca, oldpeak having outlier

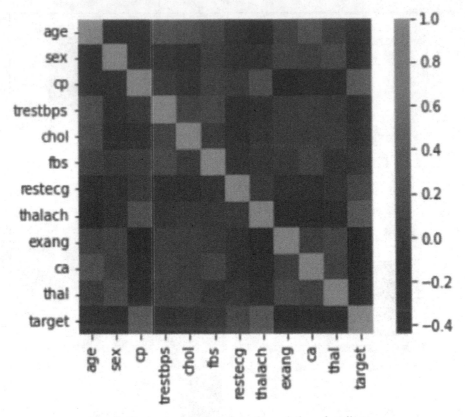

Fig. 4. Heat map representation of correlation of attributes.

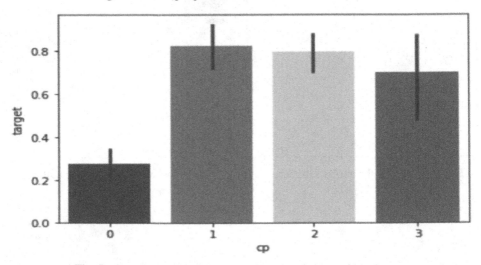

Fig. 5. Comparison graph between the types of chest pain and target

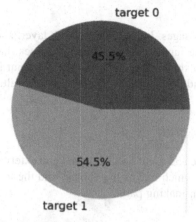

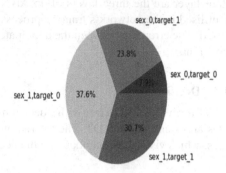

Fig. 6. Pie chart showing diseased and healthy

Fig. 7. Representation of male and female % affected from heart disease

5 Comparative Analysis

In the Previous section, results of pre-processing, feature extraction were given. In this section explained about various classification algorithms and compared the accuracy with the use of performance metrics. Some features such as chest pain, thalach helps in improving prediction accuracy.

5.1 Classification Algorithms

Classification algorithms includes SVM, LR, A-NN, K-NN, NB, and DT. Various feature selection algorithms are used for selecting the significant features such as PCA, LASSO, LLBFS, Relief, GA, MRMR, and optimization techniques, such as ACO, BFO, FFO etc. [13].

5.1.1 Linear Regression

This model is mainly suitable for binary classification problem to predict the presence of HD as 1 and absence of HD as 0 where the value of y variable y [0,1].

5.1.2 SVM

This is an excellent classification problem, and many applications uses this.

5.1.3 Naïve Bayes

The conditional probability of vectors of a class is computed using the NB's training dataset. For each vector, the conditional probability value is evaluated, and then the new vector class is determined using conditional probability.

5.1.4 Artificial Neural Network

The ANN combines the neurons that convey messages. Input layer, hidden layer, and output layer are the three layers of an ANN. The input layer receives the values that are utilised in the network's training process. For the known class, the ANN output is utilised. The error gap between the anticipated and actual class value is used to revalue the weight.

5.1.5 Decision Tree

The DT form resembles a tree with a decision node and a leaf node. Internal and external nodes are connected in a DT. The internal node, which makes the choice, and the leaf nodes, which visits the next node, are the decision-making parts.

5.1.6 K-Nearest Neighbour

This method uses the similarity of new input in the training set to its input samples. The performance of K-NN will be affected if input samples are same during the training process [14].

5.1.7 Random Forest

RF is a very effective ML technique. Bagging is a kind of ML technique. The bootstrap method for predicting a value from a data sample, such as mean. A huge collection of data samples is attained, the mean is calculated, and then average of mean values provides accurate true mean value. The similar technique is used in bagging, although DT are utilised instead of calculating the mean of each data. Many samples of the training data are considered, and models are built for each data. While a prediction for any data is needed, each model offers one, which is then be around to provide a more exact estimation of the true output [23].

5.1.8 XG Boost

Gradient Boosted decision trees are implemented in XGBoost. Many Kaggle works are dominated by XGBoost technique. In this method DT is constructed consecutively. In XGBoost, weights are very important. For all independent variables weights are given, and put into the DT, which guesses outcomes. If the tree predicts incorrect value weight of factors is raised, and these values are put into the second DT. These various classifiers are then combined to create a more precise model.

5.1.9 AdaBoost

The AdaBoost algorithm is a boosting method used in ML as an Ensemble Method. The weights are reallocated to every instance, with larger weights allocated to inappropriately categorised instances. In supervised learning, boosting is used to decrease bias and variation. With a minor variation, the AdaBoost technique operates on the similarly as boosting.

The summary of different types of algorithms, data sets, and accuracy for prediction of cardiovascular disease using IOMT are presented in Table 2. Finally, from the study we conclude that most of them uses feature extraction and optimisation techniques to improve the accuracy.

Table 2. Background study of different algorithms and accuracy percentage

Ref. No	Algorithm	Dataset	Accuracy	Research gap
[11]	Bagging-Fuzzy-GBDT	UCI	0.90	Optimize and work with the real data
[13]	Hybrid Random Forest with Linear model (HRFLM)	UCI Dataset	0.88	To develop new feature-selection methods
[2]	Modified Deep Convolutional Neural Network	UCI, Framingham, Public health and Sensor data	0.96	Feature selection algorithms and optimization techniques
[3]	MSSO-ANFIS	UCI	99.5	Feature-selection algorithms and optimization techniques
[6]	Crow Search Optimization technique-based on Cascaded Long Short-Term Memory model	UCI	96.16	hybrid metaheuristic algorithms for getting Slow search precision
[7]	Ensemble classifier model	UCI	98.18	Predicting health condition using Twitter
Proposed Methodology	XGBoost	UCI	87.4	To implement Feature Selection techniques and optimization techniques

Comparative analysis of accuracy parameters for ML algorithms are given in the Table 3, where RF: Random Forest, XG: XGBoost, DT: Decision Tree, SVM: Support Vector Machine, LR: Linear Regression, NB: Naïve Bayes, MLP: Multi-Layer Perceptron, AD: Adaboost.

Table 3. Comparative analysis of accuracy parameter for various machine learning algorithms

Performance evaluation accuracy (%)

SOURCE	KNN	SVM	AD	DT	MLP	RF	NB	LR	XG
[15]	55.7	55.3	×	52.4	47.5	55.7	×	×	×
[18]	84.8	83.2	×	82.3	×	80.3	×	83.3	×
[19]	×	×	90.2	×	×	×	×	×	92.3
[20]	87.6	81.8	×	100	×	100	×	87.6	×
Propsed work	83.6	80.2	×	81.2	×	85.4	77.9	81.1	87.4

6 Conclusion and Future Work

Early detection of diseases in people is important and will give better result by monitoring the disease. IoT based health monitoring systems reduces the cost of spending in hospital and time travelling to hospital. The proposed framework will have an important impact on improving the living quality. From the result of the dataset the male is having higher chance of getting heart disease than female.

Our future Work will be collecting real time data using IoMT devices and digitalisation of patient record will be done, and the patients are monitored real time. The limitation of the proposed method is accuracy must improve and the advantage is computationally less complex. In Future Feature-selection algorithms and optimization techniques will be implemented for increasing the accuracy of the heart disease prediction system.

In future, we will develop a IoMT based cardiac disease prediction model to improve the health of the patients by early diagnosis and treat the patients with high priority. IoMT provides an important role in increasing the quality of service, and data to researchers in a structured manner and encourages research in the field of health monitoring.

References

1. Sarmah, S.S.: An efficient IoT-based patient monitoring and heart disease prediction system using deep learning modified neural network. IEEE Access **8**, 135784–135797 (2020). https://doi.org/10.1109/ACCESS.2020.3007561
2. Khan, M.A.: An IoT framework for heart disease prediction based on MDCNN classifier. IEEE Access **8**, 34717–34727 (2020). https://doi.org/10.1109/ACCESS.2020.2974687
3. Khan, M.A., Algarni, F.: A healthcare monitoring system for the diagnosis of heart disease in the IoMT cloud environment using MSSO-ANFIS. IEEE Access **8**, 122259–122269 (2020). https://doi.org/10.1109/ACCESS.2020.3006424
4. Raj, S.: An efficient IoT-based platform for remote real-time cardiac activity monitoring. IEEE Trans. Consum. Electron. **66**(2), 106–114 (2020). https://doi.org/10.1109/TCE.2020.2981511
5. Elayan, H., Aloqaily, M., Guizani, M.: Digital twin for intelligent context-aware IoT healthcare systems. IEEE Internet of Things J. **8**(23), 16749–16757 (2021). https://doi.org/10.1109/JIOT.2021.3051158

6. Mansour, R.F., Amraoui, A.E., Nouaouri, I., Díaz, V.G., Gupta, D., Kumar, S.: Artificial intelligence and internet of things enabled disease diagnosis model for smart healthcare systems. IEEE Access **9**, 45137–45146 (2021). https://doi.org/10.1109/ACCESS.2021.3066365

7. Ashri, S.E., El-Gayar, M.M., El-Daydamony, E.M.:HDPF: heart disease prediction framework based on hybrid classifiers and genetic algorithm. IEEE Access, 9, 146797–146809 (2021). https://doi.org/10.1109/ACCESS.2021.3122789

8. Amarbayasgalan, T., Pham, V.H., Theera-Umpon, N., Piao, Y., Ryu, K.H.: An efficient prediction method for coronary heart disease risk based on two deep neural networks trained on well-ordered training datasets. IEEE Access **9**, 135210–135223 (2021). https://doi.org/10.1109/ACCESS.2021.3116974

9. Rahim, A., Rasheed, Y., Azam, F., Anwar, M.W., Rahim, M.A., Muzaffar, A.W.: An integrated machine learning framework for effective prediction of cardiovascular diseases. IEEE Access **9**, 106575–106588 (2021). https://doi.org/10.1109/ACCESS.2021.3098688

10. Ghosh, P., et al.: Efficient prediction of cardiovascular disease using machine learning algorithms with relief and LASSO feature selection techniques. IEEE Access **9**, 19304–19326 (2021). https://doi.org/10.1109/ACCESS.2021.3053759

11. Yuan, X., Chen, J., Zhang, K., Wu, Y., Yang, T.: A stable AI-based binary and multiple class heart disease prediction model for IoMT. IEEE Trans. Industr. Inf. **18**(3), 2032–2040 (2022). https://doi.org/10.1109/TII.2021.3098306

12. Li, J.P., Haq, A.U., Din, S.U., Khan, J., Khan, A., Saboor, A.: Heart Disease identification method using machine learning classification in E-healthcare. IEEE Access **8**, 107562–107582 (2020). https://doi.org/10.1109/ACCESS.2020.3001149

13. Mohan, S., Thirumalai, C., Srivastava, G.: Effective heart disease prediction using hybrid machine learning techniques. IEEE Access **7**, 81542–81554 (2019). https://doi.org/10.1109/ACCESS.2019.2923707

14. Shah, D., Patel, S., Bharti, S.K.: Heart disease prediction using machine learning techniques. SN Comput. Sci. **1**(6), 1–6 (2020). https://doi.org/10.1007/s42979-020-00365-y

15. Bharti, R., Khamparia, A., Shabaz, M., Dhiman, G., Pande, S.:Prediction of heart disease using a combination of machine learning and deep learning, Comput. Intell. Neurosci. 2021, 11 Article ID 8387680 (2021). https://doi.org/10.1155/2021/8387680

16. Satpathy, S., Mohan, P., Das, S., Debbarma, S.: A new healthcare diagnosis system using an IoT-based fuzzy classifier with FPGA. J. Supercomput. **76**(8), 5849–5861 (2019). https://doi.org/10.1007/s11227-019-03013-2

17. Kaur, P., Kumar, R., Kumar, M.: A healthcare monitoring system using random forest and internet of things (IoT). Multimedia Tools Appl. **78**(14), 19905–19916 (2019). https://doi.org/10.1007/s11042-019-7327-8

18. Hashi, E.K., Zaman, M.S.U.: Developing a hyperparameter tuning based machine learning approach of heart disease prediction. J. Appl. Sci. Process Eng. **7**, 631–647 (2020). https://doi.org/10.33736/jaspe.2639.2020

19. Majumder, A.K.M., ElSaadany, Y.A., Young, R., Ucci, D.R.: An Energy Efficient Wearable Smart IoT System to Predict Cardiac Arrest. Adv. Human Comput. Interact. 2019, 21 ArticleID 1507465 (2019). https://doi.org/10.1155/2019/1507465

20. Nashif, S., Raihan, M.R., Islam, M.R., Imam, M.H.: Heart disease detection by using machine learning algorithms and a real-time cardiovascular health monitoring system. World J. Eng. Technol. **6**, 854–873 (2018). https://doi.org/10.4236/wjet.2018.64057

21. Hosseinzadeh, M., et al.: An elderly health monitoring system based on biological and behavioral indicators in internet of things. J. Ambient Intell. Humanized Comput. 1–11 (2020)

22. Akhbarifar, S., Javadi, H.H.S., Rahmani, A.M., Hosseinzadeh, M.: A secure remote health monitoring model for early disease diagnosis in cloud-based IoT environment. Pers. Ubiquit. Comput. 1–17 (2020). https://doi.org/10.1007/s00779-020-01475-3

23. Chatrati, S.P., et al.: Smart home health monitoring system for predicting type 2 diabetes and hypertension. Comput. Inf. Sci. **34**, 862–870 (2020)

24. Wan, J., et al.: Wearable IoT enabled real-time health monitoring system. J. Wireless Commun. Networking **2018**, 1–10 (2018)

25. Shashidhar, R., Abhilash, S., Sahana, V., Alok, N.A., Roopa, M.: Iot cloud: in health monitoring system. Int. J. Sci. Technol. Res. **9**(1), 27 (2020)

26. Kadhim, K.T., Alsahlany, A.M., Wadi, S.M., Kadhum, H.T.: An overview of patient's health status monitoring system based on internet of things (IoT). Wireless Pers. Commun. **114**, 2235–2262 (2020)

27. Manas, M., Sinha, A., Sharma, S., Mahboob, M.R.: A novel approach for IoT based wearable health monitoring and messaging system. J. Ambient Intell. Humanized Comput. **10**, 2817–2828 (2018)

28. Shang, C., Chang, C.Y., Chen, G., Zhao, S., Lin, J.: Implicit irregularity detection using unsupervised learning on daily behaviors. IEEE, Biomed. Health Inform. **24**(1), 131–143 2020

29. Casaccia, S., et al.: Measurement of users' well-being through domotic sensors and machine learning algorithms. IEEE Sens. J. **20**(14), 8029–8038 (2020). https://doi.org/10.1109/JSEN. 2020.2981209

Circular BlockEntropies and Fast Legendre Moments Based Content Preserving Image Authentication

K. Alice[(✉)] [iD], M. Sindhuja[iD], and B. Pandeeswari

Department of Computing Technologies, School of Computing, SRM Institute of Science and Technology, Kattankulathur, Chennai, Tamil Nadu, India
`k_alice_suresh@yahoo.com`

Abstract. Digital Images plays widespread in multimedia information, image authentication applications have a great impact. In this research article, we propose a model using global and local entropies based on the content preserving image authentication. The images are sub-divided into equal-sized circular blocks and each block entropies are measured. These measured entropies locally define the information contained in the image on a circular basis. Moments acts as a global descriptor of the image, from which the global features of the image are extracted using Fast Legendre Moments and local entropies are used to generate the hash values. These global fast Legendre moments and generated hash function values are used to authenticate the image. The experimental results show that our proposed system outperforms against attacks for rotations in large scale is robust against content preserving manipulations along with a greater tolerance to the rotation of large angles up to 90°. The proposed system is 100% sensitive to content change in image and is also able to locate the region of change, however image recovery can only be achieve by compromising lengthy hash code.

Keywords: Circular blocks · Moments · Entropies · Fast legendre moments · Image hashing

1 Introduction

Image authentication is widely used in the field of digital image processing, which is used to authenticate the originality of the image. In traditional authentication mechanism, the content of the image is used instead of whole image. The various applications of image authentication are medical image processing, court judicial evidence image processing, property digital documentations, quality measure and control using image processing, military and research target image processing, etc.,

Content based authentication can be broadly classified into digital signatures [21] and watermarking [7]. It tolerant content preserving modification such as compression, image file format, translation, scaling, rotation, transmission errors etc., [2]. This method of authentication fails to authenticate, manipulation like deletion of object from the image, addition of object into the image, position change of objects in an image[2] etc. The general structure of content-based image authentication using image signatures is as shown in Fig. 1.

© The Author(s), under exclusive license to Springer Nature Switzerland AG 2023
K. Kottursamy et al. (Eds.): IconDeepCom 2022, CCIS 1719, pp. 119–132, 2023.
https://doi.org/10.1007/978-3-031-27622-4_10

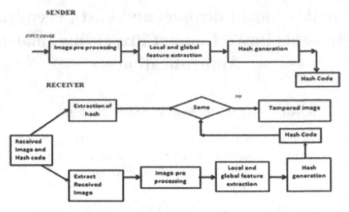

Fig. 1. Image authentication system architecture

The basic requirement of a good authentication system can be given as follows [2]: (i) The system must be robust to tolerate transformation of content, (ii) the data must be in secured and prevent from malicious attacks, (iii) any changes in the content must be notified to provide sensitivity of the data, (iv) the tampering location must be easily locatable, (v) event though the system content is tampered, it must have the ability to recovery the originality as must as possible, (vi) the process must be legitimate to the complexity level, (vii) the image authentication must be simple enough to carry within the image to provide portability.

Schneider et al. [15] were the first to handle content-based authentication system, using an image histogram to represent image content. However, the generated hash is quite large and time demanding, and the image content can be modified without modifying the histogram. Edges are used to represent content in Sobel, Canny [3], but the produced hash is lengthy and cannot recover lost data. Storck et al. [17], Wu et al. [20, 21], Lin et al. [10], Sun et al. [18], Lin et al. [21] employ transform coefficients such as DCT and DWT to describe image content; nevertheless, the produced hash cannot recover lost data. For each block of image, statistical metrics such as mean, standard deviation, kurtosis, and skewness are used to determine hash code by Kailasanathan et al. [7]. The system constructs the long hash code by combining local entropies with global descriptors to define the image description's individual moment information. Moments are employed to build the [11] hash, however if the inverse basis function includes approximation errors, the reconstruction of the completed region cannot be determined.

The majority of the hashing techniques works by fusing more than one hashing technique to yield best authentication system. Seyed Amir [16] employs a two-phase image authentication scheme that combines rigorous and selective authentication with the usage of two of the most generic approximate message authentication codes (AMAC).By combining DWT and SVD, Moataz Z. Salim [12] uses visual cryptography based watermarking approach for detection of forgery and localization. Nguyen et al. [19] created a digital watermarking. It becomes more difficult to recollect and locate altered places. Lima, Sebastian et al. [9], Yan Zhao et al. [22] Hamid Shojanazeri [6], Xingang Zhang [25] used local texture characteristics and global Zernike moment features to create a hash. It was unable to recover the information on tampering that had been lost. Obaid et al. [13] developed a watermark that uses Reed Solomon codes to perform partial recovery in the spatial and frequency domain. Machine learning methods such as HMM and SVM classifiers, as described by M. F. Hashmi et al. [10], classify images as authentic or unauthentic, but do not address localization or recovery.

The systems has drastic improvement in robustness, security, sensitivity, localization, recovery, complexity, portability because of combing the local entropies hash code and global descriptor for content-based image authentication system. The drawback of content-based authentication system is the possibility of having same feature vectors for different images [11], this vulnerability cannot be removed decisively but can be avoided by generating a combination of global and local image features.

In the existing system implementation, the image is divided into small equal sized squared local features blocks for image authentication. Though they are robust to content preserving modifications almost all system failed in rotation to larger angle. Based on the observation on image hashing techniques dividing image into circular blocks tolerate rotations to even greater angle and entropies are approximately linear to content preserving modifications [20]. Fast legendre moments are more suitable for image reconstruction [21] as it exactly calculate the content of image without any approximation errors or geometric errors.

This paper is organized in the Sect. 2 discussed about the representation of circular blocks, Sect. 3 describes about the entropies, Sect. 4 describes about the fast Legendre moments, Sect. 5 explains our proposed work, Sect. 6 narrates about the performance analysis and Sect. 7 concludes the paper.

2 Representation of Circular Blocks

Many image hashing Techniques [6, 8, 17–20] divides the image square blocks of equal size to extract local features. In all these methods content preserving operations of rotation is supported only up to very small angles less than 10 [21]. In an image if the blocks are considered as circular blocks the image pixels in that ring is almost unchanged even to larger angle rotation [1].

The Fig. 2 represents the area partitioning in equal sized circular spacing, the Fig. 3 represents the unchanged image pixels even though changing the rotating angle in a large scale.

The notated notations used for circular portioned such as number of circles/rings, pixels size, radius of rings, area of circle, center of circle, and distance matrix as mentioned in Table 1.

The algorithm for dividing into circular blocks starts with center (x_c, y_c) and set of radius r_k $(k = 1, 2, 3, ...n)$. The center of the circle is given as

$$if\ m = even \begin{cases} x_c = \frac{m}{2} + 0.5 \\ y_c = \frac{m}{2} + 0.5 \end{cases} if\ m = odd \begin{cases} x_c = \frac{(m+1)}{2} \\ y_c = \frac{(m+1)}{2} \end{cases}$$

The center of concentric circle for the radius r_k $(k = 1, 2, 3, ...n)$ is given as,

r_1 - radius of the inner circle = $\sqrt{\frac{\mu_A}{\pi}}$.

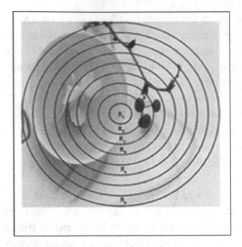

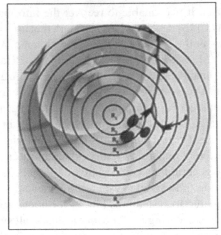

Fig. 2. Image divided into circular blocks   **Fig. 3.** Rotated version (rotated by 40°)

Table 1. Symbols used in circular block division algorithm

m x m	Image size
N	Ring count
R_k	Group of pixels that form k^m ring
f_k	Radius of k^m ring
f_l	Radius of 1^m ring
f_n	Radius of n^m ring
A	Area of circle generated by f_n
μ_A	Average area of each ring and is given as A/n
x_c, y_c	Center of the circle
$q_{ij}(x_i, y_j)$	Value of pixels in i^m row and j^m column
d_{ij}	Distance matrix containing distance of $q_{ij}(x_i, y_j)$ to the image center

r_n - radius of the outer circle = floor (m/2).

r_k - radius of the intermediate circle r_k (k = 2, 3, ... n − 1) = $\sqrt{\frac{\mu_A + \pi (r_{k-1})^2}{\pi}}$.

The Euclidean distance is used to measure the distance from $q_{ij}(x_i, y_j)$ from the center of the image x_c, y_c is given as,

$$d_{ij} = \sqrt{(x_i - x_c)^2 (y_j - y_c)^2}.$$

The circular partitioned pixels values can be measured using,

$R_1 = \{q_{ij}|d_{ij} \leq r_1\}$ and $R_k = \{q_{ij}|r_{k-1} < d_{ij} \leq r_1\}$ where k = {2, 3...n}.

The image is formed using measured pixel size in each equal circular block by R_k, where k = {1, 2, 3....n}.

3 Entropy

Entropy is a basic concept of information theory. It is the measure of average content of information in an image. For an image I, entropy can be defined as

$$H(I) = -\sum_{i=1}^{N} p(e_i).log_2 p(e_i) \tag{1}$$

where N is the number of intensity value in a image, N = 256 for gray scale image and p(e_i) probability of pixel value e_i in image I. Entropies are approximately linearly changed by content preserving modifications.

4 Fast Legendre Moments

Moments are used to retrieve the information from an image, the values from the pixel describes the content of the image. The moment values are propositional to the pixel values, circle partition area, number of rings where the information is collected. Based on the above parameters, the moment values changes, the optimal moment value is identified based on best fit information in which it retains.

The set of direct legendre moments for a grey scale image of size M × N is given as [21]

$$L_{pq} = \sum_{i=1}^{M} \sum_{j=1}^{N} I_p(x_i) I_q(y_j) f(i,j) \tag{2}$$

The moment kernel and image function for $f(i,j)$ is given as,

$$I_p(x_i) = \frac{2p+1}{2p+2}(u_{i+1}) P_p(u_{i+1}) - P_{p-1}(u_{i+1}) - (u_i) P_p(u_i) - P_{p-1}(u_i) \tag{3}$$

$$I_q(y_j) = \frac{2q+1}{2q+2}(v_{j+1}) P_q(v_{j+1}) - P_{q-1}(v_{j+1}) - (v_j) P_q(v_j) - P_{q-1}(v_j) \tag{4}$$

where $u_{i+1} = -i + i\,\Delta x_i$ and $u_i = -i + (i-1)\Delta x_i$ and $\Delta x_i = 2/M$
$v_{j+1} = -j + j\Delta y_j$ and $v_j = -j + (j-1)\Delta y_j$ and $\Delta y_j = 2/N$.

The moment kernel is calculated using the image size and moment order, and it is independent of image properties. The calculated moment kernel can be stored and used further processes.

Equation (2) is valid only for p ≥ 1 *and* q >= 1, So the first row p = 0, q = 0, 1, 2, 3 … Max is calculated using

$$L_{0q} = \frac{1}{M} \sum_{i=1}^{M} \sum_{j=1}^{N} I_q(y_j) f(i,j) \tag{5}$$

Max is calculated from the first column q = 0, p = 0, 1, 2, 3...using,

$$L_{p0} = \frac{1}{N} \sum_{i=1}^{M} \sum_{j=1}^{N} I_p(x_i)f(i,j) \tag{6}$$

For image size M x N the fast legendre moments can be calculated as two separate 1-D function given us,

$$L_{pq} = \sum_{i=1}^{M} I_p(x_i)Y_{iq} \tag{7}$$

where Y_{iq} is the qth order moment of row i

$$Y_{iq} = \sum_{j=1}^{N} I_q(y_j)f(i,j) \tag{8}$$

The approximation and geometric errors are reduced to the usage of legendre moments in our function, and it supports the reconstruction of tampered image which contains the information. The legendre polynomial over the square $[-1, 1] \times [-1, 1]$ for the image function f(x, y) is given as,

$$f_{max}(x_i, y_j) = \sum_{p=0}^{\infty} \sum_{q=0}^{\infty} L_{pq}P_p(x_i)P_q(y_j) \tag{9}$$

If the order of moment is smaller than infinity then the above Eq. (9) can be rewritten as

$$f_{max}(x_i, y_j) = \sum_{p=0}^{Max} \sum_{q=0}^{p} L_{p-q,q}P_{p-q}(x_i)P_q(y_j) \tag{10}$$

The maximum moments and total moments are used to reconstruct the image is given as,

$$N_{TOTAL} = \frac{(MAX + 1)(MAX + 2)}{2}$$

5 Proposed Authentication System

The proposed authentication system generates an image hash using local entropy features calculated on circular blocks and global fast legendre moments. Figure 4 shows the proposed system block diagram, the image is preprocessed, the hash code is generated by combining the circular block entropies and fast legendre moments.

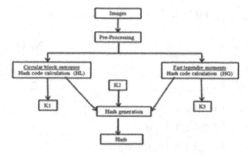

Fig. 4. Architecture of proposed system

5.1 Preprocessing

The image size of M × N is accepted as input and converted to a square image of size 512 × 512 using bilinear interpolation. The additive noise is removed using the Gaussian filter, is applied to the images. The RGB image is converted to gray scale image to extract the local and global features and to generate a hash.

5.2 Local Features Based on Circular Block Entropies

The gray scale image of size 512 × 512 is divided into circular blocks of equal sized areas. The number of circular blocks n for an image is taken as 60.The set of pixel values that constitute the circular blocks is available in R_k where k = 1, 2, 3, 4...60. For each R_k entropies are calculated using Eq. (1) where N is the number of intensity value in a image. N = 256 for gray scale image and $p(e_i)$ probability of pixel value e_i in circular block R_k. The 60 entropies thus calculated from each block are stored in H1 a row vector of size [1 × 60]. The random key generated numbers ranging from 0–255 and named it as K1 and the row vector of size [1 × 60].Generated hash code HL = (H1 + K1)mod 256 using the encrypted H1 value. HL is a row vector of size [1 × 60] is a hash formed from local entropies of circular blocks.

5.3 Global Features Based on Fast Legendre moments

Global features are extracted based on fast legendre moments, over the other existing moments like Zernike and geometric moments the approximation and geometric errors is reduced. This makes possible to calculate the information even though the image has losses. Because of this the legendre moments has a higher reconstruction capability.

The set of fast legendre moments for an image of size 512 × 512 is computed as two 1D function using Eq. (7) and Eq. (8). For an order of n = 4, 15 moments will be generated as shown in TABLE 2 and are stored in H2 a row vector of size [1 × 15].

The random key generated numbers ranging from 0 − 255 and named it as K2 and the row vector of size [1 × 15]. Generated hash code HG = (H2 + K2)mod 256 using the encrypted H2 value. HG is a row vector of size [1 × 15] is a hash formed from global features based on fast legendre moments.

Table 2. Moments of order n = 4

Order	Moments	No of moments
0	$L_{0,0}$	1
1	$L_{0,1}, L_{1,0}$	2
2	$L_{0,2}, L_{1,1}, L_{2,1}$	3
3	$L_{0,3}, L_{1,2}, L_{2,1}, L_{3,0}$	4
4	$L_{0,4}, L_{1,3}, L_{2,2}, L_{3,1}, L_{4,3}$	5
Total		15

5.4 Hash Generation

The Final hash HF is generated from HL and HG.HF is a row vector of size [1 × 75] generated by grouping HL and HG given as HF = [HLHG]. A random key K3 is generated containing numbers in the range of 0 to 255 and is a row vector of size [1 × 75]. Now HF is encrypted to generate the hash H for the image using both local and global features, H = (HF + K3)mod 256.The hash H is a row vector of size [1 × 75]. This hash H is sent with the image for authentication.

5.5 Hash Verification

At the receiver side, the hash is extracted from the image and decrypted using K3 and is called as the received hash HR. From the received image the hash is generated using the same techniques as performed by sender. This hash is called as test hash HT. For this test hash and received hash correlation co efficient is calculated using

$$S = \frac{\delta(HR.HT)}{\delta HR.\delta HT} \tag{11}$$

where $\delta(HR.HT)$- refers to the covariance and δHR, δHT-refers to standard deviation of HR and HT respectively. S the correlation coefficient lies in the range [−1, 1] i.e. 1 refers to high correlation and −1 refers to negative correlation or no correlation, here if it is greater than 0.95 the image is said to be authentic.

6 Experimental Results

The experiment was performed using 2000 images collected is used to test and performance analysis. Images downloaded from internet and CASIA database [4]. The content preserving manipulations of the images such as scaling, rotation and cropping, jpeg compression, embedding watermarking, Gamma correction, Contrast adjustment, Brightness adjustment, and zero mean Gaussian noise applied to original image together form the database.

Robustness
The system is designed to prevent the content modification, for measuring robustness

5 original images of size 512 × 512 as shown in Fig. 5 is taken. In table 3, show the list of image content preserving manipulation operation, the parameters considered are content pressuring manipulations, measured in range and number of images undergone for analysis are applied to each original image to generate 54 variant images.

Fig. 5. Original images (a) House (b) Lena (c) Pepper (d) Pirate (e) Plane

Table 3. Set of content preserving operations

Content preserving manipulation	Luminance	Geometric distribution			Additive noise	Compression	Watermarking
	Bright & contrast adjustments	Rotation	Scaling	Gamma correction	Zero mean Gaussian noise	JPEG	Text water marking of length 10
Measured in range	Scale [±10, ±20]	Degree [±1 to ±90]	% [0.5–2.5]	γ [0.3–1.0]	Variance [0.3–1.0]	Ratio [30–100]	Capacity [10–100]
Number of images	4	16	4	4	8	8	10

The software such as MATLAB 8.5 and Adobe Photoshop CC is used to attack the image, the resulted various attacks are recorded to perform analysis and shown graphically in Fig. 4(a) to 4(g). For the above image image the threshold is taken as .95 except for rotation to angle above .93. It is evidenced that our proposed system outperforms against attacks for rotations in large scale. When compared to the existing methods [14, 20], our proposed system performs well when rotation is done in larger angles.

Sensitivity
The forged image correctly specified and correctly classifies images as authentic and forged. The Table 4 shows the performance of our system in comparison with [8, 20]. The hash length is reduced when compared to [8] and it can tolerate large angle rotation

even up to ±90. Forgery localization is also supported by our system. Recovery of forged region is also possible but the system has the limitation that for recovery, the order of moments must be greater than 60 which drastically increases the hash length and computational complexity.

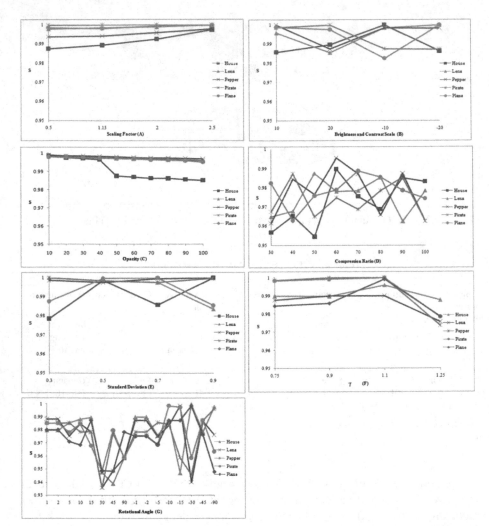

Fig. 6. Robustness validation (A) Scaling (B) Brightness contrast adjustment (C) Watermark embedding (D) JPEG compression (E) Zero Mean Gaussian noise (F) Gamma correction (G) Rotation

Figure 6 shows the characteristic curve of receiver operation, and the left corner represents the ROC and classification represented at the top.

The below Fig. 7 shows the false positive rate of ROC of proposed system.

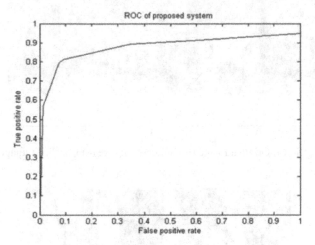

Fig. 7. False positive rate

Table 4. Comparison of hash performance

Methods	Hash length	JPEG compression	Small angle rotation	Large angle rotation	Brightness adjustment	Location	Recovery
[19]	560 bits	Yes	Yes	No	Yes	Yes	No
[7]	1200 bits	Yes	Yes	No	Yes	Yes	No
Proposed	600 bits	Yes	Yes	Yes	Yes	Yes	Yes [with limitation]

6.1 Localization and Recovery

The localization of forgery region can be identified by comparing the hashes. The hash value is used to measure the exact circular blocks by changing the hash value. The exact location of changed pixel is determined by comparing the R_k and respective d_{ij} values, this is shown in Fig. 8 below.

The use of fast Legendre moments helps in reconstruction of localized region using Eq. 10 but with cost of increased hash length. Image recovery is effective only for moments order greater than 60. If the order of moment is increased there will be drastic increase in hash length. It becomes the limitation of our proposed system. Figure 9 shows the reconstruction of Lena for orders of 60, 80,100 followed by histogram equalization.

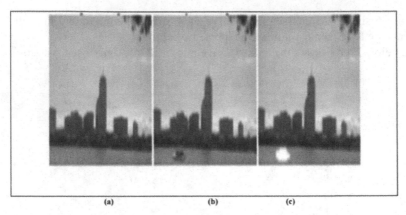

(a)   (b)   (c)

Fig. 8. (a) Original image (b) Tampered image (c) Localized image

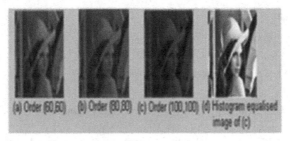

Fig. 9. Reconstruction of image using fast legendre moments of various order followed by histogram equalization

7 Conclusion

The proposed system is robust against content preserving manipulation and the values are static even though image is rotated. When compared to existing system our system outperforms other system in tolerance to larger angle of rotation. The average time of the proposed system is 2.89 s and has no significant difference with [20] that has 2.7 s. Rotation invariance is addressed in [1] uses only local haralick features and the proposed system increases the reliability in hash code by including both local and global features. The limitation of the system is the requirement to increase the hash length in order to achieve recovery. With the existing hash length of 600 bits recovery does not exist. Future work may be to concentrate on recovery without considerable change in hash length.

References

1. Alice, K., Ramaraj, N., Rajagopalan, S.P.: Rotation invariant image authentication using haralick features. Multimed. Tools Appl. **79**(1), 17211–17225 (2020)
2. Haouzia, A., Noumeir, R.: Methods for image authentication a survey. Multimed. Tools Appl. **39**, 1–46 (2008)

3. Canny, J.F.: A computational approach to edge detection. IEEE Trans. Pattern Anal. Mach. Intell. **8**(6), 679–698 (1986)
4. CASIA tampered image detection evaluation database. http://forensics/idealtest.org
5. David, M.C.: BerndGirod "a hybrid mobile visual search system with compact global signature". IEEE Trans. Multimed. **17**(7), 1019–1030 (2015)
6. Shojanazeri, H., Wan Adnan, W.A., Syed Ahmad, S.M., Rahimipour, S.: Authentication of images using Zernike moment watermarking. Multimed. Tools Appl. **76**(1), 577–606 (2015). https://doi.org/10.1007/s11042-015-3018-2
7. Kailasanathan, C., Safavi-Naini, R., Ogunbona, P.: Image authentication surviving acceptable modifications. In: IEEE-EURASIP, Workshop on Nonlinear Signal and Image Processing (2001)
8. Hosny, K.M.: Exact Legendre moment computation for gray level images. Pattern Recogn. **40**(12), 3597–3605 (2007)
9. Sebastian, L., Varghese, A., Manesh, T.: Image authentication by content preserving robust image hashing using local and global features. 1877-0509. Elsevier (2015)
10. Lin, C.Y., Chang, S.F.: A robust image authentication method distinguishing JPEG compression from malicious manipulation. CU/CTR Technical report 486-97-19 (1997)
11. Hashmi, M.F., Hambarde, A.R., Keskar, A.G.: Robust image authentication based on HMM and SVD classifiers. Eng. Lett. **22**(4) (2014)
12. Salim, M.Z., Abboud, A.J., Yildirim, R.: A visual cryptography-based watermarking approach for the detection and localization of image forgery. Electronics **11**, 136 (2022)
13. Ur Rehman, O., Tabatabaci, S.A.H.A.E., Zivic, N., Ruland, C.: Spatial and frequency domain complementary watermarks for image authentication and correction. In: SCC 2015 in Hamburg, Germany. VDE Verlag GMBH, Berlin (2015)
14. Queluz, M.P.: Content-based integrity protection of digital images. In: Proceedings of the SPIE Conference on Security and Watermarking of Multimedia Contents, San Jose, California, USA, vol. 3657, pp 85–93 (1999)
15. Schneider, M., Chang, S.-F.: A robust content based digital signature for image authentication. In: Proceedings of the IEEE International Conference on Image Processing, pp. 227–230 (1996)
16. Amir, S.: Secure and robust two-phase image authentication. IEEE Trans. Multimed. **17**(7), 945–956 (2015)
17. Storck, D.: A new approach to integrity of digital images. In: Proceedings of the IFIP Conference on Mobile Communication, pp. 309–316 (1996)
18. Sun, Q., Chang, S.F.: Semi-fragile image authentication using generic wavelet domain features and ECC. In: Proceedings of the ICIP (2002)
19. Nguyen, T.H., Duong, D.M., Doung, D.A.: Robust and high capacity watermarking for image based on DWT-SVD. In: IEEE RIVF, International Conference on Computing and Communication Technologies Research Innovation and Vision for Future (RIVF) (2015)
20. Wu, C.W.: Limitations and requirements of content based multimedia authentication systems. In: Proceedings of the IS&T/SPIE's International Symposium on Electronic Imaging: Science and Technology, San Jose, CA, vol. 4314, pp. 241–252 (2001)
21. Wu, C.W.: On the design of content based multimedia authentication systems. IEEE Trans. Multimed. **4**(3), 385–393 (2002)
22. Zhao, Y., Wang, S., Zhang, X., Yao, H.: Robust hashing for image authentication using zernike moments and local features. IEEE Trans. Inf. Forensics Secur. **8**(1), 55–63 (2013)
23. Yang, H.Z., Shu, G.N., Han, C., Toumoulin, L., Luo, M.: Efficient Legendre moment computation for grey level images. Laboratory of Image Science and Technology, Department of Biology and Medical Engineering, Southeast University, 210096 (2014)
24. Tang, Z., Zhang, X., Huaug, L., Dai, Y.: Robust image hashing using ring based entropies. Signal Process. **93**, 2061–2069 (2013)

25. Zhang, X., Yan, H., Zhang, L., Wang, H.: High-resolution remote sensing image integrity authentication method considering both global and local features. Int. J. Geo-Inf. **9**, 254 (2020)

Predictive Model for Depression and Anxiety Using Machine Learning Algorithms

Anmol Jha, M. S. Abirami[✉] [ID], and Vishal Kumar

Department of Computational Intelligence, SRM Institute of science and Technology, Kattankulathur, Tamil Nadu, India
abiramim@srmist.edu.in

Abstract. Psychological health disorders have grown quite widespread in recent decades. In this work, a few machine learning algorithms were used to predict the prevalence of psychological issues such as depression and anxiety using data from the online DASS42 application and the WESAD dataset. The algorithms were divided into four categories: probabilistic, closest neighbour, neural network, and tree-based methods. Depression and Anxiety are distinct—albeit overlapping— psychiatric maladies, as of now analyzed by self-reported-symptoms. Early recognizable proof of Sadness and Uneasiness could be a significant to begin with step towards evaluation, mediation, and backslide anticipation. Uneasiness disarranges are a kind of mental clutters characterized by imperative sentiments of fear and uneasiness. As of late, the advancement of machine learning procedures has made a difference enormously to create instruments helping specialists to foresee mental clutters and back understanding care. In this work, we used two datasets, DASS42 survey and WESAD dataset for predicting of depression and anxiety separately using various algorithms and then later using the results from the above to create a hybrid model which used both theoretical and medical symptoms to predict if a person is suffering from depression or anxiety. The accuracy varies according to type of people and equipment used. On comparing our results from the previous papers, we would like to say we did a significant work on the prediction accuracy. In the future we will achieve greater accuracy which will lead to a better recovery option for patients.

Keywords: WESAD · SVM · RespiBAN · DASS · CNN UDRP · ROC · RMSE · TSC · WEKA

1 Introduction

1.1 Depression and Anxiety

In today's world depression, anxiety, stress and dissatisfaction of people are very common. Due to this we all have started to regard them as an important aspect or to be exact an integral part of professional and everyday life. Depression is a state of in activity that can be accompanied by a loss of interest in activities that a person usually feels

© The Author(s), under exclusive license to Springer Nature Switzerland AG 2023
K. Kottursamy et al. (Eds.): IconDeepCom 2022, CCIS 1719, pp. 133–147, 2023.
https://doi.org/10.1007/978-3-031-27622-4_11

comfortable, has a change in appetite, and feels a imbalance between sleep and wakefulness. Depression is a combination of factors instead of being related to single factor. The people which are affected from it are mostly who have gone through various adverse life events like unemployment or disturbing events. Being depressed is like a start of the falling dominos as it leads to more stress and dysfunction, exacerbating an individual life and depression itself.

Anxiety is characterised by anxiety, fear, and discomfort. Sweats, agitation, and stress, as well as a quicker heartbeat. This may be a typical reaction to stress. When confronted with challenging challenges at work, for example, you may feel worried before taking an exam or making critical decisions (Fig. 1).

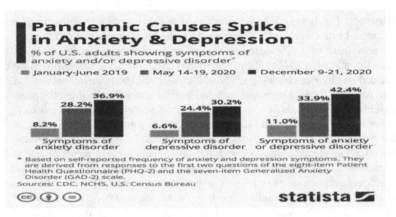

Fig. 1. Statista stats for depression and anxiety 2019–2020 [1]

1.2 Proposed Hybrid Model

As the topic of psychological problems is sensitive and distinguishing between depression, anxiety and stress cannot be easily done. As humans still cannot properly comprehend the differences, we decided to use machine learning techniques to predict the problem. We chose a DASS42 questionnaire which has 42 questions, related to stress, anxiety and depression. This will help us in assessing the core symptoms of the three. Just to be precise the research is only comparison of symptoms and prediction, not for diagnosis. The questionnaire is already medically proven thus no proper proof was given.

We then used RespiBAN and Empirica E4. RespiBAN and Empatica E4 are wearables which the users wear on their chest and non-dominant hand respectively. Both sensors are used in various households to get the readings of a person which are pretty accurate and can give us a proper detail of the medical conditions of the person. Due to the extreme price and the current pandemic instead of collecting our own data we got the dataset from the internet instead of collecting it manually. The dataset isn't publicly accessible, so we had to write a mail to the author for them to provide us the dataset. The dataset is widely known as WESAD dataset.

The DASS42 questionnaire had lots of extra questions like their age, ethnicity, work background, marriage, etc. which further helped us to group the people of one age to another. We were also able to predict which age group or people from what work background suffers the most with the psychological problems. The data collected from repiBAN were drawn, predicted, and thus were said to be depressed or not. After the two predictions were done individually, we combined the two model and made a hybrid model which helped in making a model which was more accurate than the previous two as well as we were able to do a much exhaustive prediction due to the fact, we combined theory and medical graphs thereby making it a better than a lot of models currently used.

2   Related Works

Choudhury et al. [1] contend that downturn establishes a certified test in individual. Significant quantity of persons encountered the evil impacts of misery and simply a division seeks adequate treatment consistently. They likewise researched the likelihood to use web-based systems administration to recognize and dissect any indication of critical melancholy issue in the individuals. Box their e-social organizing postings, they measured conduct credits relating to social commitment, feeling, lingo and linguistic styles, feeling self-framework, and notification of energizer meds.

O'Dea et al. [2] inspected Twitter to be dynamically investigated as techniques for perceiving psychological prosperity status, remembering despondency and suicidality for the populace. Using both human coders and a modified machine classifier, this study discovered that it is feasible to detect the level of stress in tweets about self-destruction.

Chih-Ming Cheng et al. [3] utilized confidence information estimated at mean ages 13, 16 and 22, and uneasiness issue conclusion at mean age of 33 to analyze the effect of advancement of confidence on beginning of grown-up uneasiness issue. The examination depended on a Bayesian joint model with a straight blended impacts model for the longitudinal estimations, and a summed up direct model for the paired essential endpoint.

Ishita Bhakta et al. [4] used algorithms which were widely during that time and was able to achieve a 82.6% accuracy and 84.1% precision with Catboost algorithm which was the best in compared to others like Logistic Regression, Naïve Bayes, SVM and Random Forest were used to predict depression. The survey was based on 470 seafarers.

Arkaprabha Sau et al. [5] published a paper in which five classifiers algorithm were compared according to 4 aspects – Accuracy, precision, ROC area and RMSE. Out of all the 5 classifiers used Bayes Net was found to be the best among them.

Narendra K. Kamila et al. [6] used a new algorithm which wasn't use yet, known as Apriori algorithm and it was used to predict the presence of depression at workstation. According to their result it was stated that the work can be extended at individual level to predict depression.

Raid M. Khalil et al. [7] used various classifier algorithms like SVM, F-Cmean, PNN probabilistic Neural Network, and K-Mean ML algorithms were all used to predict depression disorder and compared on the basis of accuracy and precision. This paper mostly focused on the people suffering from type 2 diabetes. As the predictions were made by a highly selected group of people, i.e., type 2 diabetic people it helps doctors to detect depression at an early stage thereby reducing severe cases. SVM classifier was chosen the best among them.

Aashie Roy Saxena et al. [8] focused on three major methods to predict depression among a group of people using Machine Learning classifiers and WEKA using imaging and Machine Learning method.

Rashmi Phalnikar et al. [9] used the CNN-UDRP technique uses a Convolution Neural Network to predict the risk of heart disease based on Unimodal disease risk prediction (CNN-UDRP). In the case of heart illness, CNN-UDRP has a 60–65% accuracy rate. As a result, the performance is better for predicting the risk of heart disease. The system's output is divided into three categories: low, medium, and high risk.

Sharath Chandra Guntuku et al. [10] concentrated on the linguistic features of data from Facebook and Twitter. In a cross-domain environment, it assesses how well models trained on Facebook data predict stress on Twitter language. As a result, the necessity for transfer learning has been established in order to apply the stress model to Twitter language, which has been trained on Facebook languages.

Chrandrasekar Vuppalapati et al. [11] suggested system is made up of three modules: a sensor (hardware circuit) device connected to a microcontroller, a mobile app for displaying the findings, and cloud storage for storing the data. Brain waves measured with electroencephalography (EEG) are a useful tool for determining stress levels. It detects stress and sends an alarm to the user via a mobile application, which may be used to help the user keep track of their stress levels at any time. The system is dependent on the datasets used as well as the machine learning methods used.

Min Chen et al. [12] suggested a CNN-based (CNN-MDRP) system, also known as a Multi-modal Disease Risk Prediction algorithm, that leverages SQL and non-SQL data (in JSON format) from Chinese hospitals. Chen concluded that the proposed system for predicting illness risk has an accuracy of about 94.80% and is faster than the CNN-UDRP algorithm.

Thomas Stutz1 et al. [13] conducted stress research, as well as data collected from sensors and smartphone usage. This research is based on a variety of observations. It collects stress data using an Android application called The Stress Collector (TSC). After installing the application using a (.apk) file on an Android phone, it operates in the background to collect mobile usage and sensor data on a regular basis.

David Liu et al. [14] stated ECG - electrocardiogram data can be used to create a method for forecasting various stress levels. The Galvanic Skin Response (GSR) data are recorded at a rate of 31 Hz, while ECG signals are constantly gathered at a rate of 496 Hz in this experiment. According to the article, predicting GSR with > 97 percent accuracy using a combination of Heart Rate Variability and ECG features is difficult if it is in the highest percentile or lowest 20 percentile. It implies that we may anticipate whether a user is stressed or not using consumer ECG monitors without the need for GSR estimations.

Tasnim et al. [15] explored different machine learning methods and acoustic characteristics in voice were used to investigate sadness detection. The AVEC 2013 dataset yielded a total of 2268 audio characteristics. Using Principal Component Analysis, these features got reduced to 791. (PCA). When these features are combined for a classification challenge, deep neural networks produce the best results.

Acharya et al. [16] presented a model for detecting depression based on EEG signals and a CNN model. The proposed method was tested using EEG signals from both the hemispheres, i.e., left and right with accuracy of 93.54 percent and 95.49 percent respectively. Employing EEG signals for depression identification might provide excellent results, the data collecting, and processing method can be time-consuming and complex.

M. P. Dooshima et al. [17] The researchers looked at demographic, biological, psychological, and environmental aspects for prediction. To validate the results, a number of mental health professionals were engaged.

S. G. Alonso et al. [18] have carried out a thorough examination of the various algorithms used to predict mental health. Various approaches were investigated, including Association Rule Mining and Randomization.

Afef Saidi et al. [19] developed a hybrid model that uses a unique audio-based technique to detect depression. Convolutional neural networks and Support Vector Machines [13] are combined in their model, with SVM replacing CNN's fully linked layers. The feature extraction in this suggested model was done with CNN, as well as the categorization was done with SVM. It achieved 68 percent efficiency utilizing the mixed model, compared to 58.57 percent using CNN model.

Dilip Singh Sisodia et al. [20] utilized a Kaggle-sourced HR analytics dataset to predict employee turnover rate by developing a model that can predict employee turnover rate. A heatmap is constructed to emphasis the link between the characteristics. In the investigational region, histogram was constructed to comparison of salary of left over employees, satisfaction level, and other parameters.

S. S. Alduayj et al. [21] measured the rate of employee attrition; a three-step experiment was conducted. In the first experiment, they employed SVM along multiple kernel functions, Random Forest, and KNN to analyze an original imbalanced dataset. They used the adaptive synthetic (ADASYN) strategy to reduce class imbalance and the latest dataset is trained using the SVM, RF, and KNN models. They are also sampled under the data to accomplish class balancing. Then, using KNN with K = 3 to train an ADASYN-balanced dataset gave us the best result, with 0.93 F1 score.

M. Deshpande et al. [22] Emotional analysis according to Twitter feeds was successfully applied, with an emphasis on depression. Based on specially prepared account of terms reflecting depression inclinations or symptoms, the feed was classed as negative. They went about doing their experiments in a novel way. They were able to predict depression tendencies with an accuracy of 83.0 percent using the Naive-Bayes Classifier and SVM.

AR Subhani et al. [23] According to research and explorations, the human brain is the one that is most affected by stress. This study aims to understand more about the changes and stress that people suffering from mental or psychological disorders, such as depression and anxiety, experience. The signal analysis of the afflicted person's Electroencephalogram can reveal a few details (EEG). The collected features were classified using algorithms like Decision Tree Classifier (DTC), Logistic regression, and others, yielding findings that were utilized to distinguish between stress levels, assisting in the identification of psychological problems.

3 Proposed Methodology

3.1 WESAD Data Set

The WESAD dataset consists of data from two sensors, RaspiBAN and Empatica E4. RespiBAN is a wearable device that is wear on chest and measures the following data like EMG, ECG, RESP. Data Format.

Two devices were used to collect raw sensor data: a chest-wearable - RespiBAN and a wrist wearable device -Expatica E4. The raw data from RespiBAN is synced with study protocol labels (similar start time). The RespiBAN and Empatica E4 data, on the other hand, must be manually synchronised. The subjects made a dual tapping gesture on their breast with their non-dominant hand (where they wore the E4). The characteristic pattern in the acceleration signal that results can be utilised to synchronise the data of the two devices. In addition, the dataset includes the SX.pkl file, which contains synced raw sensor data and labels.

3.1.1 Data from RespiBan

The RespiBAN Professional was used. At 700 Hz, all signals were captured. SX respiban.txt contains the raw data. There are ten columns in this table. The first column contains the consecutive line number. Ignore the second column. Columns 3–10 include the raw data from the eight sensor channels.

The header specifies the order of the channels. The "XYZ" entries relate to the three-channel accelerometer (thus, acceleration data is provided in 3 columns).

Each channel must be changed using the methods below to convert raw sensor readings into SI units (signal contains raw sensor values, $vcc = 3$, $chan\_bit = 2^{16}$) (Fig. 2).

$CG\,(mV): ((signal/chan\_bit - 0.5) * vcc)$

$EDA\,(\mu S): (((signal/chan\_bit) * vcc)/0.12)$

$EMG\,(mV): ((signal/chan\_bit - 0.5) * vcc)$

$TEMP(^\circ C): vout = (signal * vcc)/(chan_bit - 1.)rntc = ((10^4) * vout)/(vcc - vout) - 273.15 + 1$

$$/(1.12764514 * (10^{(-3)}) + 2.34282709 * (10^{(-4)}) * log(rntc)$$

$$+8.77303013 * (10^{(-8)}) * (log(rntc)3))$$

$XYZ\,(g): (signal - Cmin)/(Cmax - Cmin) * 2 - 1, where\ Cmin = 28000\ and\ Cmax = 38000$

$RESPIRATION\,(\%): (signal / chan\_bit - 0.5) * 100$

3.1.2 Data from Empatica E4

The E4 device was worn on the non-dominant wrist of the individuals. The sampling rate of the various sensors varied, as shown below. SX E4 Data.zip contains the raw data. The following files, when unzipped, contain derived information and should be ignored in this dataset: HR.csv, IBI.csv, and tags.csv are all csv files. The file info.txt contains information on the contents of the folder. The following files include raw data from the E4 device (the first line in each file refers to the sensor channel's global timestamp at start, and the second line refers to the sensor channel's sampling rate):

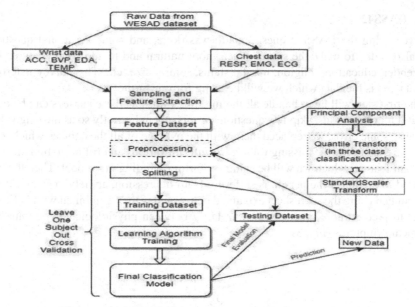

Fig. 2. Proposed prediction model for depression and anxiety using WESAD dataset

- ACC.csv: sampled at 32 Hz. The three columns refer to the three accelerometric channels. Data is provided in units of 1/64g.
- BVP.csv: sampled at 64 Hz. Data from photoplethysmography (PPG).
- EDA.csv: sampled at 4 Hz. Data is in μS.
- TEMP.csv: sampled at 4 Hz. Data is in °C

3.1.3 Synchronized Data

The raw data of the two devices was manually synchronised using the double-tap signal pattern. The results are stored in SX.pkl files, one for each subject. This file is a dictionary, and the keys are as follows:

- *'subject'*: The subject ID is SX.
- *'signal'*: consists of two fields that contain all of the raw data:
  'chest' refers to RespiBAN data (all the modalities:ECG, EDA, EMG, RESP, TEMP,ACC)
  'wrist' data from Empatica E4 (all the modalities: BVP, EDA, TEMP, ACC)
- *'label'*: 700 Hz sampling ID of the corresponding study condition of protocol. The following are the IDs that have been provided: 0 indicates that the value is undefined or temporary. 1 denotes the starting point, 2 denotes stress, 3 denotes fun, and 4 denotes meditation. In this dataset, 5/6/7 = should be omitted.

Raw data was collected and stored in the folder named WESAD with the raw data from all the sensors.

3.1.4 DASS42

A survey using the DASS42 questionnaire was done, and some additional questions were also added to make the survey much more natural and to add some features like age, gender, education, religion, marital status, family size, etc. This survey is termed raw data and is the data which we will be using for our further work.

The first step will be to handle all the missing values as these surveys can be quite tedious a lot of users just skip few questions or miss them honestly so as missing values will cause some error; we replaced them with the average of all the choices which were made. After handling the missing values, we will run various algorithms to find the most important feature, which we will be using for further building our model. Then the data was used to predict if the person is suffering from depression, anxiety or stress. It can be calculated using the scoresheet explained below and is then combined with WESAD dataset to predict more precisely the similarity between physiological symptoms and biological symptoms (Fig. 3).

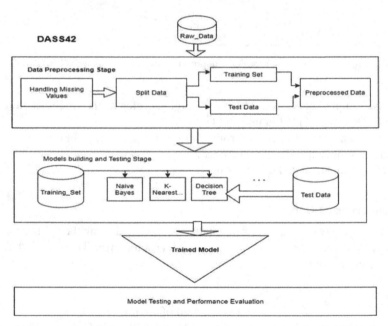

Fig. 3. Proposed prediction model for depression and anxiety using DASS42 dataset

3.2 Data Collection

We first collected our data from the given DASS42 questionnaire which contains 42 questions with 4 options for each question which differ from "did not apply to me at all" to "applied to me very much, or most of the time", that account for depression, anxiety, and stress in a person.

3.2.1 Feature Extraction and Filtration

We then filtered the collected data and extracted only the necessary features that can lead to the determination of a person's emotional status, and we also mapped the emotional traits with different personalities to ensure a more characteristic model. The data collected was then separated into three classes of depression, stress, and anxiety along with their scores. We then select the people having the majority traits of depression from the list and pass them to our second Model which uses Wearables to determine the different physical attributes that can be used to identify the depressed state. These attributes include the Motion (acceleration of chest and wrist), ECG and EMG values, and many more.

3.2.2 Data Cleaning and Pre-processing

The data collected from the wearables is cleaned and pre-processed for further process of training and testing our Machine learning Model.

We first calculate the interquartile range, then we clean up the data Outliers followed by the Normalization of the data. Then the Normalized data was split into testing and training data in the ratio of 80:20 respectively.

3.2.3 Machine Learning Models

(a) **Logistic Regression Model**

The link between a categorical dependent variable and a group of independent factors is studied using Logistic Regression.

When the dependent variable has just two categories, such as Yes and No or True and False, Simple Logistic Regression is utilized.

When the dependent variable has three or more distinct values, such as two-wheeler, three-wheeler, four- wheeler, and so on, Multinomial Logistic Regression is utilized.

The constant (b_0) in logistic regression moves the curve left and right, whereas the slope (b_1) determines the curve's steepness. The logistic regression equation may be written as an odds ratio using a simple transformation.

Finally, we might express the equation in terms of logits, which is a linear function of predictors, and takes natural log of both sides. As x is changed from one unit to another, the coefficient (b_1) represents how much logit (log-odds) changes.

(b) **Linear Discriminant Analysis (LDA)**

The aim of LDA is to reduce dimensionality by preserving the class's selective information. LDA calculates the probability of a given set of inputs and checks just to see if they belong toward any classes. The output class is the one that reflects the highest likelihood, and a forecast is produced. In the LDA classification, the Bayes Theorem is employed to estimate the probabilities (Fig. 4).

$$ln\frac{p}{1-p} = b0 + b1x \tag{1}$$

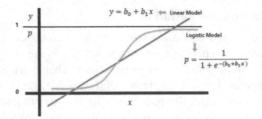

Fig. 4. Linear discriminant analysis

If data is collected from a multivariate Gaussian distribution, which is the distribution of X that can be defined by its mean (μ) and covariance (Σ), exact form of the preceding allocation rules may be accomplished. According to the Bayesian criteria, data x is classified as class j if it has the highest likelihood among all K classes for I = 1..., K:

$$\delta_i(x) = \log f_i(x) + \log \Pi_i \tag{2}$$

The above Eq. (2) is known as discriminant function. The discriminant function calculates the chances that data x belongs to each of the classes. The decision line separating any two classes, k and l, is the set of x where two discriminant functions have the similar value. As a result, any data on the decision border may originate from either of the two classes.

If the covariance among K classes is assumed to be same, then LDA is used. This means, same covariance matrix is utilized by all the classes rather than having a individual covariance matrix for every class, all classes share the same covariance matrix. The discriminant function may then look like this:

$$\delta_k(x) = x^T \Sigma^{-1} \mu k - \frac{1}{2} \mu^T{}_k \Sigma^{-1} \mu + {}_k \log \pi_k \tag{3}$$

(c) Quadratic Discriminant Analysis (QDA)

The main difference between linear discriminant analysis and quadratic discriminant analysis is that we relaxed the assumption that all classes' covariance and mean were identical. As a result, we had to calculate it independently.

The quadratic discriminant function is given by

$$\delta_k(x) = -\frac{1}{2}(x - \mu)^T_K \Sigma^{-1}_k (x - \mu) + {}_k \log \pi_k \tag{4}$$

(d) K - Nearest Neighbor (KNN)

When predicting a class label (in classification) or a continuous target value, KNN examines the k nearest neighbor (in regression).

KNN's most basic variant predicts the target class label for a given query point as the most often represented class label among the k most similar training samples.

The process of determining the nearest point to the input point from the collected data can be characterized as "determining the closest point to the input point from a given data set." The approach saves all existing samples (test data) and classifies new instances based on its K neighbors' majority votes. The initial step in creating a KNN is to convert data points into mathematical values (vectors). The approach works by calculating the distance between these points' mathematical values. It analyses if the points are likely to be like those on the exam (Table 1).

Table 1. Formula for calculating various types of distances

Distance measure	Formula
Euclidean	$D = \sqrt{\left(x_1 - y_1\right)^2 + \left(x_2 - y_2\right)^2 + \ldots + \left(x_n - y_n\right)^2}$
City block	$D = \left|x_1 - y_1\right| + \left|x_2 - y_2\right| + \ldots\ldots + \left|x_n - y_n\right|$
Cosine	$D = \dfrac{\Sigma_i\, x_i y_i}{\sqrt{\Sigma_i\, x_i^2}\,\sqrt{\Sigma_i\, y_i^2}}$
Correlation	$D = \dfrac{N\Sigma\, xy - \left(\Sigma x\right)\left(\Sigma y\right)}{\sqrt{\left[N\Sigma\, x^2 - \left(\Sigma x\right)^2\right]\left[N\Sigma\, y^2 - \left(\Sigma y\right)^2\right]}}$

(e) *Decision Tree*

One of the supervised classification algorithms is a decision tree that can be utilized for regression and classification problems; however, it is very useful for solving classification problems. Dataset features are represented by internal nodes, decision rules are indicated by tree branches, and the conclusion is delivered in the leaf nodes.

The decision tree consists of decision node and leaf node. Decisions can be taken by using choice nodes which have many branches, whereas the endpoints of the decisions are the leaf nodes.

4   Results and Discussion

We used various Machine learning classifiers to predict depression in a person. We used Logistic regression, LDA, QDA classification, KNN, and decision trees, with a different set of parameters such as cost function, nearest neighbours, value of folds in cross-validation, and many more.

4.1 Logistic Regression

We started off with logistic regression which gave us decent accuracy of 82%, the change in a penalty or regression function from lasso to the ridge was not of much improvement either, giving only percentage change in the accuracy of the order of $1e^{-1}$ (Table 2).

Table 2. Logistic regression performance parameters

	Precision	Recall	f1-score	Support
0	0.8223	0.8921	0.8558	246238
1	0.9740	0.8998	0.9354	10786
2	0.6993	0.4014	0.5100	63452
3	0.7889	0.8191	0.8037	47738
4	0.9101	0.9998	0.9529	51878
Accuracy			0.8232	420092
lAvg	0.8389	0.8024	0.8115	420092

4.2 LDA Classification

We then performed LDA classification which gave us worse results than the Logistic regression model of the accuracy of just 79%, with and without cross-validation (Table 3).

Table 3. LDA classification performance parameters

	Precision	Recall	f1-score	Support
0	0.8128	0.8674	0.8392	245716
1	0.9738	0.6511	0.7804	10738
2	0.6287	0.3745	0.4694	63486
3	0.7521	0.8109	0.7804	47778
4	0.8538	1.0000	0.9212	52374
Accuracy			0.7975	420092
lavg	0.8042	0.7408	0.7581	420092
avg	0.7873	0.7975	0.7853	420092

4.3 QDA Classification

We then used QDA classification in case our dataset has nonlinear classification boundaries, which would have not been traced properly by LDA. This model gave the better result of all the previous models > 90%, to prevent overfitting we also performed cross-validation which maintained a great accuracy of more than 90%.

4.4 KNN

Similarly, we used KNN which gave an accuracy of 85%, the best so far, with and without cross- validation (Table 4).

Table 4. KNN Performance parameters

	Precision	Recall	f1-score	Support
0	0.9249	0.8253	0.8723	1230433
1	0.9246	0.8831	0.9034	53659
2	0.7107	0.9127	0.7992	316935
3	0.7492	0.8527	0.7976	239191
4	0.9024	0.9430	0.9222	260238
Accuracy			0.8577	2100456
lavg	0.8423	0.8834	0.8589	2100456
avg	0.8698	0.8577	0.8597	2100456

4.5 Decision Tree

We then finally implemented the Simple Decision tree, whose results are on par with the KNN model (Table 5).

Among the various Machine Learning Classification Models applied, we can see that the Models having QDA implementation given better accuracy than most of the other models. This shows that our dataset is Gaussian and contains a non-linear classification boundary between the classes.

As we can see the model has an accuracy of 92%approximately. These results are better than many of the proposed papers regarding the same research topic.

Table 5. Decision tree performance parameters

	Precision	Recall	f1-score	Support
0	0.8866	0.8848	0.8857	1230433
1	0.9702	0.9373	0.9535	53659
2	0.8993	0.7566	0.8218	316935
3	0.6914	0.8289	0.7540	239191
4	0.9065	0.9307	0.9184	260238
Accuracy			0.8661	2100456
Macro lavg	0.8708	0.8677	0.8667	2100456
Weighted avg	0.8709	0.8661	0.8668	2100456

5 Conclusion and Future Enhancement

We can detect a person's depression very accurately using the readings of questionnaires and wearable devices. We hope to further improve our accuracy and expand the scope of the project to show the degree or severity of depression and the degree of stress and anxiety of a person. We will add some more questions that can describe more about a person's emotional state and can be used as a deterministic measure in estimating depression, stress, and anxiety.

Depression detection in a person is a very sensitive topic. It requires a reasonable number of psychological questions that can be used to get an estimation of the state. We will also try to improve the volume of our questionnaire with some psychological research and acquire results from a greater audience.

References

1. De Choudhury, M., et al.: Predicting depression via social media. In: Proceedings of the Seventh International AAAI Conference on Weblogs and Social Media, pp. 128–137 (2013)
2. O'Dea, B., et al.: Detecting suicidality on twitter. Internet Inventions **2**(2), 183–188 (2015)
3. Cheng, C.-M., et al.: Risk of developing major depressive disorder and anxiety disorders among adolescents and adults with atopic dermatitis: A nationwide longitudinal study. J. Affect. Disord. **178**, 60–65 (2015)
4. Sau, A., Bhakta, I.: Screening of anxiety and depression among the seafarers using machine learning technology. Inf. Med. Unlocked **16**, 100228 (2019)
5. Jena, L., Kamila, N.K.: A model for predicting human depression using Apriori algorithm. In: IEEE International Conference on Information Technology (2014).https://doi.org/10.1109/ICIT.2014.65
6. Khalil, R.M., Al-Jumaily, A.: Machine learning based prediction of depression among type 2 diabetic patients. In: IEEE International Conference on Intelligent Systems and Knowledge Engineering (2017). https://doi.org/10.1109/ISKE.2017.8258766
7. Hooda, M., Saxena, A.R., Madhulika, D., Yadav, B.: A study and comparison of prediction algorithms for depression detection among millennials-a machine learning approach. In: IEEE International Conference on Current Trends in Computer, Electrical, Electronics and Communication (2017). https://doi.org/10.1109/CTCEEC.2017.8455078

8. Ambekar, S., Phalnikar, R.: Disease risk pre-diction by using convolutional neural network. In: IEEE International Conference on Computing Communication Control and Automation (2018). https://doi.org/10.1109/ICCUBEA.2018.8697423

9. Guntuku, S.C., Buffone, A., et. al.: Understanding and measuring psychological stress using social media. In: International AAAI Conference on Web and Social Media, vol. 13 (2019)

10. Vuppalapati, C., Khan, M.S., et al.: A system to detect mental stress using machine learning and mobile development. In: International Conference on Machine Learning and Cybernetics (2018). https://doi.org/10.1109/ICMLC.2018.8527004

11. Chen, M., Hao, Y., Kai Hwang, L., Wang, and Lin Wang,: Disease prediction by machine learning over big data from healthcare communities. IEEE Access, Spec. Sect. Healthc. Big Data **5**, 8869–8879 (2017)

12. Stütz, T., et al.: Smartphone based stress prediction. In: Ricci, F., Bontcheva, K., Conlan, O., Lawless, S. (eds.) UMAP 2015. LNCS, vol. 9146, pp. 240–251. Springer, Cham (2015). https://doi.org/10.1007/978-3-319-20267-9_20

13. Liu, D., Ulric, M.: Listen to Your Heart: Stress Prediction Using Consumer Heart Rate Sensors. Machine Learning, Stanford (2014)

14. Tasnim, M., Stroulia, E.: Detecting depression from voice. In: Meurs, M.-J., Rudzicz, F. (eds.) Canadian AI 2019. LNCS (LNAI), vol. 11489, pp. 472–478. Springer, Cham (2019). https://doi.org/10.1007/978-3-030-18305-9_47

15. Acharya, U.R., Oh, S.L., Hagiwara, Y., Tan, J.H., Adeli, H., Subha, D.P.: Automated EEG-based screening of depression using deep convolutional neural network.Comput. Methods Programs Biomed. **161**, 103–113. Elsevier (2018)

16. Dooshima, M.P., Chidozie, E.N., Ademola, B.J., Sekoni, O.O., Adebayo, I.P.: A predictive model for the risk of mental illness in Nigeria using data mining. Int. J. Immunol. **6**(1), 5–16 (2018)

17. Alonso, S.G., et al.: Data mining algorithms and techniques in mental health: a systematic review. J. Med. Syst. **42**(9), 1–15 (2018). https://doi.org/10.1007/s10916-018-1018-2

18. Saidi, A., Othman, S.B., Saoud, S.B.: Hybrid CNN-SVM classifier for efficient depression detection system. In: International Conference on Advanced Systems and Emergent Technologies, Tunisia, vol. 2020, pp. 229-234 (2020)

19. Sisodia, D.S., Vishwakarma, S., Pujahari, A.: Evaluation of machine learning models for employee churn prediction. In: International Conference on Inventive Computing and Informatics. IEEE (2017). https://doi.org/10.1109/ICICI.2017.8365293

20. Alduayj, S.S., Rajpoot, K.: Predicting employee attrition using machine learning. In: International Conference on Innovations in Information Technology, Al Ain, United Arab Emirates, IEEE (2018) https://doi.org/10.1109/INNOVATIONS.2018.8605976

21. Deshpande,M., Rao, V.: Depression detection using emotion artificial intelligence. In: International Conference on Intelligent Sustainable Systems, Palladam, India, IEEE (2017). https://doi.org/10.1109/ISS1.2017.8389299

22. Subhani, A.R., Mumtaz, W., Saad, M.N.B.M., Kamel, N., Malik, A.S.: Machine learning framework for the detection of mental stress at multiple levels. IEEE Access **5**, 13545–13556 (2017)

A Deep Learning Based Species Reciprocal System for Partridge

J. Aswini[1], A. Gayathri[2(✉)], A. Revathi[3], and L. Vinoth Kumar[4]

[1] Department of AIML, Saveetha Engineering College (Autonomous), Affiliated to Anna University, Chennai, India
aswinij@saveetha.ac.in
[2] Department of Computer Science and Engineering, Saveetha School of Engineering, Saveetha Institute of Medical and Technical Sciences (SIMATS), Chennai, India
gayathribala.sse@saveetha.com
[3] Department of Computational Intelligence, School of Computing, SRM Institute of Science and Technology, Kattankulathur, Chennai, India
revathial@srmist.edu.in
[4] Department of Information Technology, R.M.K Engineering College, RSM Nagar, Chennai, India
vk.cc@rmkec.ac.in

Abstract. Bird watching is a form of wildlife observation of birds which is a recreational activity. Bird watchers make use of bird books to know about the birds. To provide handy tool to birdwatchers and to admire the splendor of birds, to recognize bird species a web based Convolutional Neural Network is used to help out users. Avifauna species images were used to localize major features in the image and it is learnt by a convolutional neural network (CNN)s. To distill the shapes and colors of the object granularities then to balance the distribution of bird species, circumscribed region of interest is performed. Then, for feature extraction convolutional neural network (CNN) is used. Finally, activation function softmax is applied on the resulting class probabilities. To identify picture uploaded by users, the erudite parameters of bird features were used. Instead of training from scratch, the concept of transfer learning is used in which pre-trained models (VGG16, Xception, ResNet, etc.) are used. Here two of these models are used namely ResNet50 and VGG16. Among these two models ResNet50 have provided better accuracy. Transfer learning helps us to increase the classification accuracy. Hence, materialization of deep learning algorithms has resulted in highly intricate cognitive for computer vision & image recognition. The deep learning model uses CNN framework for bird image classification.

Keywords: Convolution neural network · RESNET50 · Flask · Transfer learning

1 Introduction

Bird-watching as a recreational activity has gained in popularity in recent years, coinciding with the development of environmental activism. The study of birds has contributed

K. Kottursamy et al. (Eds.): IconDeepCom 2022, CCIS 1719, pp. 148–163, 2023.
https://doi.org/10.1007/978-3-031-27622-4_12

much both to the theoretical and practical aspects of biology. In classifying birds, most environmentalists have historically relied upon structural characteristics to infer evolutionary relationships. So, to help them in order to recognize the bird species A machine learning application model is build that would assist them. To classify the bird species with greater accuracy, deep learning with transfer learning model RESNET50 is used.

Machine Learning, on the other hand, is a subset of Artificial Intelligence, and Deep Learning is a subset of Machine Learning. Artificial intelligence (AI) is a general term for techniques that allow computers to mimic human nature. All of this is made possible through machine learning, which is a set of algorithms trained on data. From scratch, the conventional machine & deep learning algorithms and it techniques have been built. To solve specific tasks these algorithms are trained. The models have to be rebuilt from scratch once the feature-space distribution changes. To overcome the idea of building the problem from scratch and to utilize knowledge acquired for solving tasks transfer learning is ideated. An interface is developed to extort information from bird images by using prediction and also by adding pre-trained model RESNET50 and few dense layers. The number of neurons in the output layer is determined by the number of bird classes. A dataset of birds was taken from the Kaggle. The model is trained on this dataset. The output of this machine learning model is an array of class probabilities. The class which has higher probability will be the output. The model is saved and flask framework is use to build a web application.

2 Literature Review

Huang and Basanta developed a deep learning platform in which it assisted users in recognizing 27 species of bird's endemic to Taiwan using an application developed for mobile named the Internet of Birds (IoB) [1]. The author proposed three different models for this application. They are CNN with skip connections, a CNN, SVM classifier. Among these three CNN with skip connections produced better accuracy (96.7%). The skip connection strategy was utilized to linearly integrate the outputs of the previous and current layers to improve feature extraction. Finally, the softmax function is used to generate a probability distribution of bird species. The accuracy of the CNN model and the SVM classifier was 93.98% and 89%, respectively. The proposed system is capable of anticipating and distinguishing between images of birds and non-birds. When a user uploads an image that is not a bird, the system encourages the user to only upload bird images.

B. Qiao, Z. Zhou, H. Yang, & J. Cao (2017). Bird species recognition based on SVM classifier and decision tree. 2017 First International Conference on Electronics Instrumentation & Information Systems (EIIS).

This article proposes a bird recognition model based on a SVM decision tree. To identify birds, the SVM classifier and decision tree are combined and a new beak feature is supplied to describe the bird. Caltech's bird dataset (CUB-200-2011) was used to evaluate the proposed method, as each species consists of around 60 images. A proper classification rate of about 84% is achieved by the proposed method. By changing the beak feature, some changes in classification accuracy are achieved. However, the decision tree presents a problem of error accumulation.

Sakib, K. M., Ragib, K. M., Shithi, R. T., Haq, S. A., Hasan, M., and Farah, T. (2020). PakhiChini: Automatic Bird Species Identification Using Deep Learning. The Fourth World Conference on Smart Trends in Systems, Security and Sustainability (WorldS4) 2020.

In this research, the authors proposed a deep learning model for classifying bird species. They also recommended a deep learning model built on the pre-trained ResNet architecture. They used the base model to train the dataset, and then used the basic model in the various layers of ResNet. Using the base model they achieved an accuracy of 63.48%. Using the ResNet architecture they were able to achieve an accuracy of 96.71%. Few variants of ResNet such as ResNet101, Resnet50, ResNet34, ResNet18 are also used and attained an accuracy of 96.7%, 97.4%, 97.83%, 97.98% respectively. To freeze certain neurons, dropout was set to 0.5. Batch size was set to 128 in order to accommodate 200 classes of images. The dataset contains images from 200 classes divided into three stations: validation 2000 images, training 10000 images, and testing 2000 images with accompanying labels. A web interface has been created to which the user uploads an image which is loaded into the model. The model predicts the bird species and provides the result to the users using an API request.

In D. Gavali et al. (2020). Bird Species Identification Using Deep Learning on GPU platform. The 2020 International Conference on Emerging Trends in Information Technology and Engineering (ic-ETITE).

The author presented an approach that generated the autograph by converting the image of a bird into a format called grey scale format. Each autograph is analyzed, and then a score sheet is calculated for each node, resulting in a prediction about a bird's species based on the score sheet analysis. In training, 500 data points are labelled with labels, while 200 unlabeled data points are used for testing. The data from the [CUB-200-2011] Caltech-UCSD Birds 200 project was used for both training and testing. DCNN were employed for classification, while GPU technology was used for parallel processing. The DCNN system can predict 88.33% of bird species, according to the final results.

Marini, E., Facon, J., and Koerich, A. L. (2013). Bird Species Classification Based on Color Features. 2013 IEEE International Conference on Systems, Man, and Cybernetics.

This studies describes a brand new approach for classifying chicken species primarily based totally on colour cues retrieved from unconstrained photos. This way that the birds should seem in a number of circumstances, in addition to in a number of poses, sizes, and perspectives. The recommended approach starts through the use of a colour segmentation method to put off history factors and delimit feasible places wherein the chicken is probably gift withinside the picture. The picture is then separated into factor planes, and normalized colour histograms for every aircraft are computed from those candidate places. After that, aggregation processing is used to lower the quantity of histogram durations to a hard and fast quantity of bins.

3   Related Work

Bird species recognition has been accomplished using a variety of methods, including various Convolutional Neural Network architectures and ensemble models that combine multiple models. Some of the existing systems are mentioned in the above section. Some of these existing systems are CNN's with skip connections, basic CNN architectures, Support Vector Machines, SVM with decision trees, Vgg16, etc. Every existing system that is mentioned have their own drawbacks. The existing system [1] was developed using convolutional neural networks with skip connections. These skip connections will provide the output of the previous layers as an input to the current layers. This system has to be built from scratch. In existing system [2] SVM with decision trees have been used. It suffers from error accumulation problem. Even this system has to be built from scratch. The existing system [4] converts the grey scale images into autographs and make predictions based on the score sheet analysis. The existing system [5] uses the color segmentation technique to remove the background elements and locate the bird. Later they use the histogram bin size to recognize the bird species. They can't differentiate the minute variations using these histogram bin sizes. Easy training is the significant advantage to use the ResNet50 model as it learns residuals from the image instead of some features [6]. In these existing systems there was a problem of building a new machine learning architecture. The weights that are chosen are random values which takes time to reduce the loss. The proposed system overcomes the problem of building a model from scratch and using random weights.

4 Proposed System

In developing a bird species recognizing system a concept called transfer learning is used.

Transfer Learning
(Transfer Learning): Given a source domain Ds and learning task Ts, and a target domain Dt and learning task Tt, transfer learning aims to improve the accuracy of the target predictive model Mt in Dt using the knowledge in Dt and Ds in the case where Ds6 = Dt and/or Ts6 = Tt. In transfer learning, there are three main questions to answer: (1) what to transfer; (2) how to transfer; (3) when to transfer [12, 13]. To find answers to these questions, we need to extract application-specific metrics to measure the quality of available knowledge. Furthermore, we need to develop algorithms to transfer the knowledge in a way that increases the performance of the target domain. Finally, we need to notify the system whenever it is necessary to transfer the available knowledge. Transfer learning is technique of a machine learning in which a model that has been trained for one job and that trained model is reused for another task. With huge resources required to train deep learning models or large datasets and demanding deep learning [14]. Figure 1 shows the differences between Traditional ML and Transfer learning.

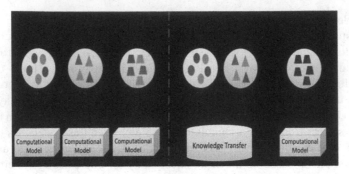

Fig. 1. Traditional ML vs Transfer learning

Transfer Learning and Fine calibration: Transfer learning is that the method of reusing a pre-trained model trained on an outsized dataset, usually on a large-scale image classification task [15, 16]. Options learned by the pre-trained model can effectively act as a generic model of the visual world, and hence the model may be used for various pc vision issues. For example, a model could also be trained on Image Net [17] (where categories are principally animals and everyday object) and then it is restated for a task like bird image classification. The base network is trained on a base dataset and task, then repurpose or transfer the learnt features to a second target network to be trained on a target dataset and task. This approach is more likely to succeed if the characteristics are generic, i.e., relevant to succeed if the traits are standard, i.e., relevant to both the base and goal tasks, in place of being precise to the base task [18]. There are many pre-educated models available for transfer learning. These pre-educated models can be used with/without their pre-trained weights. Another few extra layers can be added to these models.

Pre-trained Models
The availability of models that work well with source tasks is one of the most basic requirements for transfer learning. Many of the latest deep learning architectures have been publicly deployed by their authors. They apply to a variety of disciplines, including computer vision and natural language processing (NLP), the two most well-known deep learning applications. Pre-trained models are typically shared with respect to the millions of parameters/weights that the model achieved while being trained to steady state. Keras, a well-known deep learning Python library, has a download interface for certain popular models.

Some of the popular pre-trained models are VGG16, VGG19, Inception V3, ResNet-50, Xception, etc. In this system ResNet-50 and Vgg16 are used. Among these two models ResNet-50 produced more accuracy.

VGG-16: This deep learning strategy consists of thirteen convolutional layers out of 13 with 3 layers for categorically connected layers. The ultimate output layer consists of the a thousand categories of pictures for an input of 224×224 images. All the layers don't seem to be followed by the convolutional layers and max-pooling layers [19]. The activation perform utilized in the hidden layers is RELU.

ResNet: ResNet stands for the Residual Network and it is known as an Artificial Neural Network that builds pyramidal cells that utilizes skip connections and contains non linearity [20]. The skip connections are disbursed to beat the matter of the vanishing gradients and any makes the network a lot of straightforward [21–23].

ResNet-50 has fifty layers wherever forty eight convolution layers ar gift. It's an oversized variety of tunable parameters. It carries out the three 8×109 operations. With the appropriate capacity, a feedforward network with one layer can represent any function, according to the Universal Approximation Theorem. Otherwise, the layer can be quite large and the network can be prone to data over fitting. As a result, there is a growing consensus among researchers that our network design must become more complex. However, increasing the depth of the network does not work by simply stacking layers together. Deep networks are difficult to train due to the infamous vanishing gradient problem - since the gradient is propagated back to previous layers, multiplying many times can make the gradient infinitely small. As a result, as the network goes deeper, its performance saturates or even begins to degrade rapidly. ResNet's basic concept is to provide an "identity shortcut link" that bypasses one or more levels, as indicated in the diagram below. These are called skip connections. These skip connections are able to overcome the vanishing gradient problem.

Residual Block

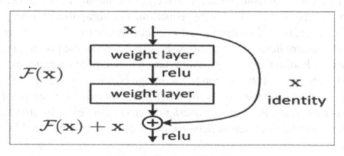

Fig. 2. Residual block

Resnets are made up from Residual Blocks. The first thing is to be noticed that there is a direct connection that bypasses certain levels in between depends on the model. The center of the residual blocks is a link known as the 'skip connection'. The output of the layer is no longer the same due to this connection jump. If this jump connection is not used, the input 'x' will be multiplied by the weight of the class, followed by an addition of a bias term. This term then passes through the activation function, f() and H(x) are taken as outputs. H(x) = f (x) + x. ResNet's skip connections alleviate the vanishing gradient problem in deep neural networks by allowing the gradient to flow along an additional shortcut channel. These connections also aid the model by helping it learn recognition functions, ensuring that the top layer performs at least as well as the bottom layer, if not better. Residual block is depicted in Fig. 2.

Architecture
The ResNet network uses a simple 34-layer network design inspired by VGG19, then a shortcut connection is added. The architecture is then transformed into a residual network by these shortened links. ResNet architecture mainly consists of the following three different kinds of layers: Fully connected layers, Pooling Layers, Convolutional Layers.

4.1 Convolutional Layers

In a convolutional neural network, the basic building blocks are convolutional layers. Convolution is the basic process of applying a filter to an input to produce a transformation. Figure 3 depicts the architecture of RestNet.

When the same filter is applied multiple times to an input, an object map is created, showing the position and magnitude of the recognized object in an input, such as an image (Fig. 4).

4.2 Pooling Layers

The Pooling layer, like the Convolutional Layer, is responsible for reducing the spatial size of the combined feature. With size reduction, the computing power required to process the data is reduced. Furthermore, it is effective in extracting dominant rotation and positional invariant dominating features. Figure 5 depicts the pooling layer.

The process of Pooling divided into two types: average pooling and maximum pooling. The maximum value of the portion of the image covered by the kernel returned by Max Pooling. Average aggregation, on the other hand, returns the average of all values of the image kernel share. ResNet uses averaging group classes in its architecture. The ith layer of the convolutional neural network consists of a convolutional layer and the Pooling Layer.

Fully Connected Layers: The fully connected layer only powers the neural network. The fully connected layers form the final layers of the network. The input to the fully connected layer is the output of the final Pooling or Convolutional Layer, which is flattened and then served into the fully connected layer.

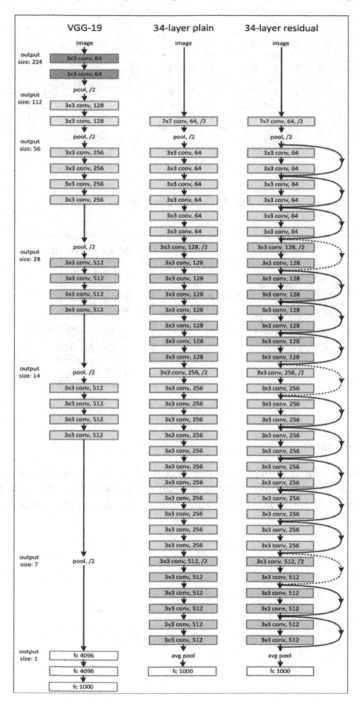

Fig. 3. ResNet architecture

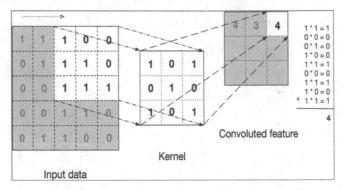

Fig. 4. Convolution layer

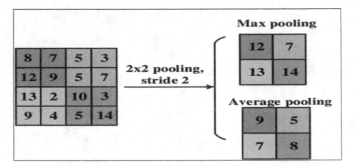

Fig. 5. Pooling layer

4.3 Implementation

Google Colab was used to implement the project. It offers notebooks with free GPU support. To complete this project, create a colab notebook and use the code below to mount the Google Drive. Figure 6, 7, 8, 9 and 10 has given the details on model creation.

Fig. 6. Mounting Google Drive

4.4 Loading the Dataset

The dataset contains train, test, valid folders which contains bird images. These images are read using ImageDataGenerator. This class helps us to perform data augmentation which is necessary to remove the class which imbalance. As a part of data augmentation, different image transformations are applied like rescale, sheer, horizontal flip, zoom. Two objects are created namely train_datagen, test_datagen which holds the training and testing/validation data.

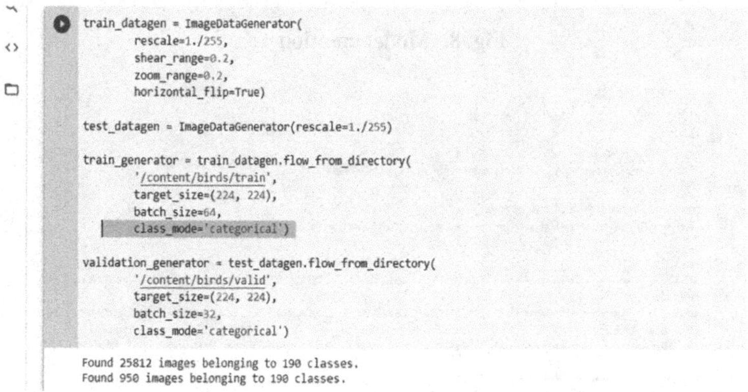

```
train_datagen = ImageDataGenerator(
        rescale=1./255,
        shear_range=0.2,
        zoom_range=0.2,
        horizontal_flip=True)

test_datagen = ImageDataGenerator(rescale=1./255)

train_generator = train_datagen.flow_from_directory(
        '/content/birds/train',
        target_size=(224, 224),
        batch_size=64,
        class_mode='categorical')

validation_generator = test_datagen.flow_from_directory(
        '/content/birds/valid',
        target_size=(224, 224),
        batch_size=32,
        class_mode='categorical')

Found 25812 images belonging to 190 classes.
Found 950 images belonging to 190 classes.
```

Fig. 7. Loading dataset

4.5 Model

Import the model from keras application and add few fully connected dense layers to it. The size of input layer is changed to (224 * 224 * 3). The weights of the pre-trained model are included. Activation functions that are used are relu and softmax. Accuracy is used as a metrics and categorical gross entropy as loss function.

4.6 Training

The training and validation data is used for training. The model is trained for 10 epochs. After each epoch the model is tested against the validation data.

4.7 Saving the Model

The model is saved to use it in other systems.

```
[ ] #from keras.applications import ResNet50
    from tensorflow.keras.applications.resnet import ResNet50
    base_resnet50 = ResNet50(weights='imagenet', include_top = False, input_shape=(224,224,3))

    Downloading data from https://storage.googleapis.com/tensorflow/keras-applications/resnet/resnet50_weights_tf_dim_ordering_tf_kernels_notop.h5
    94773248/94765736 [==============================] - 1s 0us/step

[●] out = base_resnet50.output
    out = GlobalAveragePooling2D()(out)
    out = Dense(256, activation='relu')(out)
    out = Dense(256, activation='relu')(out)
    total_classes = 190
    predictions = Dense(190, activation='softmax')(out)

[ ] model = Model(inputs=base_resnet50.input, outputs=predictions)
    # for layer in base_vgg16.layers:
    #     layer.trainable = False
    model.compile(adam(lr=.0001), loss='categorical_crossentropy', metrics=['accuracy'])
    model.summary()
```

Fig. 8. Model creation

```
<> [●] model.fit(
           train_generator,
           steps_per_epoch=train_generator.samples/train_generator.batch_size,
           epochs=10,
           validation_data=validation_generator,
           validation_steps=validation_generator.samples/validation_generator.batch_size)

    Epoch 1/10
    403/403 [==============================] - 530s 1s/step - loss: 0.1024 - accuracy: 0.9710 - val_loss: 0.2238 - val_accuracy: 0.9389
    Epoch 2/10
    403/403 [==============================] - 530s 1s/step - loss: 0.0888 - accuracy: 0.9754 - val_loss: 0.1720 - val_accuracy: 0.9463
    Epoch 3/10
    403/403 [==============================] - 531s 1s/step - loss: 0.0693 - accuracy: 0.9795 - val_loss: 0.2661 - val_accuracy: 0.9274
    Epoch 4/10
    403/403 [==============================] - 535s 1s/step - loss: 0.0694 - accuracy: 0.9799 - val_loss: 0.1784 - val_accuracy: 0.9484
    Epoch 5/10
    403/403 [==============================] - 530s 1s/step - loss: 0.0663 - accuracy: 0.9813 - val_loss: 0.2240 - val_accuracy: 0.9453
    Epoch 6/10
    403/403 [==============================] - 522s 1s/step - loss: 0.0561 - accuracy: 0.9838 - val_loss: 0.1801 - val_accuracy: 0.9432
    Epoch 7/10
    403/403 [==============================] - 522s 1s/step - loss: 0.0460 - accuracy: 0.9867 - val_loss: 0.2068 - val_accuracy: 0.9495
    Epoch 8/10
    403/403 [==============================] - 528s 1s/step - loss: 0.0481 - accuracy: 0.9861 - val_loss: 0.1544 - val_accuracy: 0.9558
    Epoch 9/10
    403/403 [==============================] - 535s 1s/step - loss: 0.0521 - accuracy: 0.9853 - val_loss: 0.2515 - val_accuracy: 0.9442
    Epoch 10/10
    403/403 [==============================] - 530s 1s/step - loss: 0.0463 - accuracy: 0.9873 - val_loss: 0.1338 - val_accuracy: 0.9611
    <tensorflow.python.keras.callbacks.History at 0x7f59400eb7d0>
```

Fig. 9. Training the model

```
[ ] model.save("resnet50-98.h5")
```
✓ 28s completed at 11:23 AM

Fig. 10. Saving the model

4.8 Execution Procedure

The project's main goal is to identify the different bird species. The actual execution process begins once the written code has been run. The application is executed on anaconda prompt using the driver code. The user will access the web page using http:// 127.0.0.1:5000/ through the browser. When the user access this URL the following web page is been displayed. The user selects the bird image from the local system and uploads the image. The application takes the image provided by the user as an input. The image is resized as per the input size of the model and is used for prediction. The model predicts the bird species and provide the result to the user.

5 Results

The application predicts the species based on the image that is provided by the user. The model extracts the features from the image and based on these features the model provides an array of class probabilities. From these class probabilities, the output is identified. When the user access the application the following web page is displayed. Figures 11, 12, 13 and 14 has depicted the output of the proposed system's results.

Fig. 11. Main page

The user selects the choose button to select the image from the local system. The application predicts the bird species and provides the output.

Output: Indigo Bunting

Fig. 12. Selecting the image

Fig. 13. Output

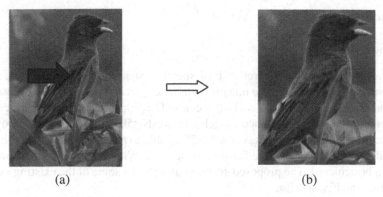

(a)   (b)

Fig. 14. (a) Input image (b) Cropped image

6 Performance Evaluation

The performance of the system is evaluated based on the metrics called accuracy.

Accuracy
One technique to determine how often a machine learning classifier correctly classifies a data point is to test its accuracy. The number of data points correctly predicted across all data points is called accuracy $(TP + TN)/(TP + TN + FP + FN)$ whereas

True Positives - TP
False Positives - FP
True Negatives - TN
False Negatives - FN

The training and validation accuracy of the system are 98.73% and 96.11% respectively.

7 Comparison

As a part of transfer learning concept, the two pre-trained models namely, ResNet50, VGG16 are used. Among these two models ResNet50 produced better accuracy (Table 1).

Table 1. Comparison table

Model	Training accuracy	Validation accuracy
ResNet50	98.73	96.11
VGG16	87.47	87.89

8 Conclusion and Future Work

8.1 Conclusion

The project's main goal is to predict bird species. Significance of this work shows that ResNet50 is able to recognize images with better precision compared to Vgg16 and Vgg19 and hence predicted the exact bird species. The proposed system uses the concept of transfer learning. The pre-trained models like ResNet50 and Vgg16 are employed as part of the transfer learning process. ResNet50 is able to provide better results than the other model when it comes to predicting bird species. With this model, an accuracy of 98.7% can be achieved. The proposed system outperforms some of the existing systems in predicting the bird species.

8.2 Future Work

Future work based on this project has a much broader scope. A few are listed here:

- Web application can convert this into a mobile application
- Whenever a new bird species is included, the model has to be re-trained which is a time-consuming task. The model that can learn from very few images can be build and that can include new species without re-training the model.
- The changes can be made in the application such that the images can directly be uploaded from the camera instead of uploading it from the folder.
- The detail information can be provided about the bird species.

References

1. Huang, Y.-P., Basanta, H.: Bird image retrieval and recognition using a deep learning platform. IEEE Access **7**, 66980–66989 (2019). https://doi.org/10.1109/ACCESS.2019.2918274
2. Qiao, B., Zhou, Z., Yang, H., Cao, J.: Bird species recognition based on SVM classifier and decision tree. In: 2017 First International Conference on Electronics Instrumentation & Information Systems (EIIS) (2017)
3. Ragib, K.M., Shithi, R.T., Haq, S.A., Hasan, M., Sakib, K.M., Farah, T.: PakhiChini: automatic bird species identification using deep learning. In: 2020 Fourth World Conference on Smart Trends in Systems, Security and Sustainability (WorldS4) (2020)
4. Gavali, P., Banu, J.S.: Bird species identification using deep learning on GPU platform. In: 2020 International Conference on Emerging Trends in Information Technology and Engineering (ic-ETITE) (2020)
5. Marini, A., Facon, J., Koerich, A.L.: Bird species classification based on color features. In: 2013 IEEE International Conference on Systems, Man, and Cybernetics (2013)
6. Zhang, Ren, Sun: Deep residual learning for image recognition. arXiv:151203385v1 (2015)
7. Cox, D.T.C., Gaston, K.J.: Likeability of garden birds: importance of species knowledge & richness in connecting people to nature. PloS One 10 (2015)
8. Marini, A., Facon, J., Koerich, A.L.: Bird species classification based on color features. In: 2013 IEEE International Conference on Systems, Man, and Cybernetics, pp. 4336–4341. IEEE (2013)

9. Keras: The Python Deep Learning library (2017). https://keras.io/
10. https://towardsdatascience.com/a-comprehensive-hands-on-guide-to-transfer-learning-with-real-world-applications-in-deep-learning-212bf3b2f27a/
11. https://towardsdatascience.com/what-is-deep-learning-and-how-does-it-work-2ce44bb692ac
12. Pan, S.J., Yang, Q.: A survey on transfer learning. IEEE Trans. Knowl. Data Eng. **22**(10), 1345–1359 (2010)
13. Torrey, L., Shavlik, J.: Transfer learning. In: Handbook of Research on Machine Learning Applications and Trends: Algorithms, Methods and Techniques, vol. 1, p. 242 (2009)
14. Saeedi, R., Ghasemzadeh, H., Gebremedhin, A.H.: Transfer learning algorithms for autonomous reconfiguration of wearable systems. In: IEEE Big Data Conference (2016)
15. Shin, H.C., et al.: Deep convolutional neural networks for computer-aided detection: CNN architectures, dataset characteristics and transfer learning. IEEE Trans. Med. Imaging **35**(5), 1285–1298 (2016)
16. Chollet, F.: Deep Learning with Python. Manning Publications (2018)
17. Deng, J., Dong, W., Socher, R., Li, L.-J., Li, K., Fei-Fei, L.: ImageNet: a large-scale hierarchical image database. In: IEEE Conference on Computer Vision and Pattern Recognition (2009)
18. Siddiqi, R.: Effectiveness of transfer learning and fine tuning in automated fruit image classification. In: ICDLT 2019. Association for Computing Machinery (2019)
19. Sitaula, C., Hossain, M.B.: Attention-based VGG-16 model for COVID-19 chest X-ray image classification. Appl. Intell. **51**(5), 2850–2863 (2020). https://doi.org/10.1007/s10489-020-02055-x
20. Farooq, M., Hafeez, A.: Covid-ResNet: a deep learning framework for screening of Covid19 from radiographs. Preprint arXiv, 14395 (2003)
21. Aleem, M., Raj, R., Khan, A.: Comparative performance analysis of the ResNet backbones of mask RCNN to segment the signs of Covid-19 in chest CT scans. Preprint arXiv, 09713 (2020)
22. Lu, S., Wang, S.H., Zhang, Y.D.: Detecting pathological brain via ResNet and randomized neural networks. Heliyon **6**, e05625 (2020)
23. Shallu, Mehra, R.: Breast cancer histology images classification: training from scratch or transfer learning? ICT Express **4** (2018). https://doi.org/10.1016/j.icte.2018.10.007

Detecting Pneumonia from the CT-Scan Images Using Convolutional Neural Networks and Transfer Learning Techniques

M. Ranjani$^{(\boxtimes)}$ and Jayant Nadar

Department of Computer Science and Engineering, SRM Institute of Science and Technology, Kancheepuram, Tamil Nadu, India
{ranjanim1,jn3284}@srmist.edu.in

Abstract. In the medical industry, diagnosis and analysis of a disease is proven to be one of the most critical things which can save a life of a person, and disease like pneumonia is one of the best examples of it. As we know that an early diagnosis of pneumonia can change save life of many people, as the time passes pneumonia can prove itself as a life-threatening disease. By some of the surveys it has proved that in India one of the three deaths takes place due to pneumonia. Currently we detect pneumonia by looking to an X-ray image of lungs but we need an expert to look at that image and predict that a person is infected by pneumonia or not. But there are not enough radiologist around the world so we need an automated system which will help to predict that a person is infected with pneumonia or not. For this study we have used a chest X-ray dataset from kaggle and we have implemented deep learning to it so that we can predict whether a person is contracted with pneumonia or not, and they can get treated earliest, if they infected.

Keywords: Deep learning · Pneumonia · Transfer learning · Convolutional neural network · Image processing · Residual networks · Inception networks

1 Introduction

Pneumonia is one of lung related disease which is caused by the bacterial infection on the lungs which range from mild to severe, the bacteria directly affects the air sacs of the lungs to fill with fluid, which creates the depletion of oxygen in the bloodstream of the patient as the fluid will create problem while breathing fresh air. This disease is very common and it is very much vulnerable to the people who are below the age of 2 and people who are above 65. Pneumonia is considered as one of the deadliest diseases in South Asia. As per some reports which prove that in 2017 in India alone there where more than 500000 deaths of children who are below the age of 5 [17].

But pneumonia can be treated if it is diagnosed at early stage, but we have observed that there is only one radiologist for three people so it is one of the problems why many people lose their lives because of pneumonia [25]. So to overcome this many computerized diagnosis are begin used which are powered by cutting edge Artificial Intelligence systems. One of the most used deep learning method used in the healthcare

K. Kottursamy et al. (Eds.): IconDeepCom 2022, CCIS 1719, pp. 164–175, 2023.
https://doi.org/10.1007/978-3-031-27622-4_13

related field is Convolutional neural network which are used to predict the output with the help of the image processing and image recognition [11].

In this following analysis we have aimed to classify the patients into two different sets, one is patients who are normal and another one is patients who are diagnosed with pneumonia. So for achieving the following we can use deep learning methods. Previously for achieving the following many researches have been following machine learning algorithm which have replaced by the deep learning methods.

By using machine learning algorithms we observed that it requires less computation power but it also comes at a cost of less accuracy, but in deep learning tend to get better accuracy compared to the machine learning algorithm but we also need large amount of data and it requires more computation power. For the following research we have used convolutional neural network (CNN) algorithm which has got better results than traditional machine learning algorithm, then we have extended our research to test and include transfer learning algorithms like ResNet [20], Inception Model [8], etc. to the existing CNN based models.

2 Related Works

Saraiva et al. [21] they have compared two artificial neural network architectures- Multilayer Perceptron and Convolution Neural Network. Using K-fold cross-validation they achieved 92.16% and 94.40% accuracy on test data respectively.Rajaraman et al. [18] they have used a custom VGG-16 and achieved an accuracy of 96.2% and 93.6% for bacterial and viral pneumonia respectively.Cohen et al. [4] applied the DenseNet-121 architecture in their research, which was later used by Rajpurkar et al. [19] to demonstrate on the chest X-Rays.

Stephen et al. [22] they have used a custom Convolutional Neural Network model which was created from scratch which gave good accuracy without using any transfer learning techniques.They achieved an accuracy of 93.73%. Rahib H. Abiyey et al. [1] they did a comparative analysis of custom-designed Backpropagation neural network (BPNN), Convolutional Neural Networks and Competitive Neural Networks (CpNN) by which they have achieved an accuracy of 80.04%, 92.4%, 89.57% on test data respectively.Ayan et al. [2] they used two transfer learning models - VGG16 and Xception Net and achieved an accuracy of 87% and 82% respectively. Kuo et al.[13] used X-rays of 185 schizophrenia patients to detect 11 different features to detect pneumonia from the X-ray images, They used decision trees, SVM and logistic regression models, but they achieved best accuracy on 94.5%.

Zubair et al. [26] they applied transfer learning approaches combined with different CNN models pre-trained using ImageNet Dataset.Jaiswal et al. [9] used image segmentation to create mask region using CNN to detect pneumonia traces, they used ResNet50 and ResNet101 for image thresholding.

3 Dataset Description

The dataset which we have used here is taken from Kaggle. Which is the 3rd of version of the dataset. The dataset has been divided in to 2 different directories which are namely

Train and test, Train folder contains 2 more directories in which one is NORMAL and another is PNEUMONIA, same goes for the Train folder also (Fig. 1).

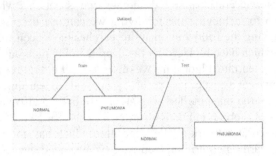

Fig. 1. Dataset hierarchy

3.1   Train Set

The train set was divided into 2 different directories i.e. normal and pneumonia, in which we have found that 1349 images where belonging to Normal class and 3883 images where belonging to Pneumonia class (Fig. 2).

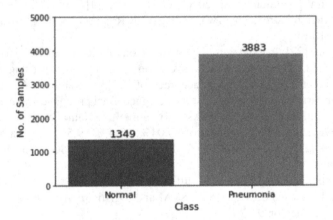

Fig. 2. Bar chart representation of train set

3.2   Test Set

The test set was also divided into 2 different directories i.e. Normal and Pneumonia, in which we have found 234 images belonging to Normal class and 390 images belonging to the Pneumonia class.

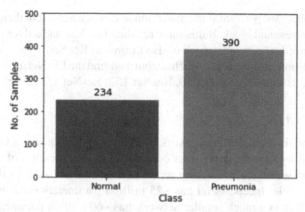

Fig. 3. Bar chart representation of test set

3.3 Validation Set

As there was no validation set available readily so we have created a validation set by dividing the train set, in which we have allocated 20% of the training set to validation set, remaining 80% of the data is allocated to the train set.

4 Proposed Model

For the following research, we have taken some of the parameters as standard like the image size is fixed as 224, then the batch size is set to 32, now these parameters can be used in our models.

So we have taken two approaches here, where the first approach is to use a standard CNN model and second approach is based on the transfer learning technique.

4.1 Standard CNN Model

A Convolutional Neural Network is one of the type of artificial neural network which is used for analyze images, CNNs are considered as better version of the Multilayer Perceptron(MLP), as we know that MLPs are very much prone to the problem of over-fitting. CNNs work on the same as a neuron work, to regularize the output and to solve the problem of overfitting we have different techniques where we follow the hierarchical pattern which can decrease the complexity level by using the simpler and smaller patterns to it.

4.2 ResNet

It is different from any other convolutional network, as in ResNet we use skip connection where we skip some of the layers by which we can achieve very accurate results even after having large number of layers, but in normal CNN algorithm we use the traditional method where we move through every layer until we reach the output layer.

This block where we perform skip connection and create a shortcut then the particular block is named as residual block. If this same residual block is stacked for multiple times then it makes a residual network which is also known as ResNet.

There are multiple architectures which are built around the ResNet architecture where some of the most common is ResNet 50, ResNet 152, ResNet 152v2 etc.

4.3 Inception Net

Inception Network is deep learning network which was earlier known as GooLeNet [15] as it was created by Google which was considered as modification of the LeNet. In inception network we basically use deep neural network but it also keeps the parameters in check For example, InceptionNet has ~25 million parameters but if we compare it with AlexNet which is a much smaller network has ~60 million parameters. Inception Network uses repeating components in its architectural design which are also known as inception modules. By which we can do faster computation, faster pattern detection, etc.

4.4 Batch Normalization Layer

A batch normalization is a method to train large and deep neural networks that helps to standardize the input into mini batches, by which stabilizes the model's learning process and also decrease the number of epochs which helps to use less computational power. Thus it makes the neural network much faster and reliable at the same time.

4.5 Max Pooling

Max pooling is used to downscale the size of the image, if the image is not used by the convolution layer. The maxpool layer tries to get only the most important parts of the image which reduces the computation as we need not to compute other blocks of image, as the name suggests 'max', in max pooling we take the maximum value of the feature map according to the filter size and the size of the kernel or stride.

4.6 Dropout Layer

A dropout layer is one of the regularization method where we drop the n number of neurons from a particular layer randomly, For example if we have kept the dropout value as 0.5 then randomly 50% of the neurons will be dropped from a layer.

4.7 Output Layer

The output layer is the final fully connected layer in a neural network in which we help us to predict the output, in our case the output will be binary so we are using a sigmoid activation function.

5 Proposed Approach and Architecture

Figure 3 shows the pipeline for building the model, first pre-process our data, then extract features from it and then analyze the results achieved (Fig. 4).

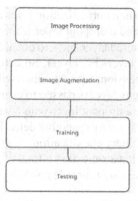

Fig. 4. Model pipeline

5.1 Image Augmentation

So as we have the datasets we have to perform the augmentation to the images so that it performs in a better for the Convolutional Neural network models and we can achieve this by keras library's inbuilt class ImageDataGenerator where we will see the different aspects of image by zooming an image, flipping of image etc.

So by this we can also convert a one color channel image into three color channel image by the repeating of the values.

5.2 Architecture

So we have test and implemented 3 different CNN architectures: A CNN model, ResNet Model and InceptionNet.

CNN MODEL

In this model first we start with the input value in which we define the size of the input which we are going to use in our case we have used 224 * 224 * 3 where 224 * 224 is the size of the image along with 3 color channels namely red,blue,green are used.

In the current model we have deployed the layers into different blocks, so if we consider the first block then there is a two dimensional convolution layer which is having a filter size set as 16 and having kernel size set at 3 then this layer is followed by a batch normalization layer where we standardize the input into mini batches so that it stabilize the learning process while training, this layer is followed by a activation layer where we have used a Relu activation function, then we have used a two dimensional max pooling layer which is followed by a dropout layer whose value is set to 0.2.

In the second block we have used a two dimensional convolutional layer which is having a filter size of 32 and having a kernel size of 3 then this layer is followed by a batch normalization layer, a Relu activation layer, a two dimensional max pooling layer and a dropout layer whose value is set to 0.2.

In the third block we have used two dimensional convolutional layer which is having a filter size of 64 and having a kernel size of 3 but the same layer is repeated twice then this layer is followed by a batch normalization layer, a ReLu activation layer, a two dimensional max pooling layer and a dropout layer whose value is set to 0.2

Now we have created the required layers now to obtain the output we have to connect this layers to a fully connected layer (FC layer), So here first we will flatten the two dimensional output into one dimensional output which will be passed to the dense layer where the output from the previous layer is passed to every neuron in this case we have 64 of them, then finally we have a dropout layer with a value of 0.5.

Then finally to receive the output we use another dense layer with a sigmoid activation function as we are predicting a binary classification.

From the above method we have generated a total of 2.621 million parameters out of which 2.620 million parameters are trainable and rest are non trainable parameters.

Resnet

In this current study we have chosen the ResNet152v2 model, as the name itself suggest that this model consist of 152 layers, and as we are using transfer learning technique, we will be using weights which were obtained from the ImageNet Dataset and we transfer that weights to the current model to train them.

And as these algorithms are pre trained so they have all their layers freezed, as these layers are freezed which will prevent the model from overfitting and the model becomes more effective overall.

So in this model initially we have created a ResNet Layer for that we will use the keras library's inbuilt function which has all the resnet models, then we will import the required ResNet152v2 model which we are going to use. Then we will unfreeze only the last layer of the model to train the model, then we will construct a fully connected layer to fetch the output from the previous layers. Here we are using a two dimensional Global Average pooling layer, then we are using a dense layer of 128 units followed by a dropout layer of 0.1 value which is passed to a dense layer with sigmoid activation function which will give us the output.

In this model we had a total of 58.59 million parameters out of which only 0.262 million parameters were trainable and rest were non trainable.

Inception Net

In this model we will use the keras inbuilt function to create the inceptionV3 Layer, and we will be using ImageNet weights here, then we used a dense layer of 512 units which is followed by a batch normalization layer to normalize the layers into mini batches which is followed by a dropout layer.

Then we have another dense layer of 128 units which is followed by a batch normalization layer and a dropout layer added to it.

Then we have one more dense layer which has 64 units which is followed by a batch normalization layer and a dropout layer added to it.

And finally a fully connected layer (dense layer) with sigmoid activation function is added which will predict the output of the model.

5.3   Sigmoid

The Sigmoid function is an activation function that we use for binary classification. The idea behind the Sigmoid Function is that a neuron will be activated if it has a value greater than 0.5 or it will be dropped. This maintains the value of the neuron in a fixed range between 0 and 1. Equation no. 1 represents the formula for the sigmoid function.

$$S(x) = 1/\left(1 + e^{(-x)}\right) \tag{1}$$

6 Parameters, Training and Results

6.1 Parameters

We have tuned our parameters to provide us with the best performance.
We have set the image size as 224 pixels.
We have set the batch size as 32.

6.2 Training

For Training we have used Convolutional Neural Network and Convolutional Neural Network with Transfer Learning Technique, In transfer learning we use a model which has been trained with the help of a large dataset and it can be used for multiple tasks, and we have used callback functions like early stopping and reduceLRplateau to reduce the number of epochs and also to adjust the learning if the accuracy dips for several epochs. Early stopping saves the model from getting overfitted, and reduceLRplateau is used to reduce the learning rate if the loss on the validation set doesn't reduce for a given number of epoch.
We have used binary_crossentropy as the loss function here.

6.3 Results

So, for the CNN model, we have set the total epochs to 50 but because of the early stopping we got our best accuracy at the 17th epoch, and for this model we got an accuracy of 93.94% on the train set and 75% accuracy on the test set (Figs. 5 and 6).

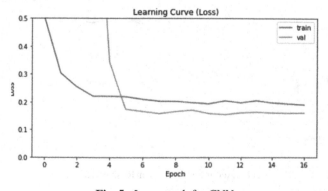

Fig. 5. Loss graph for CNN

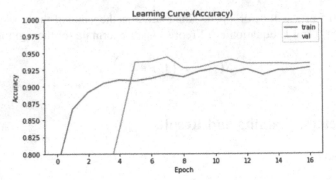

Fig. 6. Accuracy graph for CNN

For the ResNet152v2 model we have set the total epochs to 50 but because of the early stopping we got our best accuracy at the 19th epoch, and for this model we have got an accuracy of 97.03% on the train set and 90.05% on the test set (Figs. 7 and 8)

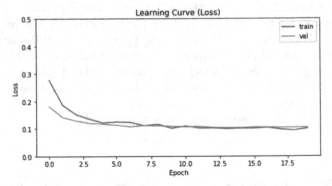

Fig. 7. Loss Graph for ResNet 152v2

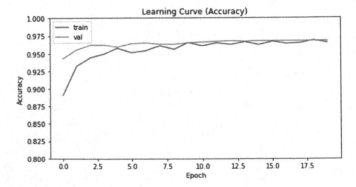

Fig. 8. Accuracy Graph for ResNet 152v2

For the Inception Net (InceptionV3) model we have set the total epochs to 50 but because of the early stopping we got our best accuracy at the 9th epoch, and for this model we have got an accuracy of 96.56% and 93.1% accuracy on the test set (Figs. 9 and 10).

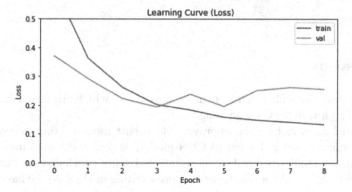

Fig. 9. Loss graph for IncpetionV3

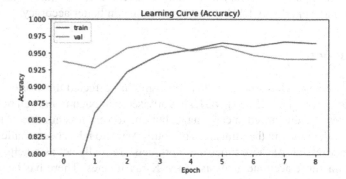

Fig. 10. Accuracy graph for InceptionV3

So from the above conclusions we can say that the Inception Net(InceptionV3) performs better than the other 2 algorithms, with a better accuracy on achieved on the test set by which we can say that for this particular study inception net is giving better results (Table 1).

Table 1. Model evaluation table

	Train set (accuracy)	Test set (accuracy)
CNN model	93.94%	75%
ResNet 152v2	97.03%	90.03%
InceptionV3	96.56%	93.10%

7   Discussions

Our model aims to provide an efficient and robust model which can detect the presence of pneumonia virus in the CT scan images.

Our model aims to be more improved and robust models from the pre-existing machine learning based and standard CNN model, as our model uses transfer learning technique to predict whether the lungs is infected or not which gives us better results when we have compared our results with the pre-existing models. As we have observed that if we have a large dataset it is advised to use deep learning algorithms as they will provide more robust results and also will avoid the problem of overfitting in some cases. One of the most important aspects which we have observed here is that we have to make sure that our data is perfectly labeled and cleaned to gain better accuracy.

8   Conclussion

In our study we have addressed that the pneumonia has affected the world with a high rate of mortality which is ~25%[7], WHO has advised that pneumonia can be prevented and cured when it is diagnosed in early stage, but due to very less number of radiologist across the world, mainly in the rural areas of South Asia. So it has been challenge which needs to be addressed. At these times these projects are really act as a helping hand to the doctors, for more accurate analysis of the X-ray images. There has been constant improvement in the following field as we have seen that many researches have taken place to improve the current operating models and there have been techniques which have improved the data augmentation which saves the models from getting overfitted. Lately Transfer learning was implement with current operating models which has been a boon for many researches as it saves training time and also provides better accuracy and performance in most of the cases.

1. References

1. Abiyev, R.H., Ma'aitah, M.K.S.: Deep convolutional neural networks for chest diseases detection. J. Healthc. Eng. (2018)
2. Ayan, E., Ünver H.M.: Diagnosis of pneumonia from chest X-ray images using deep learning. In: Proceedings of the 2019 Scientific Meeting on Electrical-Electronics & Biomedical Engineering and Computer Science (EBBT); Istanbul, Turkey (2019)
3. Szegedy, C., Vanhoucke, V.: Rethinking the inception architecture for computer vision (2016)

4. Cohen, J.P., Bertin, P., Frappier, V.: Chester: a web delivered locally computed chest x-ray disease prediction system
5. Dropout Layer. https://techvidvan.com/tutorials/keras-layers/
6. Harsh Agrawal Pneumonia Detection using Image Processing and Deep Learning
7. Healthcare, University of Utah. Pneumonia Makes List for Top 10 Causes of Death (2016). https://healthcare.utah.edu/thescope/shows.php?shows=0_riw4wti7
8. Inception V3. https://keras.io/api/applications/inceptionv3/
9. Jaiswal, A., Tiwari, P., Kumar, S., Gupta, D., Khanna, A., Rodrigues, J.: Identifying pneumonia in chest X-rays: a deep learning approach. Measurement **145**, 511–518 (2019)
10. He, K., Zhang, X., Ren, S., Sun, J.:Deep residual learning for image recognition
11. Kallianos, K.: How far have we come? Artificial intelligence for chest radiograph interpretation. Clin. Radiol. **74**, 338–345 (2019)
12. Simonyan, K., Zisserman, A.: Very large convolution networks for large scale image recognition (2014)
13. Kuo, K.M., Talley, P.C., Huang, C.H., Cheng, L.C.: Predicting hospital-acquired pneumonia among schizophrenic patients: a machine learning approach. BMC Med. Inf. Decis. Making **19**, 1–8 (2019)
14. Racic, L., Popovic, T.: Pneumonia detection using deep learning based on convolutional neural network (2021)
15. Hasan, M.M., Kabir, M.M.J., Haque, M.R., Ahmed, M.: A combined approach using image processing and deep learning to detect pneumonia from the chest X-Ray images
16. Talo, M.: Pneumonia detection from radiography images using convolution neural networks (2019)
17. Our World in Data. "Number of people dying from pneumonia by age". "Pneumonia". https://ourworldindata.org/pneumonia#burden-ofpneumonia
18. Rajaraman, S., Candemir, S., Kim, I., Thoma, G., Antani, S.: Visualization and interpretation of convolutional neural network predictions in detecting pneumonia in pediatric chest radiographs. Appl. Sci. **8**, 1715 (2018)
19. Rajpurkar, P., et al.: Chexnet: radiologist-level pneumonia detection on chest x-rays with deep learning
20. ResNet 152v2 . https://keras.io/api/applications/resnet/#resnet152v2-function
21. Saraiva, A., et al.: Models of learning to classify x-ray images for the detection of pneumonia using neural networks (2019)
22. Stephen, O., Sain, M., Maduh, U.J., Jeong, D.U.: An efficient deep learning approach to pneumonia classification in healthcare. J. Healthc. Eng. (2019)
23. Transfer Learning . https://www.tensorflow.org/guide/keras/transfer_learning
24. Liu, W., Szegedy, C.: Scott reed going deeper with convolutions
25. WHO Pneumonia is the Leading Cause of Death in Children. (2011). https://www.who.int/maternal_child_adolescent/news_events/news/2011/pneumonia/en
26. Zubair, S.: An efficient method to predict pneumonia from chest x-rays using deep learning approach. the importance of health informatics in public health during a pandemic

Emotion Recognition of People Based on Facial Expressions in Real-Time Event

C. Amuthadevi$^{(\boxtimes)}$ (iD), E. Poongothai (iD), and S. Amudha (iD)

Department of Computational Intelligence, SRM Institute of Science and Technology,
Kattankulathur 603 203, Tamilnadu, India
amuthadc@srmist.edu.in

Abstract. Technology is evolving markedly and so is the demand for brilliant everyday solutions. Perceiving the response/reaction of the partakers is significant in enhancing and boosting the performance of the particular event which makes collection and interpretation of reviews and feedback very crucial. Facial Expressions are a clear illustration of a person's emotion, intention and cognitive activity. So this project focuses on detecting faces and recognizing Facial Emotions based on Deep Learning Models such as Multi-Task Cascaded Convolutional Neural Network (MTCNN) & Convolutional Recurrent Neural Network (CRNN) respectively, which are in accordance with the CNN Model. We have utilized OpenCV libraries for pre-processing & Matplotlib to manipulate the results into a 2D graphical illustration. All of this is hosted onto a webpage through Flask API. The UI has options to collect input through webcam in real-time and also a provision for the user to drop input images directly.

Keywords: Healthcare · Support vector machine · Random forest algorithm · Elderly people

1 Introduction

Facial Expressions are extremely important for the social interaction of individuals, which can markedly express the degree of content and dismay the individual perceives. Taking part in events has become indispensable in everyone's day-to-day life, for instance small Get-Togethers, Organized Conferences, Campaigns, Concerts, Virtual Classes, Physical Classes, Ceremonies and other public events are realities that make us comprehend that we are part of several gatherings regularly. Being a partaker of events is effortless, but when it comes to organizing one, it is a big task in itself. When being an organizer of the event, the first thing they prioritize is the degree to which the event is productive and to look out for ways to enhance people's involvement. Their prime way to know it is through feedback of the people involved, through which the service delivery strategy can be adjusted. For the system, there are two alternatives when it comes to the source of the image: to utilise a webcam or to drop the image on the webpage which is then fed to the system. The first step in the process is to locate the facial area and extract the features that indicate distinct emotions. Once this information has been

K. Kottursamy et al. (Eds.): IconDeepCom 2022, CCIS 1719, pp. 176–186, 2023.
https://doi.org/10.1007/978-3-031-27622-4_14

collected, each piece of features is assigned to a set of emotions, and the following seven types are often recognised: Anger, Fear, Disgust, happy, Surprise, sad, and Neutral. And through further processing & manipulation using python libraries such as Matplotlib, a 2D Graphical illustration as shown Fig. 7 is generated.

2 Related Work

The earlier works have been assessed in terms of its relevance to the proposed work, including similar concepts, methodologies used, and comparisons of those techniques.

Weiqing Wang et al. [1] proposed a framework which is developed by integrating a Facial Expression Recognition algorithm with Online Learning platforms such as Tencent Meetings in the paper "Emotion Recognition of Students based on Facial Expression in Online Education Based on the Perspective of Computer Simulation" employed using the Convolutional Neural Network. The advantage is that it provides beneficial support for the model's overall performance, but in this approach, lighting fluctuations and various positioning of models could contaminate the feature vector, which possibly decreases the classification accuracy. Illiana Azizan et al. [3] in the paper "Facial Emotion Recognition: A Brief Review" aim to comprehend the fundamental principles of Facial Emotion Recognition and make a comparison of current research using Support Vector Machine and Multilayer Perceptron, which brought into light that there is no risk of overfitting in SVM and also that MLP has good accuracy compared to SVM. However, Long training time for huge datasets in Support Vector Machines (SVM) means that the model is difficult to analyse and comprehend, and variable weights and individual impact are not well-understood. FER has poorer SVM performance.

Shima Alizadeh et al. [4] developed a method to classify each facial image into one of the few facial emotion categories addressed in their study in the paper "Convolutional Neural Networks for Facial Expression Recognition". This is accomplished through the use of Convolutional Neural Network. Although this methodology recognizes certain emotions with good accuracy, the accuracy is low for the anger class of input image. Byoung Chul Ko [5] in the paper "A Brief Review of Facial Emotion Recognition Based on Visual Information" utilized CNN-based FER and Nearest - mean classifier, Kernel subclass discriminant analysis. It brought more emphasis on visual manifestation in interpersonal communication research. Also end-to-end learning strategy is done with FER. However, it was found that differences in the results were caused by illumination in the background and the stance in the 2D pictures. Hyeon-Jung Lee et al. [7] proposed a study which claimed that seven emotions and positive and negative emotional recognition methods were introduced utilising face picture and method-based app development, which was then implemented as an app that offers the user with seven positive and negative emotions and results in "A Study on Emotion Recognition Method and Its Application using Face Image". It was developed using the Convolutional Neural Network. The major advantage is that through deep learning, the accuracy of 50.7% was achieved, whereas with positive and negative images, 72.3% was achieved. But, the results for the positive emotion set were highly inaccurate.

Ielaf Osamah Abdul Majjed [8] in the work "Emotion Recognition System Based on Facial Expressions Using SVM" created a robust system by merging multiple computer vision and pattern recognition algorithms employing Support vector machines. It fetched an acceptable accuracy of 75.8%. However, low accuracy was attained in fear, anger classes. Renuka Deshmukh et al. [6] propose a report on a complete and illustrative analysis of the most prevalent approaches in problems regarding emotion recognition in the paper "A Comprehensive Survey on Techniques for Facial Emotion Recognition". Feed-Forward Neural Network & Multiple Deep Convolutional Neural Networks (CNN) are used. This study highlighted that, by minimising the log likelihood loss and the hinge loss in the set, the framework was able to achieve greater accuracy even though problems were faced in homogenous faces. Kaipeng Zhang et al.[9] propose a framework using cascaded architecture with three levels of deep convolutional networks meticulously constructed to coarse to fine anticipate the face and landmark position and also offer a novel hard sample mining approach online that enhances performance in practise further in the paper "Joint Face Detection and Alignment using Multitask Cascaded Convolutional Networks" using Multi-task Cascaded Convolutional Networks. (MTCNN). This method has acceptable false detection and reasonable accuracy, but the slow detection process and complicated approach are the challenges. R. Padilla et al. [10] proposed a study focusing on the assessment of facial detection classifiers with facial characteristics in "Evaluation of Haar Cascade Classifiers Designed for Face Detection" using Haar Cascade. The methodology detected faces very fast compared to any other algorithm. However, It was not able to detect faces without frontal view or upright orientation. Nicu Sebe et al.[20] propose a way to identify facial emotions in video clips in the paper "Emotion Recognition Using a Cauchy Naive Bayes Classifier" which is employed using Naive Bayes. This method generally does well if the training and testing data sets are comparable. But, it is ineffective unless the training and test datasets are comparable.

3   Proposed Work

The proposed Algorithm is a combination of two algorithms which will have less over fitting when the training data set increases In our proposed project we have utilized 2 algorithms, which are Multi-Task Cascaded Convolutional Neural Network (MTCNN) and Convolutional Recurrent Neural Network (CRNN). The purpose we have employed MTCNN is for Face Detection and CRNN is for the purpose of Face Emotion Recognition (FER). We used the Dataset from Kaggle [2] for training the FER model. Keras and TensorFlow are used to model the Convolutional Recurrent Neural Networks.

The activation functions utilised are ReLu - Rectified Linear Unit (in both the input and hidden layers) and Softmax (in the output layer). Sparse Categorical Cross entropy was used as the loss function for the Convolutional Recurrent Neural Network. The ADAM optimizer is used to compile the Neural Network. Multi-Task Cascaded Convolutional Neural Network (MTCNN) for Face Detection & Convolutional Recurrent Neural Network (CRNN) for Face Emotion Recognition (FER) (Fig. 1)

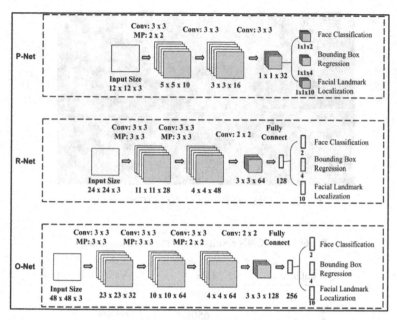

Fig. 1. MTCNN architecture

3.1 Multi-task Cascaded Convolutional Neural Network (MTCNN)

A Multi-task cascaded algorithm is used to detect facial features, which gives better results than the Haar cascade algorithm. Haar cascade uses a predefined feature matrix whereas MTCNN is a learned feature matrix from a large data set. And then using OpenCV, we crop out the detected faces and feed to the CRNN model for the result after converting it to a grayscale image.Multi-Task Cascaded Convolutional Neural Networks, a pre-trained neural network is composed of three stages that analyse facial bounding boxes and Five point facial landmarks. It was published in 2016 by Zhang et al [9]. As each step of the model processes the preceding stages' inputs, they run their inputs through a CNN, which returns candidate bounding boxes with their scores. Next, non max suppression is applied to remove any boxes that have scores over a specific threshold. The stages in Multi-Task Cascaded Neural Network is as follows:

Stage 1- Input image is scaled down multiple times to build an image pyramid and each scaled version of the image is passed through it's CNN.

Stage 2 and 3 - Extract image patches for each bounding box and resize them (24×24 in stage 2 and 48×48 in stage 3 and forward them through the CNN of that stage. Stage 3 not only computes bounding boxes and scores but also additionally computes 5 face landmarks points for each bounding box. The sample output from MTCNN is as follows (Fig. 2):

The results of MTCNN are as follows (Table 1 and Fig. 3):

Fig. 2. Input image given to the MTCNN model

Table 1. MTCNN results with different algorithms

Network	Input size	FPS	Validation accuracy
P-Net	12 × 12	8000	94.6%
R-Net	24 × 24	650	95.4%
O-Net	48 × 48	220	95.4%

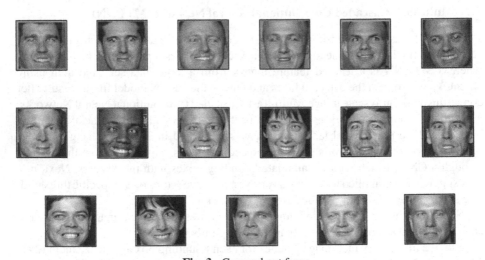

Fig. 3. Cropped out faces

3.2 Convolutional Recurrent Neural Network (CRNN)

For this research work, we have trained a Convolutional Recurrent Neural Network - CRNN (Combination of CNN and RNN). The output of the CNN is then supplied to the RNN, which in turn processes the output of the CNN. To train the CRNN model for Face Emotion Recognition, we followed the following methods.

3.2.1 Data Collection

The Kaggle dataset (consisting of roughly 35,887 well-structured 48×48 gray-scale facial pictures) was used to assist with Collection and the development of our dataset. This data set includes seven different categories of photographs, including photos of emotions such as Angry, Disgust, Fear, Happy, Sad, Surprise and Neutral.

3.2.2 Data Processing

1. The image contains the values ranging from 0–255 (Because the data set is grayscale image) so it should be scaled from 0–1.
2. Stored within objects are the Respective emotion labels and their respective pixel values.
3. sklearn's train_test_split function is used to split the data set into training and testing purposes. And 80% is used for training and 20% is used for testing.

3.2.3 Data Augmentation

Data augmentation occurs when more data is generated by applying some alteration to a training set. In cases where the training set is insufficient, it is essential to apply. Image data is generated by rotating, cropping, shifting, shearing, zooming, flipping, reflecting, and so on. For modest modifications to the training set, we have utilised the values rotation range, zoom range, width shift range, and height shift range (Fig. 4).

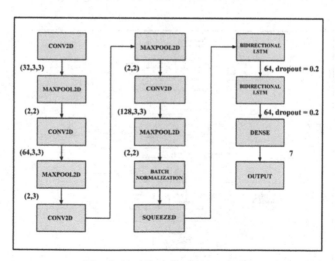

Fig. 4. Training the CRNN model

1. **Conv2d** - A kernel is a tiny matrix of weights that serve as the starting point. As part of each pixel wise multiplication, the 2D picture is used as a source for multiplication and the results are summed together to generate a single output.

2. **MaxPool2d** - To compute the maximum output value at each location, a kernel of size m * m is moved across the matrix, and for each point, the maximum value is taken and placed in the corresponding position in the output matrix.
3. **Batch Normalization** - The standardisation of inputs is performed for each mini-batch in the training of very deep neural networks using batch normalisation.
4. **Squeezed** - The squeezed layer in the model removes any dimensions of the size 'one' from the shape of a tensor.
5. **Bi directional LSTM** - Reinforcement learning with bidirectional recurrent neural networks (or RNNs) is basically using two separate reinforcement learning algorithms (or RNNs) simultaneously. In this case, it is beneficial for the networks to have information that permits both backwards and forwards navigation of the sequence.
6. **Dropout** - Each training step either removes one node with a probability of 1−p or keeps one node with a probability of p, and the resulting network is simplified accordingly.
7. **Dense** - This neural network layer has a dense layer of neurons that are all connected deeply, meaning that each neuron in the dense layer is linked to every neuron in the layer before it. This identifies seven different emotional categories. The entire network is connected to all of the neurons that came before it.

3.2.4 Validation

Validation of the trained model is carried out by taking into account the testing data set, which accounts for 20% of the total dataset used for training (Fig. 5).

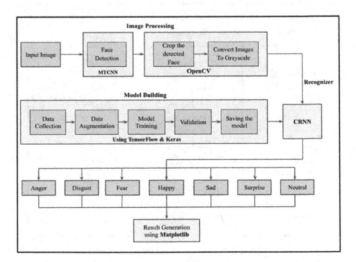

Fig. 5. The flow diagram of our proposed work

4 Structural Architecture

The procedure we followed for this particular project is as follows:

Step 1: Input images are collected from the user through two options, i.e., either using a webcam to capture images in real-time or the user can input the images through a static webpage made using Flask API.

Step 2: The collected input is fed to the trained MTCNN Model and the bounding boxes of faces and also their 5 point facial landmarks are detected & the detected faces are cropped out using a python script.

Step 3: The cropped out faces are converted to grayscale images using OpenCV libraries

Step 4: These processed images are fed to the CRNN model trained using Keras and TensorFlow, which involves the following steps: Data Collection, Data Preprocessing, Data Augmentation, Validation & Training which are clearly explained in the above headers.

Step 5: The CRNN Model does Face Emotion Recognition (FER) and classifies the recognized emotions into 7 categories as Anger, Disgust, Fear, Happy, Sad, Surprise & Neutral.

Step 6: A final 2D-Graphical representation of the entire result set of the input is generated using Matplotlib.

5 Output Snapshot

Results from running the models and calculations are compiled into a 2D Graphical Illustration and presented as a visual representation of the emotion frequencies found in the photos fed into the system (Figs. 6, 8 and 9).

Fig. 6. Sample input image

184   C. Amuthadevi et al.

Fig. 7. Faces detected using MTCNN

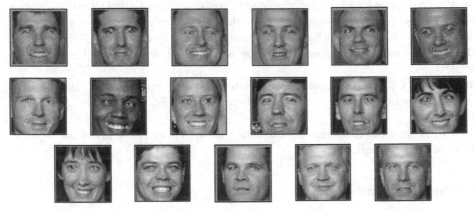

Fig. 8. Cropped out faces using OpenCV

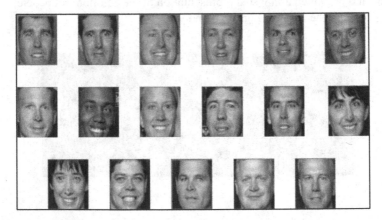

Fig. 9. Grayscale converted image using OpenCV

In order to obtain the final graph produced by Matplotlib, the clipped off faces of 48 × 48 pixels were fed to CRNN and then additional processing was done to obtain the following image (Fig. 10).

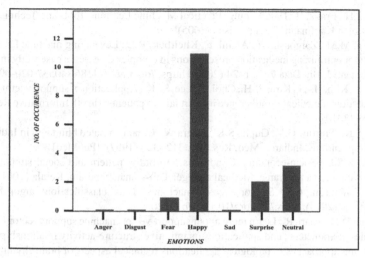

Fig. 10. Final 2D illustration depicting the number of occurrences of each emotion

While 80% of the dataset was used to train, the project recognised faces with an accuracy of 95.4% and estimated the emotions with a high accuracy of 88% when 20% of the dataset was used to test. Training and testing the data at 80:20 makes it possible to display how accurate and inaccurate the dataset will be, as well as how accurate and inaccurate the testing data will be, over the course of 50 epochs.

6 Conclusion

Life expectancy of people is increased with the help of technological and medical advancements. It ultimately leads to the necessity of increased healthcare facilities. Huge availability of medical data and technologies like AI and machine learning reduces and eases the tasks of healthcare professionals. Still the availability of correct data, relevant attributes, and selection of algorithm for processing those data are the tedious task. The proposed work considered the most critical chronic disease i.e diabetes, heart and kidney diseases that exist commonly among elder population. SVM and Random Forest Algorithms are considered to classify the disease from the dataset. The classification performance of Random Forest is comparatively better than SVM due to its ensemble nature and size of the dataset. For the small sized diabetes dataset both algorithms produced less accuracy. People who are suffered from heart or kidney aliments along with diabetes need careful suggestion and treatment from expert team comprised of nephrologists, endocrinologists, nutritionists, and cardiologists. This kind of expert's treatment can reduce repeated pills and side effects of medications.

References

1. Tran, B.X., Vu, G.T., Ha, G.H., Vuong, Q.H., Ho, M.T., Vuong, T.T., et al.: Global evolution of research in artificial intelligence in health and medicine: a bibliometric study. J ClinMed **8**(3), 360 (2019)

2. Witten, I.H., Frank, E.: Data Mining: Practical Machine Learning Tools and Techniques, 2nd edn. Morgan Kaufmann, San Fransisco (2005)
3. Hosseini, M.M., Zargoush, M., Alemi, F., Kheirbek, R.E.: Leveraging machine learning and big data for optimizing medication prescriptions in complex diseases: a case study in diabetes management. J. Big Data 7(1), 1–24 (2020). https://doi.org/10.1186/s40537-020-00302-z
4. Son, Y.-J., Kim, H.-G., Kim, E.-H., Choi, S., Lee, S.-K.: Application of support vector machine for prediction of medication adherence in heart failure patients. Health Informative Res. 16(4), 253–259 (2010)
5. Angra, S.K., Murthy, G.V., Gupta, S.K., Angra, V.: Cataract related blindness in India and its social implications. Indian J. Med. Res. 106, 312–324 (1997). [PubMed]
6. Kumari, R.S.S.: Socio-economic Conditions, morbidity pattern and social support among elderly women in a rural area. Medical college; Thiruvananthapuram, Kerala (2001)
7. Wang, P.W., Lin, C.J.: Support vector machines. Data classification: algorithms and applications (2014). https://doi.org/10.1201/b17320
8. Gholami, D., Fakhari, R.: Learn more about support vector machine support vector Machine : principles , Parameters , and applications quantitative structure-activity relationship (QSAR): modeling approaches to biological applications technical aspects of brain rhythms and sp (2017)
9. Padmavathi, J., Heena, L., Sabika, F.: Effectiveness of support vector machine in medical data mining. J. Commun. Softw. Syst. 11(1), 25–30 (2015)
10. Sreekanth, R., Suryakanthi, T.: Predicting the risk of diabetes in big data electronic health records by using scalable random forest classification algorithm. In: International Conference on Advances in Computing and Communication Engineering (ICACCE) (2016)

Deep-Recurrent Neural Network (RNN) for Industrial Informatics

A Novel Modified LSTM Deep Learning Model on Precipitation Analysis for South Indian States

P. Umamaheswari[✉] [ID] and V. Ramaswamy [ID]

Department of Computer Science and Engineering, Srinivasa Ramanujan Centre, SASTRA
Deemed University, Kumbakonam 612001, India
`pum@it.sastra.edu`

Abstract. Rainfall prediction is one of the economically beneficial scientific technologies. Saving water when it rains will lead to the betterment of human society. Agriculture is the direct beneficiary of rain because it helps to improve yield production. So analyzing precipitation is playing a vital role in many sectors. In past days linear regression and logistic regression models were being used to predict different types of precipitation levels. These traditional methods fail to work efficiently on various parameters which influence preprocessing tasks. Prediction accuracy can be improved using our proposed deep learning model. Three phases are being developed for predicting precipitation. Data preprocessing includes missing value estimation, irrelevant data removal, and data transformation. This model uses a novel modified LSTM (M-LSTM) approach for improving predictive accuracy. This approach is compared to a number of techniques, including Nave Bayes, Support vector machines, Genetic Algorithms, and Random Forest. The Indian Meteorological Department (IMD) provided the data for this study, which spans the years 1901 to 2015. It is observed that our approach can qualitatively predict rainfall more efficiently.

Keywords: Precipitation · Data mining · Genetic algorithm · Preprocessing · Modified LSTM · Deep learning

1 Introduction

Improving precipitation accuracy and forecast necessitates taking into account the entire phenomenon involving many different and reliable attributes. Emerging technologies such as statistical approaches and machine learning (ML) models are becoming more widely used. Computational intelligence and machine learning models are growing the attention of various classifiers called ensemble systems. Earlier models took into account statistical relationships between rainfall and a variety of global climate variables. Rainfall forecasting is critical because heavy and unpredictable rainfall can have serious consequences, such as crop and field destruction, damage to property, and so on. This forecast is primarily beneficial to farmers. Water resources may be used in a very efficient manner as well. Predicting rainfall is a difficult task, and the findings must be correct. Time series are observed values that are connected with previous values. When developing a model

K. Kottursamy et al. (Eds.): IconDeepCom 2022, CCIS 1719, pp. 189–201, 2023.
https://doi.org/10.1007/978-3-031-27622-4_15

in this manner, the appropriate sample procedures for training prediction models must be constructed. This section presents a brief assessment of time series analysis using an ensemble model, as well as several implementation strategies and classifier types. Generally, there are many ways to combine many learners with a final one. When it comes to time-series data, the ensemble method takes datasets and averages the findings. To create an ensemble model, the following methods were employed.A generic ensemble approach combines numerous weak classifiers to create a powerful classifier. This generates a model from the training data and then generates a second model that sccks to rectify the previous model's mistakes. It aims to boost prediction accuracy by training a series of weak models. This method combines the results of numerous classifiers based on diverse sub-samples of the same data set to reduce the variance of classifier predictions. This method makes use of a number of training examples where some observations are replicated across them.It's a type of boosting method designed to solve classification difficulties (also called discrete AdaBoost). The error rate of the weak estimator reveals the learner's weakness. The results of the other base learners are combined into a weighted sum that represents the final output of the boosted classifier.

AdaBoost is adaptive in that it tweaks succeeding weak learners in favour of instances misclassified by earlier classifiers. Anomalies and inconsistent data make AdaBoost sensitive. Several classification methods have been suggested by different authors for distinct climatic situations based on their needs. In relation to the study of precipitation data, some classifier models have been discussed. Many hardware devices that use weather factors such as temperature, humidity, and pressure to predict rainfall are available. Because malfunctioning instruments might produce erroneous data, these old methods are ineffective. Accuracy improvisation tasks have their own unique space for countries like India whose well-being depends to a large extent on Agriculture. Our suggested method allows for a comparison of different machine learning models.Creating an exact prediction strategy remains a major challenging task faced by meteorologists the world over. From time immemorial weather prediction continues to be one of the most intriguing and engaging areas of research Scientists have been attempting to forecast meteorological phenomena using a variety of methods.

2   Related Work

The K-Nearest Neighbour and Relevance Vector Machine are ideal for multi-model ensembles, according to KamalAhmeda et al. [1]. The most widely used machine learning algorithms fall into the "shallow" learning category, which means that instinct information is poorly represented. These flaws can be overcome by employing deep learning approaches, which, due to their richer representations, can improve predicting performance. According to Binh Thai Pham et al., an AI-based study [2] could aid in the speedy and precise prediction of daily rainfall. Ricardo Aguasca-Colomo et al. [3] proposed For predicting medium-term precipitation in similar geographical locations, machine learning prediction models are a viable option.A rapid greedy learning algorithm that trains the network one layer at a time and addresses the initialization problem.Rainfall, on the other hand, is influenced by a variety of land, ocean, and atmospheric systems, as well as their intricate relationships. Nikhil Oswal [4] presented a series of studies which included the use of basic machine learning approaches to construct models to predict whether it would rain tomorrow or otherwise not depending on meteorological data from key Australian cities for that specific day. J. Refonaa et al. [5, 6] tested if precision in rainfall forecast could aid in anticipating heavy rains and preventing disasters.

The physical-chemical rules of climate that characterise the rainfall process are used to construct models. Regression-based models are commonly shown to be incapable of reliably predicting rapid changes in climate, which may be seen in time series of climate variability. The trends identified by Scherrer SC et al. [7, 8] are unlikely to be random, and they are consistent with climate model estimations, theoretical understanding of an user change in the energy requirements and water cycle, and larger-scale detection and attribution investigations. TSchnideret al [9] proposed exploring a climate continuum, constraining macroscopic rules governing this climatic continuum, and placing historical and potential future climate changes in a larger context. According to the findings of SB Guerreiro et al. [10], temperature modulation overlooks reported changes in hourly rainfall variations in Australia, which has implications for evaluating the impacts of extreme rainfall. How to effectively estimate rainfall has been a highly important subject in the weather forecasting community around the world, according to Yen, Meng-Hua [11], and colleagues.

A DLNN model with 192 neurons in three hidden layers has also been proposed to build an interpretive framework that estimates variable quantities of exposure to flash floods. In most cases, the RF-based SMFM overlooks observed radar-derived rainfalls, according to Pao-ShanYu et al. [12], and the SVM-based SMFM can outperforms the RF-based SMFM. The invasion of Machine Learning (ML), according to Farheen and Nida [13], has aided in the discovery of potential solutions to problems such as predicting rainfall, soil assessment, crop management, yield prediction, crop quality, and disease detection and categorization. Without a best and most consistent or worse NWP model, Beda Luitel et al. [14] found that weather forecasting models can give skillful predictions of tropical cyclone precipitation with lead-times up to 48 h. According to Eslam Hussein et al. [15], there is also some indication that SVMs used to large-scale weather maps can provide useful tools to determine regional rainfall under certain situations, although caution must be exercised to avoid traps. Using that ideology a novel deep learning model for precipitation analysis is presented in this research.

The rest of this paper is organized as follows: The background and related work are described in Sect. 2. Section 3 introduces the suggested architecture as well as the dataset used for analysis. Section 4 contains the results and discussion, while Sect. 5 is about the conclusion and future improvements.

3 Proposed Methodology

Important tasks of the proposed model have been depicted in the following phases. Key approaches of the four phases are listed below. The overall module is depicted in Fig. 1.

- *Phase 1:* Collection of precipitation data for three south Indian states from the **India Meteorological Department** for the period from 1901–2017.
- *Phase 2*: Transformation of raw data into the normalized format by applying missing value estimation and irrelevant data removal

- *Phase 3*: Identification of accuracy prediction for classification algorithms such as Naïve Basean (NB), Supprt Vector Machine(SVM), Genetic algorithm (GA), and Random Forest (RF)
- *Phase 4*: Construction of proposed deep learning model and comparing the result with various classifiers.

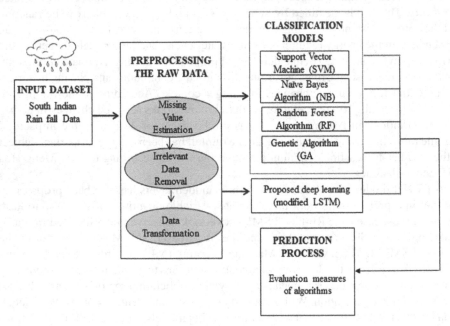

Fig. 1. Framework of the proposed work

3.1 Dataset Collection and Preprocessing

This process requires an enormous quantity of chronicled information for examination. The proposed approach starts with the initial phase involving data transformation. Standardization, grouping, and abstraction are common data processing techniques. For instance, a set of data labelled "−4, 47, 100, 99, 68" can be renamed "−0.04, 0.47,1.00, 0.99, 0.68". The data is becoming increasingly suitable for data analytics. The data turns out to be progressively appropriate for data analytics. In this phase, There are four states namely Tamil Nadu, Kerala, North Interior Karnataka and South Interior Karnataka, which are all in southern India have been taken.Rain fall dataof all four stated have been collected from IMD for the period from 1901–2017.Here the sample data set taken for Tamil Nadu is shown in Table 1. Which contains the months from Jan to July as a sample data, and Table 2. Which has a coloumn names are JF (January, Febrary), MAM (March, April, May) JJAS (June, July, August and september) and OND (October, November, December). This table consists summary information based on Meteorological Seasons.

Table 1. Sample precipitation data from IMD for Tamil Nadu from 1901–2017.

Sub division	Year	Jan	Feb	Mar	Apr	May	Jun	Jul
Tamil Nadu	1901	24.5	39.1	21.7	36	74	41.8	49.3
Tamil Nadu	1902	67.2	9.8	25.1	21.9	84.7	39.3	55.1
Tamil Nadu	1903	19.3	7.8	1.7	18.2	128.5	58.5	72.6
...	...	...	...	...	...	...	...	...
Tamil Nadu	2017	37.3	1.1	35.4	17.3	73.5	47.9	42

Table 2. Summary based on meteorological seasons

ANNUAL	JF	MAM	JJAS	OND
960.3	63.6	131.6	350.1	415
1138.2	77	131.7	306.7	622.9
1163.9	27.1	148.4	456.5	531.9
663.1	35.3	142.1	249.9	235.8
...	...	...	...	...
159.4	165.3	155.5	141.5	96.8

A basic building architecture model is presented in Fig. 2a. A component handling system performs enormous information calculations and receives and transfers the results to a different layer. As a result, the components below can perform calculations and add further layers to the final result. Rainfall is influenced by a variety of elements due to its complexity. The goal of developing LSTM was to solve the challenge of capturing long-term interdependence. LSTM has been issued in numerous versions since its inception. Memory cells replace hidden neurons in sigmoid or *tanh* functions in the LSTM approach, which uses several gates to regulate input and output. These gates control the flow of information to hidden neurons. The hidden layer of LSTM has a high level of complexity. The LSTM has four times the number of parameters as a traditional RNN. Other approaches, such as Grid LSTM and Multi-dimensional networks, have been tried to overcome the problem of long-term dependency.

The input gate is represented by Ct, the forget gate is represented by ft, and the output gate is represented by ot in the LSTM.as illustrated in Fig. 2b. This has a close connection to time series. Given that the LSTM's main focus is on complex time-related interactions. In this study, the LSTM was employed to model input data via K-means clustering. The association between the model's predicted meteorological variables and actual rainfall should be studied further after modelling. The proposed model has the potential to increase the accuracy of rainfall predictions made by models. The LSTM network is a special sort of cyclic neural network. The LSTM network has one more unit state than normal circulating neural networks, which helps to preserve long-term information and avoids the conventional circulation network gradient fading or blowing

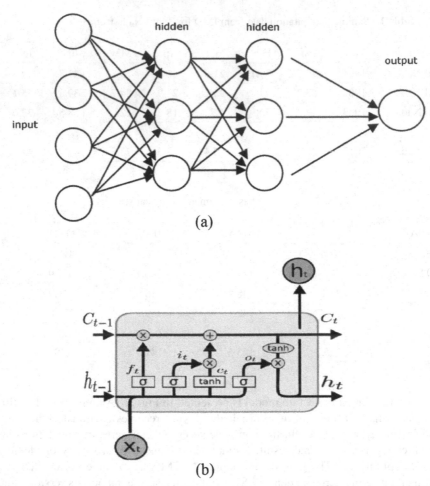

Fig. 2. (a) The neural network's basic building architecture [15] (b) The structure of LSTM [16]

up while learning. As a result, the topology of the LSTM network resembles that of a traditional cyclic neural network, with an input layer, a hidden layer, and an output layer. The hidden layer structure connects the hidden layer from the previous moment to the hidden layer from the next moment. It's critical to figure out what information will be discarded from the cell state. This type of decision is made using the forget gate and a sigmoid function.

3.2 Proposed Algorithm

Steps in the neural network algorithm:

a) *Begin the neural network algorithm's weights and biases.*
b) *Make a practise test available.*

c) *Evaluate the net input and output of each component in the covered up and output layers; distribute the inputs forward.*
d) *By back propagating the lapse to the hidden layer, it will be promoted.*
e) *To account for the scattered latency, adjust the weights and biases.*
f) *To change the system's loads and biases, scientists applied scientific approaches such as planning and improving knowledge capacity.*
g) *Putting an end to the weight-adjustment procedure.*

4 Experimental Design and Analysis

When it comes to precipitation analysis, one of the most typical issues is figuring out how to evaluate the past and make accurate predictions. If over a short time, the parameters required to predict rainfall are very intricate and fascinating. Various rainwater prediction systems have been offered to overcome this challenge. These methods, however, have performance limits due to the vast range of data variances, and the volume of data is restricted. Several techniques are employed, including the Support Vector Machine, Genetic algorithm, Naive Bayes, Random Forest and a deep learning model. Many of these tactics performed admirably and yielded favorable performance, while others did not.

4.1 Support Vector Machine

In the beginning, SVMs were created to solve forecasting and classification difficulties. During the typhoon season, other meteorological control variables such as pressure distribution, temperature, convection state, and wind velocity, which may be considered in their framework for estimating rainfall levels, are a major limitation for time-series forecasting models. It's a self-learning technique that could be used for reversion and grouping. SVMs rely on identifying the most efficient hyperplane for dividing a data is divided into two classes. In comparison to other learning machine algorithms, SVMs

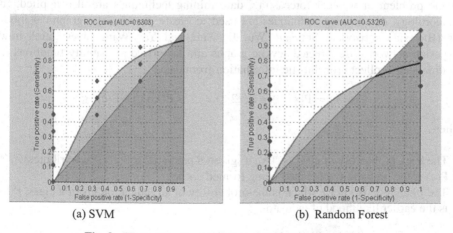

(a) SVM   (b) Random Forest

Fig. 3. TP vs. FP rate at different classification thresholds.

have a higher level of precision. The purpose of SVM is to construct a design that predicts the survey's expected information levels (Fig. 3).

4.2 Random Forest

Another sort of categorization model that was utilised as a machine learning model benchmark is random forest regression (RFR). According to Zhongrun Xiang and Ibrahim Demir [16], in each station, 456 input factors were used to predict 120 output variables. However, there are certain disadvantages to the data driven approach, such as using 4 years of data rather than 6 years of data, which reduces model accuracy substantially.Random forest is a method for generating tree classifications that requires supervision. An given input vector is placed in every rainforest tree to order a new goal from an entrance traits vector in this approach of the algorithm. The "votes" are collected from every tree in the rainforest, and the tree with the most "polls" is analysed for grouping. From the sum of "m" features, pick "k" attributes at random. By employing the best partitioning, you can spill the elements into more components. Base Classifier: This term refers to the random forest gathering's base classifier. A decision-making structure can be used as the base classifier.

- Split Measure: Whereas if Random Forest's base classifier is a decision-making structure, a part action is found at each tree node to complete the division. The Gini record is used to perform separation.
- Several Passes: It must run through the data for generating and Random Forest categorization, whether the required of passes is single or several.
- Combine strategy: All of the given classification algorithm are used for organisation in the Random. When it comes to organising, the consolidated approach is critical for bringing the findings of instance-based classifiers together.

4.3 Naive Bayes

In the problem of weather forecasting, data mining techniques are also applied. In meteorology, data mining techniques are used to create probabilistic graphical models (Bayesian networks). ShuFang Wu, Jie Zhu, and Yan Wang investigated how Bayesian networks use directed acyclic graphs and factorised probability functions to automatically collect probabilistic information from data.

$$P(c|X) = P(x1|c) * P(x2|c) * \ldots * P(xn|c) * P(c)$$

where

- The back probability of class (c, target) given a predictor is $P(c|x)$ (x, attributes).
- $P(c)$ is the probability of a class being formed earlier.
- The likelihood is $P(x|c)$, which is the probability of an indication given a class. $P(x)$ is the earlier likelihood of indicator.

4.4 Genetic Algorithm

The selection operator, crossover operator, and mutation operator will all be used by the genetic algorithm to assign strength. If the fitness value is correct, the forecast will be updated. If the fitness value is false, the fitness will be assigned again using these three operators, and finally, a specific activity will be gained. This calculation was used to estimate the value of rainfall data gathering. Choosing the best from a certain location or region aids our proposed method in swiftly forecasting the value, resulting in the best performance validation. To calculate accuracy, divide the total digits of perfect predictions by the total digits of test data. 1 – ERR is another way to express it. The best possible accuracy is 1.0, while the worst possible accuracy is 0.0 (Table 3, Figs. 4, 5 and 6).

Table 3. Comparison of the proposed method with conventional classifiers.

Classifier	Accuracy	Precision	Recall	F1 score	ROC AUC	Specificity	Standard error
Naïve Bayes	0.8045	1	0.5	0.95	0.512	0.5	0.21
Genetic algorithm	0.7938	1	0.5	0.952	0.581	0.8	0.22
Random forest	0.7938	1	0.5	0.952	0.532	0.5	0.30
SVM	0.8735	1	0.5	0.85	0.630	0.5	0.28
Proposed deep learning model	**0.9644**	1	**0.5**	**0.95**	**0.718**	**0.5**	**0.20**

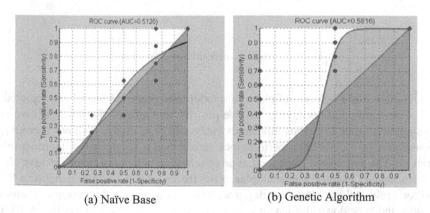

(a) Naïve Base   (b) Genetic Algorithm

Fig. 4. TP vs. FP rate at different classification thresholds.

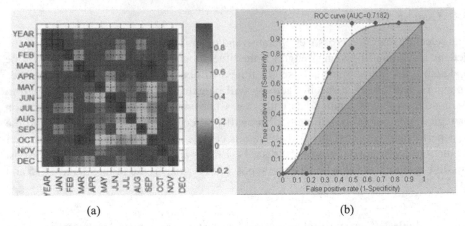

(a)   (b)

Fig. 5. a. Confusion matrix & b. TP vs. FP rate at different classification thresholds for proposed method

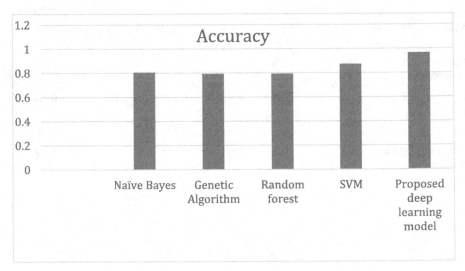

Fig. 6. Accuracuy measures of classifiers

ROC–AUC and F1-Scores of classifier models and proposed model are depicted in Fig. 7. Calculating and displaying the true positive rate against the false positive rate for a single classifier at various thresholds yields the ROC curve. It shows a graphical representation of a classifier's performance rather than a single value, as most other metrics do. The anticipated likelihood of an observation belonging to the positive class.

It is necessary to categorise examples as per their scores in order to generate a ROC curve for a probabilistic classifier. Begin with the instance with the maximum ranking and work the way down the list of cases. The process of drawing begins in (0, 0). Whether the instance's true class is positive or negative should be checked at each step, and if positive, movement should be one unit up, if negative, one unit to the right. The

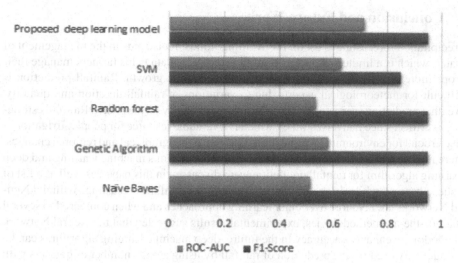

Fig. 7. ROC–AUC and F1-Scores of classifier models

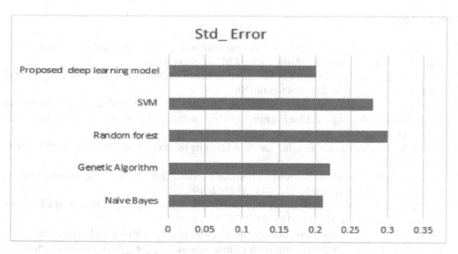

Fig. 8. Standard error for various classifiers.

method is also known as applying different score thresholds, and it ends whenever the right upper corner in (1, 1) is obtained. The number of false and positive cases in the dataset are inversely related to the horizontal and vertical unit sizes, respectively. The inverse of accuracy is the error rate. As the name implies, this metric assesses a model's performance in terms of inaccurate predictions. Figure 8 shows the standard error for rainfall prediction using Random forest, Nave bayes, Genetic algorithm, and Support Vector Machine, and it can be seen that the suggested deep leaning model outperforms with less error.

5 Conclusion and Future Work

Precipitation forecasting is useful for avoiding floods. It also aids in the management of water, which is a limited resource. Rainfall forecasting data helps farmers manage their crops more effectively, resulting in enhanced economic growth. Rainfall prediction is difficult for meteorological experts due to variations in rainfall duration and quantity. Weather prediction seems to be a top issue in every country on the planet. Rainfall estimation is critical since it involves water, which is a valuable resource for people. Irrigation is also crucial for environmental protection. Because of geographical and regional changes, there may be some fluctuations in rainfall estimates. Various machine learning and deep learning algorithm for rainfall prediction were discussed in this paper, as well as a list of issues observed while using different approaches for rainfall forecasting.Artificial Neural Networks are favoured over other learning approaches and when compared to several state-of-the-art methodologies, experimental results suggested that the Neural Network methodology enhances accuracy.In the future, deep machine learning algorithms can be productively used for the prediction of rainfall by using a large number of datasets with multiple attributes.

References

1. Ahmed, K., et al.: Multi-model ensemble predictions of precipitation and temperature using machine learning algorithms. Atmos. Res. **236**, 104806 (2020)
2. Pham, B.T., et al.: Development of advanced artificial intelligence models for daily rainfall prediction. Atmos. Res. **237**, 104845 (2020)
3. Aguasca-Colomo, R., Castellanos-Nieves, D., Méndez, M.: Comparative analysis of rainfall prediction models using machine learning in islands with complex orography: Tenerife Island. Appl. Sci. **9**(22), 4931 (2019)
4. Oswal, N.: Predicting rainfall using machine learning techniques. arXiv preprint arXiv:1910. 13827 (2019)
5. Refonaa, J., et al.: Machine learning techniques for rainfall prediction using neural network. J. Comput. Theor. Nanosci. **16**(8), 3319–3323 (2019)
6. Manandhar, S., et al.: A data-driven approach for accurate rainfall prediction. IEEE Trans. Geosci. Remote Sens. **57**(11), 9323–9331 (2019)
7. Tien Bui, D., et al.: Spatial prediction of rainfall-induced landslides for the Lao Cai area (Vietnam) using a hybrid intelligent approach of least squares support vector machines inference model and artificial bee colony optimization. Landslides **14**(2), 447–458 (2016). https://doi. org/10.1007/s10346-016-0711-9
8. Scherrer, S.C., Fischer, E.M., Posselt, R., Liniger, M.A., Croci-Maspoli, M., Knutti, R.: Emerging trends in heavy precipitation and hot temperature extremes in Switzerland. J. Geophys. Res.: Atmos. **121**(6), 2626–2637 (2016)
9. Schneider, T., O'Gorman, P.A., Levine, X.J.: Water vapor and the dynamics of climate changes. Rev. Geophys. **48**(3) (2010)
10. Guerreiro, S.B., et al.: Detection of continental-scale intensification of hourly rainfall extremes. Nat. Clim. Chang. **8**(9), 803–807 (2018)
11. Yen, M.-H., et al.: Application of the deep learning for the prediction of rainfall in Southern Taiwan. Sci. Rep. **9**(1), 1–9 (2019)
12. Yu, P.-S., Yang, T.-C., Chen, S.-Y., Kuo, C.-M., Tseng, H.-W.: Comparison of random forests and support vector machine for real-time radar-derived rainfall forecasting. J. Hydrol. **552**, 92–104 (2017)

13. Farheen, N.: Rainfall prediction and suitable crop suggestion using machine learning prediction algorithms. In: Hassanien, A.E., Bhattacharyya, S., Chakrabati, S., Bhattacharya, A., Dutta, S. (eds.) Emerging Technologies in Data Mining and Information Security. AISC, vol. 1300, pp. 497–513. Springer, Singapore (2021). https://doi.org/10.1007/978-981-33-4367-2_48
14. Luitel, B., Villarini, G., Vecchi, G.A.: Verification of the skill of numerical weather prediction models in forecasting rainfall from US landfalling tropical cyclones. J. Hydrol. **556**, 1026–1037 (2018)
15. Hussein, E., Ghaziasgar, M., Thron, C.: Regional rainfall prediction using support vector machine classification of large-scale precipitation maps. In: 2020 IEEE 23rd International Conference on Information Fusion (FUSION), pp. 1–8. IEEE (2020)
16. Rashid, T.A., Fattah, P., Awla, D.K.: Using accuracy measure for improving the training of LSTM with metaheuristic algorithms. Proc. Comput. Sci. **140**, 324–333 (2018)

Industrial Machine Learning Cloud Applications: Integrity and Confidentiality of Machine Sensitive Data

Munisamy Eswara Narayanan[1,2]($\boxtimes$) and Balasundaram Muthukumar[3]

[1] Sathyabama Institute of Science and Technology, Chennai, India
eswaranarayanan@gmail.com
[2] HCL Technologies Ltd., Chennai, India
[3] Department of Computer Science and Engineering, DMI College of Engineering, Chennai, India

Abstract. Many industries have adopted an industrial 4.0 environment to improve manufacturing processes and productivity through continuous monitoring of machine-sensitive trained dataset that is frequently shared between local and global cloud storage. It has enabled cloud collaborative editing with high security and quick user revocation for extracting features from a cloud-based trained dataset. Furthermore, it provides secure access to the accumulated data across multiple cloud terminals. Sometimes, the process may shut down unexpectedly due to interrupt of unknown entry anywhere, resulting in the entire manufacturing modality collapsing. Therefore, this paper proposes a Machine Learning Used Confidential (MLC) protocol for enhancing integrity and confidentiality service of machine sensitive data in industries cloud applications. It divides machine data into several segmented copies, each of which is encrypted before being stored in multiple cloud terminals. Additionally, if the actual machine data is changed in the field, the stored secured data is automatically updated. The local and global cloud servers keep track of all of these functions securely. Finally, the experimental results demonstrate that the proposed MLC protocol outperformed the others in terms of the performance and efficiency of the security provision.

Keywords: MLC protocol · Sensitive data · Integrity and confidentiality · CNN

1 Introduction

Smart manufacturing is defined as a man-machine integrated smart system with machines and human specialists is an unavoidable trend in the modern manufacturing industry that has sustained evolution [1]. This industrial data security has sparked a lot of academic attention in recent years to the rapid growth of Industrial Internet technologies [2]. A massive amount of sensitive data is produced throughout the industrial production process including the manufacturing processing data, production expense data, operations data, marketing method, intellectual property protection, and user details. When this confidential data is released, it could result in severe commercial informational loss or potentially harm an organization's reputation. Information leakage has been a frequent occurrence in recent times wherein the industrial data such as predictive maintenance information in today's smart factories must be analyzed in contemporaneous real-world circumstances.

Cloud computing service is rapidly reforming the technique of data storage and retrieval [3]. It benefits data consumers by permitting them to access and utilize storage resources that a service provider (SP) has demanded and therefore, many organizations are relying on the cloud to store their sensitive data. In a pay-n-use structure, cloud computing delivers low security for users, and their stored data. This cloud can be accessed by users at any time and from any location. It enhances cloud fraud by allowing unrestricted cloud utilization. As online malevolent people steal huge money losses, numerous financial businesses are affected by fraudulent persons and their operations. Many economic sectors such as medical, healthcare, and company data are mostly lost due to insured persons. Hence, these cloud computing applications demand a highly secure framework for their communication, data, and financial interactions. By taking into account all features of cloud applications, Fig. 1 depicts a comprehensive security infrastructure in the aspect of users, obtained data, and data storage. Data integrity and data confidentiality are used to guarantee storage-level data security.

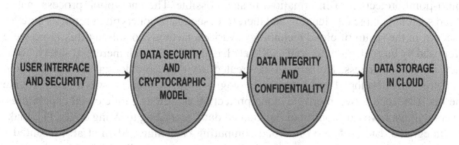

Fig. 1. Cloud computing-based data storage structure.

2   Contribution

A machine learning (ML) software is essential for balancing data accessibility within your firm with its security consequences. Even if accessibility to sensitive information is restricted, users require insights from the raw machine dataset to aid ML training. To accomplish these objectives, machine learning algorithms can be trained on machine data, or the complete dataset after applying a variety of aggregation techniques. Complex data streams and autonomous in-built procedures that require data alterations are driving the rapid growth of machine learning models. To enable the DI, a dataset is managed with specific limitations described via rules set based on data manipulation actions such as insertion, detection, and updating.

- The proposed MLC protocol explains how to use a security paradigm that combines data integrity and confidentiality. In cloud computing applications, the proposed MLC uses a highly protected and optimized cloud cooperative editing mechanism, as well as an effective user revocation method.

- The proposed method provides an extremely secure and simplified cloud cooperative editing method in which users with a set of machine data into multiple segments are stored in distinct cloud terminals, and under the cipher-access text's policy, the user is permitted to read as well as write encryption data preserved in the cloud terminals. If required they are allowed to do a modification that will be updated in the cloud.
- The proposed machine learning CNN model verifies the data/user access and notifies the data owner if there is the possibility of unauthorized access.

3 Prior Works

Data protection in cloud storage has gained a lot of interest in the last several decades from both industries and academia. Several scholars and researchers are presenting solutions to this problem. Since data is transmitted via SSL, Hou et al. proposed protection mechanisms that use encrypted information by its system [4]. Feng presented a method for encrypting data in a confined cloud infrastructure to address the issue of information theft because of increased cloud server load [5]. One-time encryption, as well as multi-point protection of information, is also possible. The encryption process makes cloud searching more challenging and therefore, searchable encryption remains a major concern in the realm of cloud technology. Various methods to solving this issue were proposed by Fu et al. [6–8] as well as Xia et al. [9], each of which increased safety, accuracy, and effectiveness. Kulkarni et al. created a virtual confidential storage solution using recently developed encryption technologies [10]. This service was able to provide the finest balance between private cloud protection as well as public cloud capabilities. Users will not have true control of outsourced data, according to Wang et al. [11], making integrated data protection in cloud computing challenges. Shen et al. presented a public auditing system that incorporates a location array as well as a doubly connected data table [12]. The experimental analysis demonstrates that the proposed technique can minimize computation and communication overheads while also achieving efficiency.

Differences in Cloud computing were described by Khorshed et al. as trust difficulties among consumers and Cloud service providers, wherein users' mistrust rules were secret from them [13]. Cloud providers were concerned that users would exploit their facilities and may attack utilizing them. The objectives of the organizations, as well as the services received from a certain provider, were the most important factors in choosing a service provider. As per Modi et al., the vulnerability was Cloud security gaps that an adversary might exploit to get the network access and infrastructure resources. A cloud risk was a potentially harmful event that was purposeful or unintentional. Vulnerability exploitation would impact Cloud computing accessibility and financial rewards [14]. An attack includes a Cloud resource degradation action, and exploitation might affect the Cloud accessing and financial rewards.

HABE was obtained as a solution for secure and effective data sharing in cloud computing [15]. They created solutions for important difficulties such as providing cooperative security write functionality on important management complexity, ciphertext, and significant computation burden on the consumer, as cooperative consumers might read as well as write information via any device. The fine-grained controlled access of ciphertext, as well as protected data writing action, can be performed using ABE with attribute-based signature (ABS). Half decryption and signature constructions were also presented to hand away from the majority of the computing cost on the user towards the cloud service contributing. SECO is an efficient, safe, and scalable data cooperation mechanism described by Dong et al. [16]. To ensure data security versus insecure cloud, the creators of SECO used multi-level hierarchical identity encryption (HIE). They assumed that their research was the first to look into secured cloud data collaborative services that minimize information leakage while also allowing encryption models, data rewriting, and fine-grained controlled access.

Wang et al. propose a novel auditing mechanism publicly for shared data dependability that includes capable user revocation [17]. Even if a portion of the shared information had been again signed by cloud, an examiner was able to verify and incorporate without having to retrieve the complete shared data. Regarding ciphertext-policy ABE (CP-ABE) systems, Xu and Martin presented a dynamic user revocation with a key refreshing approach [18]. A major feature of their architecture was the ability to recover system keys or remove accessibility from users independent of issuing fresh keys to other consumers or re-encrypting previous ciphertexts in generic CP-ABE systems.

Their methodology proved effective and well-suited to use in cloud storage systems. They cited BSW's CP-ABE method as an instance of how their approach may be adapted to a CP-ABE method. An ABE with time-specific features (KP-TSABE) has been proposed by Xiong et al. [19]. Each ciphertext was regarded as a time interval in the KP-TSABE system, whereas the private key had linked to a time instantaneously. When the time instant has been permitted, i.e. the timeframe and the qualities connected with the ciphertext suit the key's structure access, the ciphertext may be decoded. Li et al. suggested a key-updating as well as an authenticator-evolving method for safe cloud data monitoring with zero privacy information of the preserved files [20–23]. The cost of transmission and processing is reduced as a result of this substantial technique, resulting in attractive security.

4   Preliminaries

The Data Integrity (DI) model examines the input machine data, evaluates it, removes duplicates, maintains the data, and backs it up. It audits the trails as well as verifies to maintain the controlled access permission. When a data breach occurs, the DI investigates the origins of the vital information. The listing of risks is emphasized as a feature of data security that protects the DI, then lowers the risk towards the companies in which the data has been used. It is critical to verify the input when it comes from an unfamiliar data owner, program, or any regular or atypical user. It guarantees that the data entry is highly precise. The integrity of the processing data is then checked. It is derived by checking the information, the organization's attributes, and requirements. When sharing data throughout several departments of a business, it is important to keep duplicate data to a minimum.

DI Problems

Data checks in the software are used to detect DI vulnerabilities. The ML system code includes an invoke code that checks the whole training machine dataset or testing dataset for DI problems. It's a big task to include lost values, range violations, and type mismatches as features. Rule-set policies regularly examine the input data before sending it into ML seems to be an effective way for detecting DI errors. If a data input obtained from the database is sent to this prototype, then certain rules/policies become enabled.

As prototype inference, the data checks are incorporated with this system. The proposed ML protocol is tested using a sample machine dataset as input. It aids in the evaluation of this model depending on data and policies. Once the ML detects the DI faults, it sends an alert to the administrator or programmer. The data checks may fix the problem and help the developer figure out what kind of DI problem he or she is dealing with. The proposed model performance is harmed by flaws that go undetected. As a result, this model must incorporate the following components:

Local and Global Analyzation
By combining ML inferences with DI concerns and evaluating the model's impacts, a fine-grained model begins the best practices of the essential usage scenarios for prediction assessment. The machine learning model is designed to comprehend the contextual data to swiftly identify issues. It implies that it must occasionally perform as a black box system. As a result, this model became time-consuming. To detect DI errors, it reconstructs all of the elements depending on the contextual data. It's difficult to again produce the result that hasn't been properly versioned.

To resolve the complexity of the DI concerns, the proposed model's global analysis has been applied. It entails a thorough analysis of data properties to discover difficulties at the time of development. The data is changed at the same time as new products are released. As a result, queries prompted for data tampering might include the DI concerns with a specific code, as well as data releases allowing quick reversing. These are sent into the proposed model as data drifting, with a corresponding output drift depending on their effects. As a result, an analysis model is used to determine its origins.

The methods described are appropriate for DI difficulties; otherwise, it will result in DI breaches. Local data and global data analytics aid in identifying and assessing this problem in the ML process. As a result, the proposed model includes data-check-points to ensure data quality, identify errors, and resolve DI problems.

All data is retrieved from the user database, and the RAID is created. Any files can be downloaded and validated using the customer account as well as other data. The customer and the information are validated if the file segmentation is accurate and present in the user-account-based database. It claims that the information is accurate because no data has been lost. Thus, Machine learning user confidential (MLC) protocol with the CNN algorithm has been utilized to improve the DI.

Data Confidentiality
The proposed MLC has been utilized to encrypt followed by performing the decryption of user data, ensuring data confidentiality is the most legitimate and efficient accessible method in today's technological environment. It's a cryptographic hybrid encryption system that's commonly used for certain security and transmission of information referred to as an asymmetric cryptosystem since it employs two distinct mathematically related

keys during the encryption process and decryption process, with the receiver and transmitter. The public key and private key are the keys employed in encryption as well as the decryption process. The public key has been utilized for encrypting the information without the requirement of sharing it with the private key is widely known and freely disseminated. The only person who knows about the private key is the individual who possesses it. Simply the user with this key may decrypt once the encryption is successfully performed.

The MLC produces the above-mentioned key generation mechanism and provides it extremely valuable for secure data exchange, allowing data secrecy to be maintained. It doesn't utilize identical private keys for encryption as well as decryption process, with exception of the symmetric method. The difficulty of factoring huge integers that are the multiplication of two big prime numbers is the basis for this RSA algorithm. Even with supercomputers, finding its actual prime numbers from the total factoring is impossible. The encryption strength is determined by the key size, which is commonly measured in bits. All public key creation necessitates that pair mathematical operations are the most important and difficult element.

4.1 Machine Learning Used Confidential (MLC) Protocol

Utilizing the functional segment and a meta tag with an index such as $I = 0$, 1, 2..., n for determining a specific segment), where the input 'Z' file is segmented into 'n' number of segmented copies ($\{Z_0, Z_1, Z_2, \ldots, Z_n\}$). The resulting ciphertext $\left(CT_{p0}, CT_{p1}, CT_{p2}, \ldots, CT_{pn}\right)$ has now transferred to the multiple cloud terminals along with each meta tag of the file using an access rule (T) as well as public key (PK).

Utilizing the centralized authority, the framework establishes function is used to choose the 'K' parameter randomly. This function generates the public key (PK) and the master key (MK-0) for authorized individuals as well as domain authority, both of which are kept private. The security factor (λ) is used as a source input for the proposed system. The outcome of the proposed system are the master secret key (MSK), as well as PK. The competitors use to set value 1λ to obtain these output. The generator (G) choose the parameters μ, and, followed by h_1 as well as h_2 hash functions are used in the configuration function. The following are the expression of PK and MK-0:

$$\text{\rule{2cm}{0.3ex}} \quad (1)$$

$$\text{\rule{1.5cm}{0.3ex}} \ 0 = \tilde{n}_{\eta} \ \text{\rule{0.5cm}{0.3ex}} \quad (2)$$

The configuration procedure $G(1\lambda)$ is executed initially to acquire $\left(p, q, r, G, GT, e^{\wedge}\right)$ using s; where G denotes cyclic groupings and then order $N = pqr$. Expression (3) shows the public key value whereas expression (4) shows the master key value.

$$PK = \left(A_0 = g_p.R_0, \left\{A_{i,j} = g_p^{a_{i,j}}\right\} 1 \le i \le n, 1 \le j \le l, g_r, Y = e \wedge \left(g_p, g_p\right)^w\right) \quad (3)$$

$$MSK = \left(g_p, \left\{a_{i,j}\right\} 1 \le i \le n, 1 \le j \le l, w\right) \quad (4)$$

The domain method (DM) is used to select the distinct values U_l as well as $U_{l,i}\epsilon\beta_0$ per attribute in $S = \{a_1, a_2, \ldots, a_n\}$. . Then, the MSK (MK-1) for the level-1 authority domain is determined as follows:

$$MK - 1 = \left(S, D_1 = G^{(\eta+U_l)\mu}\right) \tag{5}$$

Here, S represents the attributes, whereas D_1 represents the encrypted data.

$$D_{1,i} = G^{U_l\mu}h_1(i)^{U_{l,i}} \text{ and } \left\{D'_{1,i} = G^{U_{l,i}}\right\}_{i\epsilon s} \tag{6}$$

The keys with DM_i are produced using the DM algorithm. During the next stage, TTP uses this algorithm to produce master keys for internally authorized parties. The level-1 authority domain employs this DM procedure, with the master key from the prior stage $MK - 1$ serving as the level-1 authority domain's input. With $S' = \{a_1, a_2, \ldots, a_n\}$, this procedure is used to select the random numbers ω_l and $\omega_{1,i}\epsilon\beta_0$ per attribute. The succeeding stage master key i.e. $MK - 1 + 1$ is submitted to the level-2 domain using the 'S' attribute set and the $MK - 1 + 1$ is the preceding stage, which is calculated as follows:

$$MK - 1 + 1 = \left(S', D_{1+1} = D_1 \cdot G^{\omega_1\mu} = G^{(\eta+U_l+\omega_1)\mu}\right) \tag{7}$$

In formula (7),

$$D_{1+1,i} = D_{1,i} \cdot G^{\omega_1\mu}h_1(i)^{\omega_{1,i}} = G^{(U_l+\omega_1)\mu}h_1(i)^{U_{l,i}+\omega_{1,i}} \tag{8}$$

$$D'_{1+1,i} = D'_{1,i}.G^{\omega_1\mu} = G^{U_{l,i}+\omega_{1,i}} \tag{9}$$

The relevant authority domain uses the key generation technique using $MK - 1$ to choose a random $\varepsilon \epsilon \beta_0$ per attribute of the customer to choose a random $\varepsilon \epsilon \beta_0$ for the customer. Following this, the attribute with the secret key has calculated:

$$SK = \left(S, D = D'_1.(G^\mu)^\varepsilon\right) = G^{(U_l+\omega_1)\mu} \tag{10}$$

$$\left\{D_i = D'_{l,i}.G^{\varepsilon\mu}h_1(i)^{\varepsilon_i} = G^{(U_l+\varepsilon)\mu}, D'_i = D'_{1,i}.G^{\varepsilon_i} = G^{U_{l,i}+\varepsilon_i}\right\}_{i\epsilon S} \tag{11}$$

The key server accepts the secret data γ t and an attribute set AS as source input for the customer Ut. The resultant ASK attribute key element $ASK_{A,t}$ is obtained. The master key has been used as a source of data. It gives you a private key that corresponds to the identification ID.

Utilizing the segment functions, the user divides the actual 'Z' plaintext data into several segmented copies $Z_0, Z_1, Z_2, \ldots, Z_n$ during the process of data encryption. To determine the specific segment for modifications, a single Meta tag T_k has been given segment during segmentation. $T_k = \{t_{k,i}\}_{i\epsilon[1,2,\ldots,n]}$ denotes the Meta tags are obtained as follows,

$$t_i = \left\{h(SK_h, W_i).\pi_{j=1}^s Z_j^{Zij}\right\}^{SK_t} \tag{12}$$

$$T_k = \{t_{k,i}\}_{i \in [1,2,\dots,n]} \tag{13}$$

The encryption method uses the access policy (T) to encrypt every individual segment piece $(Z_0, Z_1, Z_2, \dots, Z_n)$ as well as return the ciphertext towards the CSP when the user needs the data the segmented data are retrieved together this might reduce the vulnerable action; therefore, randomly, $(\varphi \in \beta_0)$ has been chosen for data encryption. The data owner selects the p_b polynomial for every (b) leaf node within accessing tree in a top-down way. In this tree, p_b polynomial has d_b degree where d_b is fixed when the (K_b) the threshold value is lower than 1 $(db = K_b - 1)$. This encryption algorithm picks $p_v(0)$ randomly from the initial root node (S_R) is assigns to $(p_v(0) = v)$, on the other hand, the degree (d_v) is chosen from p_v polynomial to finish the process.

The degree d_a has been randomly chosen from the other (p_a) polynomial to fix the parent node i.e. $p_a(0) = p_{parent(a)}(index(a))$. Further, the decrypted fragments of ciphertext are computed using the structural tree access γ is given as follows:

$$CT(CT_0, CT_1, CT_2, \dots, CT_n)$$
$$= \left(\gamma, E = Enc_\varphi(Z_0, Z_1, Z_2, \dots, Z_n), CT - \varphi.\hat{e}(G, G)^{\eta\mu\nu}, CT - G^a\right) \tag{14}$$

$$CT'_a = G^{p_a(0)}, CT'_a = h_1(attry_a)^{p_a(0)} \ here, a \in A \tag{15}$$

Here, T represents an access tree, whereas M represents a message. The source input being feed is a public key (PK) for which the corresponding output obtained is ciphertext (CT). The identification ID of the user is an input for which a message M must be encrypted to get the resultant CT. This is implemented by leveraging the sender's encryption.

The files $Z_0, Z_1, Z_2, \dots, Z_n$ are decrypted by users with its secret key (SK) attribute after getting $(CT_{p0}, CT_{p1}, CT_{p2}, \dots, CT_{pn})$. The user decrypts $CT_0, CT_1, CT_2, \dots, CT_n$ and recovers the actual file.

$$CT'/\left(\hat{e}(CT\varphi/A) = \varphi.\frac{\hat{e}(G, G)^{\eta\mu s}}{\left(\hat{e}(G^s, G^{(\eta, U_l+\varepsilon)})\hat{e}(G, G)^{(U_l+\varepsilon)\mu s}\right)} = \varphi\right) \tag{16}$$

Then, the segment files $Z_0, Z_1, Z_2, \dots, Z_n$ with φ is decrypted by the user, and it is given as follows:

$$Z_0, Z_1, Z_2, \dots, Z_n = Dec_\varphi(Enc) \tag{17}$$

The ML core framework and functionality are developed for establishing and analyzing Data Integrity and Confidentiality (DIC) is shown in Fig. 2. There are two primary processing phases in the proposed paradigm. The machine learning Convolution Neural Network (CNN) method is applied as a supervised learning technique initially and is trained using numerous layers. To achieve better feature retrieval, the CNN employs many hidden layers and a feed-forward ANN. To begin, replicate all data from multiple cloud users, their data, and IoT data as (X) traffic data. These data with their meta-data are fed into CNN as (X) source input. When the user uploads and downloads data from a database, the DI improves the quality of data and validates it. Thus, it is possible to

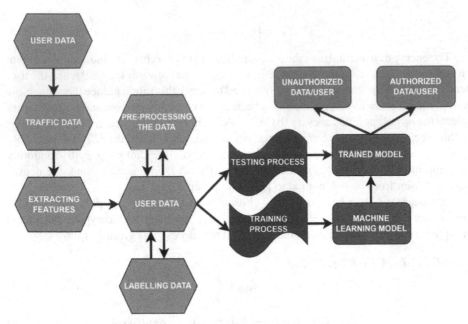

Fig. 2. Proposed machine learning framework.

categorize owner and malicious users based on the validation. When a user is found to be malicious, then they are immediately refused and removed from the customer table.

CNN's complete model that examines three separate data sets derived from publicly accessible standard datasets and tested by previous techniques is shown in Fig. 3. This has a number of layers at various stages. The input machine data is fed into CNN, wherein the convolution layers examine the machine data into several segmented copies and retrieve (X) data features, which are then fed into hidden layers. The 4-CNN has four different kernel sizes: 32 numbers, 64 numbers, 128 numbers, and 128 numbers. These layers decrease dimensionality by learning the similarities of characteristics based on context, as well as syntax. Weight numbers supplied to every x are used to normalize the data and feature values. The concealed layers are the pooling layers. The fully-connected layers summarize and collect the final data groups, as well as offer output classes like a harmful user, inaccurate data, and harmful storage.

For encrypted activities, the machine learning CNN model is more effective. This model includes native plaintext is considered as a cyclotomic polynomial ring, allowing numerous plaintext values to be divided into multiple copies are stored in different cloud terminals. Via SIMD procedures, this ciphertext package allows parallel processing of addition as well as multiplication operations. Furthermore, it should be noted that the following packing is not feasible to read values in isolated ciphertext segments randomly. Because a ciphertext can specifically perform restricted operation sets, the advantages of SIMD operations are completely realized if there is a minimum connection among the segment. As a result, a more conservative as well as straightforward method is chosen to ciphertext packing, amortization computation time via processing datasets

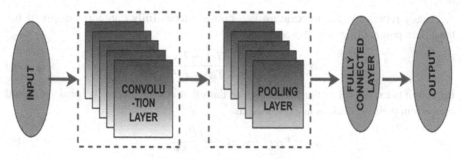

Fig. 3. CNN model.

in parallel. A polynomial approximation is used to construct a ReLU functioning. To reduce computational complexity, the model is well-trained to improve testing precision. During the training phase, the data investigation included checkpoints to improve data quality. This also prevents data validation errors. To measure the outcome, the testing method is used to unfamiliar data. Thus, it will prevent sensitive data leakage. This model enables the authorized user to read/write and perform some modification operation in the stored data. Since the data is divided and stored in the cloud platform, this method can be implemented in many organizations to store sensitive data.

5 Result and Discussion

The proposed MLC model implemented in NetBeans IDE has a Cloud-Sim that enables it to activate cloud functionalities, using the JAVA language. Java-NetBeans is implemented on an Inteli7 Pentium 3.0 GHz PC having 8 GB RAM as well as a 1TB hard drive. The dataset is used to test the proposed module, which calculates a few evaluation measures to determine the MLC performance to improve the integrity and confidentiality of machine data. To evaluate the outcomes, the processing is performed by modifying the dataset.

- True-Positive appropriately recognizes and categorizes abnormal users and their data as unauthorized users and data.
- True-Negative wrongly recognizes and categorizes the anomalous user/data as authorized.
- False-Positive accurately recognizes and qualifies normal users and their data as authorized users and data.
- False-Negative wrongly classifies and distinguishes normal users and their data as unauthorized users and data.

The MLC's performance parameters are analyzed using the above-mentioned evaluation metrics and are as follows:

- Accuracy represents the maximum data points successfully categorized out of the total data points utilized in the computation.

$$Accuracy = \frac{TP + TN}{TP + TN + FP + FN} \tag{18}$$

- Precision is expressed as the percentage of data that is projected to be positive based on current positive classes is expressed as

$$Precision = \frac{TP}{TP + FP} \tag{19}$$

- The performance factor, namely recall, defines whether the proposed model remains adequate or not. When the recall value is higher, then FP value will be lower, and vice-versa is expressed as follows:

$$Recall = \frac{TP}{TP + FN} \tag{20}$$

The proposed MLC is assessed based on the experimental results by assessing several aspects like F1-Score, time, CPU consumption, loss prediction, and accuracy comparisons. Initially, the time-based number of accessing demand that the web server can be tackled is computed. The demand handled by web servers decreases as time passes. Figure 4 depicts the outcome of this study.

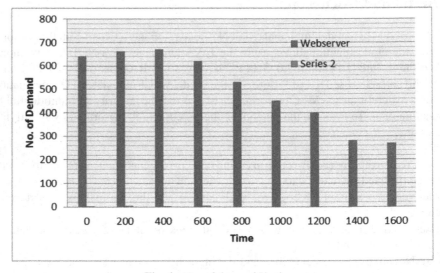

Fig. 4. No. of demand Vs time.

The CPU utilization is then calculated based on the time. If there is an increase If time grows, the number of demand and implementation rises. As a result, CPU consumption for time-based demand and application functionality has increased. The program may not be performed in the virtualization software at times, such as during off-hours. As a result, CPU use is not consistent and varies over time. Figure 5 depicts the outcome.

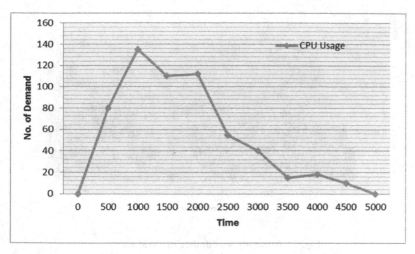

Fig. 5. CPU usage with respect to time.

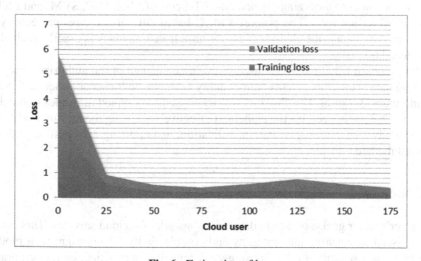

Fig. 6. Estimation of loss.

By measuring the loss yields, the MLC performance is evaluated. The loss is caused by decreased data quality, a slow response to demand, and the total web server applications running at the same time. It depends on the virtual machine, the resources accessibility, as well as the cloud's resource provisioning procedures. Losses may arise as a result of a congested path or a lack of resources. Figure 6 depicts the loss difference during the testing and validation process. For an increased number of cloud customers, the loss fell abruptly and remained steady. Then, the experiment's accuracy is being contrasted to the actual and estimated results. In cloud technology, accuracy improves as the number of users grows is shown in Fig. 7.

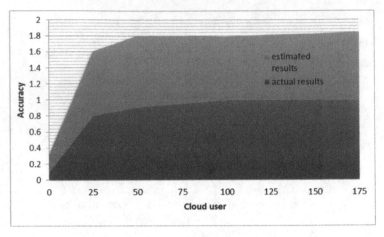

Fig. 7. Accuracy Vs number of cloud users.

When it comes to analyzing log data, the F1-Score of MLC-DIC, SVM, and LSTM are 98%, 93%, and 89%. The proposed MLC-based DIC offers superior security in storing sensitive data in the cloud because the anticipated accuracy is exactly equivalent to the actual accuracy.

The proposed MLC method is used to evaluate the data of the authorized user for accessing data in the cloud. Data confidentiality is employed for security needs, flexible and fine-grained control. The cloud service receives the encrypted messages of the data files. The CSP partly decrypts the ciphertext effectively allowing the user to modify the data. Partially signature, segmentation, validation, and updating are possible with the proposed method.

6 Conclusion

This paper's major goal is to ensure data and its security for cloud services. This can be accomplished by ensuring data integrity and confidentiality. The conventional models provide a lower security level. This subject is regarded as a critical cloud computing issue, and the purpose of this study is to build and develop MLC for security assurance. The proposed MLC includes the encryption scheme to protect data stored in the cloud, data accessibility, and modification authorization. The proposed technique reduces the encryption overhead in this case. Because the user count and the data size are large, the CNN model has been employed to evaluate the data and forecast unauthorized access. From the entire dataset, 80% of data is used in the training stage and 20% of data is used in the testing stage. The experimental findings prove that the enhanced MLC protocol is effective in terms of security protection. Additional changed functionalities such as segmentation, data retrieval, and file updates are included in the proposed approach. In the future, several real-time cloud apps will be used to test and evaluate the ML-DIC model performance.

References

1. Tseng, M., Edmunds, T., Canaran, L., et al.: Introduction to Edge Computing in IIoT. Industrial Internet Consortium, Need-ham (2018)
2. Hui, H., Zhou, C., Xu, S., Lin, F.: A novel secure data transmission scheme in industrial internet of things. China Commun. **17**(1), 73–88 (2020)
3. Hazela, B., Gupta, S.K., Soni, N., Saranya, C.N.: Securing the confidentiality and integrity of cloud computing data (2021). https://spast.org/techrep/article/view/2449
4. Shaw, S., Singh, A.K.: A survey on cloud computing. In: Proceedings of 2014 International Conference on Green Computing Communication and Electrical Engineering, Coimbatore, India (2014)
5. Hou, Q., Wu, Y., Zheng, W., Yang, G.: A method on protection of user data privacy in cloud storage platform. J. Comput. Res. Dev. **48**(7), 1146–1154 (2011)
6. Feng, G.: A data privacy protection scheme of cloud storage. Softw. Guide **14**(12), 174–176 (2015)
7. Fu, Z., Wu, X., Guan, C., Sun, X., Ren, K.: Toward efficient multi-keyword fuzzy search over encrypted outsourced data with accuracy improvement. IEEE Trans. Inf. Forensics Secur. **11**(12), 2706–2716 (2016)
8. Fu, Z., Ren, K., Shu, J., Sun, X., Huang, F.: Enabling personalized search over encrypted outsourced data with efficiency improvement. IEEE Trans. Parallel Distrib. Syst. **27**(9), 2546–2559 (2016)
9. Singhal, P., Singh, P., Hazela, B., Singh, V., Singh, V.: Machine learning algorithm: wine quality prediction. SPAST Abstracts **1**(01) (2021). Smart Green Connected Societies
10. Fu, Z., Huang, F., Sun, X., Vasilakos, A., Yang, C.-N.: Enabling semantic search based on conceptual graphs over encrypted out-sourced data. IEEE Trans. Serv. Comput. **12**(5), 813–823 (2016)
11. Xia, Z., Wang, X., Sun, X., Wang, Q.: A secure and dynamic multi-keyword ranked search scheme over encrypted cloud data. IEEE Trans. Parallel Distrib. Syst. **27**(2), 340–352 (2016)
12. Kulkarni, G., Waghmare, R., Palwe, R., et al.: Cloud storage architecture. In: Proceedings of the 2012 7th International Conference on Telecommunication Systems, Services, and Applications, Bali, Indonesia, pp. 76–81 (2012)
13. Wang, C., Chow, S.S.M., Wang, Q., Ren, K., Lou, W.: Privacy-preserving public auditing for secure cloud storage. IEEE Trans. Comput. **62**(2), 362–375 (2013)
14. Shen, J., Shen, J., Chen, X., Huang, X., Susilo, W.: An efficient public auditing protocol with novel dynamic structure for cloud data. IEEE Trans. Inf. Forensics Secur. **12**(10), 2402–2415 (2017)
15. Khorshed, M.T., Shawkat Ali, A.B.M., Wasimi, S.A.: Trust issues that create threats for cyber-attacks in cloud computing. In: Proceedings of the International Conference on Parallel and Distributed Systems – ICPADS (2011). https://doi.org/10.1109/ICPADS.2011.156
16. Modi, C., Patel, D., Borisaniya, B., Patel, A., Rajarajan, M.: A survey on security issues and solutions at different layers of cloud computing. J. Supercomput. **63**, 561–592 (2013). https://doi.org/10.1007/s11227-012-0831-5
17. Huang, Q., Yang, Y., Shen, M.: Secure and efficient data collaboration with hierarchical attribute-based encryption in cloud computing. Futur. Gener. Comput. Syst. **72**, 239–249 (2017)
18. Dong, X., Yu, J., Zhu, Y., Chen, Y., Luo, Y., Li, M.: SECO: secure and scalable data collaboration services in cloud computing. Comput. Secur. **50**, 91–105 (2015)
19. Wang, B., Li, B., Li, H.: Panda: public auditing for shared data with efficient user revocation in the cloud. IEEE Trans. Serv. Comput. **8**(1), 82–106 (2015)

20. Xu, Z., Martin, K.M.: Dynamic user revocation and key refreshing for attribute-based encryption in cloud storage. Paper presented at: IEEE International Conference on Trust, Security and Privacy in Computing and Communications, Liverpool, UK (2012)
21. Xiong, J., Liu, X., Yao, Z., et al.: A secure data self-destructing scheme in cloud computing. IEEE Trans. Cloud Comput. 2(4), 448–458 (2014)
22. Li, Y., Yu, Y., Yang, B., Min, G., Wu, H.: Privacy preserving cloud data auditing with efficient key update. Futur. Gener. Comput. Syst. 78, 789–798 (2018)
23. Gupta, S.K., Tiwari, S., Jamil, A.A., Singh, P.: Faster as well as early measurements from big data predictive analytics model. SPAST Abstracts 1(01) (2021). Smart Green Connected Societies

Classification of Dermoscopy Textures with an Ensemble Feedback of Multilayer Perceptron

A. Prabhu Chakkaravarthy[1]([⊠]), T. R. Saravanan[2], Sridhar Udayakumar[3], · and C. A. Subasini[4]

[1] Department of Networking and Communications, School of Computing, College of Engineering and Technology, SRM Institute of Science and Technology, Kattankulathur, India
prabhuca@srmist.edu.in
[2] Department of Computational Intelligence, SRM Institute of Science and Technology, Kattankulathur Campus, Chennai, India
saravant1@srmist.edu.in
[3] Department of Information Technology, Mettu University, Mettu, Ethiopia
sridhar.udayakumar@meu.edu.et
[4] St. Joseph's Institute of Technology, Old Mamallapuram Road, Chennai, India

Abstract. Aim: To build a perfection classification of skin cancer dataset in the form of textured parameters. The input images are taken from ISIC 2019 dataset. The images are converted into textures like contrast, homogeneity, energy and correlation using GLCM feature extraction. **Materials and method:** Multilayer perceptron's, or MLPs, can approximate any continuous function with a single hidden layer. They can be used in supervised learning to model the correlation of inputs and outputs between pairs of inputs and outputs. To optimize performance, models are trained to minimize error by adjusting their parameters, or weights and biases. **Result:** The input classification elements like contrast, correlation, energy and homogeneity are taken for classification, the initial with normal Multi-layer perceptron classification generates the sample input of 65.5% but the object is carried over ensemble classification again with Multi-layer perceptron generates 93.5% classification accuracy. **Conclusion:** On comparing the outcomes from the normal classification and the ensemble classification with Multi-Layer Perceptron, the ensemble model generates the maximum classification accuracy without breaking the sample of classification dataset.

Keywords: ISIC 2019 dataset · Multilayer perceptron · Ensemble model · GLCM · Melanoma · Activation function

1 Introduction

Melanoma tumour can cause a genuine perilous issue in people, whenever left unprocessed for quite a while lacking early analysis [7]. It is more critical to create narrative strategies depending on the biophysics analysis, atomic waits until acknowledgements,

K. Kottursamy et al. (Eds.): IconDeepCom 2022, CCIS 1719, pp. 217–231, 2023.
https://doi.org/10.1007/978-3-031-27622-4_17

and new image investigation measures received for early determination of melanoma. One of the quickest developing diseases in human cell is skin malignant growth. At first, it begins at the external layer of the skin called epidermis and expands unevenly up to a diameter. An arrangement of the skin malignancy relies upon the shortcoming of the skin cell. To locate the ideal finding, dermatologists should utilize the computational strategy [8]. It is very difficult to identify the skin disease at an early stage by the dermatologists but the computational technique portrays out impeccably.

2   Literature Review

For picture recuperation and suggestion, framework finish is broadly utilized [1]. Consequently, this paper proposes an original network fruition model in light of the MLP integrating kernel regularization (MCKR). The proposed model uses the MLP to extricate highlight, which can consequently remove connection component of missing information and observational information. Besides, novel portion regularization has been determined in light of a non-direct planning between low-layered inactive subspace and the schatten p-standard as a method for lessening the commotion of a finished lattice. Three freely accessible datasets are inspected to decide the pertinence and legitimacy of this proposed model. Multi-layer perceptron (MLP), Matrix factorization (MF), expertise matrix factorization (EMF) and Logistic matrix factorization (LMF) are comparable to our proposed model.

It is expected to create RSS values for each reference point (RP) by the customary RSS-based unique mark confinement calculation [2]. An increment in the quantity of passageways will bring about a lot of unique finger impression information gathered by the APs, which possesses a ton of extra room in huge scope indoor conditions. It indicates the networks on which the intrigued target shows up generally in the checking area that has been isolated into mathematical frameworks to carry out another dependable limitation calculation that uses quantized RSS. Multi-layer Perceptron (MLP) to compute the limitation brings about non-isomorphic lattice districts utilizing reference point organizations. With a similar sending of areo-morphic areas, it is vital for train just one model to supplant the others, along these lines extraordinarily lessening the calculation expected by neural organizations. In light of exploratory outcomes, the proposed unique mark limitation calculation decreases the size of finger impression data sets by more than 80% contrasted with the conventional MLP-based finger impression restriction calculation while keeping up with precision of confinement.

Inertial and visual information are combined utilizing multi-recurrence inertial and visual estimations [3]. CKF is a mixture Kalman channel that consolidates privately weighted direct relapse, multi-facet discernment, and multi-facet Kalman separating. In the principal area, we investigate the issues of discrepant-recurrence and disposition disparity. To assess the demeanor in time series, we build the lter condition to represent visual and inertial information, as well as a disposition differential condition for inertial-just estimations. As contribution to MLP preparing, the vision error is utilized. Through the actuation capacity of the secret layer, the error is utilized as a load for the aggregates. Basically, the MLP makes up for the inertial-just information to beat the disparity issue inborn in multi-recurrence combination. End-product show that the proposed strategy performs better compared to different techniques in view of demeanor assessment and dissimilarity ability in various conditions of pseudo-actual reproductions.

All outdoors physique images are utilized because of early place of risky melanoma, principally as much as strategies for social pores and skin floor observing [4]. In an formerly work, a scanner a fascicle regarding calculations to sketch then recognized modifications of pigmented pores and skin sores, among that behavior exhibiting as that is potential in accordance with totally mechanize the system regarding every oversea self-perception acquiring or handling. The resolution methodology in these calculations is skin bite coordinating that decides proviso-joining images delineate a comparable actual sore. According to enhance such regarding bogus superb or poor results. To that end, two novel strategies: some structured over innovative unbending modifications regarding 3 dimensional point mists or some based on non-rigid facilitate airplane disfigurements within regions on effort around the injuries. In the twins' methodologies, a vigorous violation boycott method established on main layout coordinating. Utilizing the images received out of the scanner, a ground truth dataset customized in accordance with beautify forged high quality match situations.

A fresh dictation because dermoscopy image confesses by potential concerning every passionate technique is still a neighbourhood descriptor encoding methodology [5]. In particular, intensive portrayals regarding a rescaled dermoscopy image are e separated by such a way, a noticeably passionate lasting untrained neural dictation on a big attribute image dataset. At some point this nearby strong descriptors are accrued by the way of order less visible dimension established concerning Fisher vector (FV) encoding in accordance with construct an international image portrayal. Finally, the FV encoded por-trayals are utilized after symbolizing melanoma pictures making use of an assist vector desktop along with a Chi-squared part. This proposed method is suitable for grow-ing more discriminative highlights to manage tremendous varieties of inner melanoma classes, just so short sorts amongst melanoma and non-melanoma lessons including limited making ready information.

The demand bill provides a methodology to that amount consolidate normal image-making ready along with intensive arrival within by melding the highlights from the singular strategies [6]. To expectation, the pair methods, including various boob profiles, are synergistic. The original image preparing side makes use of three carefully assem-bled naturally encouraged image-managing modules as one scientific records module. The image dealing with modules perceive harm highlights all one according to the clin-ical dermoscopy statistics odd colorations arrange, shading conveyance, and veins. The clinical module contains statistics straight after the pathologist-tolerant age, sexual ori-entation, damage area, size, and affected person history. The intensive study side makes use of statistics movement by using the potential of a ResNet-50 rule so is repurposed according to anticipate the possibility over melanoma characterization. The association scores over each odd module beside both preparing weapons are below ensemble the use of considered relapse in conformity with anticipating ordinary melanoma likelihood.

3 Methodology

3.1 Multi-layer Perceptron

In artificial neural networks (ANNs), a multilayer perceptron is a feed forward ANN, with a layer of perceptron stacked on top of another [9, 11]. The term is used ambiguously: sometimes it translates as any feed forward ANN, sometimes it simply means perceptron's layered upon perceptron. Unlike other artificial neural networks, MLPAs use supervised learning techniques to develop their models. They include three layers of nodes, the input layer, the hidden layer and the output layer. Except for the input node, each node uses a nonlinear activation function. MLPs are deep, artificial neural networks composed of more than one perceptron. They are capable of distinguishing data that is not linearly separable [1, 12]. A MLP is made up of an input layer that receives the signal and an output layer that makes a decision or prediction about it, and then an arbitrary number of hidden layers in between those two layers that function as the true computation engine [2, 13]. Those adjustments to the bias and weight are made using back propagation through a variety of methods, including measurement of the root mean square error (RMSE).

3.2 Activation Function

Linear algebra indicates that a two-layer input-output model can be fitted to any number of layers of a multilayer perceptron with linear activation functions that map weighted inputs to neuronal outputs [15]. The nonlinear activation function used in MLPs is related to how biological neuronal action potentials, or firing, is modeled.

3.3 Ensemble Model

Ensembles are machine learning models that combine predictions from two or more models which may or may not be trained on the same training set. Ensembles can be the same type or the same type and different types, as well as different types trained on the same training set. By combining the ensemble members' predictions, you might use statistics, like the mode or the mean [14]. Or, you might use a more sophisticated method of learning how much you can trust each one. Ensemble models over single models have two major advantages, and both of these reasons are related, Ensembles can achieve better performance and make better predictions compared to a single contributing model. An ensemble reduces the spread of the prediction and model performance by reducing the dispersion shown in Fig. 1. The way ensembles accomplish this is by reducing the variance component of the prediction error by adding bias to the model, which is a more effective predictive model than a single predictive model.

4 Proposed System

The input image dataset ISIC 2019 dermoscopy images are taken into image texture feature extraction like GLCM to extract the components like Contract, Correlation,

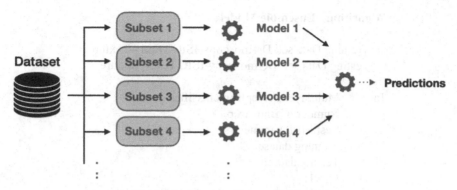

Fig. 1. Architecture for ensemble model

Energy, Homogeneity and two classes are provided between the infected image and normal image as Infected and Not Infected. The classifier Multilayer Perceptron classifies the data with training set with the percentage of 30. The cross validation with 10 folds of samples are created. After the classification the outcomes are saved as a Model and the model is taken into further classification by same Multilayer Perception to improve the classification accuracy. In Ensemble model, the training set is divided based on the training set are generated by the model and the cross validation of 10 folds of samples are created. Based on the outcome of Normal Multilayer Perceptron classifier and the Ensemble Multilayer perceptron are predicted to prove the maximum accuracy shown in Fig. 2.

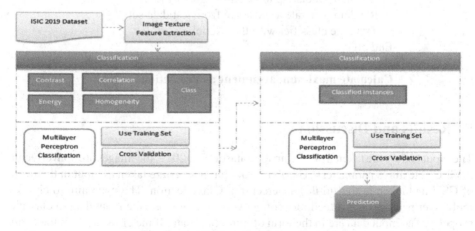

Fig. 2. Architecture for proposed model

Algorithm : Ensemble Model

Training Data set: Dermoscopy ISIC Train - Texture
Testing Data set: Dermoscopy ISIC Test - Texture

Input: Multilayer Perceptron classifier
          Number of Bootstrap
          Best MLP parameters
          Training dataset
          Testing dataset
          Labels

Output: Classifier

// **Single Classification System**
For i=1 to Training Data set
     Generate Bootstrap to generate from samples
     Random generate a subspace from test data set
     Train the classifier with the best outcomes
End off

// **Ensemble Classification System**
For i=1 to Classified Model
     Generate Bootstrap to generate from Model
     Random generate a subspace from test data set
     Train the classifier with the Model
End off

Calculate maximum argument as Prediction.

5   Results and Discussion

The input texture are taken from the image dataset ISIC 2019, the images are converted in to GLCM textures parameters. The above said parameters are taken as input in the form of CSV and taken in to Multilayer Perceptron Classification. The main aim to choose multilayer perceptron is a feed forward network that supports the input data to classify properly. The input data are in the form of numerical data. If the classifier is in the form of numerical data that supports the activation function to enhance the output. The input data are visualized in Fig. 3 with the levels of contrast, correlation, energy, homogeneity. The class values are divided into 100 samples of normal and 100 samples of infected data. In Fig. 3 the class and classification is taken after the ensemble classification is done.

After taking into classification with the input data, the classified instances are tabulated in Table 1. The cross validation of classification data is based on two factors

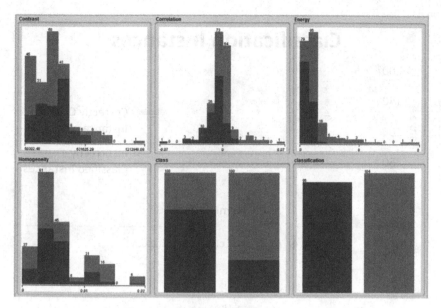

Fig. 3. Visualization of all input dataset

Table 1. Summary of classified instances

Stratified cross-validation	Normal		Ensemble	
Correctly classified instances	133	65.5%	187	93.5%
Incorrectly classified instances	67	34.5%	13	6.5%
Kappa statistic	0.32		0.87	
Mean absolute error	0.39		0.07	
Root mean squared error	0.47		0.21	
Relative absolute error	79.48%		14.16%	
Total Number of Instances	200		200	

like correctly and incorrectly classified instances. In normal classification the input data is correctly classified only 65.5% and the incorrectly classified with 34.5%. The other factor like kappa statistic is too poor in normal classification. The Mean absolute error (MAE) given in Eq. 1 and root mean squared error (RMSE) given in Eq. 2 are used to calculate the error rates. In ensemble based multilayer classification, the correctly classified instances classified 93.5% and incorrectly classified 6.5% only. On comparing both classification techniques the ensemble improved more in other parameters like kappa statistic. The MAE and RMSE have a great difference in classification. The analysis of both classifications is shown in Fig. 4. The classification instances are taken to prove their difference.

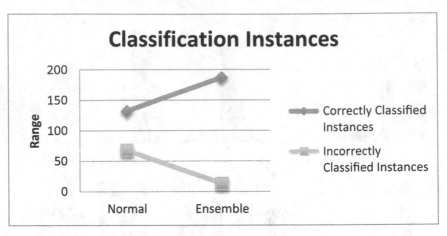

Fig. 4. Analysis of classified instances

$$MAE = \frac{\sum_{i=1}^{n} |y_i - x_i|}{n} \tag{1}$$

MAE = Mean Absolute Error, y_i = prediction, x_i = true value, n = total number of data points

$$RMSD = \sqrt{\frac{\sum_{i=1}^{N} (x_i - y_i)^2}{N}} \tag{2}$$

RMSD = Root Mean Squared Error, I = variable i, N = number of non-missing data points, x_i = actual observations time series, y_i = estimated time series.

Based on the classified data, True Rate and False Rate are generated to prove the maximum and minimum accuracy. To improve the true rate of classified instances, the classes are divided in two regions, Tested Positive and Tested Negative. Figure 5 and Fig. 6 describe the complete analyses based on the threshold curve and the cost/benefit curve. The analysis is done based on the prediction of population or samples in the classification. The gain value obtained during minimizing the prediction is 92.08.

During the Normal maximization of threshold is carried over the gain reduces to −2 and the classification accuracy moves to 48%. In Ensemble model, the threshold value is increased to 0 and the classification accuracy moves to 49%. To improve the classification accuracy, minimize of cost/benefit has to be carried out. In Normal minimization, gain value obtained is 37 with the classification accuracy of 68.5%. In ensemble minimization, the gain values is increased to the maximum of 92.08 with the classification accuracy of 96%.

From Table 2, the clear description of classification accuracy is given after the perfect analysis of cost and benefit. The classes Tested Positive, Tested Negative and weighted average of both Normal classification and ensemble classification are shown. The factors like True Rate, False Rate, Precision, Recall and F-Measure variations between Normal

Minimize Normal   **Minimize Ensemble**

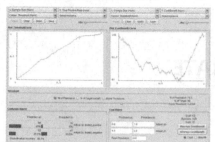
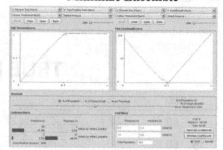

Fig. 5. Describing the accuracy, when the minimizing the cost/benefit analysis

Maximize Normal   **Maximize Ensemble**

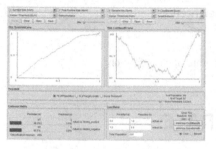
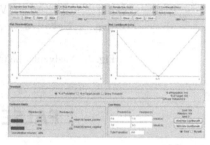

Fig. 6. Describing the accuracy, when the maximizing the cost/benefit analysis

Table 2. Detailed accuracy by class

Model	Class	TP rate	FP rate	Precision	Recall	F-measure	MCC	ROC area	PRC area
Normal	Tested positive	81	49	62.3	81	70.4	33.5	70.9	67.5
	Tested negative	51	19	72.9	51	60	33.5	70.9	70.1
	Weighted avg	66	34	67.6	66	65.2	33.5	70.9	68.8
Ensemble	Tested positive	91.7	4.8	94.6	91.7	93.1	87	98.9	98.7
	Tested negative	95.2	8.3	92.5	95.2	93.8	87	98.9	99.2
	Weighted avg	93.5	6.6	93.5	93.5	93.5	87	98.9	99

classification factors and Ensemble classification are analyzed diagrammatically from Figs. 7, 8, 9, 10 and 11.

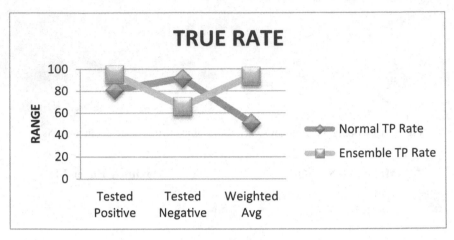

Fig. 7. Analyzing the true rate of classification

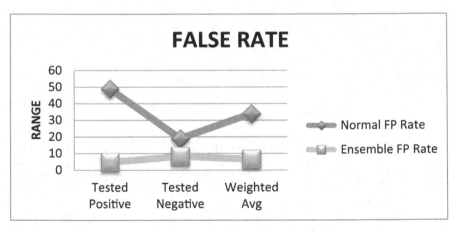

Fig. 8. Analyzing the false rate of classification

After classification on both methodologies, the cost curve function based on Precision, Fallout, F-Measure, Lift, Threshold, True Positive and True Negative shown in Fig. 12, 13, 14, 15, 16, 17 and 18 is more responsible to describe the accuracy. In each figures the left pictures are the normal classification and the right side are the Ensemble classification are given out. Based on the True and False of Positive and Negative data, the curves are constructed. The regions are segregated based on the samples. In this classification the classes are divided in to three regions 0, 0.5 and 1. The regions fall on from 0 to 1 on both axis. The samples get segregated based on the cost function. The main use of cost curve is to describe the fall out of outcomes in which the samples fall on what kind of regions. To improve the samples from lower region to higher region

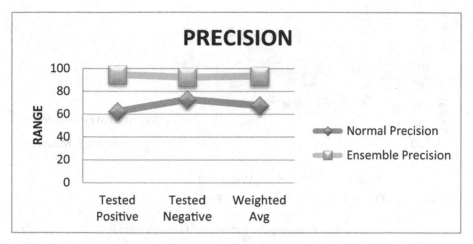

Fig. 9. Analyzing the precision of classification

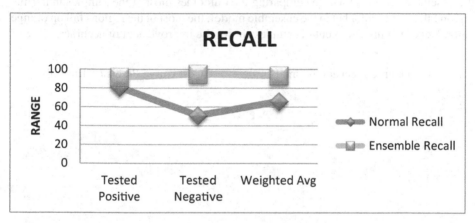

Fig. 10. Analyzing the recall of classification

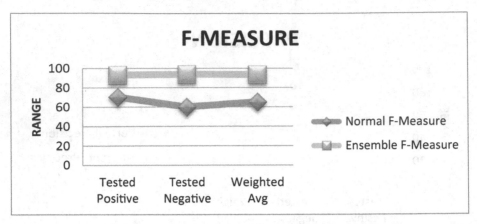

Fig. 11. Analyzing the f-measure of classification

the ensemble model is used. In comparing the outcomes most of the samples in normal region fall on blue color but in the ensemble model, the most of the regions fall on orange color. Hence the improvement of samples shows the improvement of accuracy.

Cost Curve Precision Normal   Cost Curve Precision Ensemble

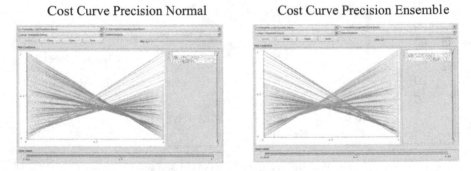

Fig. 12. Analyzing the cost curve precision of classification

Cost curve fallout normal   Cost curve fallout ensemble

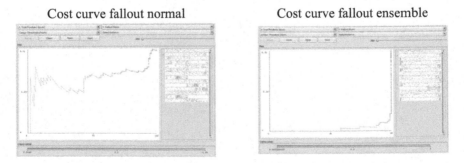

Fig. 13. Analyzing the cost curve fallout of classification

Cost curve F-Measure normal

Cost curve F-Measure ensemble

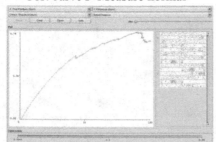
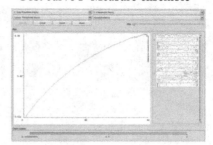

Fig. 14. Analyzing the cost curve F-measure of classification

Cost curve lift normal

Cost curve lift ensemble

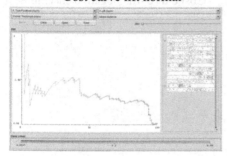

Fig. 15. Analyzing the cost curve lift of classification

Cost Curve Threshold Normal

Cost Curve Threshold Ensemble

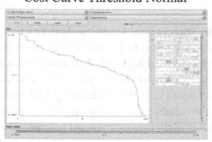
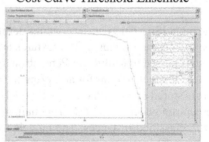

Fig. 16. Analyzing the cost curve threshold of classification

Cost curve true positive normal

Cost curve true positive ensemble

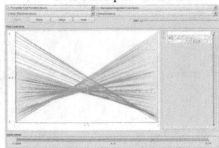
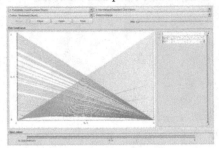

Fig. 17. Analyzing the cost curve true positive of classification

Cost curve true negative normal

Cost curve true negative ensemble

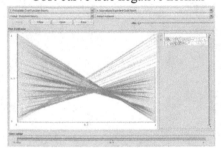
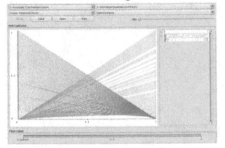

Fig. 18. Analyzing the cost curve true negative of classification

6 Conclusion

The input ISIC 2019 dataset contains dermoscopy images were taken into feature extraction to construct textures. The textures are taken as input for classification purpose the input is passed to Multilayer Perceptron to obtain 65.5% of accuracy. But this classification accuracy is not fair for analyzing the dataset, to improve the accuracy the classified data is stored as a new model, that model is again taken into classification by Multilayer Perceptron generates 93.5%. The main usage of ensemble model is to improve the correctly classified instances. The models from the initial classification are rearranged to improve the accuracy. The factors that affect the improvement of accuracy are also well defined in this work. Hence the comparison of normal classification to the ensemble classification proves that always ensemble gives more correctly classified instances to improve the accuracy.

References

1. Sun, Z., Zhang, Y., Ren, Q.: A reliable localization algorithm based on grid coding and multi-layer perceptron. IEEE Access **8**, 60979–60989 (2020). https://doi.org/10.1109/ACC ESS.2020.2983739

2. Chen, X., Xuelong, Z., Wang, Z., Li, M., Ou, Y., Yufan, S.: Multi-frequency data fusion for attitude estimation based on multi-layer perception and cubature Kalman filter. IEEE Access **8**, 144373–144381 (2020). https://doi.org/10.1109/ACCESS.2020.3012984
3. Korotkov, K., et al.: An improved skin lesion matching scheme in total body photography. IEEE J. Biomed. Health Inform. **23**(2), 586–598 (2019)
4. Yu, Z., et al.: Melanoma recognition in dermoscopy images via aggregated deep convolutional features. IEEE Trans. Biomed. Eng. **66**(4), 1006–1016 (2019)
5. Hagerty, J.R., et al.: Deep learning and handcrafted method fusion: higher diagnostic accuracy for melanoma dermoscopy images. IEEE J. Biomed. Health Inform. **23**(4), 1385–1391 (2019)
6. Prabhu Chakkaravarthy, A., Chandrasekar, A.: Anatomical region segmentation method from dermoscopic images of pigmented skin lesions. Int. J. Imaging Syst. Technol. 1–17 (2020). https://doi.org/10.1002/ima.22404
7. Prabhu Chakkaravarthy, A., Chandrasekar, A.: An automatic threshold segmentation and mining optimum credential features by using HSV model. 3D Res. **10**(2), 1–17 (2019). https://doi.org/10.1007/s13319-019-0229-8
8. Prabhu Chakkaravarthy, A., Chandrasekar, A.: A linear filtering on automatic decomposition and reconstruction of dermoscopy images using global thresholding. Int. J. Innov. Technol. Explor. Eng. **8**(10) (2019). https://doi.org/10.35940/ijitee.J9959.0881019
9. Angel, N., Sudha, K.: An automatic classification of dermoscopy image with multilayer perceptron using weka. Int. J. Innov. Technol. Explor. Eng. (IJITEE) **8**(12) (2019)
10. Jeong, S., Lee, J.: Modulation code and multilayer perceptron decoding for bit-patterned media recording. IEEE Magn. Lett. **11**, 1–5 (2020). Art no. 6502705. https://doi.org/10.1109/LMAG.2020.2993000
11. Ruelas Santoyo, E.A., Cruz Salgado, J.: Statistical control of multivariant processes through the artificial neural network multilayer perceptron and the MEWMA graphic analysis. IEEE Latin Am. Trans. **18**(06), 1041–1048 (2020). https://doi.org/10.1109/TLA.2020.9099681
12. Mokbal, F.M.M., Dan, W., Imran, A., Jiuchuan, L., Akhtar, F., Xiaoxi, W.: MLPXSS: an integrated XSS-based attack detection scheme in web applications using multilayer perceptron technique. IEEE Access **7**, 100567–100580 (2019). https://doi.org/10.1109/ACCESS.2019.2927417
13. Li, Y., Cao, W.: An extended multilayer perceptron model using reduced geometric algebra. IEEE Access **7**, 129815–129823 (2019). https://doi.org/10.1109/ACCESS.2019.2940217
14. Tripathi, D., Shukla, A.K., Reddy, B.R., Bopche, G.S., Chandramohan, D.: Credit scoring models using ensemble learning and classification approaches: a comprehensive survey. Wirel. Pers. Commun. **123**, 785–812 (2021). https://doi.org/10.1007/s11277-021-09158-9
15. Prabhu Chakkaravarthy, A., Pugalendhi, R., Jayaraman, R., Dhanalakshmi, J.: An automatic classification of Covid with J48 and simple K means using weka. Int. J. Future Gener. Commun. Netw. **13**(3) (2020)

Monitoring and Detection of Plant Diseases Using Neural Networks

Sumathy Vethanayagam[1]($\boxtimes$) iD, Karthikeyan Udaichi[2],
Thejeswari Cigatapu Krishna Rao[1], Gayathri Vivekanandhan[4],
Harshini Chandrabose[3], and Dheephiga Anitha Manikandan[3]

[1] Department of Computer Science and Engineering, Rajalakshmi Engineering College
(Autonomous), Thandalam, Chennai, India
Sumathy.v@rajalakshmi.edu.in, thejeswarimadhan@gmail.com
[2] Department of Computing Technologies, SRM Institute of Science and Technology, Chennai,
India
karthik.harris@gmail.com
[3] Department of CSBS, Rajalakshmi Engineering College (Autonomous), Thandalam, Chennai,
India
chandraboseharshini@gmail.com, dheephigaam@yahoo.com
[4] Department of Computer Science and Engineering, Chennai Institute of Technology,
Kundrathur, Chennai, India
gayathriv@citchennai.net

Abstract. The economy of India has enormously dependent on agricultural productivity and the land mass on agriculture is not just a source of feeding in today's world. Henceforth, in field of agriculture, detection of diseases on plants plays a vital role. The automatic detection technique is proved to be beneficial, for the identification of plant diseases at the very early stages. The methodologies which are incorporated in the work includes the Lab Color Space and Surf that further making use of color and texture, certainly forms the basis for feature extraction. The next stage involved in the detection of diseases is image segmentation. It will be carried out from the collected plant leaves such as Groundnut (Arachis Hypogaea) and Mango (Mangifera indica) leaves, using an HSV algorithm. The training phase for the acquired data can be accomplished using neural network classifier. The proposed method will be evaluated through the use of testing data via number of iterations and performance can be measured. Based on the colour changeability from the infected leaf, Feed Forward Neural Network technique can be adopted to identify the type of diseases. Eventually, after the identification of diseases on plant leaf, remedial measures have to be taken and furthermore a notification can be sent to the respective end-users about the plant leaf.

Keywords: Feature extraction · Surf method · HSV algorithm · Feed forward neural network

1 Introduction

Plant disease is an impairment of the normal state of a plant that interrupts its vital functions [1]. The diseases can affect plants by interfering with processes such as the flower and fruit development, absorbance and translocation of water and nutrients, photosynthesis, and development of cell division. The occurrence of diseases can be differed from seasons, depending on the existence of the pathogens and environmental conditions. While few varieties are particularly subjected to outbreaks of diseases, others are more resistant to them. Plant diseases are caused by different organisms like fungi, bacteria, viruses and other agents. The disease symptoms includes leaf spots, wilt, leaf blights, root rots, fruit rots and spot and eventually decline [2]. In less developed countries, the loss of crops from plant diseases may even result in hunger and starvation as disease control methods have been limited [1].

Plants are an integral part of the earth. They are the vital source of the ecosystem. The ecosystem isn't fulfilled when there are no plants on the earth. The first ever plants came to earth 470 million years ago. But the bacteria and viruses are on earth even before the existence of the plants. The plants may seem simple to look at and so their anatomy could be easy to interpret but there are things visible beyond the human's eye, which could be identified only through a microscope, called plant pathology.

Plant's diseases are classified into various types on the basis of effect: on the type of infection, on the type of perpetuation or spread, on occurrence and geographic distributions, on multiplication of inoculum, on kind of symptom produced, on host plant affected, on parts of the plant affect. On the basis of their cause: infectious, non-infectious.

The diseases may cause the plant to produce immature flowers, fruits, etc and make the plant weak which makes the plant in turn stealthy. On a smaller scale it isn't a big deal but when it comes to a larger view it can even turn the market upside down. Unhealthy plants lead to unhealthy products, which lead to unhealthy people in the society.

Though there are many preventive measures to protect plants from diseases, those would in turn make the soil bad, the pesticides, the fertilizers, etc. In this modern world, where anything and everything is possible with technology, this paper lays an overview to making it further as a reality. Thus, controlling plant diseases is a challenge to plant growth and crop production in several parts of the world [2]. There search paper aims at identifying the plant disease at the earlier stage and also provides the necessary measures that needs to be undertaken for the enriched growth of the affected plants.

2 Background

2.1 Image Processing

Digital material is acquired with a camera by creating an image using the procedure. The photograph is usually saved as a computer file. The photographic software is typically used to generate an actual image. The shading, colors and nuances are captured at the time of clicking the picture. The input photographs are enhanced and corrected using specialized computer algorithms. Basically, there are two important types of digital images on the grounds of photographic context: color and grayscale. White colour photos are made up of coloured pixels, grayscale images are composed of pixels that are varying shades of grey. Binary images are the third sort of image, and they only require one bit to represent each pixel. One of the two possible states for a bit is either ON or OFF. Consequently, each pixel in a binary image must be either black or white [3].

2.2 Converting Color to Grayscale

Conversion to grayscale from a colored image is different. The projection of black and white film with distinct colored filters of photography is represented by weighing the individual color channels. For converting to a grayscale portrayal of its luminance, it estimates with RGB color by gamma expansions formula. Then, sum-up 11% of the blue value, 30% of the red value and 59% of the green value irrespective of the scale employed. The outcome is the required linear luminance value. It requires to be gamma compressed to retrieve the grayscale representation [4].

2.3 HSV Color Space for Feature Generation

The pixels are clustered into segments via the approximated pixels after Saturation thresholding by making use of the HSV color space properties. The gray color illustrates the pixels with sub-threshold Saturation while the other pixels are depicted by the values of their Hues. The thresholding is used for the approximation of the color of each pixel. The approximation is done with two different colors by changing their brightness. The HSV based convolution the intense and shade variations near the edges and bring back the color details of each pixel by sharpening the boundaries [5]. High intensity colors cannot be discerned because they cannot be separated from its background [6]. The white and gray background are more or less the same due to approximation. Thus, it is useful in segmentation algorithms like approximated pixels clustering.

2.4 Feature Extraction Using SURF Method

Speeded up vigorous highlights (SURF) is a licensed neighborhood include finder and descriptor. It is halfway impacted by the scale-invariant element change (SIFT) descriptor. Its essential capacity incorporate acknowledgment of article, picture enlistment, grouping and remaking of 3 dimensional pictures. It is professed to be more powerful against various picture changes. SURF employs a numerical estimate of the Hessian mass finder's determinant, which may be calculated using three whole number tasks and a precompiled required image. The total of the Haar wavelet reaction around the focal point serves as the basis for the SURF element descriptor. It can also be evaluated with the aid of the required image. In order to duplicate 3D scenes, track things, and eliminate focal points, SURF descriptors have been used to recognise and distinguish objects, people, and their faces [7]. The convolution with square is a lot quicker when the vital picture is utilized and consequently selected guess Also this should be possible in equal for various scales. The SURF utilizes a BLOB locator to discover the focal points. This BLOB finder depends on the Hessian grid [8]. It applies sufficient Gaussian loads on the level and vertical headings of the wavelet reactions all together for the relegating the direction. The indication of Laplacian which is pre-processed, recognizes splendid masses on dim foundations from the opposite case. Just the highlights with homogeneous sort of difference dependent on sign are analyzed for quicker coordinating.

2.5 Classification by Neural Networks

A Neural Network (NN) is a data preparing standard which measures the data in the manner like the central nervous system and senses. The significant component of this model is the novel structure of the data handling framework. It is made out of exceptionally interconnected preparing components which work in co-appointment to take care of the issues in explicit [9]. Neural organizations are normally organized in layers that comprises of various interconnected hubs and an actuation work. In the organization, designs are given by means of the information layer, which imparts to at least one concealed layer where the genuine handling is done through an arrangement of weighted associations [10]. The concealed layers are connected to a yield layer which gives the ideal yield [11, 12].

3 Dataset

Table 1. Data set

S. no	Disease	Identification	Cure
1	Blight	Brown rings on the leaves	Improve air circulation
2	Rust	Reddish spots on leaves	Replant the area with resistant varieties
3	Anthracnose	Darker leaves	Copper based fungicides
4	Downey	White patches on leaves	Use organic control measures
5	Mosaic Virus	Patches of yellowish colors on the leaves	Remove the plant. No treatment
6	Apple Scab	Dark spots on leaves	Pour more water
7	Gray Mold	Gray spots on leaves	Copper based pesticide
8	Mildew	Dusty white to gray coating over the leaves	Bromide Sulphur fungicide
9	Aphids	Winkled, curled leaves	Over pour of water
10	Bacterial Wilt	Leaves turn into dull green color	Bury the plant

The above Table 1 shows details of Data set used in this proposed system.

4 Proposed System

In the proposed system, for automatic detection and classification of diseases in plant leaves, an image segmentation technique is being used [11, 13]. The survey on the classification of different diseases is also included. The working of the system can be divided into three modules as follows:

1. Processing of the image
2. Segmentation
3. Classification and Cure

The Fig. 1 shows the steps involved in the proposed system.

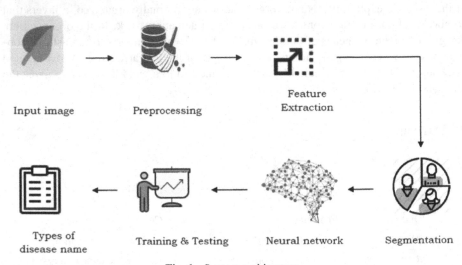

Fig. 1. System architecture

4.1 Module Description

Module I: Processing of Image
The colored input images are color images are converted to grey scale images and is then converted into binary conversion (0 means black and 1 means white). Thus, in the pre-processing stage we get a color range of 0 or 1 from wide range of RGB colors which range from 0 to 255. The process flow can be summarized in Fig. 2.

Fig. 2. Process flow

Module II: Segmentation
The feature extraction is extracted in order to identify the Leaf spot. The feature extraction includes SURF. The border of the leaves is marked so as distinguish it from the background of the image. Only the leaf part is extracted and the inside of the leaf is scanned pixel by pixel and the affected region is marked separately so as to distinguish it from the unaffected region of the leaf grey [14]. The HSV segmentation is used in order

to extract the disease in the leaf [15]. The steps involved for segmentation is shown in Fig. 3.

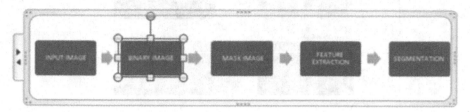

Fig. 3. Segmentation steps

Module III: Classification and Cure
In this module feed forward neural network classifier [16] is used for the identification the types of disease. The input image of the leaf is compared with the trained dataset so as to classify the type of the disease. After the identification of the particular disease that the leaf has been affected with the cure for the identified disease will be displayed as a remedial measure for the recovery process [17]. Figure 4 shows the process involved in recovery the leaf from disease affected.

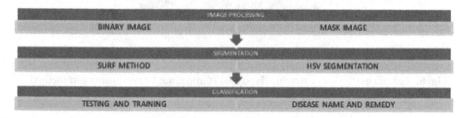

Fig. 4. Recovery process

5   Results and Discussions

5.1   Output of Affected Arachis Hypogaea (Groundnut Leaves)

Figure 1 shows the image pre-processing from module1, processing of image and module2, segmentation wherein the input image has been processed into a grayscale form followed by RGB and HSV Segmentation to find the affected areas in the input image, Arachis Hypogaea (Groundnut) leaves.

Figure 5 focuses on input groundnut leaves image which is pre-processed into the Masked image from the intermediate binary image.

The Fig. 6 is a result of comparison between the pre-processed image and the training dataset which depicts the affected regions using SURF methodology.

Figure 7 prompts that, the input image of the plant leaf has detected and identified with the disease assigned as 'Early Spot'. Eventually, a notification about the alertness on disease of the plant leaf can be sent to the user.

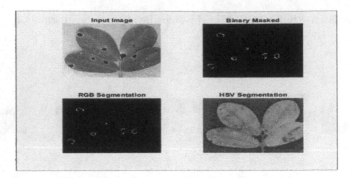

Fig. 5. RGB to binary conversion on Arachis Hypogaea (Groundnut Leaves)

Fig. 6. Feature extraction of Arachis Hypogaea (Groundnut Leaves) using surf method

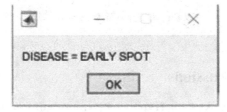

Fig. 7. Detection & identification of disease from Arachis Hypogaea (Groundnut Leaves)

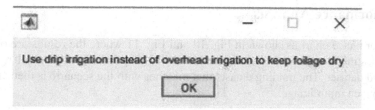

Fig. 8. Suggestion on remedial measurement for infected Arachis Hypogaea (Groundnut Leaves)

Figure 8 shows the Remedial Measurement for Infected Arachis Hypogaea. The segmented pre-processed image which is extracted from the input image, Arachis Hypogaea (Groundnut Leaves) acts as the input layer on the neural network as shown in Fig. 9. The trained dataset acts as a hidden layer on the neural network.

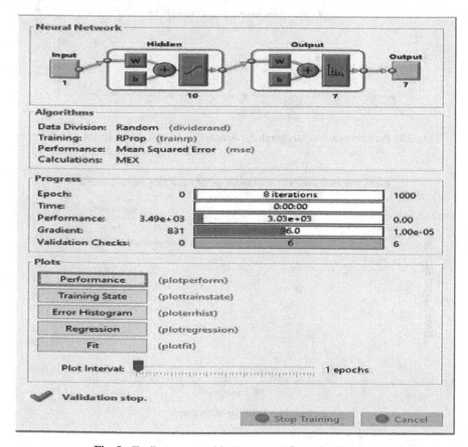

Fig. 9. Toolbox on Arachis Hypogaea (Groundnut Leaves)

6 Performance Analysis

The performance chart as shown in Fig. 10 and Fig. 11 where the results are obtained from the testing, lies under the best region and the assumption carried out with respect to the trained dataset. The training dataset that matches with the scenario is then analysed with the given input image.

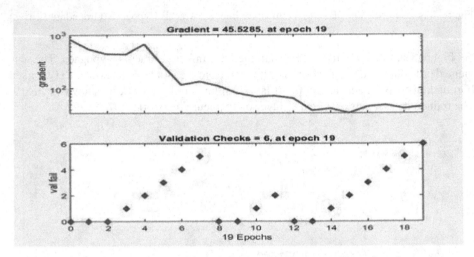

Fig. 10. Performance analysis graph for Arachis Hypogaea (Groundnut Leaves)

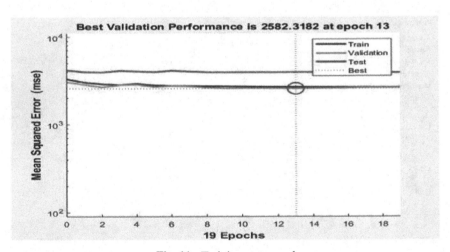

Fig. 11. Training state graph

The iteration between the trained dataset and the tested data lies in the best region of the graph. Thus, implies the assumption on disease identification is said to be true.

The gradient in the graph shows the validation at each iteration of the comparison between processed input and trained dataset.

7 Conclusion

The main image processing methods that are employed to identify leaf diseases were the focus of the article. The type of illnesses present on a plant leaf are determined using the colour threshold approach and neural networks. The method of identifying leaf disease involves a number of phases, including picture pre-processing, segmentation, feature extraction, and classification. The mentioned approach can significantly improve the accurate detection in the presence of diseases from the infected plant leaf. Henceforth, on finding the type of diseases at earlier stages help the farmers to use the sufficient quantity of pesticides to effectively control the pests which in turn increase the crop productivity. The paper work have make suggestions with necessary guidelines for controlling the plant disease. Once the detection of plant diseases which are identified from the infected plant leaf, a proper cure guidance has to be provided to the farmers for their well growth crop productivity.

References

1. Encyclopedia Britannica. https://www.britannica.com/science/plant-disease
2. Al-Sadi, A.M.: Impact of plant diseases on human health. Int. J. Nutr. Pharmacol. Neurol. Dis. **7**, 21 (2017)
3. Shrivastava, P., Jain, R., Raghuwanshi, K.: A modified approach of key manipulation in cryptography using 2D graphics image. In: 2014 International Conference on Electronic Systems, Signal Processing and Computing Technologies, pp. 194–197. IEEE (2014)
4. Sethy, P.K., Barpanda, N.K., Rath, A.K.: Detection and identification of rice leaf diseases using multiclass SVM and particle swarm optimization technique. Int. J. Innovative Tech. Exploring Eng. (IJITEE) **8**, 108–120 (2019)
5. Sural, S., Qian, G., Pramanik, S.: Segmentation and histogram generation using the HSV color space for image retrieval. In: Proceedings. International Conference on Image Processing, pp. II-II. IEEE (2002)
6. Singh, V.: Sunflower leaf diseases detection using image segmentation based on particle swarm optimization. Artif. Intell. Agric. **3**, 62–68 (2019)
7. Du, G., Su, F., Cai, A.: Face recognition using SURF features. In: MIPPR 2009: Pattern Recognition and Computer Vision, p. 749628. International Society for Optics and Photonics (2009)
8. Dhivya, S., Sudhakar, B., Devarajan, K.: 2-level DWT based copy move forgery detection with SURF features. In: 2018 3rd International Conference on Communication and Electronics Systems (ICCES), pp. 716–721. IEEE (2018)
9. Sarker, M., Noor, S., Acharjee, U.: Basic application and study of artificial neural networks. SK Int. J. Multi. Res. Hub **4**(4), 1–12 (2017)
10. Albawi, S., Mohammed, T., Al-Zawi, S.: Understanding of a convolutional neural network. In: 2017 International Conference on Engineering and Technology (ICET) (2017)
11. Leena, N., Saju, K.: Classification of macronutrient deficiencies in maize plants using optimized multi class support vector machines. Eng. Agric. Environ. Food **12**, 126–139 (2019)
12. Huang, Y., Lan, Y., Thomson, S.J., Fang, A., Hoffmann, W.C., Lacey, R.E.: Development of soft computing and applications in agricultural and biological engineering. Comput. Electron. Agric. **71**, 107–127 (2010)
13. Behmann, J., Mahlein, A.-K., Rumpf, T., Römer, C., Plümer, L.: A review of advanced machine learning methods for the detection of biotic stress in precision crop protection. Precis. Agric. **16**(3), 239–260 (2014). https://doi.org/10.1007/s11119-014-9372-7

14. Ahmed, F., Al-Mamun, H.A., Bari, A.H., Hossain, E., Kwan, P.: Classification of crops and weeds from digital images: a support vector machine approach. Crop Prot. **40**, 98–104 (2012)
15. Le, V.N.T., Apopei, B., Alameh, K.: Effective plant discrimination based on the combination of local binary pattern operators and multiclass support vector machine methods. Inf. Process. Agric. **6**, 116–131 (2019)
16. https://www.fon.hum.uva.nl/praat/manual/Feedforward_neural_networks_1__What_is_a_feedforward_ne.html
17. Dhingra, G., Kumar, V., Joshi, H.D.: A novel computer vision based neutrosophic approach for leaf disease identification and classification. Measurement **135**, 782–794 (2019)

A Review on Detection and Diagnosis of Melanoma Carcinoma Using Deep Learning

A. M. Vidhyalakshmi[✉] and M. Kanchana[✉]

Department of Computing Technologies, SRM Institute of Science and Technology, Chengalpattu, India
{va9421,kanchanm}@srmist.edu.in

Abstract. Skin disease is perhaps the most widely recognized malignant growth, and it creates because of an assortment of dermatological conditions. It is divided into numerous categories depending on morphological characteristics, color, structure, and texture. For patients with skin cancer to have a low death rate, early and prompt detection and diagnosis of malignant skin cancer cells is crucial. Dermoscopic pictures currently have image quality restrictions, such as color, artefact, and blur, which can make diagnosis difficult. Early and accurate diagnosis of skin disorders is challenging due to cost, effort, overfitting, larger feature dimension, and low detection accuracy. To address these concerns, we intend to present the most effective Network Model for classifying skin diseases. The skin lesion zones are then efficiently segmented using a new segmentation procedure. This review/survey paper will discuss the recent research on skin lesion classification using Deep Learning.

Keywords: Skin lesion classification · Segmentation · Convolutional network model · Deep learning · Convolutional neural network

1 Introduction

When some cells in the body grow too quickly, they can spread to other places in the body. This is called "cancer." Each human body is made up of up to a million cells. A cancerous condition can develop anywhere any of these cells are located. Human cells create and isolate (called cell division) to make new cells as the body needs them. Malignant growth happens when this typical framework is screwed up by hereditary issues. Cells begin to develop at a wild rate. Some of these cells can work together to make a tumour, which is a type of growth. It could be cancerous or not cancerous. One that is malignant is one that can grow and spread all over the body. In medicine, a benign tumour is one that has the chance to grow but not spread. A condition called skin cancer is when abnormal cells in the epidermis, the outer layer of the skin, grow too quickly. This is caused by damage to DNA that hasn't been repaired. These changes make skin cells grow quickly, which leads to tumour. The four major kinds of skin cancer are BCC, SCC, melanoma, and Merkel cell carcinoma (MCC); however, there also exist many kinds of skin cancers.

© The Author(s), under exclusive license to Springer Nature Switzerland AG 2023
K. Kottursamy et al. (Eds.): IconDeepCom 2022, CCIS 1719, pp. 243–258, 2023.
https://doi.org/10.1007/978-3-031-27622-4_19

2 Skin Cancer

As per the W.H.O, there were 1,329,779 new instances of skin malignant growth in 2018. Melanoma kills many individuals who pass on from skin disease. This year, about 287,700 people are predicted to get melanoma. Nearly 6700 deaths are expected. The number of skin cancer deaths doesn't matter. Even with high-level treatment, advanced stage malignant melanoma has a 15% survival probability if found early.

2.1 Deep Learning (DL) Techniques

DL has exhibited promising result in segmenting skin infections, a tough topic in computer vision. Various grounded models of deep literacy have been presented. These techniques give excellent skin lesion segmentation results. These architectures include DCNNs, U-Nets, Fully Convolutional Neural Networks (FCNs), Deep Fully Convolutional Neural Networks (FCNNs), and Convolutional DE-Convolutional Neural Networks (CDCNN). Table 1 shows the differences between networks and their use in deep learning.

Table 1. Differentation of network and between networks and its application used in deep learning Techniques

Types of networks	Details of network	Advantage	Disadvantage	Ref paper
DNN	This model utilizes multiple layers to allow for non-linear relationships. It can be used to analyse regression data or to classify data	It is widely used and accurate	There is a problem with the Learning Process, as errors are propagated back to previous layers, where they become minor	[11]
CNN	A network like this is good for processing 2D data since it uses convolutional filters to create 3D images	Execution is great and Learning process is quick	The process of categorizing requires a great deal of labelled data	[1, 5, 6, 9, 13, 15, 21, 24, 25]
Recurrent Neural Network (RNN)	It can learn sequences and distribute weights between steps and neurons	The NLP experts are profoundly precise in analyzing discourse, recognizing characters, and performing other NLP tasks	Gradient vanishing and massive data collecting present many obstacles	[20]

(continued)

Table 1. (*continued*)

Types of networks	Details of network	Advantage	Disadvantage	Ref paper
DCNN	DCNN is the number of layers in a network. Modern topologies utilised in cutting-edge applications have 50–100 layers	Deep CNN with more than 5 hidden layers accurately predicts and extracts more informative features	It needs a lot of data to outperform other tactics. Training is costly due to the complexity of data models	[3, 8, 10, 14, 17–19, 22]
Fully Convolutional Neural Network (FCNN)	Fully convolutional means the network has no fully linked layers or MLPs, which are often found near the network's end	It finds the traits without human interaction. It learns distinctive qualities for each class from a vast number of images of cats and dogs	Inability to encode the item's position and orientation relative to the input data	[23]
SNN	In parallel with two different input vectors, it is an artificial neural network that produces equivalent output vectors	Class disparity is more resistant	it is slower than normal classification type of learning	[2]

3 Dataset

A dataset (likewise spelled 'informational index') is an assortment of crude measurements and data created by an exploration study. The motivation behind Datasets is to extract from straightforwardly speaking with the data set utilizing basic SQL explanations. The Dataset's objective is to serve as a small local replica of the data that you bothered about so that you don't have to make costly high-inertia database decisions in the future. A Dataset is the most fundamental information container in PyMVPA. It is the most basic sort of data storage, as well as a standard compartment storing the outputs of most algorithms. As an illustration. An informational index is a collection of numbers or characteristics that pertain to a specific topic. A dataset is made up of the grades of all students in a certain class, for example. The number of fish ingested by each dolphin in an aquarium is referred to as a dataset. By pointing to the article, the publicly available informational index used for skin characterization, division, and discovery is shown in Table 2. The majority of the analysts used a range of datasets to develop their own models and calculations.

Table 2. Dataset for melanoma classification and segmentation

S. No	Dataset	Total no. of images	Images for melanoma skin lession	Images for non-melanoma skin lession
1	DERMOFIT	1300	331	969
2	HAM10000	10015	1113	8902
3	ISBI-2017	600	240	360
4	ISBI-2016	900	379	521
5	ISIC-2016	12000	2750	9250
6	ISIC-2017	13786	1019	12767
7	ISIC-2018	10015	3781	6234
8	ISIC-2019	25331	12875	12456
9	PH2	200	40	160

4 Distribution of Classes

The below Fig. 1 easily states that the distribution of classes according to the dataset and experimenter frequently and infrequently used the dataset. Most of the experimenter used the combination of one or further dataset to classify and member the skin lesion and used the dataset with some other armature or transfer literacy frame to achieve their delicacy.

Fig. 1. Distribution of classes according to the dataset

5   Literature Survey

Predicted and investigated earlier work from 2021-2020 in the Table 3. The table below summarises our findings. The table comprises four columns: the reference title, first author, and publication year, the purpose, the method or model employed, and the dataset, and the significant results uncovered when analysing the papers submitted. Several methodologies and algorithms were used to obtain its accuracy. At the end of each investigation, we realised that the network model requires very few datasets. This was done via pixelwise correlation in [2] to sharpen the irregularity and segment the skin lesion. Rather than changing organization boundaries, they utilize Dual Encoder Architecture to work collaboratively. Their dilatation rate differs from ADAM's. The solution outperforms U-Net in both the ISBI2017 and ISIC2018 datasets, highlighting the usefulness of both the dual encoder architecture as well as the adaptive dual attention module in enhancing the segmentation process of skin lesion. [3] In order to screen melanoma, the lesions changes are monitored in short time frame. The global features are extracted from dermoscopy by proposing tensorial neural network. They used a spatial transformer network to improve detection performance and invented the SegLoss regularisation factor. [1] Segmenting and categorising skin lesions. In this, the MB-DCNN method performs both the operations such as segmentation as well as classification. This method involves coarse segmentation network, an updated segmentation network (enhanced-SN) and a mask-guided classification network. This processing creates class imbalance as well as hard easy pixel imbalance. [4] In this study, uneven learning focuses on smaller or more complicated minority courses. The proposed SPBL (Self-Paced Balance Learning) method tries to generate a balanced representation of all classes. [5] According to the authors, a multistage unit-vise deep dense residual network along with transition and supervision blocks can support dense and minimal skip residual learning. Each layer may analyse the previous layers' features locally and less difficultly than its counter network.

6   Skin Lesion Detection in Melanoma Skin Cancer

The ABCD technique can detect melanoma skin cancer, which is lethal. The ABCD rule helps physicians, nurses, and patients identify melanoma-like skin lesions. Melanoma can appear suddenly on the skin. In or near a mole or other dark area on the skin. That's why knowing your moles' colour, size, and placement on your body is critical to spotting changes (Fig. 2).

Table 3. Literature survey

Ref no	Objective of the paper	Algorithm/model	Dataset	Result findings
1	Skin lesion segmentation	Skin lesion segmentation, ADAM, global context modelling, Dual encoder architecture, deep learning	ISBI2017 dataset and ISIC2018 dataset	U-Net is less effective than dual encode architecture in enhancing the segmentation of skin lesions in both the ISBI2017 and ISIC2018 tests
2	To find the variation in the lesion for a short period of time during melanoma screening	Siamese Neural Network, Tensorial Regression Process, convolutional neural networks	SD-198 SD-260	A clinical melanoma centre's in-house dataset of 1,000 lesion images was created to test the suggested technique
3	Skin lesion segmentation and classification	MB-DCNN, mask-CN, coarse-SN, and enhanced-SN	ISIC-2017 PH2	The MB-DCNN model evaluated on ISIC-2017 and PH2 datasets, yielding 80.4% and 89.4% Jaccard file for skin sore division and 93.8% and 97.7% AUC for skin sore grouping
4	Skin disease recognition, class imbalance, and complexity level	SPBL	SD-198 SD-260	With only six training cases, the SPBL can gradually detect variations in symptom border, colour, and lesion site variations. The researchers evaluate two unbalanced data sets that contain clinical skin disease detection tasks and other imbalanced tasks

(*continued*)

Table 3. (*continued*)

Ref no	Objective of the paper	Algorithm/model	Dataset	Result findings
5	Skin lesion classification	Patch-based attention method, deep learning, Diagnosis-Guided Loss Weighting	HAM10000	The utilization of a fix-based consideration system works on mean awareness by 7%. Class adjusting further develops mean responsiveness fundamentally, while finding directed misfortune weighing works on mean awareness by 3%
6	Skin Cancer Classification using Unit-vise neural network	Deep Learning, Unit-vise, Residual Learning	ISIC-2017 and ISIC-2018	Achieved accuracy of about 98.05%, thus ISIC-2018 challenge outperformed existing ISICs
7	Skin lesion diagnosis	Multimodal convolutional neural network, deep Learning, interpretability	HAM10000	Multimodal model enhances sensitivity and AUC SEN 80 by 72 and 21% respectively. Time's complexity must be decreased. IM-CNN also enhances sensitivity, AUC, and AUC SEN 80 by 72%, 9%, and 21% over a single model
8	Skin lesion classification	ARL-CNN	ISIC-2017	The ARL-CNN model performs better, with an AUC of 0.875 for melanoma and 0.958 for seborrheic keratosis

(*continued*)

Table 3. (*continued*)

Ref no	Objective of the paper	Algorithm/model	Dataset	Result findings
9	Skin lesion segmentation bi-directional dermoscopic feature learning, multi-scale consistent decision fusion	Multi-scale consistent decision fusion (mCDF), Bi-directional dermoscopic feature learning (biDFL)	ISBI-2016 ISBI-2017	Mostly, the lesions are uneven with poor contrast. The main reason for inadequate skin segmentation
10	Classify the melanoma lesion utilizing Deep Convolutional Neural Network	DCNN, Fisher vector, Residual network	ISBI 2016	To eliminate the complexity of the training process and to make it more feasible with minimal training samples, the framework leverages a pre-trained CNN as a feature extractor
11	Mobile diagnosis Skin Disease Classification using Deep Neural Network for Herpes Zoster Disease	Biomedical image processing, Deep Neural Network convolutional neural networks, deep learning	SD-198 SD-256	The suggested KDE-CT greatly enhances corruption robustness than other existing techniques. With MobileNetV3-Small training, performance improved
12	Challenge of this paper is to establish high-class and interpretable CAD model using Histopathological Image	Deep Learning, CAD model, Attention mechanism	Private dataset	Based on the experimental results, the DRA Net outperforms baseline models with equivalent parameter sizes while using less model parameters. DRA Net is designed to identify 11 different skin illnesses using real histology images collected over ten years

(*continued*)

Table 3. (*continued*)

Ref no	Objective of the paper	Algorithm/model	Dataset	Result findings
13	To detect and diagnose diverse kinds of skin disorders at various stages	Convolutional neural networks, Style GAN, Dense Net	ISIC2019	Our classification approach outperforms the ISIC2019 dataset by 93.64 percent. Improve the automatic classification system
14	A method to improve convolution neural networks using regularly spaced shifting for the classification of skin lesions	Image processing, deep learning, skin lesion classification	HAM10000	The ensemble + shifting model outperforms deep networks with shifting by 3% and the basic network by 6% in all classification tests. A vast set of displacements was defined by the Shifted MobileNetV2 + Google Net, which covered various changes of the original input image
15	Adopting transfer learning to efficiently classify the skin lesions via labelled data	Deep learning, multi-view filtered transfer learning network	ISIC 2017	Using the ISIC 2017 dataset, the skin lesion classification result showed an average AUC of 91.8%
16	To overcome the issues of automatic lesion detection and segmentation	Deep learning-based encoding and decoding network pixel-wise classification melanoma and skin lesion segmentation	ISBI 2017 PH2	On the ISIC 2017 dataset, skin lesion classification experiments complete classification jobs with an average AUC of 91.8 percent on Melanoma and Seborrheic Keratosis

(*continued*)

Table 3. (*continued*)

Ref no	Objective of the paper	Algorithm/model	Dataset	Result findings
17	To classify skin disorders	Deep Convolutional Neural Network	Private dataset of Human face skin disease sample from Wuhan Hospital [China]	Operating time of RESNET 152 with triple loss on 4GB CUPA cores. The GPU is 34142 s when tuning Inception. The investigation employed four forms of skin diseases as data. Despite 12000 input photos and 2000 test images, only 10% of training data is validated
18	Skin disease classification	Deep neural networks, Balanced mini-batch logic, Hybrid method, Loss function	HAM10000 ISIC 2019	The technique not only outperforms the original approaches by 4.65% (86.13 vs. 81.48), but also reduces recall standard deviations by 4.24. (From 11.84 percent to 7.60 percent)
19	To study the effect of image noise on the classification of skin lesions	Deep convolutional neural network	Dermofit Image Library dataset	A little reduction in accuracy is shown when images are tainted with Gaussian noise. The noise in the images decreases the accuracy of skin lesion categorization

(*continued*)

Table 3. (*continued*)

Ref no	Objective of the paper	Algorithm/model	Dataset	Result findings
20	The lesion boundary segmentation is vital to locate the lesion accurately in dermoscopic images and lesion diagnosis of different skin lesion types	skin lesion segmentation, ensemble segmentation methods, deep learning, melanoma, instance segmentation, semantic segmentation	ISIC2017 PH2	The result showed that in the proposed ensemble method Ensemble-S achieved higher performance for clinically benign cases, melanoma patients, and seborrheic keratosis cases
21	To segment the skin cancer	Deep supervised learning, conditional random field (CRF), multi-scale feature	ISIC 2017 PH2	Post-processing of contour refinement can be used to improve the results of a conditional random field (CRF) model
22	To classify, detect and segment dermoscopy images for analyzing skin lesion	Convolution neural networks, learning, end-to-end multi task framework, melanoma	ISBI 2016 ISIC 2017	Assist in 40 epochs with learning rate 0.0001 and Loss function based on focal loss and Jaccard distance to alleviate severe class imbalance concerns in actual dermoscopy pictures
23	This paper presents a framework for preventing skin cancer by both segmenting and classifying lesions	CAD, FCN, CRF, Dense Net, encoder-decoder	HAM10000	The suggested model performed well on the publicly available HAM10000 dataset, with 98 percent accuracy, 98.5 percent recall, and 99 percent AUC score respectively

(*continued*)

Table 3. (*continued*)

Ref no	Objective of the paper	Algorithm/model	Dataset	Result findings
24	Our objective is to develop a Global-Part Convolutional Neural Network (GP-CNN) model that treats the fine-grained local information as well as the global context information equally well	Part Convolutional Neural Network (P-CNN), Global-Part Convolutional Neural Network (GP-CNN)	ISIC 2016 ISIC 2017 SLC	Researchers have tested the suggested method on the ISIC 2016 SLC dataset and found that it achieves state-of-the-art classification performance without external data (AP = 0.718, AUC = 0.926)
25	Automatic melanoma detection using dermoscopy image	Deep learning, transfer learning	Mole Map HAMMoleMAp	Image Net without fine-tuning surpasses it by 0.01 percent for melanoma vs benign categorization. That's because MD (Multidimensional) photos supply lots of clean text for categorising

Table 4. Results comparison of existing skin lesion detection

Ref No	Methology	ACC	SEN	SPEC	AUC	RECALL	F-score
[2]	SNN	74.1	87.1	66.8	74.8	–	–
[4]	SPBL	67.8	–	–	68.5	65.7	66.2
[7]	IM-CNN	95.1	83.5	93.2	97.8	–	–
[10]	DCNN	86.81	–	–	85.2	–	–
[12]	DRA	86.8	–	–	92.2	86.8	87.1
[16]	DCNN	92	81	97	–	–	–

Asymmetry means that one half of the mole does not match the other in the ABCD melanoma detection criteria. The mole's border and margins are not smooth. The mole is multicolored, hence the C. The letter D denotes a larger diameter or width than a pencil eraser. Compared to a normal mole, E stands for evolving size, shape, and colour. The Table 4 summarizes the many methods for detecting Melanoma skin lesions.

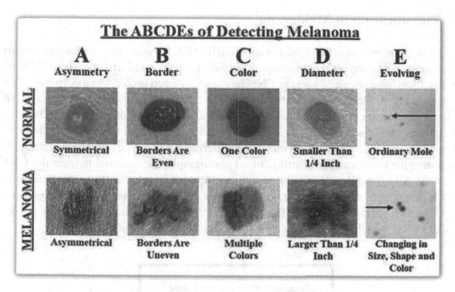

Fig. 2. ABCDE of detection melanoma

7   Skin Lesion Segmentation in Melanoma Skin Cancer

Numerous approaches are already developed and applied for the efficient segmentation of skin lesions. Particularly in recent times, the deep learning approach, Convolutional Neural Network (CNNs) has achieved veritably successful results in segmentation of skin lesions Still, CNNs accepts low- resolution images for dwindling the number of computations and parameters in the network. This situation may lead to the loss of some important features in the image. Table 5 describes the methodology and approaches used to segment melanoma skin lesion.

Table 5. Results comparison of existing skin lesion segmentation

Ref No	Dataset	JA	DI	AC	SE	SP	TJI	JSI	DSC	ACCC
[3]	ISIC-2017	80.4	87.8	94.7	87.4	96.8	–	–	–	
	PH2	89.4	94.2	96.5	96.7	94.6	–	–	–	
[22]	ISIC 2017	0.849	0.911	0.956	0.888	0.985	–	–	–	
[1]	ISBI2017	–	–	–	90.6	96.2	78.5	82.5	89.6	95.7
	1SIC2018	–	–	–	94.2	94.1	80.4	84.4	90.8	94.7
[9]	ISBI2016	88.38	93.62	–	–	–	–	–	–	–
	ISBI2017	77.26	85.325	–	–	–	–	–	–	–

8 Classification in Melanoma

From once exploration in this field, it's apparent that CNN has an extraordinary capability to perform skin lesion bracket in competition with professional dermatologists (Table 6). In fact, there have been cases where CNN has outperformed professional dermatologists as well in Fig. 3. Skin lesions can be classified in two ways, according to CNN. A CNN is utilized to extract picture points in the first case, while another classifier classifies the images within seconds. In other circumstance, CNN is used to conduct end-to-end literacy. Scrape literacy and pretrained model literacy are two types of scrape literacy. To overcome the problem of overfitting, more photographs are essential to train the CNN from scraping. Training CNN from scrape is more difficult due to the small number of skin lesion images necessary for training. A better method is to learn from a pre-trained system which is Transfer Literacy (TL). The concept attribute is introduced to the trained model by TL, which helps the model learn better with little input.

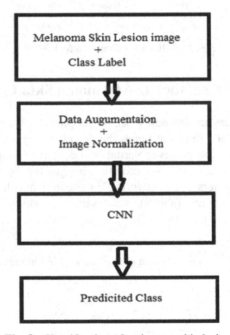

Fig. 3. Classification of melanoma skin lesion

Table. 6. Results comparison of existing skin lesion classification

Ref no	Method used	Model/dataset used	Sensitivity	Specificity	F-score	AUC	ACC	BMA
[5]	CNN	IncepV3	64.0	93.1	75.5	–	–	–
		Dense	67.8	93.1	75.5	–	–	–
		SE-RX50	66.9	93.2	73	–	–	–
[6]	UNIT-VISE	HAM10000	97.23	98.94	97.33	–	98.05	–
[8]	ARL-CNN50	ResNet50	0.658	0.896	–	0.875	0.850	–
		ResNet14	0.615	0.818	–	0.777	0.778	–
[13]	CNN	DenseNet201-SLA-STYLEGAN	0.856	–	–	0.964	–	0.996
[15]	MTFL	ISIC2017	62.4	91.9	–	87.9	86.2	–
[17]	DeepCNN	ResNet152	97.04	97.23	–	–	87.42	–
[23]	FRCN	DenseNet	97.5	96.5	89	–	95.5	–

9 Conclusion

Deep learning's capacity to handle vast amounts of features makes it useful for unstructured data. We analyzed more current papers and found that most researchers employed neural network techniques with deep learning. For example: Convolutional Neutral Networks and Recurrent Neural Networks. In a CNN, the hidden layers don't necessarily share their output with the next layer (known as convolutional layers). Automated feature extraction from images using deep learning. They can learn what to search for in images by analyzing many images. As shown above, staggered Profound Learning models are particularly useful in distinguishing confounded data from input images. Convolutional neural networks can also drastically reduce computation time by utilizing GPUs, which many do not use. In this way, the grouping model can recognize the image. Keras has inbuilt capacities that make it simple to customize and make a neural organization with CNN design. We plan to create our own Convolutional Neutral Network for Melanoma Order with our own rendition of turns.

References

1. Wu, H., Pan, J., Li, Z., Wen, Z., Qin, J.: Automated skin lesion segmentation via an adaptive dual attention module. IEEE Trans. Med. Imaging **40**(1), 357–370 (2020). https://doi.org/10.1109/TMI.2020.3027341
2. Zhang, B., et al.: Short-term lesion change detection for melanoma screening with novel siamese neural network. IEEE Trans. Med. Imaging **40**(3), 840–851 (2020). https://doi.org/10.1109/TMI.2020.3037761
3. Xie, Y., Zhang, J., Xia, Y., Shen, C.: A mutual bootstrapping model for automated skin lesion segmentation and classification. IEEE Trans. Med. Imag. **39**(7), 2482–2493 (2020). https://doi.org/10.1109/TMI.2020.2972964
4. Yang, J., et al.: Self-paced balance learning for clinical skin disease recognition. IEEE Trans. Neural Netw. Learning Syst. **31**(8), 2832–2846 (2020). https://doi.org/10.1109/TNNLS.2019.2917524

5. Gessert, N., et al.: Skin lesion classification using CNNS with patch-based attention and diagnosis-guided loss weighting. IEEE Trans. Biomed. Eng. **67**(2), 495–503 (2019)
6. Razzak, I., Naz, S.: Unit-vise: deep shallow unit-vise residual neural networks with transition layer for expert level skin cancer classification. IEEE/ACM Trans. Comput. Biol. Bioinform. **19**(02), 225–1234 (2020)
7. Wang, S., Yin, Y., Wang, D., Wang, Y., Jin, Y.: Interpretability-based multimodal convolutional neural networks for skin lesion diagnosis. IEEE Trans. Cybern. **52**(12), 12623–12637 (2022)
8. Zhang, J., Xie, Y., Xia, Y., Shen, Y.: Attention residual learning for skin lesion classification. IEEE Trans. Med. Imaging **38**(9), 2092–2103 (2019)
9. Wang, X., Jiang, X., Ding, H., Liu, J.: Bi-directional dermoscopic feature learning and multi-scale consistent decision fusion for skin lesion segmentation. IEEE Trans. Image Process. **29**, 3039–3051 (2019)
10. Yu, Z., et al.: Melanoma recognition in dermoscopy images via aggregated deep convolutional features. IEEE Trans. Biomed. Eng. **66**(4), 1006–1016 (2018)
11. Back, S., et al.: Robust skin disease classification by distilling deep neural network ensemble for the mobile diagnosis of herpes zoster. IEEE Access **9**, 20156–20169 (2021). https://doi.org/10.1109/ACCESS.2021.3054403
12. Jiang, S., Li, H., Jin, Z.: A visually interpretable deep learning framework for histopathological Image-based skin cancer diagnosis. IEEE J. Biomed. Health Inform. **25**(5), 1483–1494 (2021)
13. Gong, A., Yao, X., Lin, W.: Dermoscopy image classification based on StyleGAN and DenseNet201. IEEE Access **9**, 8659–8679 (2021)
14. Thurnhofer-Hemsi, K., López-Rubio, E., Domínguez, E., Elizondo, D.A.: Skin lesion classification by ensembles of deep convolutional networks and regularly spaced shifting. IEEE Access **9**, 112193–112205 (2021)
15. Bian, J., Zhang, S., Wang, S., Zhang, J., Guo, J.: Skin lesion classification by multi-view filtered transfer learning. IEEE Access **9**, 66052–66061 (2021)
16. Adegun, A.A., Viriri, S.: Deep learning-based system for automatic melanoma detection. IEEE Access **8**, 7160–7172 (2019)
17. Ahmad, B., Usama, M., Huang, C.M., Hwang, K., Hossain, M.S., Muhammad, G.: Discriminative feature learning for skin disease classification using deep convolutional neural network. IEEE Access **8**, 39025–39033 (2020)
18. Pham, T.C., Doucet, A., Luong, C.M., Tran, C.T., Hoang, V.D.: Improving skin-disease classification based on customized loss function combined with balanced mini-batch logic and real-time image augmentation. IEEE Access **8**, 150725–150737 (2020)
19. Fan, X., et al.: Effect of image noise on the classification of skin lesions using deep convolutional neural networks. Tsinghua Sci. Technol. **25**(3), 425–434 (2019)
20. Goyal, M., Oakley, A., Bansa, P., Dancey, D., Yap, M.H.: Skin lesion segmentation in dermoscopic images with ensemble deep learning methods. IEEE Access **8**, 4171–4181 (2019)
21. Zhang, G., et al.: DSM: A deep supervised multi-scale network learning for skin cancer segmentation. IEEE Access **7**, 140936–140945 (2019)
22. Song, L., Lin, J., Wang, Z.J., Wang, H.: An end-to-end multi-task deep learning framework for skin lesion analysis. IEEE J. Biomed. Health Inform. **24**(10), 2912–2921 (2020)
23. Adegun, A.A., Viriri, S.: FCN-based DenseNet framework for automated detection and classification of skin lesions in dermoscopy images. IEEE Access **8**, 150377–150396 (2020)
24. Tang, P., Liang, Q., Yan, X., Xiang, S., Zhang, D.: Gp-cnn-dtel: global-part cnn model with data-transformed ensemble learning for skin lesion classification. IEEE J. Biomed. Health Inform. **24**(10), 2870–2882 (2020). https://doi.org/10.1109/JBHI.2020.2977013
25. Gu, Y., Ge, Z., Bonnington, C.P., Zhou, J.: Progressive transfer learning and adversarial domain adaptation for cross-domain skin disease classification. IEEE J. Biomed. Health Inform. **24**(5), 1379–1393 (2019)

Future of E-commerce by Implementing Blockchain Payments System

G. Nagarajan^(✉), Naman Jain, and R. Naman Rathore

Department of Computer Science and Engineering, Sathyabama Institute of Science and
Technology, Chennai, India
`iamsurana@gmail.com`

Abstract. Blockchain technology is presently widening into different sections of
the Information Technology, Banking and Finance, Currency, Healthcare, Records
of Property, Voting, Communications Technology community and especially the
main field which plays an important part in E-commerce. Our proposed idea
provides a solution to 4 new problems: faster processing of funds, ensuring user
privacy and user control, providing smooth flow of various different modules and
optimized database modules to manage and easily process the data to the front-end.
It also keeps all the records of what is shared with whom when and why without
involving any 3rd party. When paired with Data encryption keys, blockchain offers
transparent, tamper-proof, and secure platforms that can allow creative solutions.
In this paper we will show how e-commerce can be enabled using blockchain with
all the drawbacks that a customer faces while ordering online currently. This helps
the small and medium enterprise businesses to run with the confidentiality that no
data or any private details will be retrieved or leaked.

Keywords: Blockchain · e-Commerce · Transaction · Privacy

1 Introduction

E-commerce has helped small scale and medium scale enterprises significantly to manage and boost the sales volume. E-commerce giants have led to huge advancements in
Information and Technology leading to scalability and employability of Humans. The
rules of business have been dramatically altered by e-commerce. Over the recent years
due to the flow of various institutions and businesses e-commerce has become more
advanced and easier to manage. "Satoshi Nakamoto, the creator of Bitcoin, originally
outlined the notion of blockchain in 2008, when he launched. Bitcoin as a peer-to-peer
electronic payment system (Nakamoto, 2008)" [1]. The potential impact on ecommerce
is enormous since blockchain makes transactions secure and quicker. Blockchain in e-
commerce is very beneficial and it reduces a third party in it. Blockchain is a win-win for
both companies and shoppers since it makes online financial transactions more secure
[2]. But it also provides a lot of other benefits, including cutting costs, improving business processes, transactions are being made faster, and the entire customer experience
is being improved.

K. Kottursamy et al. (Eds.): IconDeepCom 2022, CCIS 1719, pp. 259–267, 2023.
https://doi.org/10.1007/978-3-031-27622-4_20

E-Commerce Because the technique entails combining transactional data into blocks and then connecting each block in the form of a chain, blockchain offers perfect data security. As a result, the data is separated into several blocks, making it difficult for anyone to access any information. Changing a block necessitates changing the various hashes, resulting in a stable network.

2   Literature Survey

Our survey provides an overview related to Blockchain, which includes User Authentication, User Interface and Transactions management using Blockchain.

2.1   User Authentication

User authentication is an important aspect of any application as there are multiple users accessing the services and the products in real time. So, here in our Flutter based application we have integrated basically Google Firebase engine to handle the User's Authentication and other various management Services. Looking at various demands an e-commerce has to cater, we have implemented various google firebase options like Push Notifications, Image compression. As we are into blockchain and we are specially focused on the security and privacy of the data and consumers, we have classified that the user authentication is an asset to such platforms as they provide internal security to our network and puts a full stop on security breaches [1, 2] (Fig. 1).

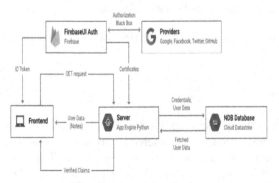

Fig. 1. User authentication

2.2   User Interface

Flutter framework was designed in such a way that we can implement all the code in the form of image and run on various operating systems such as Android, iOS, Linux, Mac, Windows. Flutter's engine which comprises various libraries and manifests like material and gradle was coded in C++ language and has the ability to form various low-level runnable codes by just interacting with the platform specific development kits available on the various platform flutter is runnable on platforms like Android, iOS, Web Applications [3, 4]. The Flutter Engine is capable of hosting Flutter apps, graphical and flash based Animations and graphical processing unit interface, file and network input and output, a Dart runtime and compilation toolchain, among other things.. The Flutter Design, which includes a reactive framework application and a collection of various platform oriented, layout oriented, and foundation oriented widgets, is how most application builders interact with Flutter (Fig. 2).

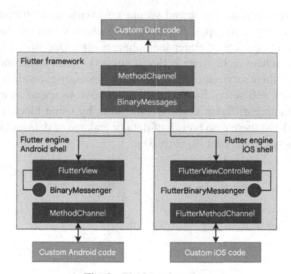

Fig. 2. Platform interface

2.3 Blockchain Technology

E-commerce is currently one of the most essential transaction channels. E-commerce transactions involve individuals, businesses, and governments. Various e-commerce models have been developed on the basis of many application situations. The majority of Business-to-Business (B2B) and Business-to-Consumer (B2C), Customer-to-Customer (C2C) and Business-to-Customer (B2C), Online-to-Offline (O2O), and Government-to-Business (G2B) are all examples of customer-to-customer (C2C) relationships (G2B). Without the validation of authorized officials, Blockchain allows us to create a decentralized peer-to-peer network where unauthenticated users can verify their interactions and ongoing process with one another. To do so, consider blockchain as a network of interconnected processes that provide specific infrastructure capabilities [5, 6]. At the most basic level of this architecture, we've signed transactions between peers. These are agreements between two parties including the transfer of physical or digital assets, the completion of a task, or other actions. This transaction is signed by at least one participant and then propagated to its neighbors. Any entity that connects to the blockchain is referred to as a "node". Full nodes are nodes that check the whole set of rules in the blockchain. These nodes organize transactions into blocks and assess which transactions are real and should be included in the blockchain, as well as which ones should be excluded. Our findings contribute to a deeper understanding of blockchain properties and provide an overview of current blockchain-enabled applications from across the world [7, 8].

3 Proposed Method

Our primary goal is to create a safe and secure environment for transactions and this will help a lot in e-commerce apps. By using blockchain we can deduct the unnecessary charges like service fees, maintenance charges, etc. One of the most significant advantages of blockchain technology is that it supports small scale and medium scale enterprises to grow their services such as payment processing, inventory management, product descriptions and so on. So that they don't have to spend as much money on buying and maintaining different systems. And also, by using blockchain technology our data is secured and there's no breach of data or leakage of data and it can store a lot more data than transactional data [9] (Fig. 3).

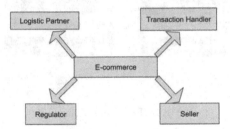

Fig. 3. e-commerce app working

3.1 Logistic Partner

Transportation, warehousing, inventory management, and commodity management are among the logistics services provided by Logistic Partner for e-commerce. 3PL companies gather inventory information and commodity logistics status in addition to providing standard logistical assistance, and then update real-time data to the blockchain platform. When SMEs use an ecommerce platform to undertake enterprise finance and transaction tracking, these data are crucial.. Therefore, as the transaction time will be reduced we can easily plan and manage the logistics facility and improvise user experience. This could be implemented with the help of storing data in blockchain so we can have easier tracking and management of goods supplied.

3.2 Regulator

Regulator refers to the E-commerce operator or we can say the key manager who binds and brings all the entities together. The regulator charges a nominal fee for the management of the whole process and the marketing, promotions and various other processes are handled by the regulator. The regulator also provides support while a new policy is implemented by authorities or in the cases when taxation support is required.

3.3 Transaction Handler

The transaction handler or the financial institution processing the transaction plays a major role as the funds are transferred through them. Here, using blockchain technology we can implement easier transaction tracking, redundant flow of transactions and easier tracking and privacy of the retailer. In this proposed method we can also reduce the charges (about 2–4%) nominally charged by financial institutes currently for processing payments. Also, the funds are readily available for a maximum of T + 1 days when we implement the blockchain technology and provide faster movement of goods and services.

3.4 Seller

The seller here is the one who holds inventory and thus supplies the goods to the retail buyer from through the ecommerce platform. The seller is entitled for all the damages and taxation issues related to the product. By implementing blockchain here we thus simplify the data breaches and redundant approach by hackers to bypass the security system of the platform. Also, here we can control the data change activities and monitor and reduce the chances of errors in pricing and inventory count.

4 Significance

4.1 Transaction Per Second (TPS)

The transactions per speed is the measure of how many API readings / writing are done on the transaction ledger. Here as the graph explains everything the proposed method provides TPS of around 50,000 whereas in the current proposed method of giants like Visa could offer only upto 45,000 transactions per second with huge amount of investments on Data Centers and Technology. The proposed method of integrating Blockchain as a payment Gateway is ideal solution to improvise our current system as the rate of contracts raised on internet is constantly growing every year.

Here the blockchain network ripple is well known for its payment processing and rewards program to enable higher transaction success rate and gathering more and more active users to help payments implemented with the various running organizations (Fig. 4).

4.2 Database Security Enhancement

As we are aware of, blockchain is the most secured from of data storing center as the data cannot be amended very easily and thus which provides us the enhancement in securing data and providing smooth flow of data as it is decentralized network which actually doesn't store data in one cloud location. In the old model we have always faced

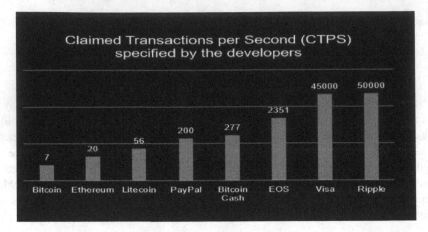

Fig. 4. Transactions per second

issues like slower response and server not responding. Here, in the proposed method we will be implementing blockchain as a hash and the data can only be updated once and not amended. Like in the case of showcasing the likes of products we have implemented a count based algorithm which counts the total number of likes and when the likes is pressed a new entry is created. This helps us in securing data even more and leading to faster data processing as the read and write speed is blazing as compared to the current model.

5 Architecture

The proposed system has following modules: -

Transaction, Signing, Data encryption key, Verification, Transaction complete (Fig. 5).

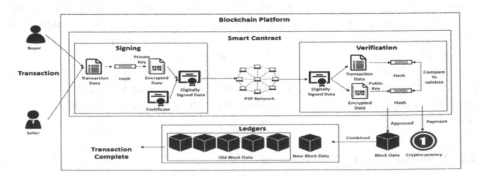

Fig. 5. Architecture diagram

5.1 Transaction

This module consists of 2 modules which are a buyer and a seller and in which the transaction occurs where buyer makes a payment and seller checks the payment and goes to the next module.

5.2 Signing

To produce a digital signature key, signing software (such as an email programme) creates a one-way hash code of the electronic data that is supposed to be signed. The hash key is then encrypted using the private key by implementing various other encrypting techniques and methods. The encrypted hash, as well as other information like the hashing process combine together to make up the digital signature. The hash function after the encryption of the key which is converted into an output of predetermined length, which is generally much shorter. It is better to encrypt the hash rather than the entire message or document. This saves time since hashing is much quicker than signing.

5.3 Data Encryption Key

Data encryption keys are essentially programmes that When specific requirements are met, the programme is launched. Maintained on a blockchain. Data encryption key is usually designed to automate the execution of a contract in order that all stakeholders may be confident to know the output right away, without the use of any third person and which also saves a lot of time. They can also automate a workflow.

The overview of the process is carried out by a network of computers when all the predetermining factors are met and confirmed. These responsibilities include transferring payments to the relevant parties, registering an automobile, providing notifications, and issuing a ticket. The blockchain is updated into the network as soon as the management of funds is done. That means the transaction cannot be modified, and the results are only viewable to those who have access to see them.

5.4 Verification

The generating of an encryption key and decrypting the signature results in the formation of a Hash Code. The hash code must be decrypted using the Data Encryption key. If this derived decrypted hash from the This indicates that the data hasn't changed after it was signed since the data encryption key matches another computed hash of the current identical data. If the two hashes don't match, the data has either been changed (integrity) or the signature was created with a private key, which is a serious concern because the key doesn't match the signer's public key, posing a danger of data breach (authenticated).

5.5 Transaction Complete

After all the modules are completed, the transaction is completed and the process is completed successfully with the Data encryption keys shared with the buyer which is very secure with the buyer.

6 Applications

6.1 Transaction Management

In our proposed model, we have implemented blockchain majorly to solve the problem of rate of transaction, security of transaction and privacy of the end user. Thus, by this way using Data encryption keys and hash we simplify the payments processing and also easier management of transactions for the regulator. According to the intelligent matching result, the seller and buyer finalizes the transaction contract and constructs a Data encryption key based on the contract. When the Data encryption key's requirements are completed, the seller will automatically start processing the orders from their end, and the buyer will finish the transaction by processing funds for the commodities. The Data encryption key will automatically stop the subsequent transaction if the vendor fails to deliver the products on time or the customer fails to make the requisite payment of the seller or the buyer and upload the transaction results to the Sustainability 2021, 13, 8158 10 of 14 platform. Because of the data's openness and unforgeability, it will have a bigger influence on the company's following transactions, forcing it to actively comply to the rules of the contract and avoid opportunistic misbehaviors.

6.2 Data Security

While in the current system, we face a lot of issues related to pricing mismanagement and inventory management. In our proposed model, we have simplified data processing with blockchain technology and encrypted the data to not to be manipulatable. In this process we can track the data very easily and find where exactly the error is occurring.

7 Conclusion

Due to a host of possible real-world applications like faster cross-border payments and Data encryption keys, blockchain technology is here to stay.. As more businesses see how blockchain may benefit them, they'll invest more resources, money, and time in the technology, resulting in even more use cases. While we recognise that blockchain technology will continue to be a difficult issue for many, it does not have to be so for you.

Blockchain can act as the spine of e-commerce and provide a major ease and various solutions to managing funds and easier storage of transactions and smooth processing of orders. Besides being faster and cheaper, blockchains facilitate all the activities that current e-commerce is in need of. Using blockchain in all fields will increase our economy. Data sharing is done in the private blockchain network and among the members of blockchain holding people and no public member can easily access the data in Blockchain. So, there won't be any leakage of any kind of data. So, our paper concludes that using Blockchain in E-commerce is very safe, secure and pocket friendly. Blockchain is not only in e-commerce it can be used in other sectors like the financial field, cyber security, digital advertising, and if to be improved in the e-commerce industry much more technology can be used like artificial intelligence and machine learning to make the e-commerce industry more exciting.

References

1. Zennaro, I., Finco, S., Calzavara, M., Persona, A.: Implementing e-commerce from logistic perspective: literature review and methodological framework. Sustainability **14**, 911 (2022)
2. IEEE draft standard for application technical specification of blockchain-based e-commerce transaction evidence collecting. In: IEEE P3802/D2.0, May 2021, pp.1–20, 22 Sep 2021
3. Xie, C., Xiao, X.: Research on decision support system of e-commerce agricultural products based on blockchain. In: 2020 International Conference on E-Commerce and Internet Technology (ECIT), pp. 24–27 (2020)
4. Wu, Y., Fan, H., Wang, X., Zou, G.: A regulated digital currency. Sci. China Inf. Sci. **62**, 32109 (2019)
5. Li, X., Wang, Y., Vijayakumar, P., He, D., Kumar, N., Ma, J.: Blockchain based mutual-healing group key distribution scheme in unmanned aerial vehicles ad-hoc network. IEEE Trans. Veh. Technol. **68**(11), 11309–11322 (2019)
6. Fuchsbauer, G., Orrù, M., Seurin, Y.: Aggregate cash systems: a cryptographic investigation of mimblewimble. In: Ishai, Y., Rijmen, V. (eds.) EUROCRYPT 2019. LNCS, vol. 11476, pp. 657–689. Springer, Cham (2019). https://doi.org/10.1007/978-3-030-17653-2_22
7. Koshy, P., Koshy, D., McDaniel, P.: An analysis of anonymity in bitcoin using P2P network traffic. In: Christin, N., Safavi-Naini, R. (eds.) FC 2014. LNCS, vol. 8437, pp. 469–485. Springer, Heidelberg (2014). https://doi.org/10.1007/978-3-662-45472-5_30
8. Nagarajan, G., Minu, R.I., Sasikala, T.: Intrusion (hybrid) detection system for cloud computing environments. In: Borah, S., Kumar Mi, S., Mishra, Brojo K., Emilia Balas, V., Polkowski, Z. (eds.) Advances in Data Science and Management: Proceedings of ICDSM 2021, pp. 463–471. Springer Nature Singapore, Singapore (2022). https://doi.org/10.1007/978-981-16-5685-9_45
9. Sajith, P.J., Nagarajan, G.: Intrusion detection system using deep belief network & particle swarm optimization. Wireless Pers. Commun. **125**, 1385–1403 (2022)

Cluster-Centric Based Hybrid Approach for Cricket Sports Analytics Using Machine Learning

Rudra Patil, Ankita Duraphe, Pranav Motarwar, G. Suganya[✉], and M. Premalatha

Vellore Institute of Technology, Chennai, India
suganya.g@vit.ac.in

Abstract. Sports Analytics is now playing a vital role in the sports industry playing a multifaceted role including decision making. Analytics in sports can be used by various stakeholders like the investors, sponsors, sports viewers and the team themselves. Analytics in cricket, being one of the most popular games of the world, pulls research interest in a greater way. Cricket related data includes statistics of players in the particular tournament or overall career statistics, team statistics, tournament statistics, etc. and the data may take a wide range related to the tournament or any particular team or any particular player of the team. Team's performance is based on selection of players and hence the need for predicting the outcome of a match based on selected players becomes important. The proposed methodology uses a predictive machine learning model for predicting the outcome of the match based on the performance of a particular batsman or bowler. The increased impact of perfect selection adds a challenging aspect to the tournament which enhances the tournament's popularity. This in turn will improve television contracts, fans store merchandise, sponsorship, ticket sales. The proposed methodology used various machine learning approaches such as Linear SVM, Logistic Regression, Decision Tree, KNN, and Gaussian Naive Bayes. A detailed comparison is made on the usage of these models. The proposed model is implemented using Python with Flask and is validated using the T20 International World Cup 2021 dataset. The results from all the machine learning models are compared and recorded. Logistic regression is proven to perform best out of all models to predict the winning probability of a cricket team.

Keywords: Predictive modeling · Linear SVM · Decision tree · KNN · Gaussian NB · Logistic regression · Sports analytics

1 Introduction

Sports has always been a domain of competition and evolution. Technology transformation has been the key factor and resulted in innovation and resulted in data driven decision making. The International Cricket Association (ICC) has shown the growing popularity of cricket as a sport with one billion fans worldwide and growing. The game is played in three formats which are Test, One-day, T20. The increasing popularity of

K. Kottursamy et al. (Eds.): IconDeepCom 2022, CCIS 1719, pp. 268–283, 2023.
https://doi.org/10.1007/978-3-031-27622-4_21

cricket and growing popularity of the short format of T20 has resulted in new leagues coming up across the globe. Recently analytics is getting increasingly popular in the research domain. Historical data analysis is becoming increasingly important to predict the future game results. The main aspect of the analytical field in almost all fields is machine learning where the independent variables are used to predict the outcome variable using various enhanced models.

The collection of relevant, historical statistics about any sports that can afford a competitive advantage to a team or individual is known as Sports analytics. Digitization and availability of huge storage enables easier data collection and storage. A detailed statistics including player performance against teams, player's home/away status etc., is available at stake for usage. On-field analytics deals with improving the on-field performance of teams and players. It digs deep into aspects such as game tactics and player fitness. Machine learning models perform better in sports analytics trying to better perform predictive analysis [1]. For example, predictive models may determine players' best position, given the game condition and opponents with whom the players are facing.

Despite its tremendous growth, sports analytics confronts numerous hurdles. Various criticisms are raised by prominent stakeholders of the field contending that humans are capable of capturing and processing critical information of the sports. Certain aspects, such as player diving in the game, fooling the opponent, and player yelling, are claimed not captured by statistics, according to sports analytics skeptics. Keeping these doubts aside, various researches are going on in the field to predict various parameters of the sports making the platform easy for user community to use and enjoy. The proposed methodology covers the individual performance impact on the outcome of the match which can be used by the team management for selecting the next player according to the live match scenario.

The organization of the paper is as follows: The first section provides the background for the research in the sports analytics field. The next section includes discussion of the previous work done in cricket analytics using machine learning. It is followed by the brief explanation of the proposed framework and deployment for the model. The next section includes the description of the dataset with detailed discussion about the results. Finally, the concluding remarks are recorded and the scope for extension of work is presented.

2   Literature Review

The statistical techniques were utilized in literature to predict the outcome of a match using several methods. In order to develop a prediction model, a multiple regression model is first tested. Using runs scored per over in the first and second innings, algorithms such as Logistic Regression with multi-variable linear regression and Random Forest [11] are used to forecast the final result. To deal with the data structure and implement the algorithms, Anaconda and Python libraries such as pandas, NumPy, and IPython were used [2, 3]. Kapadia and Kumash [1] investigate the use of machine learning technology to solve the problem of being able to forecast the results of a cricket match using the match data of IPL (Indian Premier League). Prediction models were built which used distinct features which were generated by filtering methods like Correlation based feature selection, wrapper and relief. formed two distinct subgroups, one which was based on advantages for the home team and the other was based on tossing of the coin.

Prafulla and Harshit [2] implemented various machine learning models, which include Logistic Regression, SVM (Support Vector Machine), K Nearest Neighbours, Random forest classification and Naïve bayes which could predict the winner of the game and increase the model accuracy. The emphasis of choosing the best players for the cricket match is discussed by Kalpdrum and Niravkumar [3]. They have taken multiple factors into consideration like the venue, opposition, and the current form of the player. The player statistics are also explored which can help choose the playing squad for the particular match. The players metrics like the wickets taken by the individual bowler and runs scored by the batsman are given as a forecasting output of the model.

Harshal and Deepak [5] use machine learning and artificial intelligence approaches to anticipate player performance during a match, or to predict which players should be selected based on their current performance, form, morale, and other factors, using detailed details, characteristics, and parameters. Some of these strategies are discussed, as well as a brief comparison between them. In this paper, the author [7] proposes a Convolutional Neural Network of 13 layers, dubbed "Shot-Net," to classify six types of cricket shots. Arnab Santra [8] provides a method for predicting bowler rating based on a player's previous profile. On previous IPL data, the solution utilized a supervised machine learning technique to forecast top bowlers.

Ashish and Praveen [9] projected the match outcome of the World cup event by considering a variety of criteria that have a part in determining a game's final outcome. Akhil and Nimmagadda [10] developed a model that uses Multiple Variable Linear Regression to forecast the score in each of the innings. Pathak and Wadhwa [2] studied the prediction of cricket game results utilizing data mining techniques. They tried projecting the outcome of ODI (One Day International) matches based on a range of factors such as the home venue, toss decision, innings, team player fitness, and other dynamic strategies. In addition to the approaches used by [13], a Support Vector Machine (SVM) method was used to forecast the result [12].

For a more in-depth analysis, a model was constructed for easy prediction, and then more research was done on intricate elements. The team statistical analyses were performed first, backed by the player data. The features were defined using Chi Square testing, mutual information, and Pearson correlation. The authors employed Naive Bayes, Logistic Regression, Random Forests, and Gradient Decision Trees on the data's important differentiating [4, 8].

The work discussed in the above section is focused on the static match results. The more work can be done in the dynamic format for the live match analysis. This will add more competition to the game and the stakeholders will be truly benefited by the analysis. The management will have a better overview about the next player selection by the analysis done during the live match.

3 Proposed Methodology

The dataset of T20 World cup 2021 was explored to plot the points on the standard space with three-dimensional functionality to capture defined features that are considered for constructing the model. The dataset is pre-processed by eliminating any incomplete records so that there are no missing values in the dataset and the raw dataset is modified with attributes like Runs > 30, 50 < Runs < 70, Runs < 70. A proposed ranking algorithm is applied for adding the mean points attribute in the final dataset for the Cluster model. Feature selection is implemented to eliminate all the features that have no direct impact on the result. The dataset consisted of 102 top batsmen and 102 top bowlers from the tournament in 2021.

The dataset for the Predictive model was constructed from the 45 datasets for 45 matches conducted during the T20 world cup 2021. All instances for each player along with the ranking provided for each player by the Cluster model are considered for constructing the final dataset for the Predictive model (Table 1).

Table 1. Attribute description table

Attribute	Description
Mat	Number of matches played
Inns	Number of innings played
Runs	Number of runs scored
HS	Highest runs scored
Ave	Average runs scored
SR	Strike rate
100s	Number of times runs scored above 100
50s	Number of times runs scored above 50
4s	Number of boundaries scored
6s	Number of sixes scored

The defined features were retrieved by finding the relationship between the predictor variables and the target. It was found that the predictor variables having significant impact on the target variable were having a non-linear relationship with the target variable. While some of the predictor variables were showing linear relationships. The factors are then checked for the Variance inflation factor. This will quantify the multicollinearity for least square regression analysis. This provides an index for measuring the deviation of variance of a regression coefficient due to collinearity. The variance inflation factor for the model is as follows:

$$VIF = \frac{1}{(1 - R^2)} \tag{1}$$

In expression (1) higher the R value, higher the variance inflation score meaning two Var1 is collinear with Var2 and Var3. The variables with VIF score greater than 1.5 were avoided for regression.

Based on the output of the above analogy, the six defined variables were considered for the k-means clustering model. The ratio within the similarity group and different group:

$$SDR = \frac{\left(\frac{R^2}{c-1}\right)}{\left(\frac{1-R^2}{n-c}\right)} \tag{2}$$

where,

$$R^2 = \frac{SST - SSE}{SST} \tag{3}$$

and SST signifies cluster difference between the point and SSE signifies cluster similarity.

$$SST = \sum_{i=1}^{a}\sum_{j=1}^{b}\sum_{k=1}^{c}(V^k{}_{ij} - V^k)^2 \tag{4}$$

$$SST = \sum_{i=1}^{a}\sum_{j=1}^{b}\sum_{k=1}^{c}(V^k{}_{ij} - Vt^k)^2 \tag{5}$$

where,

n = count of features
b = count of features for cluster i
a = count of classes
c = count of variables for the cluster
$V^k{}_{ij}$ = value for k'th variable in j'th feature of i'th cluster
V^k = mean value of k'th variable
Vt_i^k = mean value of k'th variable of i'th cluster

The above devised clustering algorithm is applied on the batsmen dataset and the bowler dataset separately for clustering the batsmen into 3 categories and also the bowler into 3 categories. The proposed algorithm for the hybrid approach of Clustering and Predicting is explained in this section.

3.1 Batsmen Algorithm

The factors for construction of the proposed clustering model are presented in Table 2. The factors for the predictive model are presented in Table 3.

We created a Ranking Algorithm to rank all the batsmen for the T20 World Cup 2021.

Parameter 1. Man of the Match 50 Points.
Parameter 2. Run scored: 1 Points.
Parameter 3. Six runs (off one ball) bonus*: 2 Points.
Parameter 4. Four runs (off one ball) bonus*: 1 Point.
Parameter 5. Dismissed for duck: −10 Points.
Parameter 6. Strike rate bonus (for batsmen scoring 10 runs/10 balls or more).

I.   Between 0.00 and 49.99: -10 Points

Table 2. Factors for clustering model

Player ID	Matches	Innings	Not Out	Runs	Average	Strike Rate	100	50	0

4s	6s	Runs>30	50<Runs<70	Runs>70	Total Rank Points	Mean Points

Table 3. Factors for predictive model

Player ID	SR<Mean	Man of the match	Wickets in Hands	Match Type

Innings Type	Opposition	Runs	Cluster Rank

II. Between 50.00 and 99.99: 0 Points
III. Between 100.00 and 149.99: 10 Points
IV. Above 150.00: 20 Points

Parameter 7. Milestone bonus.

I.   On reaching 30 runs: 10 Points
II. On reaching 50 runs: 20 Points
III. On reaching 70 runs: 30 Points

The Total Rank Points parameter is calculated as the combination of all the above seven parameters for each batsman. It provides normalized weightage to the players for categorizing them into particular sections. This has increased the prediction accuracy for the proposed model.

Total Rank Points =
Parameter 1*(No. of Man of the match) + Parameter 2*(No. of runs scored) +
Parameter 3*(No. of times six runs scored on last ball) + Parameter 4*(No. of times four runs scored) + Parameter 5*(No. of times dismissed on duck) + Parameter 6 +
Parameter 7*(No. of times 30-50 runs + No. of times 51-70 runs + No. of times 71-above runs)

Mean Points = Total Rank Points/Matches

The proposed methodology is presented as per below section.

Step 1: Dataset loading – T20 World Cup 2021

Data preprocessing by dropping null values and duplicate rows

Step 2: Structurize the data for Cluster Model

Total Rank Points =

I.   Parameter 1*(No. of Man of the match)
II. Parameter 2*(No. of runs scored)
III. Parameter 3*(No. of times six runs scored)
IV. Parameter 4*(No. of times four runs scored)
V.   Parameter 5*(No. of times dismissed on duck)
VI. Parameter 6
VII. Parameter 7*(No. of times 30–50 * 1 + No. of times 51–70 * 2 + No. of time 71-above * 3)

Step 3: Perform clustering on the data with the above added 'Total Rank Points' and 'Mean Points' factors. Assign the cluster rank provided by the cluster model to each player.

Step 4: Exploratory data analysis for the data of the Predictive Model.

Step 5: Training the predictive model which predicts the match output based on the performance of the batsmen.

Step 6: Testing the predictive model on the testing data and finally evaluating the model on the basis of the output.

Step 7: Performance evaluation of the predictive model. The results of the proposed model are presented in the next section.

3.2 Bowler Algorithm

The factors for construction of the proposed clustering model are presented in Table 4. The factors for the predictive model are presented in Table 5.

Table 4. Factors for clustering model

Player ID	Matches Innings	Overs	Runs	Wickets	Avg. Economy
4s	6s	2 W	3-4 W	5W	Total Rank Points

We created a Ranking Algorithm to rank all the bowlers for the T20 World Cup 2021.

Parameter 1. Man of the Match: 50 Points

Parameter 2. Wicket: 20 Points

Parameter 3. Maiden over: 40 Points

Parameter 4. Runs conceded: −1 Point

Table 5. Factors for predictive model

Player ID	Economy<Mean	Man of the match	Match Type

Innings Type	Opposition	Wickets	Cluster Rank

Parameter 5. Six conceded: -10 Points
Parameter 6. Economy rate bonus (for bowlers bowling 2 overs or more)

I.   Between 00.00 and 02.99 runs per over: 30 Points
II. Between 03.00 and 05.99 runs per over: 20 Points
III. Between 06.00 and 08.99 runs per over: 0 Points
IV. Between 09.00 and 11.99 runs per over: −10 Points
V.   Above 12.00 runs per over: −20 Points

Parameter 7. Milestone bonus

I.   On taking 2 wickets: 10 Points
II. On taking 3–4 wickets: 20 Points
III. On taking 5 wickets: 30 Points

The Total Rank Points parameter is calculated as the combination of all the above seven parameters for each bowler. It provides normalized weightage to the players for categorizing them into particular sections. This has increased the prediction accuracy for the proposed model.

Total Rank Points =
Parameter 1*(No. of Man of the match) + Parameter 2*(No. of wickets taken) + Parameter 3*(No. of maiden overs) + Parameter 4*(No. of runs conceded) + Parameter 5*(No. of six conceded) + Parameter 6 + Parameter 7*(No. of times 2 wickets + No. of times 3 -4 wickets + No. of times 5 or more wickets)

Mean Points = Total Rank Points/Matches
The proposed methodology is presented as per below section.
Step 1: Dataset loading – T20 World Cup 2021
Data preprocessing by dropping null values and duplicate rows
Step 2: Structure the data for Cluster Model
Total Rank Points =

I.   Parameter 1*(No. of Man of the match)
II. Parameter 2*(No. of wickets taken)
III. Parameter 3*(No. of maiden overs)

IV.   Parameter 4*(No. of runs conceded)
V.   Parameter 5*(No. of six conceded)
VI.   Parameter 6
VII.   Parameter 7*(No. of times 2 wickets * 1 + No. of times 3–4 wickets * 2 + No. of times 5 or more wickets * 3)

Step 3: Perform clustering on the data with the above added 'Total Rank Points' and 'Mean Points' factors. Assign the cluster rank provided by the cluster model to each player.

Step 4: Exploratory data analysis for the data of the Predictive Model.

Step 5: Training the predictive model which predicts the match output based on the performance of the bowler.

Step 6: Testing the predictive model on the testing data and finally evaluating the model on the basis of the output.

Step 7: Performance evaluation of the predictive model. The results of the proposed model are presented in the next section.

The proposed methodology predicts the match outcome using different machine learning algorithms by analyzing the performance of each player. This study proposes two models, one of which depicts the prediction of match outcome based on the performance of specific batsmen. The other depicts the prediction of match outcome based on the performance of a specific bowler. The framework methodology which is being used to build the models is depicted in Fig. 3. The preprocessing is done on the scraped data. It is done by removing any NA entries, ensuring the dataset is completely filled. More crucially, In the proposed methodology, we use feature selection to exclude features that have rather lower impact using the ranking feature in the feature selection process. Prior to the machine learning techniques' training phase, features such as Match Number, Date of the Match, and Venue of the Match, among others, were deleted.

A traditional algorithm produces a result by combining data with the logic expressed in code. In the proposed methodology, machine learning algorithms are incorporated which takes an input and an output and creates logic that can be applied to new data to obtain new results.

After preprocessing the scraped data, now the data is further divided into 2 feature sets: the first of the set is for batters features and another for bowler features. Following the preprocessing of the dataset, the clustering model is applied for assigning clustering rank of the batsmen for the batsmen model and assigning clustering rank of the bowler for the bowler model. Then a variety of learning techniques are used on the sets in order to develop various ml models. The classifiers were developed using ten-fold cross validation and also measured using different statistical measures. These models are then compared in order to determine which can be used to forecast match results. Logistic Regression, Linear SVM, Decision Tree, Gaussian NB, KNN are the machine learning methods used to create the predictive models. The approaches used are based on the various learning methods used to construct the models (Fig. 1 and 2).

The Graphical User Interface of this program was created using the Python Flask API. The tool is designed to make adding new classifiers easier in the future by keeping the computing part independent. It predicts the outcome of the match. Flask is a web application framework in python that uses the WSGI protocol. Flask is very interactive

PlayerId	Mat	Inns	NO	Runs	Ave	SR	100	50	0	4s	6s	Runs>30	50<Runs<70	Runs>70	Total points	Mean points
1	8	8	4	332	83	167.67	1	4	0	23	21	3	1	2	607	75.88
2	7	7	2	326	65.2	170.68	0	3	0	27	19	2	1	1	541	77.29
3	8	8	0	296	37	190.96	0	4	0	34	20	1	2	1	510	63.75
4	7	7	0	291	41.57	149.23	0	2	0	23	21	1	1	2	506	72.29
5	7	7	0	295	42.14	186.7	0	2	0	20	27	3	0	1	489	69.86

Fig. 1. Sample data for clustering model for batsman

PlayerId	StrikeRate>Mean	Manofthematch	Wickets_inhand	MatchType	InningsType	Opposition	Runs	Cluster Rank	Result
1	1	0	6	3	0	NZ	54	6	0
1	1	0	7	2	1	NZ	32	6	1
1	1	0	8	1	0	NZ	36	6	1
2	1	1	7	1	1	AUS	79	2	1
3	0	0	8	1	1	IN	39	12	1

Fig. 2. Sample data for predictive model for batsman

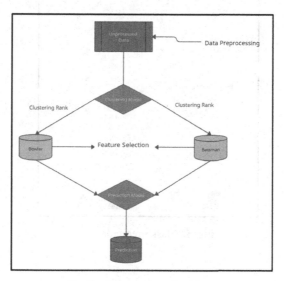

Fig. 3. Proposed methodology

and simple to use. It was created with the goal of making implementation easier and faster, in keeping with the scope of most common projects. While it may take some time to discover the correct libraries, Flask's small base makes it ideal for constructing the web application.

Machine learning model deployment, also known as putting models into production, refers to making your models available to end users or systems. The deployment of machine learning models, on the other hand, is complicated. The purpose of the proposed method is to use the Flask API to put trained machine learning models into production (Figs. 4 and 5).

Data
Training
Machine Learning Algorithms
Machine Learning Model
Write
Prediction
REST API
Calls
NGiNX
Flask Module

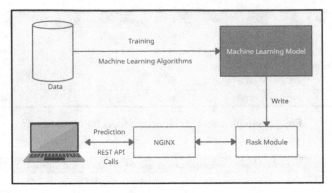

Fig. 4. Deployment methodology

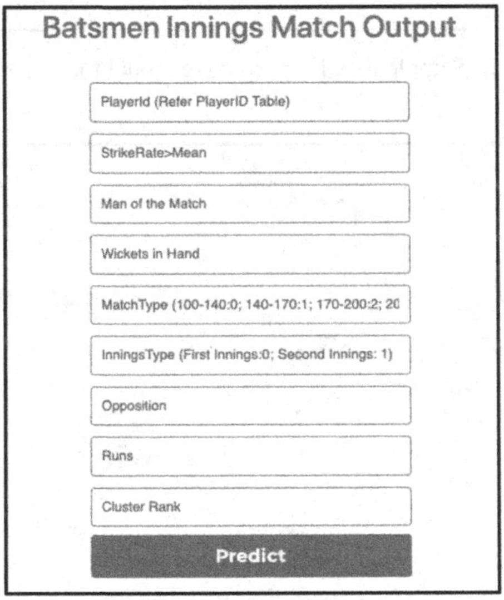

Batsmen Innings Match Output
PlayerId (Refer PlayerID Table)
StrikeRate>Mean
Man of the Match
Wickets in Hand
MatchType (100-140:0; 140-170:1; 170-200:2; 20
InningsType (First Innings:0; Second Innings: 1)
Opposition
Runs
Cluster Rank
Predict

Fig. 5. Flask predictor tool

4 Result

4.1 Dataset Description

To do prediction analysis, historical data from the T20 International World Cup 2021 is collected. The solution collects data for T20 International World Cup 2021 Cricket matches and puts them in a dataset. Beautiful Soup was used to scrape the dataset, which has 9 variables. Table 6 shows the variables in the dataset for bowler model and Table 7 shows the variables in the dataset for batsman model.

Table 6. Dataset attribute of bowler

Attribute	Description
Played Id	Unique ID for player identification
Economy < mean	Economy of the bowler is less than mean economy of match
Man of the match	Player winning man of the match in Boolean manner
Match type	Match type categorized based on the runs scored
Innings type	Identify first innings or second innings
Opposition	Name of opposition team
Wickets	Wickets taken by the player
Cluster rank	Rank provided by the proposed clustering model

Table 7. Dataset attribute of batsman

Attribute	Description
Played Id	Unique ID for player identification
Strike rate > mean	Player strike rate is greater than average match strike rate
Man of the match	Player winning man of the match in Boolean manner
Wickets in hand	Remaining wickets at the time player proceeded his innings
Match type	Match type categorized based on the runs scored
Innings type	Identify first innings or second innings
Opposition	Name of opposition team
Runs	Runs scored by the player
Cluster rank	Rank provided by the proposed clustering model

4.2 Feature Selection

To obtain the influential properties of the considered dataset, various feature selection strategies were evaluated. The fitted attribute feature importance provides the methods to be used, which are computed as the mean and standard deviation of impurity decrease accumulation within each tree.

4.3 Evaluation measures

Logistic Regression, Linear SVM, Decision Tree, Gaussian NB, KNN are some of the algorithms used to solve the research challenge. These algorithms were chosen because they use distinct learning methods. The confusion matrix is drawn for the result of each model and the different measures like accuracy, f1 score, recall, precision are checked for the same. The splitting of the training data is the major basis for the validation of all the models. The k fold cross validation method is used with k being 10 here. Here it is splitting the data in 9 folds and testing on the last fold that is left. By checking the same for all the combinations of the data, the overall average is considered for showcasing the final results. The accurate aspect about this method is that all the sets are covered in various combinations. The variance and the SD is also checked for maintaining the stability for different data inputs in all the folds.

4.4 Deployment

Once the Flask API has been created. The model can be used from the front end. By creating a test website, we were able to confirm our findings. The input screen is shown in Fig. 6. When the user clicks on 'Predict,' it will tell them whether the match will end in a 1 or a 0 score (1 for Win, 0 for Loss).

5 Result and Analysis

We used GT20 matches to evaluate the prediction of cricket game outcomes using several models, eliminating matches abandoned due to technical reasons and draws. We gathered data from 48 matches, and our data set covers 96 historical cases by considering both target setting and chasing innings in a match. The implemented methodology performs unique analysis for the bowler as well as batsman. Precision and Recall parameters are also evaluated for the bowler and batsman scenario.

The Linear Support Vector Machine, Logistic Regression, Decision Tree, K Nearest Neighbors, and Gaussian Naive Bayes are all trained and tested using this feature set. The results are presented in Tables 3 and 4.

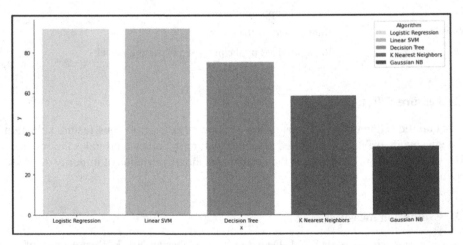

Fig. 6. Accuracy for various machine learning models for bowler

The above figure shows us the result accuracy for various machine learning models. It is observed that Linear SVM and Logistic regression resulted in the highest accuracy of 91.6% with an F1 Score of 0.947364 for both the models (Figs. 7, 8, and 9).

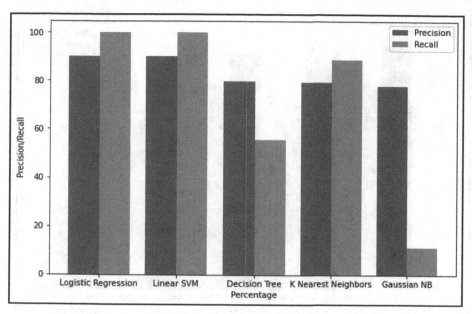

Fig. 7. Precision and recall for various machine learning models for bowler

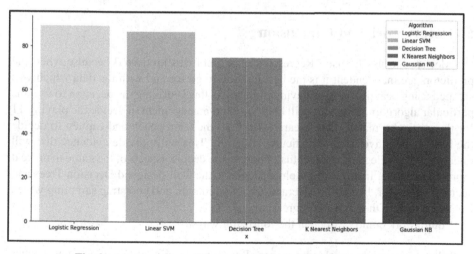

Fig. 8. Accuracy for various machine learning models for batsman

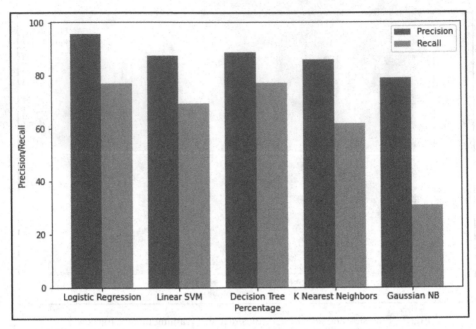

Fig. 9. Precision and recall for various machine learning models for batsman

6 Future work and Conclusion

Our decision to use Logistic Regression classifiers was motivated because when the predictors are independent it is the best method to go for and with the data which was scraped using beautiful soup is having imbalance, this is driving the decision to use this particular algorithm. The study will help the team management to decide the playing 11 for the particular match. The research will help the team coach and captain to decide the best suited player in that particular situation. This will provide evidence that will underpin better selection and eventually help in the deeper aspects of the game to make it more competitive. In terms of absolute accuracy, the well-designed Decision Trees and accurate separator, like SVM, leverages cross-validation and bootstrap sampling which is comparative to the Logistic Regression.

Future work could be done in the following ways:

- Today AI is rapidly developing across all the sectors, with a slew of new approaches being invented and old techniques being tweaked to improve performance. This defines our derived sports model to expand in further aspects of the game with inclusion of live match prediction, overall team winner prediction with new algorithms in place.
- Along with the models that are already considered for prediction during live matches, such as live stream prediction, further features could be included.
- Although our research focused on T20 matches, these models can be modified to cover the needs of other formats of the game as well.
- Other sports, including baseball and football, can use classification systems as well, albeit the manner of application may differ from one sport to the next.

References

1. Kapadia, K., et al.: Sport analytics for cricket game results using machine learning: an experimental study. Appl. Comput. Inform. (2020)
2. Praffulla Kumar, D., Suri, H., Gupta, S.: Naïve Bayes algorithm based match winner prediction model for T20 cricket. In: Intelligent Computing and Applications, pp. 435–446. Springer, Singapore (2021)
3. Pathak, N., Wadhwa, H.: Applications of modern classification techniques to predict the outcome of ODI cricket. Procedia Comput. Sci. **87**, 55–60 (2016)
4. Bhatia, V.: A review of machine learning based recommendation approaches for cricket. In: 2020 Sixth International Conference on Parallel, Distributed and Grid Computing (PDGC). IEEE (2020)
5. Mittal, H., et al.: A Study on Machine Learning Approaches for Player Performance and Match Results Prediction. arXiv preprint arXiv:2108.10125 (2021)
6. Foysal, M.F.A., et al.: Shot-Net: A convolutional neural network for classifying different cricket shots. In: International Conference on Recent Trends in Image Processing and Pattern Recognition. Springer, Singapore (2018)
7. Santra, A., et al.: Prediction of most valuable bowlers of Indian Premier League (IPL). In: Data Management, Analytics and Innovation, pp. 211–223. Springer, Singapore (2021)
8. Das, A., Ranjan Parida, A., Srivastava, P.R.: ICC cricket world cup prediction model. In: Information Systems Design and Intelligent Applications, pp. 529–539. Springer, New Delhi (2016)
9. Nimmagadda, A., et al.: Cricket score and winning prediction using data mining. Int. J. Adv. Res. Dev. **3**(3), 299–302 (2018)
10. Böhning, D.: Multinomial logistic regression algorithm. Ann. Inst. Stat. Math. **44**(1), 197–200 (1992)
11. Gunn, Steve R.: Support vector machines for classification and regression. ISIS Tech. Rep. **14**(1), 5–16 (1998)
12. Kampakis, S., Thomas, W.: Using machine learning to predict the outcome of English county twenty over cricket matches. arXiv preprint arXiv:1511.05837 (2015)
13. Hemanta, S., Bhattacharjee, D., Mukherjee, D.: Cricket, statistics, and data mining. In: Cricket Performance Management, pp. 1–22. Springer, Singapore (2016)
14. Stevenson, O.G., Brewer, B.J.: Finding your feet: a Gaussian process model for estimating the abilities of batsmen in test cricket. J. R. Stat. Soc. Ser. C: Appl. Stat. **70**(2), 481–506 (2021)
15. Prakash, C.D., Patvardhan, C., Vasantha Lakshmi, C.: AI Methodology for Automated Selection of Playing XI in IPL Cricket (2017)
16. Behera, S.R., Vijaya Saradhi, V.: Learning Strength and Weakness Rules of Cricket Players Using Association Rule Mining
17. Brefeld, U., et al.: Machine learning and data mining for sports analytics. In: 5th International Workshop, MLSA (2018)

Extended AI for Heterogeneous Edge

PPA Based MAC Unit Using Vedic Multiplier and XOR Logic

M. S. Sharook Salman$^{(\boxtimes)}$ and K. Yogeshwaran

Department of Electronics and Communication Engineering, Kalaignar Karunanidhi Institute of Technology, Coimbatore, India
cbesharook@gmail.com

Abstract. The multiply-accumulate (MAC) process is required by the majority of computer circuits. An accumulator is used to store the result of this calculation, which is either added or subtracted from the accumulator. When designing the multiplier, keep in mind that the least amount of power and time delay is critical considerations. Since any MAC unit would not be complete without a multiplier, this is an obvious fact. A basic operation that is commonly used in signal processing as well as other applications is known as the multiply and accumulate (MAC) function. Digital Signal Processors often include multipliers as one of its fundamental building blocks (DSPs). Components like as power, LUT, and latency all have a role in determining the overall performance of a DSP. The multiply-accumulate (MAC) process is required by the majority of computer circuits. Despite its age, Vedic mathematics continues to be a simple and effective instrument to compute mathematical operations. In Vedic mathematics, there are 16 different formulae that are recognized and used all over the world. In order to carry out the process of multiplication, we make use of the UT sutra in our work. In the beginning of our investigation, we created a 32-bit MAC unit by constructing it out of xor gates and a 16-bit Vedic multiplier. MAC contains a built-in add/sub module that outputs a 64-bit output. In Xilinx Vivado, the design is then generated and implemented by utilizing Verilog HDL. Synopsys DC may also be utilized for examining characteristics of **PPA** (Power Performance Area). When compared to conventional methods, the new method has a power reduction of roughly 3%.

Keywords: Vedic multiplier · MAC unit · Urdhva-Tiryagbyham (UT) · Verilog HDL · Xilinx Vivado · Synopsys DC

1 Introduction

In digital signal processing field, some of the most used operations are filtering, convolution, the Fast Fourier Transform (FFT), and the multiply and accumulate unit (MAC). In digital signal processing, one of the most fundamental processes is called the multiplication-accumulation, which is also the basic computational kernel [2]. Because the MAC unit is such an important component of the DSP architecture, it is often located on the critical path. This is because it is responsible for determining the speed of the entire framework. The development of a MAC unit with high performance is an essential

© The Author(s), under exclusive license to Springer Nature Switzerland AG 2023
K. Kottursamy et al. (Eds.): IconDeepCom 2022, CCIS 1719, pp. 287–299, 2023.
https://doi.org/10.1007/978-3-031-27622-4_22

component of continuous DSP applications. Furthermore, with the ever-increasing need for small electronic devices, an electronic section that uses less power and occupies less space is critical from a commercial standpoint. As a consequence of this, Real-time video coding and digital signal processing (DSP) demand a MAC unit with high speed performance, low space constraints, and low power consumption. As semiconductor technology advances, there is a greater demand for embedded and portable Digital Signal Processing (DSP) systems. The vast majority of digital and top-execution systems, including microprocessors, FIR filters, digital signal processors, and amongst others, have an essential piece of hardware known as a multiplier [14]. The multiplier is also a critical component in almost every DSP application. As a result, low power, high speed multipliers are required for high speed DSP. Vedic multiplier is one of the fastest multipliers because of its regular structure and ease of design.

In addition to being essential components of computer systems and mobile phones, multipliers are also often required for the majority of digital video and audio recordings. MAC (Multiply Accumulate), FFT (Fast Fourier Transforms), IDCT (Inverse Discrete Cosine), are three important functions, which implement multiplier [1]. Array multiplication and booth multiplication are two well-known methods of conventional multiplication in math coprocessors, each with its own set of constraints. A parallel version of multiplication is carried out by the array multiplier. Using a parallel multiplication approach, partial products can be computed in parallel. However, many logic gates are utilized, in an array multiplier the delay is a measure of how long it takes for signals to pass through the multiplication array [13].

In comparison, The Vedic multiplier, which is based on the Urdhva Tiryagbyham Sutra (Crosswise and Vertical technique), is considered to be the most effective multipliers. These Sutras have historically been employed for the decimal number system multiplication of two numbers. Within the scope of this investigation, our suggested method is digital hardware compatible because of the comparable concepts used to the binary number system [4]. The Vertical and Crosswise Algorithms found in ancient Indian Vedic mathematics serve as the conceptual foundation for the Multiplier Architecture. As a result, because multiplier dominates system execution time, it has a vital role to play in determining performance of system. Hence, tuning the multiplier for power and speed limits is a main undertaking. Using old Vedic mathematics to solve this problem might be a good solution. In this case, the multiplier must be powerful and fast [11]. One of these multipliers is the Vedic multiplier, which combines old Vedic math. Despite its antiquity, even today, doing mathematical computations using vedic mathematics is a straightforward and efficient process. There are sixteen equations in Vedic mathematics. Implementing as well as designing a 32-bit MAC that uses a 16-bit Vedic multiplier may be done with the help of the Urdhva-Tiryagbyham approach [9]. MAC unit is intended to store the outcomes of the product that is found from the Vedic multiplier after being subjected to repeated operations of addition and subtraction. The manner in which addition or subtraction is performed will vary according on the mode that is chosen.

2 Performance – Oriented Multipliers

The speed of multiple operations is very important in digital signal processing along with in ordinary processors nowadays, particularly since media processing has taken off. Formally, multiplication was usually accomplished through a series of addition, subtraction, along with shift operations.

2.1 Binary Multiplier

A digital or combinational logic circuit is referred to as a binary multiplier when it is employed for the purpose of multiplying two binary integers. The result is called a product, and the two integers that are multiplied together are called the multiplicand and the multiplier, respectively. Both the multiplicand and the multiplier may have bit widths of their own choosing. The bit size of the multiplicand as well as the multiplier serve as the basis for determining the bit size of the result. The bit size of the result is determined by adding together the bit sizes of both the multiplier and the multiplicand [6]. Multiplying decimal values by binary ones is the same as multiplying decimal ones. When multiplying integers containing more than one bit using binary, there are two processes involved. In the first phase of the process, a single bit-wise multiplication, also known as a partial product, is carried out. In the second step, all of the partial products are combined into a single product.

2.2 Wallace Multiplier

It is more efficient to use the Wallace tree multiplier as an implementation of a digital circuit than to use a basic array multiplier. For a parallel multiplier that reduces latency, a Wallace tree multiplier is one that multiplies two unsigned integers [7]. It sums partial products in stages using a set of full and half adders (the Wallace tree or Wallace reduction) until only two numbers remain. Wallace multipliers try to reduce as much as possible on each layer, whereas Dadda multipliers try to reduce as many gates as possible on the upper layers. It is also a parallel multiplier that reduces latency by employing the carry save addition algorithm.

2.3 Booth Multiplier

Using either full or half adders, we may design a booth multiplier. The advancement of digital multipliers is being pursued using a variety of methods. Digital signal processing (DSP) developments often include it. Radices are used to create multipliers, and the delay and power consumption of these devices vary widely [6]. They are used to do high-speed computations on complicated problems.

In order to build efficient microprocessor architectures, several multipliers are employed in various applications. Because the multiplication procedure requires a larger number of elements and is a more difficult operation, proceed at a slower pace. Several ideas have been presented to incorporate digital multipliers [2]. The addition operation is used to multiply binary values in the array multiplier, and this process should be continuous. The Vedic multiplier factors use less energy and have fewer aspects, such as power and latency dissipation, when contrasted with the factors of a few multipliers that were explained before in this paragraph.

3 Vedic Multiplication Scheme

Vedic Mathematics was written by Jagadguru Swami Sri Bharati Krsna Tirthaji Maharaja (1884–1960) (Sankaracharya of Govardhana Matha, Puri, Orissa, India). It clarifies a wide range of mathematical concepts, such as calculus, factorization, quadratic equations, trigonometry, geometry (coordinate, plane), arithmetic, and among others. The Vedic Sutras address almost every aspect of mathematics. It is possible to employ them to solve even the most difficult mathematical issues. In comparison to existing formal approaches, the Sutras provide a time- and effort-saving alternative [5]. The Sutras' application is perfectly rational and comprehensible, despite the fact that the solutions appear to be miraculous. The Sutras' ideas are adhered to in certain respects by the calculations conducted on computers. Not only do the Sutras provide calculating procedures, but they also contain ways of thinking about how to employ them.

An ancient Indian method of mathematics known as Vedic mathematics has been found in the early 20th century in the form of mathematics written on antique Indian sculptures (Vedas). This study suggests the development of a Vedic Multiplier that operates at a high speed by using Vedic Mathematics approaches that have been modified to achieve increased levels of performance [2]. Many DSP and conventional CPUs rely on multipliers as a critical hardware component for achieving high processing speeds. Vedic Mathematics employs a one-of-a-kind mathematical approach based on 16 Sutras [12]. A total of sixteen aphorisms, known as sutras, form the foundation of the Vedic mathematics system. These sutras address a broad variety of mathematical concepts, such as geometry, algebra, arithmetic, and many more. The following table provides a comprehensive list of the 16 sutras, as well as their respective corollaries and subsutras (Table 1).

3.1 Urdhva-Tiryakbhyam (UT) Sutra

Sanskrit literature inspired the phrases "Urdhva" and "Tiryagbhyam." Urdhva means "vertically" and Tiryagbyham yam means "crosswise." It is based on the groundbreaking idea that all partial products may be formed by adding partial products at the same time. Anyone may observe how using the Vedic technique improves mental calculations. To mentally multiply, one must first recollect the first row, then the second row, and so on, before adding them all together [1]. In some situations, recalling so many numbers at once might be difficult. Visualizing a line diagram and continually adding two successive product terms utilising this Vedic technique is simpler to do while doing calculations manually. There are only a few digits that must be remembered. As a consequence, Vedic multiplication might be more efficient.

3.2 Urdhva-Tiryagbhyam Sutra for Binary Numbers

Because binary systems only utilize the numbers 0 and 1, the AND logic operator replaces multiplication in the Urdhva-tiryagbhyam formula, also known as the vertically-crosswise formula. AND logic is used to perform multiplication between two binary numbers, and binary logic is used to perform addition. When it comes to the binary number system, the Vedic way of multiplication is used. In other words, multiplying two bits like a0 and b0 is simply an AND operation that can be performed with a basic AND gate [6].

The term "Vedic mathematics" refers to a set of mathematical methods that originate back to ancient times and are claimed to be effective in addition to being instantly applicable in a number of different domains. It consists of sixteen sutras, only two of which are meant to be multiplied, hence it may be considered quite rational.

NND (Nikhilam Navatashcaramam Dashatah), and UT (Urdhva Tiryakbyham) as was mentioned before, are the two sutras that must be said in order to perform multiplication using any two numbers. Because it needs the computation of two lower bit integers, the UT sutra technique was selected as the appropriate approach for this project.

Urdhva Tiryakbyham means 'vertically and crosswise'. An important component of the approach is that incomplete goods are made and then added in parallel. An instance of two four-bit integers, a [3:0] and b [3:0], is utilized for showing "multiplication.

Step 1: $c0d0 = a0b0$
Step 2: $c1d1 = a0b1 + a1b0 + c0$
Step 3: $c2d2 = a0b2 + a1b1 + a2b0 + c1$
Step 4: $c3d3 = a0b3 + a1b2 + a2b1 + a3b0 + c2$
Step 5: $c4d4 = a1b3 + a2b2 + a3b1 + c3$
Step 6: $c5d5 = a2b3 + a3b2 + c4$
Step 7: $c6d6 = a3b3 + c5$"

Finally, the result is c6d6d5d4d3d2d1d0, which is an 8-bit integer. The carry is represented by c [3:0], and the output is represented by d [3:0]. This principle may also be applied to any amount of bits. The number of bits that are used in the calculation is directly proportional to the increase in the number of steps that are necessary. The UT sutra has been originally developed utilizing decimal number systems. This has been later expanded for representing binary number systems, as most digital circuits require binary numbers for storage and calculation.

Suppose the product of two four-bit values, 1101 and 1010, resulting in a decimal value of 130. The following is the outcome of applying the UT sutra.

4 Design of MAC Unit

Figure 1 depicts the basic MAC module's construction.

A Vedic multiplier is used in this situation, and the output is either added to or subtracted first from data stored in the accumulator. Our study presents a 32-bit MAC using a 16×16 Vedic multiplier/xor gate and an accumulator register. Fig. 2 depicts the suggested design's block diagram.

Sixteen Sutras and their corollaries

Sl. No	Sutras	Sub sutras or Corollaries
1.	Ekādhikena Pūrvena (also a corollary)	Ānurūpyena
2.	Nikhilam Navataścaramam Daśatah	Śisyate Śesamjnah
3.	Ūrdhva - tiryagbhyām	Ādyamādyenantyamantyena
4.	Parāvartya Yojayet	Kevalaih Saptakam Gunÿat
5.	Sūnyam Samyasamuccaye	Vestanam
6.	(Ānurūpye) Śūnyamanyat	Yāvadūnam Tāvadūnam
7.	Sankalana - vyavakalanābhyām	Yāvadūnam Tāvadūnīkrtya Vargañca Yojayet
8.	Puranāpuranābhyām	Antyayordasake' pi
9.	Calanā kalanābhyām	Antyayoreva
10.	Yāvadūnam	Samuccayagunitah
11.	Vyastisamastih	Lopanasthāpanabhyām
12.	Śesānyankena Caramena	Vilokanam
13.	Sopantyadvayamantyam	Gunitasamuccayah Samuccayagunitah
14.	Ekanyūnena Pūrvena	
15.	Gunitasamuccayah	
16.	Gunakasamuccayah	

Fig. 1. Sixteen sutras of Vedic math

4.1 Vedic Multiplier

The first step in building a 16-bit Vedic multiplier is to create a 2 × 2 Vedic multiplier that uses the UT sutra for two 4-bit number multiplication. This is one of the many processes that go into the design of a 16-bit Vedic multiplier. In a later level, a 4 × 4 multiplier is created by using the 2 × 2 multiplier that was constructed in the previous stage. In a way similar, an 8 × 8 multiplier may be constructed out of multiplier bricks measuring 4 × 4. In the end, a multiplier block with dimensions of 8 by 8 is used to produce a Vedic multiplier with dimensions of 16 by 16. Mux is utilized for choosing the mode, which determines whether or not the value is added or subtracted.

4.2 MAC Unit

A clock signal activates the MAC process. For example, the MAC unit is sometimes claimed to be capable of performing tasks such as "x + ab," where ab is defined as the 16-bit Vedic multiplier output. Repetitive addition and subtraction are possible depending

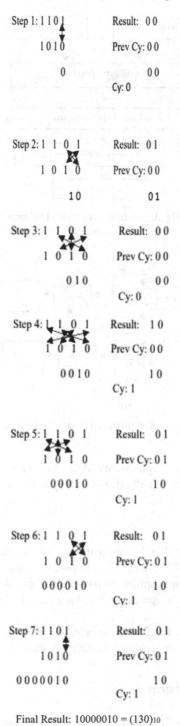

Step 1: 1 1 0 1   Result: 0 0

      1 0 1 0   Prev Cy: 0 0

           0   0 0
                          Cy: 0

Step 2: 1 1 0 1   Result: 0 1

       1 0 1 0   Prev Cy: 0 0

           1 0   0 1

Step 3: 1 1 0 1   Result: 0 0

       1 0 1 0   Prev Cy: 0 0

          0 1 0   0 0
                         Cy: 0

Step 4: 1 1 0 1   Result: 1 0

       1 0 1 0   Prev Cy: 0 0

         0 0 1 0   1 0
                         Cy: 1

Step 5: 1 1 0 1   Result: 0 1

       1 0 1 0   Prev Cy: 0 1

        0 0 0 1 0   1 0
                         Cy: 1

Step 6: 1 1 0 1   Result: 0 1

       1 0 1 0   Prev Cy: 0 1

       0 0 0 0 1 0   1 0
                         Cy: 1

Step 7: 1 1 0 1   Result: 0 1

      1 0 1 0   Prev Cy: 0 1

    0 0 0 0 0 1 0   1 0
                         Cy: 1

Final Result: 10000010 = (130)$_{10}$

Fig. 2. Product of two 4-bit Binary number using Urdhva Tiryakbyham algorithm

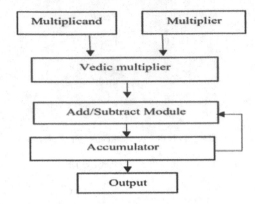

Fig. 3. Basic structure of MAC unit

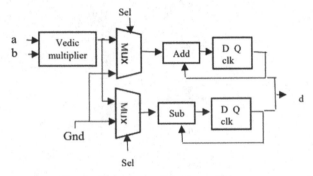

Fig. 4. The proposed design architecture

on the mux's mode settings. A high-quality MAC module is essential since it is the core of any digital signal processing method. According to the MAC, the output is 64-bits.

4.3 XOR Logic

While designing a 2 bit multiplier, UT sutra and half adders have been utilized for adding the partial products. A 4×4 Vedic multiplier was constructed by combining four 2×2 multiplier blocks with xor logic applied to partial products. As a result, hardware is both simplified and made more transparent. 8-bit along with 16-bit multipliers are designed in the same way.

The Verilog HDL is used in Xilinx Vivado to simulate and synthesize the design. The simulation's outcomes are explored in the next section.

5 Results and Discussion

Figures 3, 4, and 5 depicts the simulation outcomes. Vedic multipliers are shown in Fig. 3, whereas MAC units are shown in Figs. 4, 5, 6, and 7.

Fig. 5. 16 × 16 Vedic multiplier output

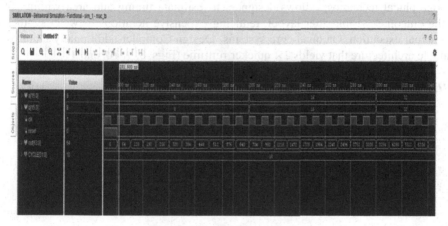

Fig. 6. MAC addition output

5.1 DC Compiler PPA Results

The Design Compiler® RTL synthesis solution allows users to meet today's design difficulties by meeting PPA (Performance, Power, Area) and test at the same time. Among Synopsys' synthesis products, Design Compiler is the most important. Optimized designs are provided by Design Compiler in order to produce the fastest as well as lowest logical representation of any given function. HDL descriptions are synthesized into technology-dependent, optimized, along with gate-level designs with the help of these tools. It can optimize for area, speed, as well as power in both sequential and combinational designs and supports a broad variety of hierarchical and flat design patterns.

For an introduction to logic- and gate-level, Design Compiler features cutting-edge topographical technology that ensures a consistent flow and speedier time to results.

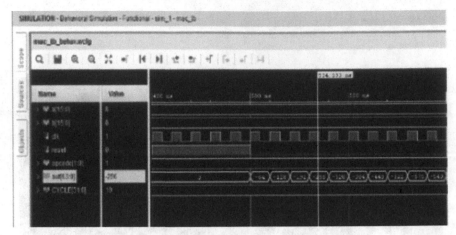

Fig. 7. MAC subtraction output

Topographical technology allows designers to estimate timing and area within 10% of the outcomes visible after layout, reducing expensive iterations between synthesis and actual execution. On quad-core systems, Design Compiler additionally features a scalable architecture that yields 2× quicker runtime (Figs. 8, 9, 10, and 11).

AREA

```
******************************************
Report : area
Design : vedic_multiplier_16x16
Version: J-2014.09-SP5-4
Date   : Sat Nov  2 18:26:12 2019
******************************************

Information: Updating design information... (UID-85)
Library(s) Used:

    saed90nm_max (File: /home/synopsys/90nmtech/SAED_EDK90nm/Digital_Standard_cell_Library/synopsys/models/saed90nm_max.db)

Number of ports:                       64
Number of nets:                       112
Number of cells:                       20
Number of combinational cells:         16
Number of sequential cells:             0
Number of macros/black boxes:           0
Number of buf/inv:                      0
Number of references:                   5

Combinational area:            8021.606567
Buf/Inv area:                  1415.577637
Noncombinational area:            0.000000
Macro/Black Box area:             0.000000
Net Interconnect area:          206.284368

Total cell area:               8021.606567
Total area:                    8227.890936
```

Fig. 8. Synthesized DC report for area of 16 × 16 Vedic multiplier

```
*************************************
Report : area
Design : accumulator_1
Version: J-2014.09-SP5-4
Date    : Sat Nov  2 17:41:19 2019
*************************************

Library(s) Used:

    saed90nm_max (File: /home/synopsys/90nmtech/SAED_EDK90nm/Digital_Standard_cell_Library/synopsys/models/saed90nm_max.db)

Number of ports:                         98
Number of nets:                         199
Number of cells:                         70
Number of combinational cells:            4
Number of sequential cells:              64
Number of macros/black boxes:             0
Number of buf/inv:                        4
Number of references:                     5

Combinational area:             9650.995360
Buf/Inv area:                   1440.460837
Noncombinational area:          2064.384033
Macro/Black Box area:              0.000000
Net Interconnect area:           355.055703

Total cell area:               11715.379393
Total area:                    12070.435096
```

Fig. 9. Synthesized DC report for area of accumulator

POWER

```
*********************************************
Report : power
       -analysis_effort low
Design : vedic_multiplier_16x16
Version: J-2014.09-SP5-4
Date    : Sat Nov  2 20:22:43 2019
*********************************************

Library(s) Used:

    gtech (File: /home/synopsys/designcompiler_vJ-2014.09-SP5-4/libraries/syn/gtech.db)

Operating Conditions: WORST   Library: saed90nm_max
Wire Load Model Mode: enclosed

Design              Wire Load Model          Library
------------------------------------------------------
vedic_multiplier_16x16  ForQA                saed90nm_max
vedic_multiplier_8x8    ForQA                saed90nm_max
vedic_multiplier_4x4    ForQA                saed90nm_max
vedic_multiplier_2x2    ForQA                saed90nm_max
half_adder              ForQA                saed90nm_max

Global Operating Voltage = 0.7
Power-specific unit information :
    Voltage Units = 1V
    Capacitance Units = 1.000000ff
    Time Units = 1ns
    Dynamic Power Units = 1uW      (derived from V,C,T units)
    Leakage Power Units = 1pW

   Cell Internal Power  =    0.0000 uW     (0%)
   Net Switching Power  =   10.7569 uW   (100%)
                          ----------
Total Dynamic Power     =   10.7569 uW   (100%)
```

Fig. 10. Synthesized DC report for power of 16×16 Vedic multiplier

5.2 Comparison of Power and Area

The recommended design is generated in 90 nm technology utilizing Synopsys Design Compiler in addition to being implemented in Xilinx Vivado for synthesis and implementation purposes. The Synopsys Design Compiler will provide the area and power that were achieved for the multiplier and accumulator modules.

The MAC power results obtained in Vivado for the suggested design is shown in Table 2, which is significantly less than the previous design reported in [6]. It is a well-known fact that power consumption rises linearly with bit input count. The current MAC

```
Report : power
          -analysis_effort low
Design : accumulator_1
Version: J-2014.09-SP5-4
Date   : Sat Nov  2 17:40:33 2019
****************************************
Global Operating Voltage = 0.7
Power-specific unit information :
    Voltage Units = 1V
    Capacitance Units = 1.000000ff
    Time Units = 1ns
    Dynamic Power Units = 1uW     (derived from V,C,T units)
    Leakage Power Units = 1pW


    Cell Internal Power  = 567.1113 uW   (77%)
    Net Switching Power  = 174.0386 uW   (23%)
                           ---------
Total Dynamic Power      = 741.1499 uW  (100%)

Cell Leakage Power       =  41.3475 uW

Information: report_power power group summary does not include estimated clock tree power. (PWR-789)

                Internal      Switching       Leakage         Total
Power Group     Power         Power           Power           Power    (   %   ) Attrs
-----------------------------------------------------------------------------------------------
io_pad            0.0000        0.0000          0.0000          0.0000  (   0.00%)
memory            0.0000        0.0000          0.0000          0.0000  (   0.00%)
black_box         0.0000        0.0000          0.0000          0.0000  (   0.00%)
clock_network     0.0000        0.0000          0.0000          0.0000  (   0.00%)
register          0.0000        0.0000          0.0000          0.0000  (   0.00%)
sequential       48.5519        1.4716       6.0004e+06        56.0240  (   7.16%)
combinational   518.5612      172.5671       3.5347e+07       726.4736  (  92.84%)
-----------------------------------------------------------------------------------------------
Total           567.1132 uW   174.0387 uW    4.1347e+07 pW    782.4976 uW
```

Fig. 11. Synthesized DC report for power of accumulator

Table 1. Power and area values

Parameter \ Circuit	Multiplier	Accumulator
Total Power (uW)	10.7569	545.8040
Total Area (sq. um)	8227.8909	5555.9737

Table 2. Comparison of power values of MAC

Parameter \ Design	Existing[6]	Proposed
Bits	16	32
Power (W)	0.124	0.241

unit uses more power than the recommended one in this case when the bit values are greater.

6 Conclusion

The MAC power results obtained in Vivado for the suggested design which is significantly less than the previous design reported above. It is a well-established fact that the amount of power required rises in proportion to the number of bits present at the input. Under these conditions, the current MAC unit uses more power as compared to the suggested one because it handles greater bit values.

A MAC unit based on the Urdhva-Tiryagbyham sutra was designed utilizing a 16 bit Vedic multiplier. In Synopsys DC and Xilinx, the design is then implemented. About a 3.2% increase in power was found to be significant. As a consequence of this, the proposed MAC unit has the potential to enhance the performance of a wide range of signal processing applications.

References

1. Dwivedi, K., Sharma, R.K., Chunduri, A.: Hybrid multiplier-based optimized MAC unit. In: 9th International Conference on Computing, Communication and Networking Technologies (ICCCNT) (2018)
2. Krishna Vamsi, A.S., Ramesh, S.R.: An efficient design of 16 bit MAC unit using Vedic mathematics. In: 2019 International Conference on Communication and Signal Processing (ICCSP), Chennai, India, pp. 0319–0322 (2019)
3. Jithin, S., Prabhu, E.: Parallel multiplier – accumulator unit based on vedic mathematics. ARPN J. Eng. Appl. Sci. **10**(8), 3608–3613 (2015)
4. Ahish, S., Kumar, Y.B.N., Sharma, D., Vasantha, M.H.: Design of high performance multiply accumulate computation unit. In: IEEE International Advance Computing Conference (IACC), pp. 915–918, June (2015)
5. Yuvraj, M., Bhaskar, N., Kailath, B.J.: Design of optimized MAC unit using integrated Vedic multiplier. In: International Conference on Microelectronic Devices, Circuits and Systems (ICMDCS) (2017)
6. Gadakh, S.N., Khade, A.K.: Design and optimization of 16×16 bit multiplier using Vedic mathematics. In: Proc. Int. Conf. on Automatic Control and Dynamic Optimization Techniques (2016)
7. Balakumaran, R., Prabhu, E.: Design of high speed multiplier using modified booth algorithm with hybrid carry look-ahead adder. In: 2016 International Conference on Circuit, Power and Computing Technologies (ICCPCT), Nagercoil, pp. 1–7 (2016)
8. Rakesh, S., Vijula Grace, K.S.: VLSI based low power multiply accumulate unit employing Kogge stone adder with modified pre-processing and post-processing stages. Int. J. Eng. Adv. Technol. **8**(4), 295–299 (2019)
9. Ranganath, L., Jay Kumar, D., Siva Nagendra Reddy, P.: Design of MAC unit in artificial neural network architecture using Verilog HDL. In: International Conference on Signal Processing, Communication, Power and Embedded System (SCOPES), pp. 607–612 (2016)
10. Akhter, S.: VHDL implementation of fast $N \times N$ multiplier based on Vedic Mathematics. IEEE. ISBN: 978-1-4244-1341-6, ECCTD (2007)
11. Bathija, R.K., Meena, R.S., Sarkar, S., Tinjrit, R.S.: Low power high speed 16×16 bit multiplier using Vedic mathematics. Int. J. Comput. Appl. **59**(6), 41–44 (2012)
12. Senthilpari, C., Singh, A.K., Diwadkar, K.: Low Power and High Speed 8×8 Bit Multiplier Using Non-clocked Pass Transistor Logic. IEEE (2007). 1-4244-1355-9/07
13. Kunchigi, V.: High Speed Area Efficient Vedic Multiplier. IEEE (2012). ISBN: 978-1-4577-1545-7
14. Law, C.F., Rofail, S.S., Yeo, K.S.: A low-power 16×16-bit parallel multiplier utilizing pass-transistor logic. IEEE J. Solid State Circ. **34**(10), 1395–1399 (1999)
15. Marimuthu, C.N., Thiangaraj, P.: Low Power High Performance Multiplier, vol. 8. ICGST-PDCS (2008)

Nowcasting - Rain Intensity Prediction Using Machine Learning Models with Markov Chain Process

Sudharsan Nagarajan, Sivagami Manickam, Jeganathan Lakshmanan, Maheswari Nachimuthu, and Pradeep Kumar Thimma Subramanian[✉]

Vellore Institute of Technology, Chennai, India
pradeepkumarts@ieee.org, {msivagami,jeganathan.l,maheswari.n, tspradeepkumar}@vit.ac.in

Abstract. Cloudbursts are weather phenomena with very high rain intensity and can result in flash floods causing large scale destruction and are extremely complex to forecast. The main aim of this research is to develop a model which would be capable of predicting cloudbursts by forecasting rain intensity. A model, combination of machine learning models with Markov Chain process, capable of forecasting rainfall intensity and in turn cloudbursts, has been proposed in this paper. The model uses Markov chain technique, in which prediction has been done based on the weather data from the past seven days. This proposed model has been implemented in two different ways, assigned each day of the previous seven days with (i) constant weights (ii) incremental weights, with closer days being considered more important. The results of the proposed model have been verified with the PRISM data set and the results have been tabulated. This result of the research shows that a multilayer perceptron with Markov chain process using incremental weights works better quantitatively.

Keywords: Precipitation · Weather forecasting · Artificial neural network · Multilayer perceptron · Weather parameters

1 Introduction

A cloudburst is defined as an extreme amount of precipitation in a very short period of time. For heavy rainfall to be classified as a cloudburst, the rate of rainfall should be greater than or equal to 100 mm per hour. Cloudbursts are a rare phenomenon as they occur only when an air mass is forced from low elevation to a higher elevation as it moves over rising terrain or occasionally when warm air mixes with cooler air, resulting in sudden condensation and large amounts of water. Most cloudbursts come from convective clouds that form thunderstorms and the amount of moisture required for a heavy downpour, which could lead to flash floods and which in turn can result in large scale destruction to human lives and properties. During a rainstorm, the air flowing upward contains a large quantity of water. When this upward current of air ends, all the

K. Kottursamy et al. (Eds.): IconDeepCom 2022, CCIS 1719, pp. 300–317, 2023.
https://doi.org/10.1007/978-3-031-27622-4_23

water is released quickly onto a small area, causing it to flood due to the extremely fast condensation and resulting in mass destruction.

Cloudburst occurrences in India has caused great damage and numerous loss of lives. More than 5000 people were killed in Kedarnath in Uttarakhand due to a cloudburst on June 15, 2013. The reason for the occurrence of floods was that the rainfall received was more than the regular rainfall the state usually received. The destruction of bridges and roads left about 300,000 pilgrims and tourists trapped in the valleys. On August 6, 2010, more than 1000 people were killed in Leh in Ladakh due to a cloudburst which also devastated 71 towns and villages including the main town in the area. On September 28, 1908, cloudbursts resulted in flooding in which 15,000 people lost their lives and more than 80,000 houses were destroyed along the banks of the Musi river. Around 1500 people were killed due to a cloudburst in Shimla in Himachal Pradesh on August 15, 1997. There have been many such occurrences of cloudbursts in India and all over the world, which have caused unimaginable amounts of destruction. Moreover, the rate of cloudburst occurrences have been increasing over the past few years, which could be the result of climate change, and currently there are no models which are capable of predicting cloudbursts, which further emphasizes the need for a prediction model.

The objective of this research is to build a system which would be capable of predicting cloudbursts by forecasting rainfall intensity. The goal of this model is to both nowcast and forecast rainfall intensity by using historical data. Rainfall intensity can then be used to predict cloudbursts. Early prediction of cloudbursts and warning of such severe weather systems is essential in mitigating societal impact arising from the accompanying flash floods.

For predicting cloudbursts, it is first essential to know the importance of each factor and the significance of the role they play in the formation of cloudbursts. However, there are a few challenges when it comes to building a cloudburst prediction model. Cloudburst is an extremely rare phenomenon, and might have not occurred multiple times in a single location. Hence, in most cases we are limited to one or two days of cloudburst datasets. This presents a challenge to build a model with high accuracy. Every location has a set of characteristics which define the default conditions. The traits of different regions could be vastly different and hence a generalised cloudburst detection model which can be used for more than one region is not possible. Cloudbursts can occur in various seasons, which makes it even more difficult to come up with a generalized model.

In this research, importance of weather parameters such as temperature, dew point temperature and vapour pressure deficit affecting precipitation has been noted. Using the role these factors play and their significance towards rainfall, rainfall intensity prediction models have been generated and compared with the existing models. For the purpose of this research, the PRISM Climate Group dataset has been used. The dataset consists of weather details for Autauga county in the state of Alabama in United States for 19 years from Jan 1, 2000 to Dec 31, 2018, having the parameters precipitation, minimum temperature, mean temperature, maximum temperature, dew point temperature, minimum vapour pressure deficit and maximum vapour pressure deficit.

Since the dataset is a time series dataset, the auto regressive integrated moving average (ARIMA) model has been implemented. An ARIMA model explains a given time series based on its own past values. It then uses that equation to forecast future values. The dataset has been divided into clusters based on the amount of precipitation. The ARIMA model results are compared with the other machine learning models such as linear regression, logistic regression, naive Bayes, k-nearest neighbours (KNN), random forests, support vector machine (SVM), perceptron and multilayer perceptron (MLP). This research paper proposes two novel methods which can be used to predict the rate of rainfall, which in turn can further be extended for both nowcasting and forecasting of cloudbursts. One of them uses a cluster based model which forecasts the intensity of rainfall for the next day given the previous day weather conditions, and the other uses a Markov chain model which predicts the intensity of rainfall for the next day given the parameter values of the previous seven days.

The main goal of this research is to generate a model capable of nowcasting and forecasting rainfall intensity in a particular location. Analysis of various machine learning models also need to be carried out by comparing their accuracy in predicting the rainfall intensity. Then, the aim is to incorporate these models with a unique mathematical approach and compare the rainfall intensity prediction results of the different models along with the mathematical approach.

The traditional methods used for predicting cloudbursts are weather forecasting, weather prediction by modeling meteorological data, data mining techniques and using manned and unmanned aerospace vehicles for laser beam atmospheric extinction measurements. These techniques are more expensive and time consuming along with an uncertainty of accurate prediction.

A less expensive method was an Arduino based cloudburst predetermination system as suggesfted by Tiwari and Verma (2019) which was able to calculate rainfall intensity in real time by using a rain gauge. This however does not help in prediction of cloudbursts and taking essential measures to prevent the damages is not possible. The Himalayan cloudburst event was further studied and numerical simulations were performed using the Weather Research and Forecasting model used by Chaudhuri et al. (2015) and MM5 model suggested by Das et al. (2006), however the location of the cloudburst was largely displaced. Various forecasting techniques for cloudbursts were surveyed and forecasting using big data analytics was found to give the best solution given by Olaiya and Adeyemo (2012). KNN clustering technique was also used to forecast cloudbursts by interpreting numerical weather prediction output products mentioned in Pabreja (2012). In one research namely Fowler et al. (2008), high levels of precipitation were classified into two categories, namely, cloudbursts and short intensity rainfall, and statistics of occurrences of these types of rainfall have been provided. Clustering plays an important role in data mining. The advantages and importance of clustering was analysed and explained in a research mentioned by Saluja et al. (2021).

Simulation of rainfall events were also carried out using MLP models suggested by Misra et al. (2018), and rainfall was found to be dependent on geopotential height, specific humidity, zonal, and meridional wind at four different levels of pressure. This model had its limitations and did not perform well when precipitation levels were high. Rainfall drop size was found out to play an important role in the type and rate of rainfall predicted by Ekerte et al. (2015). Exponential distribution was widely accepted as a suitable model for standard statistical distributions. Lognormal distributions, gamma distributions and Gaussian mixture models were also found out to provide more accurate computations for rate of rainfall. Monthly rainfall rate prediction has also been analysed and forecasted using MLP in which the number of hidden layers were equal to the number of input nodes which is recommended by Abdullah et al. (2016). The type of rain could also play a major role in determining the severity of rainfall. Methods to classify rain types into convective and stratiform using machine learning have been carried out by Ghada et al. (2019). The interdependence of rainfall and temperature were analysed to know the exact role and contribution of temperature in precipitation by Cong and Brady (2012). The results portrayed that rainfall and temperature were negatively correlated. One study evaluated the effect of climate change on everyday rainfall by assuming that the rainfall occurrences followed the Markov chain process used by Yoo et al. (2016). It concluded that the effect of climate change could cause more intense rainfalls but not significantly vary the number of rainfall days throughout the year.

There has been quite a large number of weather forecasting techniques claiming to outperform the other models and giving better results. One particular research suggested by Wang et al. (2017), states that weather forecasting carried out using artificial neural networks, decision trees and other data mining techniques give the most accurate results. Artificial neural networks and support vector machine models were developed and compared for predicting daily rainfall using a few weather parameters experimented by Pham et al. (2020). It concluded that SVM was the best method for predicting rainfall by using various quality assessment measures. A linear regressing and a functional regression model was used to forecast the maximum and minimum temperatures for seven days using the data received from the previous two days which is used by Holmstrom et al. (2016). This model however could not outperform the professional weather forecasting ones. A thorough evaluation and comparison of various machine learning models and a rainfall prediction model using Markov chain were done by Cramer et al. (2017). The machine learning models were able to outperform the current state of the art ones. A model using deep learning was proposed for predicting the total precipitation for the next day in Sumi et al. (2012). It used an autoencoder, which is a type of an artificial neural network, and a MLP for training and predicting.

To maintain high accuracy, the evaluation metrics are of extreme importance. Correlation is an important metric in evaluating the relation between 2 parameters. Correlation coefficients can range from -1 to +1, depending on the relation between the variables. The interpretation of correlation coefficients such as Pearson's and Spearman's rank has been detailed the appropriate method to use these correlation metrices has explained in this research done by Schober et al. (2018). The significance of Pearson's correlation has further been compared with other testing methods and comparisons of Statistical Package for Social Sciences (SPSS), Fisher's Z-transformation and t-distribution were carried out Sedgwick (2014). Kendall's rank correlation was testing using the Bayesian method and has been compared to Pearson's correlation given by Van Doorn et al. (2018). In some works, like Malhotra et al. (2019), the machine learning models are being used for the proactive measurement of the walking aid for the physically challenged ones. The datasets were trained with the same model what it was used in this work.

Prediction of precipitation has also been done using support vector machines (SVM) and particle swarm optimization (PSO) methods mentioned by Du et al. (2017). This uses the PSO algorithm instead of a linear threshold and finds the optimal parameters.

This paper states that the prediction model has a better accuracy than a direct prediction model. Nowcasting methods help in estimating the immediate weather conditions or gives the current conditions. Long short term memory (LSTM) algorithm was used for training a model by feeding it historical data, which was estimated by using the pyramid optical flow technique by Su et al. (2020). Their results portrayed that their model was capable of precisely simulating non-linear trends. Forecasting of long term seasonal spring rainfall was carried out using an artificial neural network and multiple regression suggested by Mekanik et al. (2013). The developed models were evaluated using mean square error and mean absolute error and showed potential for future growth. Since nowcasting, which is the prediction of rainfall for a maximum of six hours, is difficult due to the nonuniform characterization of weather, an architecture called Convast was used to predict the rainfall for short periods of time used by Kumar et al. (2020). However, this method used data from the satellite and was trained using ten continuous datasets.

2 Materials and Methods

This paper analyses the machine learning models and predicts the rain intensity for the day based on:

a) the current day's data
b) the previous day's data

Using the current day's data gives better results in comparison to using the previous day's data. This is mainly due to the reason that the current weather conditions play a larger role in determining the present situation.

The paper uses machine learning along with Markov chain approach and predicts the rain intensity for the eighth day using the data from the previous seven days. Two types of Markov chain processes have been used:

a) Days with constant weights
b) Days with incremental weights

The multilayer perceptron model with the previous seven days being assigned incremental weights gives the best results among all the prediction models.

For the purpose of this research, the PRISM Climate Group dataset has been used. The dataset consists of weather details for Autauga county in the state of Alabama in United States for 19 years from Jan 1, 2000 to Dec 31, 2018, having parameters such as precipitation, minimum temperature, mean temperature, maximum temperature, dew point temperature, minimum vapour pressure deficit and maximum vapour pressure deficit. This dataset contains the time series values for individual locations. It contains climate data observed from a wide range of monitoring networks. The dataset has been developed by applying numerous quality control measures to detect short term and long term weather patterns. Figure 1 shows a few sample records from the dataset and the parameter details are provided in Table 1

	Date	ppt (mm)	tmin (degrees C)	tmean (degrees C)	tmax (degrees C)	tdmean (degrees C)	vpdmin (hPa)	vpdmax (hPa)
0	2000-01-01	7.22	0.6	3.3	6.0	3.3	0.02	1.02
1	2000-01-02	9.84	3.4	5.4	7.5	3.7	0.14	2.59
2	2000-01-03	7.10	3.8	4.9	6.1	3.5	0.12	1.90
3	2000-01-04	12.86	4.7	6.9	9.1	5.9	0.21	1.80
4	2000-01-05	1.72	4.2	7.0	9.8	5.0	0.23	3.33

Fig. 1. Sample records from the PRISM dataset

Table 1. Parameter notations of the PRISM dataset

Notation	Parameter
ppt	Precipitation
tmin	Minimum temperature
tmean	Mean temperature
tmax	Maximum temperature
Tdmean	Mean dewpoint temperature
vpdmin	Minimum vapour pressure deficit
vpdmax	Maximum vapour pressure deficit

2.1 Nowcasting Using Machine Learning Models

Nowcasting is a type of weather forecasting technique which forecasts weather for short periods from two hours to six hours. Various machine learning algorithms such as single layer perceptron, linear regression, logistic regression, naive Bayes, KNN, random forests, support vector machine and multilayer perceptron have been used to predict the intensity of rainfall. This paper attempts to identify the best machine learning algorithm to predict the rain intensity with better accuracy.

The PRISM dataset contains 19 years of data from 2000 to 2018. For training the machine learning models, a randomized 70% of the dataset was used and the remaining 30% was used for testing. This model tries to predict the rainfall intensity using a single day's data, either the current day or the previous day, so the models were trained and tested with individual day's data and the precipitation values were assigned accordingly. The model was built using the PRISM dataset, and a single day's data has been used for the purpose of testing.

Linear Regression. A linear regression model is one in which the relationship between the dependent variables and the independent variables is computed through a linear equation, where 'y' is dependent and 'x' is independent. The main objective of the linear regression model is to find the optimum values of the coefficients of the linear equation. Mean square error is used as the cost function and is minimized to find the optimum coefficients.

$$y = b_0 + \sum\nolimits_{i=1}^{n} (b_i X_i) \tag{1}$$

In this model, 70% of the dataset was used for training and the remaining 30% was used for testing. The precipitation values of the current day or next day was used along with the other parameters. So, for testing, given the values of the temperature, dewpoint temperature and vapour pressure deficit, the model predicts the precipitation amount and the accuracy got was 37.7% for the current day's data and 15.2% for the previous day's data.

Logistic Regression. Logistic regression models are similar to the linear regression models but are used for classification purposes, whereas the linear regression models are used in the regression tasks such as to predict or to forecast values. The output of the logistic regression is the probability value of an event occurring, thus the range is between zero to one. Sigmoid function is used to calculate the probabilities.

$$p = {}^1\!\big/\!{(1 + e^{-(b_0 + \sum_{i=1}^{n} (b_i X_i))})} \tag{2}$$

In this model, 70% of the dataset was used for training. So, for testing, the model uses 30% of the dataset, and given the values of the weather parameters, the model predicts the precipitation intensity with an accuracy of 67.3% for the present day's data and 55.2% for the previous day's data.

Perceptron. A perceptron is a supervised learning algorithm that helps in the classification of the given input data. It basically divides the input signal into two classes, yes and no. The perceptron model was inspired by the biological structure of human neurons. When a single perceptron combines with many others, it forms an ANN. A perceptron algorithm that detects features from the input data by performing various computations and is used for supervised learning of binary classifiers. This algorithm processes the elements in the training dataset and enables the neurons to learn. The perceptron algorithm is used to classify groups and patterns by finding the linear separation between different objects and patterns that are received through numeric or visual input (Fig. 2).

$$f(x) = \sum\nolimits_{i=1}^{n} (w_i x_i) + \theta \tag{3}$$

$$y = \begin{cases} 1, & \text{if } f(x) \geq 0 \\ 0, & \text{if } f(x) < 0 \end{cases} \tag{4}$$

For the perceptron algorithm, the total number of iterations or epochs were set to 10,000 and the computation was terminated if the values or weights were not altered for more than 5 iterations. The learning rate was set to 0.0001. The perceptron model first assigns random weights to the parameters. In each iteration, it changes the weights for every parameter, making sure that the accuracy is greater than the previous iteration. At one point, it attains the maximum accuracy and the process is terminated.

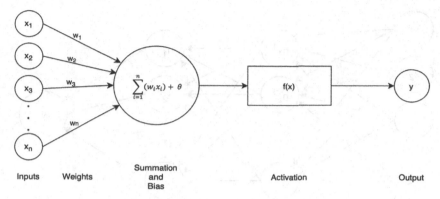

Fig. 2. Single layer perceptron

The dataset was split up into training sets and testing tests, with 70% being used for training. The precipitation values of the current day or next day was used along with the other parameters. So after feeding the temperature, dew point temperature and vapour pressure deficit values, the model uses the remaining 30% of test data, and predicts the intensity of rainfall for the current day with an accuracy of 65.5% and the next day with an accuracy of 55.2%.

Multilayer Perceptron. A multilayer perceptron is an extended version of a perceptron model. A single layer perceptron has one layer, whereas a multilayer perceptron, as the name suggests, consists of multiple layers. In a multilayer perceptron, the layers in between the input layer and the output layer are called hidden layers. A MLP is a deep, artificial neural network. It consists of more than one perceptron and has of an input layer which receives the signal, a number of hidden layers which carry out the computations and an output layer that makes a decision. A multilayer perceptron uses the input-output pairs to train itself, and learns to model the relationship between those inputs and outputs. While training, the model changes the weights to minimize the error which is done by using backpropagation in which the weights and bias adjustments are carried out relative to the error (Fig. 3).

$$f_j^1(x) = \sum_{i=1}^{n} (w_i x_i) + \theta \tag{5}$$

$$h_j^1 = \begin{cases} 1, & \text{if } f_j(x) \geq 0 \\ 0, & \text{if } f_j(x) < 0 \end{cases} \tag{6}$$

$$h_j^1 = \begin{cases} 1, & \text{if } f_j(x) \geq 0 \\ 0, & \text{if } f_j(x) < 0 \end{cases} \tag{7}$$

$$h_j^k = \begin{cases} 1, & \text{if } f_j^k(x) \geq 0 \\ 0, & \text{if } f_j^k(x) < 0 \end{cases} \tag{8}$$

$$y = \begin{cases} 1, & \text{if } f^n(x) \geq 0 \\ 0, & \text{if } f^n(x) < 0 \end{cases} \tag{9}$$

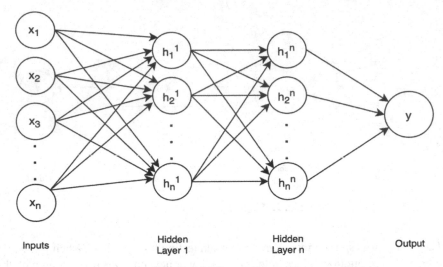

Fig. 3. Multilayer perceptron

For the multilayer perceptron algorithm, the total number of iterations or epochs were set to 10,000 and the computation was terminated if the values or weights were not altered for more than 10 iterations. The learning rate was set to 0.001 and the MLP had 8 hidden layers with each layer having 10 nodes. The activation function was changed from default the rectified linear unit function, 'relu', to a hyperbolic tan function, 'tanh'. An inverse scaling learning rate, which gradually decreases the learning rate at each step was used instead of the constant learning rate. For weight optimization, the 'lbfgs' solver, which is an optimizer in the family of quasi-Newton methods was used, instead of the default 'adam' solver, a stochastic gradient-based optimizer.

In this model, 70% of the dataset was used for training and the remaining 30% for testing. Given the values of the temperature, dew point temperature and vapour pressure deficit parameters, this model gives an accuracy of 68.5% for the present day's data and 60.2% for the previous day's data.

2.1.1 K-Nearest Neighbours

K-nearest neighbours is an algorithm used to find similar data points that exist in the close proximity of a given data point. There is no learning process for KNNs, rather the entire data is stored for finding out the similar points. Thus, each prediction is done using the training data itself. The K represents the number of similar instances that the algorithm will find (Fig. 4).

$$d(p, q) = d(q, p) = \sqrt{\sum_{i=1}^{n} (q_i - p_i)^2} \tag{10}$$

In this model, 70% of the dataset was used for training. The precipitation values of the current day or next day were used along with the other parameters. So, for testing the

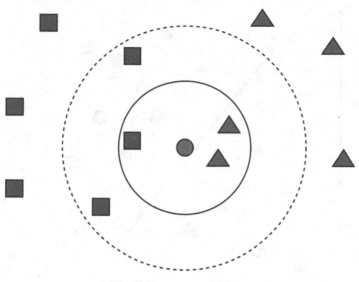

Fig. 4. K-nearest neighbours

remaining 30% of the dataset was used, and given the values of the parameters such as temperature, dew point temperature and vapour pressure deficit, the model predicts the precipitation amount with an accuracy of 64.1% for the present day's data and 55.4% for the previous day's data.

Support Vector Machine. Support vector machines are used to find the optimal hyperplane in a K-dimension feature space that distinctively classifies the data, where K is the total number of features. These hyperplanes act as a decision boundary to help classify the data. SVMs are capable of doing both classification and regressions (Fig. 5).

$$g(x) = \omega^T x + b \tag{11}$$

Having used 70% of the dataset for training, the testing was carried out using the remaining 30% of the dataset. This model gave an accuracy of 68.4% by using the current day's data, and 58.7% by using the previous day's data after feeding the values of the temperature, dewpoint temperature and vapour pressure deficit for the remaining 30% of the dataset.

2.2 Nowcasting Using Machine Learning Models with Markov Chain Process

In this paper machine learning models have been analysed with and without Markov Chain process. A new model has been proposed which can be used to predict the intensity of rainfall and in turn can be used to nowcast and forecast cloudbursts. The target variable for this research is precipitation and the range of this parameter varies broadly.

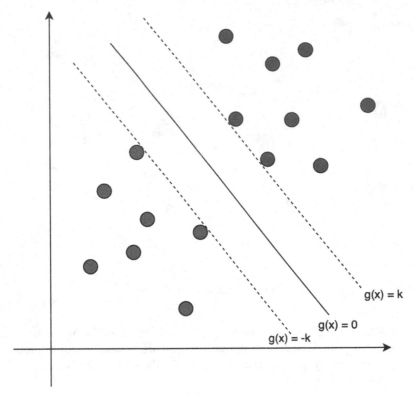

$$g(x) = k$$

$$g(x) = 0$$

$$g(x) = -k$$

Fig. 5. Support vector machine

Various machine learning algorithms such as single layer perceptron, linear regression, logistic regression, naive Bayes, KNN, random forests, support vector machine and multilayer perceptron are used to predict rainfall intensity. These models are then used along with Markov chain approach, which assigns different weightage for the days based on the proximity of that day.

These machine learning models are trained by giving more weightage to the important factors. In this Markov chain approach model the data from the previous 7 days has been used to predict the conditions for the 8th day. This model uses machine learning algorithms such as MLP, perceptron, KNN, random forests, SVM, logistic regression and linear regression for rainfall prediction and Markov chain process for assigning weights of the previous days and compares the results. Rain intensity prediction has been done by applying the machine learning models. In order to improve the accuracy of the results from the machine learning algorithms, the Markov chain process has been used. A Markov chain model is a stochastic model, so the pattern cannot be predicted precisely. It is one in which the probability of each event depends only on the state attained in the previous event. A Markov chain model is a mathematical system that consists of a sequence of possible events, where the probability of each event is completely dependent on the state attained in the previous event and the transitions from one state to another according to certain probabilistic rules. So, the next state of the process does not depend on the sequence of states but only depends on the previous state.

Markov chain model was used so that the impact of the previous day datasets could be varied. So, to streamline the variation, the Markov chain process has been implemented in two different ways, by assigning constant weights and incremental weights, and in both these methods, the most recent day is given the highest weightage. In the first method, equal weightage is given to the first six days, and in the second method, the weightage for each day doubles, going from the last day to the most recent day. In the constant weights method, a weight of 0.8 is assigned to the most recent day, while a total weight of 0.2 is assigned to the remaining six days, with each day being given equal importance. Compared to this, in the incremental weights method, a weight of 0.7 is assigned to the most recent day and a total weight of 0.3 is assigned to the remaining six days, with the weight of the fifth day being half of the sixth day, the weight of the fourth day being half of the fifth day, and so on. The Figs. 6 and 7 show how the machine learning algorithms are used with Markov chain approach for both constant weights and incremental weights respectively.

All these machine learning based Markov chain algorithms are trained and tested, and the results have been compared to find the best machine learning based Markov chain approach model.

Constant Weights Based Markov Chain Process With Machine Learning Algorithms

In this method, the most recent day is considered to be more important than the others. So it is given a greater weightage of 0.8 while the remaining 6 days together is given a weightage of 0.2 with each day given equal weights. This is then used for training and testing the machine learning models.

```
Algorithm:
X_new = [ ] y_new = [ ]
for i in range(6, len(X)-1):
            A = X[i] * 0.8
            B = sum(X[i-6:i])/6 * 0.2
X_new.append(A+B)
y_new.append(y[i+1])
For predicting X8, the equation used is:
        X7 * 0.8 + ( X6 + X5 + X4 + X3 + X2 + X1 )/6 * 0.2    (Eq.12)
        where X1-8 are the days.
Eg. For predicting a Monday. . .
        Sun * 0.8 + (Mon + Tue + Wed + Thu + Fri + Sat)/6 * 0.2 is
used.
```

This constant weights approach was implemented using the machine learning models. The parameters were calculated using Eq. 12, and the precipitation of the eighth day was assigned to it. The machine learning models were then trained and tested.

Incremental Weights Based Markov Chain Process with Machine Learning Algorithms

In this method, incremental weights are used and recent days are considered to be more important. On further analysis, the previous day's weather condition was found out to

312   S. Nagarajan et al.

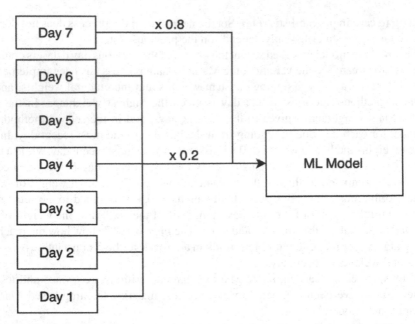

Fig. 6. Block diagram of constant weights based rain intensity prediction using ML models

have a far greater impact on the very next day. So, it has been given a weightage of 0.7, while the remaining six days together make up a total of 0.3 with each day assigned a different weight, and the more recent days getting the higher weights. This is then used for training and testing the machine learning models.

```
Algorithm:
X_new = []
y_new = []
for i in range(6, len(X)-1):
    A = X[i] * 0.7
    B = 0
    k = 32
    for j in range(6):
        B = B + X[i-1-j]*k
        k = k/2
    B = B/63
    B = B*0.3
    X_new.append(A+B)
    y_new.append(y[i+1])
For predicting X8, the equation used is:
        X7 * 0.7 + ( X6*(32/63) + X5*(16/63) + X4*(8/63)+ X3*(4/63) +
X2*(2/63) + X1*(1/63) ) * 0.3 (Eq.13)
        where X1-8 are the days.
Eg. For predicting a Monday. . .
Sun*0.7  +   Sat*(32/63)*0.3  +  Fri*(16/63)*0.3  +  Thu*(8/63)*0.3  +
Wed*(4/63)*0.3 + Tue*(2/63)*0.3 + Mon*(1/63)*0.3 is used.
```

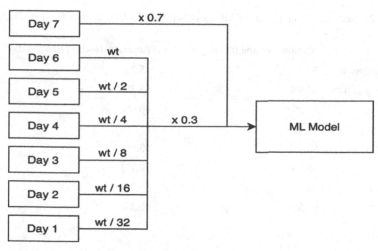

Fig. 7. Block diagram of incremental weights based rain intensity prediction using ML models

This incremental weights approach was implemented using the machine learning models. The parameters were calculated using Eq. 13, and the precipitation of the eighth day was assigned to it. The machine learning models were then trained and tested.

3 Results and Discussions

The comparisons and implementation of the models were done using a Jupyter notebook in a 2.3 GHz Quad-Core, 8th generation Intel Core i5 system. For the purpose of this research, the PRISM Climate Group dataset was used. The dataset consists of weather details for Autauga county in the state of Alabama in United States for 19 years from Jan 1, 2000 to Dec 31, 2018, having parameters such as precipitation, minimum temperature, mean temperature, maximum temperature, dew point temperature, minimum vapour pressure deficit and maximum vapour pressure deficit.

The models such as linear regression, logistic regression, k-nearest neighbours (KNN), random forests, support vector machine (SVM), perceptron and multilayer perceptron (MLP) were implemented without using Markov chain and the results are compared in Table 2. The performance of most of the models were almost in the same range with MLP giving the best results. The current day's data was used to calculate the current day's precipitation and the results have been tabulated in the first column in Table 2. Since the current day's data is used, this method cannot be used for nowcasting or forecasting. The previous day's data was also used to calculate the current day's precipitation and the results have been tabulated in the second column in Table 2. Figure 8 shows the comparison of models implemented by using the current day's data and the previous day's data.

The machine learning models with Markov chain approach gives the prediction for the next day based on the data from the last seven days. The ML models were trained by using the data obtained from the implemented Markov chain approach. For these models,

Table 2. Accuracy comparisons of ML models for the PRISM dataset from 2000–2018

Model	Accuracy (using that day's data)	Accuracy (using previous day's data)
Linear regression	37.7%	15.2%
Logistic regression	67.3%	55.2%
Naive bayes	60.9%	46.6%
KNN	64.1%	55.4%
Random forests	62.3%	53.4%
SVM	68.4%	58.7%
Perceptron	65.5%	55.2%
MLP	68.5%	60.2%

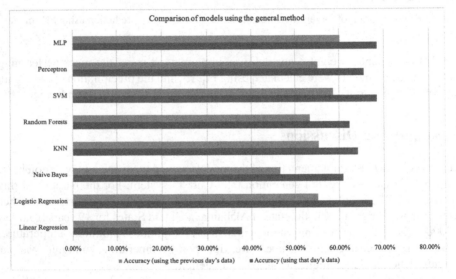

Fig. 8. Accuracy comparisons of ML models for the PRISM dataset from 2000–2018

a randomized 70% of the complete dataset was used for training and the remaining 30% was used for testing.

The accuracy got from these models varied over a large range. The maximum accuracy was got from the MLP with Markov chain model and was equal to 62.3% for the constant weights method and was equal to 64.1% for the incremental weights method. The results of the Markov chain process implemented with MLP, perceptron, KNN, random forests, SVM, logistic regression and linear regression are tabulated in Table 3. Figure 9 shows that MLP with Markov chain model clearly outperforms the other models.

The MLP with Markov chain models proposed in this paper, predicts the amount of precipitation and in turn cloudbursts based on the data of the previous days, perform

Table 3. Accuracy comparisons of ML models with Markov chain process implemented with constant weights and incremental weights for the PRISM dataset from 2000–2018

Model	Constant weights accuracy	Incremental weights accuracy
MLP	62.3%	64.1%
Perceptron	53.5%	57.0%
KNN	56.6%	55.7%
Random forests	56.5%	57.1%
SVM	60.3%	60.1%
Naive Bayes	50.8%	50.4%
Logistic regression	59.8%	59.3%
Linear regression	20.7%	20.2%

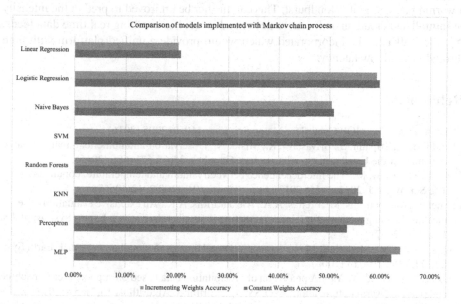

Fig. 9. Accuracy comparisons of ML models with Markov chain process implemented with constant weights and incremental weights for the PRISM dataset from 2000–2018

well and show significant improvements when compared to the other machine learning models mentioned in Table 2 which also need the current day's data for estimation. If the intensity of rainfall is greater than 100 mm, the model assigns this as a cloudburst and gives out an advanced warning.

4 Conclusion

Cloudbursts are an extremely difficult event to predict directly due to the lack of historical data and also due to its low frequency of occurrence. So, in this paper rainfall intensity has been used as a metric to forecast cloudbursts. Comparisons of various machine learning models such as linear regression, logistic regression, naive Bayes, k-nearest neighbours (KNN), random forests, support vector machine (SVM), perceptron and multilayer perceptron (MLP) applied on a weather dataset to predict the rainfall intensity have been carried out. The model proposed in this paper can be used for nowcasting and forecasting the intensity of rainfall, which in turn can be used to predict cloudbursts. A Markov chain approach, in which the states are only dependent on the previous state, is integrated and implemented with the existing machine learning models. The MLP based Markov chain model gives the best results among the machine learning models. The proposed models perform well and show significant improvements when compared to the existing models. If the rainfall intensity is greater than 100 mm, the model gives out a warning of a possible cloudburst. This can further be improved to predict the intensity of rainfall and cloudbursts for more days in advance. For handling real time data feeds, Apache Kafka can be incorporated which would provide a unified platform with high throughput and low latency.

References

Make, M.R.A., et al.: IOP Conf. Ser.: Mater. Sci. Eng. **160**, 012005 (2016)

Chaudhuri, C., Tripathi, S., Srivastava, R., Misra, A.: Observation-and numerical-analysis-based dynamics of the Uttarkashi cloudburst. Ann. Geophys. **33**(6), 671–686 (2015)

Cong, R.-G., Brady, M.: The interdependence between rainfall and temperature: copula analyses. The Sci. World J. **2012**, 1–11 (2012). https://doi.org/10.1100/2012/405675

Cramer, S., Kampouridis, M., Freitas, A.A., Alexandridis, A.K.: An extensive evaluation of seven machine learning methods for rainfall prediction in weather derivatives. Expert Syst. Appl. **85**, 169–181 (2017)

Das, S., Ashrit, R., Moncrieff, M.W.: Simulation of a Himalayan cloudburst event. J. Earth Syst. Sci. **115**(3), 299–313 (2006)

Du, J., Liu, Y., Yu, Y.: W Yan: A prediction of precipitation data based on support vector machine and particle swarm optimization (PSO-SVM) algorithms. Algorithms **10**(2), 57 (2017)

Fowler, A.M., Boswijk, G., Gergis, J., Lorrey, A.: ENSO history recorded in Agathis australis (kauri) tree rings. Part A: kauri's potential as an ENSO proxy. Int. J. Climatol. **28**(1), 1–20 (2007). https://doi.org/10.1002/joc.1525

Ghada, W., Estrella, N., Menzel, A.: Machine learning approach to classify rain type based on Thies disdrometers and cloud observations. Atmosphere **10**(5), 251 (2019)

Hernández, E., Sanchez-Anguix, V., Julian, V., Palanca, J., Duque, N.: Rainfall prediction: a deep learning approach. In: Martínez-Álvarez, F., Troncoso, A., Quintián, H., Corchado, E. (eds.) Hybrid Artificial Intelligent Systems, pp. 151–162. Springer International Publishing, Cham (2016). https://doi.org/10.1007/978-3-319-32034-2_13

Holmstrom, M., Dylan, L., Christopher, V.: Machine learning applied to weather forecasting. Meteorol. Appl. 1–5 (2016)

Ekerete, K.E., Hunt, F.H., Jeffery, J.L., Otung, I.E.: Modeling rainfall drop size distribution in southern England using a Gaussian Mixture Model. Radio Sci. **50**(9), 876–885 (2015)

Kumar, A., Islam, T., Sekimoto, Y., Mattmann, C., Wilson, B.: Convcast: An embedded convolutional LSTM based architecture for precipitation nowcasting using satellite data. PLOS ONE **15**(3), e0230114 (2020). https://doi.org/10.1371/journal.pone.0230114

Mekanik, F., Imteaz, M.A., Gato-Trinidad, S., Elmahdi, A.: Multiple regression and Artificial Neural Network for long-term rainfall forecasting using large scale climate modes. J. Hydrol. **503**, 11–21 (2013)

Misra, U., Deshamukhya, A., Sharma, S., Pal, S.: Simulation of daily rainfall from concurrent meteorological parameters over core monsoon region of India: a novel approach. Adv. Meteorol. **2018**, 1–18 (2018). https://doi.org/10.1155/2018/3053640

Olaiya, F., Adeyemo, A.B.: Application of data mining techniques in weather prediction and climate change studies. IJ Inform. Eng. Electron. Bus. **1**, 2074–9031 (2012)

Pabreja, Kavita: Clustering technique to interpret Numerical Weather Prediction output products for forecast of Cloudburst. Int. J. Comput. Sci. Inform. Technol. (IJCSIT) **3**(1), 2996–2999 (2012)

Pham, B.T., et al.: Development of advanced artificial intelligence models for daily rainfall prediction. Atmos. Res. **237**, 104845 (2020)

Schober, P., Christa, B., Schwarte, L.A.: Correlation coefficients: appropriate use and interpretation. Anesth. Analg. **126**(5), 1763–1768 (2018)

Sedgwick, P.: Understanding statistical hypothesis testing. BMJ **348**(may30 1), g3557–g3557 (2014). https://doi.org/10.1136/bmj.g3557

Shi, F., Su, X., Qian, H., Yang, N., Han, W.: Research on the fusion of dependent evidence based on rank correlation coefficient. Sensors **17**(10), 2362 (2017)

Malhotra, S., Balasubramanian, K., Parveen Sultana, H.: An IoT-ML based proactive walking aid for the visually challenged. Int. J. Eng. Adv. Technol. **9**(1), 6032–6036 (2019). https://doi.org/10.35940/ijeat.A1867.109119

Su, A., Li, H., Cui, L., Chen, Y.: A convection nowcasting method based on machine learning. Adv. Meteorol. **2020**, 1–13 (2020). https://doi.org/10.1155/2020/5124274

Sumi, S., Monira, M., Faisal, Z., Hideo, H.: A rainfall forecasting method using machine learning models and its application to the Fukuoka city case. Int. J. Appl. Math. Comput. Sci. **22**, 841–854 (2012)

Thirumalai, C., Sri Harsha, K., Lakshmi Deepak, M., Chaitanya Krishna, K.: Heuristic prediction of rainfall using machine learning techniques. In: 2017 International Conference on Trends in Electronics and Informatics (ICEI), pp. 1114–1117. IEEE (2017)

Tiwari, A., Verma, S.K.: Cloudburst predetermination system. ISOR J. Comput. Eng. **17**, 44–56 (2015)

van Doorn, J., Ly, A., Marsman, M., Wagenmakers, E.-J.: Bayesian inference for Kendall's rank correlation coefficient. The Am. Stat. **72**(4), 303–308 (2018). https://doi.org/10.1080/00031305.2016.1264998

Wang, Z., Mazharul Mujib, A.B.M.: The weather forecast using data mining research based on cloud computing. J. Phys. Conf. Series **910**(1), 012020 (2017)

Yeh, H.-F., Hsu, H.-L.: Using the Markov chain to analyze precipitation and groundwater drought characteristics and linkage with atmospheric circulation. Sustainability **11**(6), 1817 (2019). https://doi.org/10.3390/su11061817

Yoo, C., Lee, J., Ro, Y.: Markov chain decomposition of monthly rainfall into daily rainfall: evaluation of climate change impact. Adv. Meteorol, **2016**, 1–10 (2016). https://doi.org/10.1155/2016/7957490

A Survey of WSN Efficient Network Restoration Model Using Genetic Algorithms

Vishal Patil$^{(\boxtimes)}$ and Ninad More

Department of Computer Science and Engineering, Chhatrapati Shivaji Maharaj University,
Panvel, Navi Mumbai, Maharashtra, India
`vishal180109@csmu.ac.in`

Abstract. Recently, wireless sensor networks (WSNs) are attaining a lot of attention and application, particularly in challenging environments like battle-field reconnaissance. Small indicator nodes, that are lower-cost, lower-power, and multi-functional are one type of WSN usage. These tiny indication nodes communicate across short distances. Since conversational power consumption is a considerable power drain, the number of attacks must be reduced to achieve increased battery life. These networks can be damaged on a wide scale, causing several nodes to malfunction and then network is divided into discontinuous portions. In this instance, restoring network connection is critical to prevent harmful consequences on the programme. In this paper, how to restore connection in WSNs has been studied, and describe the key directions and research outcomes in recent times, categorize connectivity restoration solutions for WSNs, and identify gaps and possible research directions.

Keywords: Index terms—efficient network restoration model · Wireless sensor networks · Genetic algorithm · Next generation (xG) applications

1 Introduction

A metaheuristic-inspired evolving algorithm namely the Genetic Algorithm belongs to a vast class of algorithms. John Holland discovered GA in 1970. These are created to imitate a few of the processes that occur in nature. To solve issue, GA replicates "survival of the fittest" between individuals across several generations. Charles Darwin established this idea and said that the fittest person wins out over the weakest. Each one in a group is forced to go into an evolutionary process. Scalability, production cost, and security are all important considerations in WSNs. Implementation, scope, deployment, and density are few WSN's distinguishing features. The sensors include thoroughly embedded devices which are fully linked with their physical surroundings and capabilities of obtaining, processing, communicating, contextual awareness computing, and basic calculation activities. Whereas this novel networking class has the ability to allow a wide application range, on the other hand, faces significant hurdles in areas such as routing, data collecting and dissemination, rapid network topology modification, and fault-tolerant [1]. WSNs are a well-known and much studied wireless communication model. These networks

© The Author(s), under exclusive license to Springer Nature Switzerland AG 2023
K. Kottursamy et al. (Eds.): IconDeepCom 2022, CCIS 1719, pp. 318–331, 2023.
https://doi.org/10.1007/978-3-031-27622-4_24

have proven to be widely used and efficient wireless communication ideas to present. Sensing devices are attached to items and dispersed within a geographical region to detect particular localised circumstances and transmit in timely information, which is a fundamental definition of WSNs. Its observations of perceived local circumstances are delivered from end-to-end sensors in the dispersed network topologies, whereas findings are forwarded from every sensor towards a central controlling unit in centralized topologies. The observations are utilised in both circumstances to make crucial network choices that can assist the network in making quick actions for complete functioning and maintenance of communication networks wherein WSNs have been installed [2, 3]. Despite the fact that these networks are no more a novel technology, its importance continues to rise rapidly as improved technologies emerge which need sensing, monitoring, and feedback in order to function. WSNs become the most essential technologies in advancing next-generation (xG) wireless networking prospects in modern wireless communications world.

There are substantial progresses in the creation of novel and contemporary WSN concepts in current years. Furthermore, the sensor nodes (SNs) currently created and implemented for WSNs generally have quality, size, and durability restrictions. Because many SNs are primarily battery-powered, their lifespan is restricted. Many SNs' processing capabilities as well as memory spaces have currently quite poor, owing to their small size, restricting their resource capacity. Because of WSN as well as SN constraints, WSN deployments and application malfunctions are always a potential. When malfunctions are not effectively handled, it can have a significant impact on the WSNs performance and reliability [4]. Mistakes in WSN apps increase the consequences of malfunctions in xG techniques, in which the required amount of throughput, latency, dependability, and other factors are crucial. SNs failure in WSNs, for example, might lead to the network's shortest transmission path being lost. This can lengthen the transmission path, resulting in an enhancement in transmission latency or networking energy usage [5]. Failure's impact disastrous repercussions on WSNs when it is not treated properly, particularly when these WSNs are used or implemented for xG apps. Whereas the WSN-style method that people develop in that functionality is standard, it needs various application-specific elements, like those contained in the precision agricultural structure to demonstrate the effectiveness of the produced algorithm [1]. Table 1 shows the various classification of papers with respect to failure.

2 Network Failure Types

2.1 Actor Failure

If other channels between the harmed actors aren't accessible, an actor malfunction might result in the loss of many inter-actor network systems, potentially partitioning the network. Thus, such a circumstance will stymie the players' participation, negatively impacting the WSANs applications. The majority of this WSAN research is focused on the proper positioning/actor participation to maximise coverage and response [6, 7]. Inter-actor connection has been explored in terms of actor placement, ignoring the possibility of inter-actor connectivity breakdowns. In [8], an actor coverage has been increased while maintaining connectedness.

Table 1. Classification of papers based on actor/node failure and connectivity failure for network restoring model

Research Papers	Proposed Method	Actor/Node Failure	Connectivity/Link Failure
Abuelenin et al	Enhanced Failure recovery Method	✓	×
Zonouz et al	Hybrid Wireless Sensor Networks	✓	×
Akkaya et al	COLA: Coverage and Latency aware Actor	✓	×
Melodia et al	Distributed Coordination Framework	✓	
Younis et al	Coverage-aware and Connectivity constrained Actor Positioning	✓	✓
NeeloferTamboli et al	Coverage-Aware Connectivity Restoration	×	✓
Akkaya et al	Coverage and Latency Aware Actor Placement Mechanisms	✓	×
Wang et al	Movement-Assisted Sensor Deployment	✓	×
Wang et al	Sensor Relocation	✓	×
Basu et al	Fault-Tolerant Ad Hoc Robot Networks	✓	×
Younis et al	Localized Self-healing Algorithm	✓	×
Abbasi et al	Distributed Connectivity Restoration Algorithm	×	✓
Mohamed et al	Restoring Internode Connectivity	✓	✓
Heo et al	Energy-Efficient Mobile Sensor Networks	✓	×
Wang et al	Proxy-based Mobile Sensor Networks	✓	×
Wu et al	Scan-Based Movement-Assisted Sensor Deployment Method	✓	×
Cortés et al	Mobile Sensing Networks Coverage Control	✓	✓
Zhang et al	Link fault identification		✓
Tay et al	Impact of node failures and unreliable communications	✓	×
Sitanayah et al	Fault-tolerant relay placement algorithm	✓	×
Almasaeid et al	Minimum K-Connectivity Repair	×	✓
Tang et al	Relay node placement	✓	×
Deniz et al	Adaptive, energy-aware and distributed fault-tolerant topology-control algorithm	✓	×
Abbasi et al	Movement-assisted connectivity restoration	×	✓
Gokturk et al	Cooperation with multiple relays	✓	×
Cardei et al	Topology control in ad hoc wireless networks	✓	×
Wang et al	Adaptive connectivity restoration from node failure	✓	✓
Ramezani	Distributed method to reconstruct connection	×	✓
Akkaya et al	Distributed recovery in movable sensor/actor networks	✓	×
Imran et al	Partitioning detection and connectivity restoration algorithm	✓	×
Haider et al	Analysis of reactive connectivity restoration algorithms	✓	✓

2.2 Connectivity

A group of mobile SNs will be used to cooperatively examine a subject of concern and track particular occurrences in some applications, including space discovery, border and coastal security, military field reconnaissance, search and rescue. While engaging in the job execution, nodes have been intended to create a network and synchronize their actions once deployed. Nodes in numerous configurations, including a disaster management system, must work together to successfully seek for survivors, evaluate damage, and find safer escape routes. Inter-node communication is critical not just for application efficiency and for network access. It's preferable if connectivity can be restored quickly. Recovery in high-risk locations, such as battle zones, must be a self-healing procedure employing current sensor nodes [9].

The issue of node relocation has been well researched [10]. Some techniques simply enable mobility among the initial enhancement and the start-up of the applications. Wang, Cao, as well as La Porta proposed methods to disperse the sensors and optimise coverage [11]. With exception of C3 R, [12] and [13] are more concerned with avoiding coverage gaps than with sustaining connection. Post-deployment node displacement is proposed by COCOLA, and C2 AP to increase connection and coverage simultaneously improving other network characteristics. [10, 12] do not address the consequences of a node dropout. Wang et al. [13] presented cascaded migration of neighbouring nodes towards the failing node as a way to restore from node malfunction. Basu and J. Redi [14], such as C3 R do not anticipate that spare nodes will be available. They shift a nodes' subset in blocks, dissimilar to C3 R. RIM [15], as well as DARA [16] are the most similar methods to C3 R whereas these do not consider coverage and instead use cascaded relocation.

2.3 Internode Connectivity

The network operation can be disrupted if a node fails unexpectedly. A node might fail as a result of external damage caused by the hostile environment. The loss occurred in these nodes might disrupt network connectivity and render most of their neighbours unavailable. In worst scenario, the network could be divided into many discontinuous parts and rendered inoperable. As a result, sensors must be able to identify and retrieve from failure. Given that WSNs are often self-contained and untreated, recovery must be a network-wide self-healing procedure carried out in a dispersed way [17]. Mini-max, VEC, and VOR, are three similar algorithms developed by Wang et al. [12] enabling post-deployment relocation. Heo, and Varshney [18] adopt an identical technique that mimics Coulomb's law yet ignores the Voronoi polygon of nodes. Every node rather advances a distance proportionate to the node density in its immediate vicinity. Wang et al. [19] propose a second strategy that allows nodes to model these motions before relocating to the finalized site. Rather, Wu and Yang [20] developed the SMART algorithm, which controls nodes in clusters. The sensing area has been split into grids, further these grids are filled with the equal number of nodes. Another important paper on post-deployment node location based on coverage by Corte et al. [21].

2.4 Single Node Failure

Network partitioning owing to one or multiple backbone action nodes malfunction, i.e. when certain network section is separated from the other network has become a key challenge for WSANs in hostile conditions. Further mobile nodes, like as robots or unmanned aerial vehicles (UAVs) can occasionally be utilised to recover such divisions [22]. However, because of the unattended environment specific positions are unfamiliar, such mobile nodes typically exceedingly expensive and sometimes hard to implement. Rather than explicitly moving some more mobile nodes, such implicit appropriate action nodes are utilized for mending network segmentation in WSANs for price efficiency and real-time functioning.

3 Related Works

In this part, we'll look at the critical topic of network malfunctions and how to restore and safeguard wireless networks from errors. In specific, we look at present initiatives in the research arena to guarantee that network communications are protected from failures using existing network restoration concepts and methods. A communication defect was stated as a forceful, temporary network change, primarily as a consequence of a disturbance in the actual flow structure or traffic that typically leads to a reduction in the ability of impacted connectivity/nodes in the network occasionally to zero [23]. Connectivity problems and node problems were the two sorts of problems that can occur. A connectivity problem in wireless communication occurred whenever the connection among two different nodes in the network (i.e. node and central control unit) malfunctions [24]. When a connectivity failure occurs, the problem was commonly solved through redirecting/redistributing the faulty traffic connection to other nearby functional connections with adequate ability to handle the additional load. A node failure occurred if one or several nodes (routers, switches, control hubs, and so forth) malfunction [25]. Like a general assessment, it appeared that much more work had gone into protecting/restoring communication systems from connectivity disruptions than from those node failures. It could be attributed to a variety of factors. One of these reasons was the realisation that resolving node failure issues was far more difficult and time-consuming than addressing connectivity failure issues. An explanation could be the assumption that connectivity faults are highly important than node faults because it occurred more frequently. Furthermore, node failures occurred frequently as connectivity faults in current wireless communication systems like new-generation WSNs. As a result, node failures were as important as, if not highly important as, connectivity problems. Furthermore, newly established xG wireless communication solutions integrate the usage of multiple techniques like the internet-of-things (IoT), cloud computing, fifth-generation, and heterogeneous networks techniques at the same time. Vehicle-to-vehicle communication would be an excellent illustration of how such coupled technologies might be used. The needs of higher precision, reduced latency, and uninterrupted service delivery in the xG systems necessitate that the possibility of all forms of faults (connectivity/node) be kept to a minimal, if not totally avoided. Moreover, these xG requirements necessitate prompt detection of any failures (whether connection or node), as well as full network restoration in extremely shorter time frames when these problems happen. They evaluate current efforts on fault prediction and optimal network restoration options focusing on WSNs supporting xG communications. As per the functioning concept, existing methods can be divided into two different categories namely proactive and reactive.

3.1 Proactive Methods

To compensate the failed nodal loss, proactive approaches necessitate redundancy resources. To tackle this issue, K-connectivity [26–28] was presented. Because any node pair can have K-disjoint paths, the algorithms might withstand the malfunction of K-1 members. 2CRNDC tries to equalize a two-connected topological network having a small amount of relay nodes to attain a superior fault-tolerant property [29]. Owing to its diversity, it does not need connectivity restoration while the required relay nodes were limited. Deniz et al. proposed the Adaptive Disjointable Path Vector (ADPV) method for heterogeneity WSNs, which is an adaptable, energy-aware, and maybe even distributive fault-tolerant topology-control technique [30]. In contrast to proactive strategies, recovery mechanisms in reactive alternatives begin when a fault is discovered. Whenever a network was divided, the primary solution is to transform a faulty node with an appropriate backup node via inward motion, and also most recent research have found this to be an effective technique. DARA [31], for example, seeks a coordinated translocation to recover the disrupted communication routes between the damaged neighbours' node. The node was either a cut-vertex or else not using information from two-hop neighbours by this DARA. When a node fails, it chooses the best candidates (BC) from the failed neighbour's node based on their distance, degree, and node Identity, and subsequently relocate the BC to the faulty node's place to recover connectivity. Whether any BC's neighbours are unable to interact with the BC following its mobility, the BC's neighbours commence the procedure, and a cascaded motion was offered to remedy the issue.

3.2 Reactive Methods

The CSFR-M algorithm and CCRA algorithm were reactive processes that deal with node faults largely through collaborative communication and mobility potential as a backup technique if a CC-link cannot be created. Gokturk et al. [32] evaluated the energy efficiency of collaborative communication. This was obvious that node motions would take far higher energy rather than communication among nodes, and the communicating energy usage would be underestimated since the recovery procedure might be overlooked in comparison to node motions. Reactive restoration methods, unlike proactive restoration methods are passive and initiate a recovery procedure whenever a node fault occurs. It does not necessitate the allocation of unnecessary resources. The primary aim is to rejoin the neighboring of the failing node. Collaborative communication and node relocation are the two main methods. [33] is the first to describe collaborative communication. It enables a node to communicate with its surroundings exceeding its communication zone. The acquired mean signal-to-noise ratio (SNR) must be greater rather than fixed threshold for network entities to interact. Signal strength decreases as transmission distance increases, and overlays appear at the endpoint. To recover connectivity, CSFR uses cooperative communication [34]. Taking advantages of a neighbor's transportation information did not result in a significant rise in the neighbor's energy utilization. Although this appeared to have lower overhead in the short term, this is a long-term procedure that consumes a huge energy in the longer term. Furthermore, selecting the help nodes was inconvenient and time-consuming.

3.2.1 Distributed Actor Recovery Algorithm (DARA)

DARA is a decentralised technique that relies on the failing node's neighbours to initiate the recovery process. The cut-vertex node failure that used to connect them prevents them from cooperating. Rather, they repeat the same steps. It includes the following steps to ensure a smooth rehabilitation process: Regular Neighbor List Upkeep: The list of neighbouring actors is the only pre-failure information required. Actors must be informed of their one-hop and two-hop neighbours and keep this information current. Finding an Actor's Failure and Starting the Recovery Period: Missed heartbeat signals indicate actor failure. Depending on the actor's network structure, massive or zero recovery may be required. As previously stated, a node failure does not affect the remaining nodes' connections, requiring no network changes. Choosing the Ideal Candidate: For each lost actor, DARA replaces one 1-hop neighbour. This method can repair broken links and eliminates any uncertainty about signal propagation. Moving a Cascaded Node: The BC actors plan to move to the failed parent actor's position and estimate the time required. Also, before moving, the BC will check for nearby children.

3.2.2 Connected Dominating Set-Detection and Recovery Algorithm (CDS-DRA)

An actor's failure to connect to a network can be minor or major. If the missing actor is a node leaf, no actors are affected. When used as a networking gateway node, however, the failing actor's network connection suffers. These are called cut-vertices. Cut-vertex evaluation: It is easy to tell if a node is cut-vertex using first depth search trees (DFS) [35]. This method requires a network overload and may be costly in terms of message cost. So they look for a distributed solution. The inter-actor network's connection dominant set (CDS). Cleaning a Cut-vertex Failings: In order to restore inter-actor internet connection, find an actor within the area and replace the defective node. Message exchanged in advance: It's best to deal with the cut-vertex node loss as soon as possible because its neighbour cannot interact. Locating the nearest dominatee reduces movement distance. Connectivity is restored by moving the nearest dominatee to the failed cut-vertex. MMI would also be abnormally high due to the possibility of a long movement. However, this method is unbalanced and causes the moving actor to die much faster than the rest of the network. Figure 1 depicts this algorithmic approach.

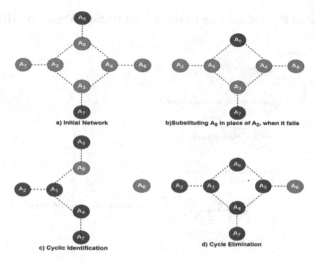

Fig. 1. CDS-DRA algorithm.

3.2.3 An Application-Oriented Fault Detection and Recovery Algorithm (AFDR)

WSANs with actors and sensors can use AFDR. Its sensors detect and communicate with actors. To design the best coordinated reaction, these actors collect and analyse sensor data. The communication length of an actor's radio is its maximum Euclidean distance. To communicate with another actor or a sensor, an actor has two transmitters. To facilitate evaluation, nodes are assumed to have the same communication range. Actors and sensors were randomly placed in a target area. Actors should be able to identify each other after deployment and form a network [36]. An actor should be ready to act on demand and notify its backups so it isn't mistaken for defective. Figure 2 depicts the network with critical and non-critical actors.

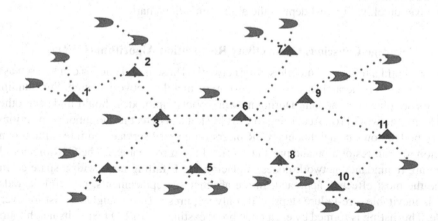

Fig. 2. Representation of non-critical and critical network in connected interactor network.

3.2.4   Distributed Prioritized Connectivity Restoration Algorithm (DPCRA)

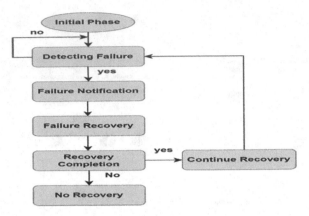

Fig. 3. DPCRA flowchart.

In hazardous situations where recovering a divided network is difficult, DPCRA is suitable. After installation, each actor node broadcasts a hello message to its neighbours, including its Id and position. Actor nodes send a heartbeat signal to update details on a regular basis. No heartbeat signal from an adjacent actor node confirms node failure, and the authorised FH initiates recovery action immediately. DPCRA uses mobile nodes and also the accessibility of the closest steady dominatee nodes to reduce the number of participating nodes for such recovery. The suggested method has two stages: A node's pre-failure knowledge is kept aggressively up to 2-hop neighbours and updated regularly with piggybacked heartrate signals. (ii) The next stage is restoration, which covers the situation after network division and how to react. Best feature of this DPCRA is whether it uses cascaded motion with nearby accessible dominatee nodes (non-cut vertex nodes) to recover quickly. Figure 3 depicts the algorithm's flowchart.

3.2.5   Coverage Conscious Connectivity Restoration Algorithm (C3R)

C3R can build a node for a mobile sensor network. These mobile nodes can be used as a second layer in a hierarchical network design, or in a flat network design. Surrounding sensors are placed at random. During network bootstrap, nodes should find each other and form a network [16]. According to C3R [37], it can detect its neighbours' positions. Every node knows its neighbours. C3R offers temporary service and intermittent connection to limit restoration and prevent service loss in some areas. The C3R method: If there are redundancy network nodes, replacing the F failing node with a spare seems to be the most effective approach. In the absence of replacements, graceful degradation is inevitable. Pre-failure steps: C3R only requires a 1-hop neighbour list for every node. This listing is formed by each node broadcasting a HELLO text to its neighbours. Identifies its neighbours' positions and IDs. Neighbour synchronisation: When node A detects F's failure, it starts the restoration process, unless it is already involved in another node's restoration. Because cut-vertex identification is difficult, C3R uses the recovery technique if F failed node is a cut vertex. A recovery plan: A node informs its neighbours of its temporary move to F to avoid being viewed as defective. Until A returns, neighbours who route data through A will have to find alternate buffers/routes. Implementing the rehabilitation strategy: The coordinator's recovery plan instructs each affected node. Avoided nodes revert to their original positions and functions. A participant node's task is to travel to F's location, stay for a while, and then return home. While in F, node A connects to all of F's neighbours to provide network access. This algorithm is shown in Fig. 4.

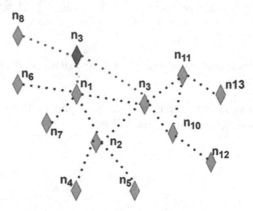

Fig. 4. C3R sample design.

4 Experimental Analysis

This section examines the network restoration model, which includes both proactive and reactive approaches. The proactive model finds the fault occurring prior to the sensor nodes in WSNs, whereas the reactive model finds the fault occurring between the two sensor nodes in WSNs. This study compares the genetic algorithm's network restoration model to show its advantages and disadvantages in WSNs. Also, we compared various proposed methodologies in various papers. Also, which methods help in the failure recovery process. The Fig. 5 shows various articles published in terms of network restoration from 2006 to 2020. Figure 6 shows various papers' proposed methods for actor/node and connectivity failure in WSNs. Figure 7 compares the performance of various proposed methods for restoring the network from Table 1. Using a genetic algorithm to repair a network failure has been proposed many times. It mostly talks about node/actor failures or connectivity/link failures. This survey helps identify the most efficient way to diagnose and fix problems in a wireless sensor network. This survey used older and newer methods. So we found the diverse growth in this field. This also aids in restoring a network's timeline.

Figure 5, is the plot of the number of survey papers that we have considered for performing this survey and also helps in segregating the methods and upgradation in it based on the published years. Figure 6, provides the information about the papers that

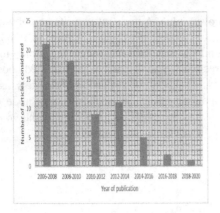

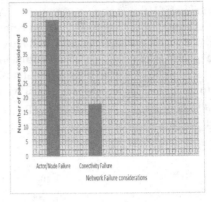

Fig. 5. No. of articles vs publication year.   **Fig. 6.** Failure vs no. of papers considered.

discussed node failure and connectivity failure. Few papers discussed about both the failures and the methods to overcome those failures.

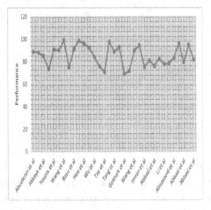

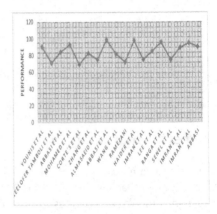

Fig. 7. a: Comparison of various methodologies. b: Comparison of various methodologies.

Figure 7a provides the data of the performance percentage of each of the proposed methods in terms of restoring a node failure. In these papers different methods have been proposed and various technologies and algorithm have been used. This provides the information of the methods that outperforms the need over the past ten years. Similarly, Fig. 7b describes the data about the performance of the methods proposed for restoring the connectivity failure in the links.

The Fig. 8a shows the performance of the various algorithms with respect to node travel during the restoration process. Many algorithms have been compared with one another with this parameter of using the genetic algorithm for network restoration. The C3R outperforms all other four algorithms in this parameter. The Fig. 8b gives us the comparison between the algorithms namely DARS, CDS-DRA, AFDR, DPCRA and C3R. In this comparison also we could find that the C3R algorithm performs better than

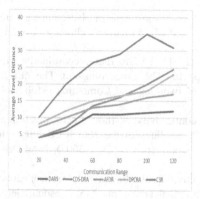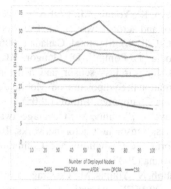

Fig. 8. a: Average node distance during restoration. b: The analysis of network size for various algorithms.

all other algorithms compared to in this figure. The size of the network doesn't influence the average distance travelled.

5 Conclusion

In this paper, we have discussed about the WSN (Wireless Sensor Networks) and its applications. We have undergone a survey on finding the efficient network model for restoring the failures occurring in the network. This genetic algorithm is a versatile algorithm that has been used in the methods for finding the failures and restoring them. Many research papers have been considered and its performance has been evaluated and we were able to come up with the efficient method for network restoration using the genetic algorithm in WSN.

References

1. Kaur, H., Tejpal, G., Sharma, S.: A review article on genetic algorithm in wireless sensor network. In: Proceedings of the 2nd International Conference on Communication and Electronics Systems (ICCES 2017) IEEE Xplore Compliant - Part Number: CFP17AWO-ART (2017)
2. Kumar, M., Gupta, V.: A review paper on sensor deployment techniques for target coverage in wireless sensor networks. In: 2016 International Conference on Control, Instrumentation, Communication and Computational Technologies (ICCICCT), pp. 452–456 (2016)
3. Verma, G., Sharma, V.: A survey on hardware design issues in RF energy harvesting for wireless sensor networks (WSN). In: 2016 5th International Conference on Wireless Networks and Embedded Systems (WECON), pp. 1–9 (2016)
4. Abuelenin, S., Dawood, S., Atwan, A.: Enhancing failure recovery in wireless sensor network based on grade diffusion. In: 2016 11th International Conference on Computer Engineering Systems (ICCES), pp. 334–339 (2016)
5. Zonouz, A.E., Xing, L., Vokkarane, V.M., Sun, Y.L.: Reliability based optimization in hybrid wireless sensor networks. In: 2015 Annual Reliability and Maintainability Symposium (RAMS), pp. 1–7 (2015)

6. Akkaya, K., Younis, M.: COLA: a coverage and latency aware actor placement for wireless sensor and actor networks. In: The Proceedings of IEEE Vehicular Technology Conference (VTC-Fall'06), Montreal, Canada (2006)
7. Melodia, T., Pompili, D., Gungor, V.C., Akyildiz, I.F.: A distributed coordination framework for wireless sensor and actor networks. In: The Proceedings of The 6th ACM International Symposium on Mobile Ad Hoc Networking and Computing (Mobihoc'05), Urbana-Champaign, Illinois (2005)
8. Akkaya, K., Younis, M.: Coverage-aware and connectivityconstrained actor positioning in wireless sensor and actor networks. In: The Proceedings of the 26th IEEE International Performance Computing and Communications Conference (IPCCC 2007), New Orleans, Louisiana (2007)
9. Tamboli, N., Younis, M.: Coverage-aware connectivity restoration in mobile sensor networks. In: 2009 IEEE International Conference on Communications. pp. 1–5. Dresden, Germany (2009)
10. Younis, M., Akkaya, K.: Strategies and techniques for node placement in wireless sensor networks: a survey. J. Ad-Hoc Netw. 6(4), 621–655 (2008)
11. Akkaya, K., Younis, M.: Coverage and latency aware actor placement mechanisms in WSANs. Int. J. Sensor Netw. 3(3), 152 (2008)
12. Wang, G., Cao, G., La Porta, T.: Movement-assisted sensor deployment. In: Proceedings of the INFOCOM'04, Hong Kong (2004)
13. Wang, G., Cao, G., La Porta, T., Zhang, W.: Sensor relocation in mobile sensor networks. In: Proceedings IEEE 24th Annual Joint Conference of the IEEE Computer and Communications Societies, vol. 4, pp. 2302–2312. Miami, FL, USA (2005)
14. Basu, P., Redi, J.: Movement control algorithms for realization of fault-tolerant ad hoc robot networks. IEEE Netw. 18(4), 36–44 (2004)
15. Younis, M., Lee, S., Gupta, S., Fisher, K.: A localized self-healing algorithm for networks of moveable sensor nodes. In: IEEE GLOBECOM 2008 – 2008 IEEE Global Telecommunications Conference, pp. 1–5. New Orleans, LA, USA (2008)
16. Abbasi, A., Akkaya, K., Younis, M.: A distributed connectivity restoration algorithm in wireless sensor and actor networks. In: Proceedings of 32nd Conference on Local Computer Networks, Dublin, Ireland (2007)
17. Younis, M., Lee, S., Abbasi, A.A.: A localized algorithm for restoring internode connectivity in networks of moveable sensors. IEEE Trans. Comput. 59(12), 1669–1682 (2010). https://doi.org/10.1109/TC.2010.174
18. Heo, N., Varshney, P.K.: Energy-efficient deployment of intelligent mobile sensor networks. IEEE Trans. Syst., Man, Cybern. A 35(1), 78–92 (2005)
19. Wang, G., Cao, G., La Porta, T.: Proxy-based sensor deployment for mobile sensor networks. In: Proceedings of the First IEEE International Conference Mobile Ad-hoc and Sensor Systems (MASS '04) (2004)
20. Wu, J., Yang, S.: SMART: a scan-based movement-assisted sensor deployment method in wireless sensor networks. In: Proceedings of the IEEE INFOCOM, '05 Mar 2005
21. Cortes, J., Martinez, S., Karatas, T., Bullo, F.: Coverage control for mobile sensing networks. IEEE Trans. Robot. Automat. 20(2), 243–255 (2004). https://doi.org/10.1109/TRA.2004.824698
22. Akyildiz, I.F., Kasimoglu, I.: Wireless sensor and actuator networks: research challenges. Ad Hoc Netw. 2(4), 351–367 (2004)
23. Franklin, P.H., Tavrovsky, I., Ames, R.: A strategy for optimal management of spares. In: 2016 Annual Reliability and Maintainability Symposium (RAMS), pp. 1–6 (2016)
24. Zhang, X., Zhang, Z.: Link fault identification using dependent failure in wireless communication networks. Electron. Lett. 52(2), 163–165 (2016)

25. Tay, W.P., Tsitsiklis, J.N., Win, M.Z.: On the impact of node failures and unreliable communications in dense sensor networks. IEEE Trans. Signal Process. **56**(6), 2535–2546 (2008)

26. Sitanayah, L., Brown, K.N., Sreenan, C.J.: A fault-tolerant relay placement algorithm for ensuring k vertex-disjoint shortest paths in wireless sensor networks. Ad Hoc Netw. **23**, 145–162 (2014)

27. Sitanayah, L., Brown, K., Sreenan, C.: Planning the deployment of multiple sinks and relays in wireless sensor networks. J. Heuristics **21**(2), 197–232 (2014). https://doi.org/10.1007/s10 732-014-9256-z

28. Almasaeid, H.M.; Kamal, A.E. On the Minimum K-Connectivity Repair in Wireless Sensor Networks. In Proceedings of the IEEE International Conference on Communications (ICC '09), Dresden, Germany, 14–18 June 2009; pp. 1–5.

29. Tang, J., Hao, B., Sen, A.: Relay node placement in large scale wireless sensor networks. Comput. Commun. **29**, 490–501 (2006)

30. Deniz, F., Bagci, H., Korpeoglu, I., Yazıcı, A.: An adaptive, energy-aware and distributed fault-tolerant topology-control algorithm for heterogeneous wireless sensor networks. Ad Hoc Netw. **44**, 104–117 (2016)

31. Abbasi, A.A., Younis, M., Akkaya, K.: Movement-assisted connectivity restoration in wireless sensor and actor networks. IEEE Trans. Parallel Distrib. Syst. **20**, 1366–1379 (2009)

32. Gokturk, M.S., Gurbuz, O.: Cooperation with multiple relays in wireless sensor networks: Optimal cooperator selection and power assignment. Wirel. Netw. **20**, 209–225 (2013)

33. Cardei, M., Wu, J., Yang, S.: Topology control in ad hoc wireless networks using cooperative communication. IEEE Trans. Mobile Comput. **5**(6), 711–724 (2006)

34. Wang, H., Ding, X., Huang, C., Wu, X.: Adaptive connectivity restoration from node failure (s) in wireless sensor networks. Sensors **16**(10), 1487 (2016)

35. Cormen, T.H., Leiserson, C.E., Rivest, R.L., Stein, C.: Introduction to Algorithms, 2nd edn. MIT Press and McGraw-Hill (2001)

36. Akkaya, K., Thimrnapuram, A., Senel, F., Uludag, S.: Distributed recovery of actor failures in wireless sensor and actor networks, In: Proceedings of the IEEE Wireless Communications and Networking Conference (WCNC'08), pp. 2480–2485., Los Vegas, Nev, USA (2008)

37. Bulusu, N., Heidemann, J., Estrin, D.: GPS-less Low-cost Outdoor Localization for Very Small Devices. IEEE Pers. Commun. **7**(5), 28–34 (2000)

An Evaluation on the Performance of Privacy Preserving Split Neural Networks Using EMNIST Dataset

Vimaladevi Madhivanan[1]([✉]) [iD] and Padmapriya Mathivanan[2]

[1] SRM Institute of Science and Technology, Kattankulathur, Tamilnadu, India
vimaladm@srmist.edu.in
[2] DXC Technologies, Singapore, Singapore

Abstract. Preserving the Privacy of user data is a raising concern in the current scenario, since the usage of client's data from edge devices play a vital role in the field of artificial intelligence and deep learning. Distributed learning is presented as a solution to the scenario, where there are restrictions in exposing the data to gain meaningful insights. Split Learning is a distributed collaborative learning technique in which the neural network is split into multiple sections for training. Each of these sections are trained on a different collaborating client and the training of the network is done only by transferring the weights between the layers of the sections without any raw data transfer. In this study, the focus is given on the application of EMNIST as a challenging dataset for the evaluation of performance of Split Neural Networks (SNNs) and Federated Learning (FL). The FL model gives an accuracy of 97.49% and 96.8% for MNIST and EMNIST dataset respectively. Also, SNNs implemented using a vanilla architecture over multiple clients provide better results in comparison with simple CNN models with an accuracy of 97.83% and 88.05% for MNIST and EMNIST dataset respectively. The experimental results prove that EMNIST can be used apart from popularly used MNIST and CIFAR 10 datasets and SplitNNs can be used to overcome the drawbacks of FL.

Keywords: Distributed learning · Federated learning · Split learning · Split neural networks · Partitioning of neural networks · Collaborative learning

1 Introduction

Recent advancements in Deep Learning and the availability of data and computing resources have made the task of pattern recognition in images as well as speech to perform with greater accuracy. This makes the application of Artificial Intelligence (AI) in almost all the fields. One of the raising concerns in the vast application of AI is the security and preserving the privacy of the user data. The success of any AI system depends on the amount of data available for training. But some data, even though available in large quantities, cannot be exposed publicly. Examples of such data include medical and clinical health, payment and transaction data, etc. A traditional AI system requires

© The Author(s), under exclusive license to Springer Nature Switzerland AG 2023
K. Kottursamy et al. (Eds.): IconDeepCom 2022, CCIS 1719, pp. 332–344, 2023.
https://doi.org/10.1007/978-3-031-27622-4_25

the data to be present in a centralized single machine or a server. This type of machine learning algorithm model requires all the data collected from different sources or clients to be sent to a central server.

Since the data is generated at frequent intervals, it is required to re-train the model for improved accuracy and performance. Hence, it is essential to use a suitable training model that does not interrupt the workflow and apply a parallelization and distributed model of computation. Federated Learning (FL) and Split Neural Network (SNN), also called Split Learning (SL), are examples of such an approach which uses collaborative distributed style of model training. These distributed learning models work in a decentralized way in training the prediction model. Instead of uploading the raw data to a central or edge server, the edge devices compute the model updates using their local data and send the updates of the model's parameters to the server, which then computes the aggregation operation. In this way, the client's raw data is protected, communication cost is reduced, and a reduction in latency is achieved. With the advent of storage and computational capabilities on the edge devices, these collaborative learning models can bring edge intelligence into reality.

This work aims to perform a study on the performance of the distributed learning approach, namely the Split Leaning model using popular datasets MNIST and EMINST. Existing literature studies the performances of FL and SL using CIFAR10 and MNIST datasets. The MNIST database was derived from NIST Special Database 19. This database contains handwritten digits, uppercase letters and lowercase letters. MNIST dataset is widely used in the character recognition and computer vision applications. This MNIST dataset was able to achieve very high accuracies of the order of above 99.7%, which puts the dataset labeling into question. Hence, it is required to use a more challenging dataset to validate the classifier system and arrive at more meaningful insights. Extended MNIST (EMNIST) dataset constitutes a more challenging classification task. For this it involves letters and digits, and this EMNIST uses the same parameters and image structure as the original MNIST. To the best of our knowledge, EMINST is not used to study the performances of the classifier models trained using Split Leaning collaborative models. Hence, in this study the performance of Split Learning using MNIST and EMNIST implemented using VGG16 is studied along with the performance of Federated Learning.

The rest of the paper is organized into various sections as follows. Section 1.1 provides an overview of image classification using deep learning models. Section 1.2 discusses the concepts of Collaborative Distributed Learning and explains the concepts of FL and SL. The summary of the literature study is given in Sect. 1.3. With the findings of the literature survey done, the problem formulation and research objective setting for this work is done in Sect. 2. The methodology of the study performed is given in Sect. 3 and the results and performance analysis are discussed in Sect. 4. Section 5 concludes this study.

1.1 Image Classification Using Neural Networks

Convolutional neural networks (CNN) is a recent breakthrough and the ubiquitous concept in image and computer vision space. Even though the history of CNN dates back from the 1980s, the researchers were able to achieve successful results in terms of high accuracy only in the 2010s with the advent of GPUs and large availability of data. A simple Convolutional Neural Network (CNN) is a deep learning model that uses three or more layers of Artificial Neural Network (ANN) to implement the task of image recognition, for example. Each layer extracts one of more features of the input images. Extraction of features is required for classification of the image and the training data is a large dataset that consists of multiple images for such feature extraction. Such a dataset where the images are annotated with the classification is called the supervised learning model.

CNN finds its application in various use cases such as medical imaging, social media analytics, facial search and much more. This section discusses some of the works that use CNN for image classification. Spanhol et al. [1] proposed a preliminary work on the use on CNN to classify breast cancer histopathological images. High resolution images are used as input for training the CNN and extraction of the image patches for classification. CNN models are able to provide better results compared to hand-crafted methods. Bora et al. [2] applied CNN for classification of cervical dysplasia using Pap smear images. The performances of the two classifiers namely, Least Square Support Vector Machine (LSSVM) and Softmax Regression are compared. Alos, the proposed system is compared with that of the conventional systems with publicly available dataset and the experimental results show that CNN outperforms the existing methods. Patil et al. [3] proposed a Convolutional Neural Network (CNN), Recurrent Neural Network (RNN) merging technique along with canonical correlation analysis for White Blood Cells Image Classification determines higher accuracy compared to other state-of-the-art blood cell classification techniques. Rostami et al. [4] developed an ensemble of Deep Convolutional Neural Network-based classifiers to categorize wound images into multiple classes including surgical, diabetic, and venous ulcers. The proposed system is applied for binary and 3-class classification problems and high accuracy results are achieved to be applied in decision support systems in classification of wound images. Diakite, Jiangsheng, and Xiaping, [5] proposed a 3D2D CNN for hyperspectral image classification. Four datasets were used in the experiment and the proposed method achieved excellent results compared with existing methods. Wang et al. [6] has taken SVM and CNN and compared them with traditional machine learning and deep learning image classification algorithms for large mnist dataset and small COREL1000 dataset. The results show that traditional machine learning performs better on small sample data sets, and for large datasets, the deep learning model has higher recognition accuracy.

1.2 Distributed Collaborative Learning

Distributed Collaborative Learning is a framework in which multiple clients participate in the learning of a machine learning model. These clients train the model locally with their own data and share only the model parameters to a central coordination server. This server aggregates the parameters received from multiple clients and updates the model parameters back to the participating clients. In this way, the machine learning model is trained multiple times with data generated frequently at the clients side. The major advantage of this method of model training is privacy preservation. The raw data that is available with the clients is not shared with the central server or the other participating clients. Federated Learning and Split Learning are examples of such distributed collaborative learning methods.

The FL approach was first introduced by Google AI researchers in 2016. FL is a privacy preserving method of model training that addresses many issues such as security, privacy, data access, and access to heterogeneous data. Gupta and Raskar [7] introduced a method to train deep neural networks in a distributed manner. The performance has been compared with models trained on a regular machine. The algorithm can be used to train the model without sharing raw data directly. Yang et al. [8] has proposed a Federated semi-supervied based learning algorithm for COVID region segmentation using chest CT. FL has been used successfully in this scenario to avoid the need for sensitive data sharing.Sharma et al. [9] proposed a blockchain and federated learning-based framework for defense for sustainable society. The Internet of Battle Things in the defense system is connected using blockchain and the model performs well even with limited data. The outcomes in terms of accuracy and loss are promising. McMahan et al. [10] proposed a method for FL based on iterative model averaging. Here, stochastic gradient descent (SGD) optimization is applied to federated optimization problems. In this approach, single batch gradient calculation is done per round of communication. The experiment has been demonstrated with different architectures, using multi-layer perceptrons, convolutional neural networks, and LSTM for promising results. Bonawitz et al. [11] proposed an architecture for Federated Learning approach based on TensorFlow. The protocol and the device configuration are explained along with the challenges and open problems. Song et al. [12] explored the user-level privacy leakage by the attack from a malicious server. A framework incorporating GAN with a multi-task discriminator, Auxiliary Identification is proposed. This framework simultaneously discriminates category, reality, and client identity of input samples without interfering with the federated learning process. Nguyen et al. [13]. Proposed an algorithm called FOLB for convergence and efficient communication in FL. This solves the problem of delay in communication and cost of network resources. This novel scheme that takes into account the statistical and system heterogeneity is used. The FOLB algorithm significantly reduces the number of rounds to attain desired level of loss value and accuracy.

Split Learning, also called as Split Neural Network (SNN), is yet another distributed and collaborative learning approach in which a deep neural network is split into multiple sections, each of which is trained on a different client. Here, the training is carried out by transferring the weights of the last layer of each section to the next section. This last layer of each section is called the cut layer. Similar to federated learning, in split learning also, no raw data of the clients are shared outside. Poirot et al. [14] applied split learning for the first time for healthcare and compared with centrally hosted and non collaborative configurations such as binary classification and multiclass classification problems. The results show performance benefits of SNN with an increase in the number of clients. Vepakomma et al. [15] has applied split neural networks to health care in which multiple entities holding patient data collaborate in the diagnosis without sharing patients data. The performance comparison of this SNN based method is done with that of the federated learning approach, large batch synchronous stochastic gradient descent and better results are achieved. Thapa et al. [16], combined the SL and Fl approaches for improved privacy and robustness. SL provides better model privacy but performs slower than FL. A novel approach called, splitfed learning (SFL) has been proposed that combines the benefits of SL and FL along with a refined architecture. The results show that the proposed SFL model gives similar accuracy and communication efficiency as SL while decreasing the computation time.

1.3 Summary of Literature

The survey carried out on the study and application of federated learning and split neural networks shows that the majority of the work uses benchmarked datasets such as NIST's MNIST dataset, and CIFAR 10. Much work has been done with respect to the use cases and applications in the field of healthcare and image recognition. The need to perform the performance analysis of the learning models and the classifiers with a more challenging dataset is often overlooked. Also, the application of Split neural networks as an alternative to federated learning is limited and the literature shows that SNNs can overcome the drawbacks of federated learning. Hence, there is a need to explore this recent technique of SNNs for various applications and selection of a challenging dataset to validate such usage is mandatory.

2 Problem Formulation

2.1 Learning Model Selection

In a typical Supervised deep learning model, the image classification task consists of the following 3 tasks:

1. Data organized in a central repository.
2. Acquiring labels or ground truth annotations for these data.
3. Training and evaluating a Deep Learning model with these annotated data for classification.

The centralized model poses some practical challenges in terms of large dataset collection in a central repository and security and privacy of the data that need to be shared outside the client premises. Also, the generation of data by various connected devices is tremendous and frequent movement of such large amounts of data is impractical. Federated Learning is proposed as a solution to resolve the above mentioned problem of privacy and data collection, in which each client trains a model with their local data and a central server performing the aggregation and model update.

Even though FL has many advantages over the centralized learning model, there are also some disadvantages with Federated Learning as mentioned below:

1. Irrespective of the contribution made by each and every client, all the clients have the same final ML model. A client who may not possess good data may also get the final model.
2. There are chances of adversarial effects such as data corruption by the clients.

SplitNNs, first introduced by MIT in the year 2018, represent a new architectural mechanic for preserving the privacy in machine learning model training. It is a framework that leverages the implementation of distributed neural networks. This allows processing of the data remotely, in a decentralized way with multiple collaborating clients. SNNs have the advantage of dramatic reduction of the computational resources and higher accuracies [17]. As the number of participating clients increase in the training process, SNNs provide efficient bandwidth usage [17]. SplitNNs can provide a solution to the above stated issues in which the final deep learning model is not shared with all the clients. Every client trains a partial deep learning network up to a specific layer known as the cut layer and only the wisdom is shared with other contributing clients. There is no single final learning model. Hence, in this work, the evaluation of the Split NNs over Federated learning with a more challenging dataset of EMNIST is chosen.

2.2 Popular Datasets

Friction in sharing of sensitive information such as clinical and finance data poses a greater challenge in machine learning. Collaborative techniques such as Federated Learning and Split Learning are proposed as a solution to address this problem. For the analysis of the literature, it is found that federated learning has been successfully applied in various use cases where privacy and heterogeneity of the data is a primary concern and also split learning serves to be an effective alternative and a variant that can be applied in such an environment. The performances of these FL and SL methods are evaluated individually for the use cases chosen. But there is limited work available to compare the performance of both the learning methods with a better dataset.

The popular data sets used for the study of the machine learning models are MNIST and CIFAR 10 and 100 datasets. MNIST is a subset of the larger NIST special database 19 [18]. As explained earlier, this dataset has handwritten letters and numerals published from 3600 writers and 810,000 character images especially used for image classification tasks. The NIST database had some drawbacks such as difficulty in accessing and using such as high cost and storage requirement. MNIST is a modified NIST dataset and a subset of the NIST database. In MNIST, the datasets are stored in an efficient and compact manner. This dataset was created by re-mixing the samples from NIST's original datasets and normalized to fit into a 28×28 pixel bounding box. It consists of 70,000 handwritten images out of which 60,000 images are used for training, and the rest of 10,000 images are used for training validation.

The CIFAR-10 and CIFAR-100 are datasets of tiny images which consists of a subset from 80 million labeled images. The CIFAR-10 consists of 60,000 images from 10 classes of 32×32 pixels out of which 50,000 images are used for training and 10,000 for testing. The CIFAR-100 dataset is similar to CIFAR-10, except it has 100 classes containing 600 images in each class. Out of this, 500 images are used for training and 100 images are used for testing under each class. In CIFAR-100, these 100 classes are grouped into 20 superclasses and each image has 2 labels, the "fine" and "coarse" labels to denote the class and superclass respectively.

2.3 The EMNIST Dataset

Extended MNIST (EMNIST), is a variant of the full NIST dataset and this EMNIST poses a more challenging task with respect to classification involving letters and digits [19]. This dataset uses the same image structure and parameters, and the conversion mechanism used to create the MNIST dataset.

The original NIST dataset provides samples with five different data hierarchies such as By_Page, By_Author, By_Field, By_Class, and By_Merge. From these, the By_Class and By_Merge data organizations encompass the classification tasks that are made compatible with the standard MNIST dataset.

The EMNIST dataset consists of six datasets as shown in Table 1.

Table 1. EMNIST dataset classification

Dataset	No. of classes	Total samples
By_Class	62	814,255
By_Merge	47	814,255
Balanced	47	131,600
Digits	10	280,000
Letters	37	130,600
MNIST	10	70,000

The introduction of the EMNIST dataset is to be a widely used dataset, since it contains a balanced subset of all the By_Merge classes. To avoid errors that may result from misclassification between uppercase and lowercase letters, this 47-class dataset was chosen compared to the By_Class dataset.

The current trends favoring the need and applicability of distributed collaborative learning techniques, such as the Federated and Split learnings, it is required to evaluate the performance of these models with a more challenging dataset such as the EMNIST dataset discussed so far.

2.4 Research Objectives

Due to the more challenging and balanced design of the EMNIST dataset, in this work, it is curious to perform a performance study of the Split Neural Networks on this EMNIST dataset. With this primary objective, following research questions are set forth and experimented.

RO1: Can the EMNIST dataset can be used as a challenging dataset to validate the performance of the classifiers trained using FL and SplitNN over MNIST?
RO2: To study the performance of Split Learning by providing a comparison on MNIST and EMNIST datasets.
RO3: To compare the performance of single CNN and Split Learning methods for these MNIST and EMNIST datasets.

3 Methodology

3.1 Split Neural Networks Training

The training of a deep learning model is split across two or more clients. Each client holds a segment of the model. Each of these segments is a NN that feeds into the segment in front. In Fig. 1, an example of such a network is shown [7]. Here, each client named Alice has some unlabelled training data and the bottom of the network and the corresponding labels are available with Bob and the top of the network. There are multiple Alices with some amount of data. After completion of training, the first Alice sends a copy of the bottom model to the next Alice and so on till all the Alices have trained.

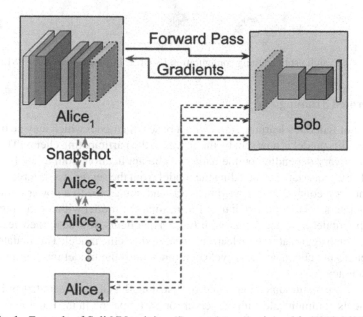

Fig. 1. Example of SplitNN training (Source: https://arxiv.org/abs/1810.06060)

Simple Vanilla Configuration for Split Learning
There are three different basic configurations suggested in literature for SNNs. They are the simple vanilla configuration, U-shaped configurations without label sharing and Vertically partitioned data configurations [15]. In this study, the simplest of splitNN configurations, namely the vanilla configuration is used. This is illustrated in Fig. 2.

In this setup each client (Alice as in our earlier example) trains a partial deep network up to cut layers. The outputs at the cut layer are sent to the server (Bob as in our earlier example), which completes the remainder of the training without any data. The gradients are back propagated at the server until the cut layer, which is sent back to clients, which continues back propagating until the entire network model is trained. The entire training takes place without looking at each other's data.

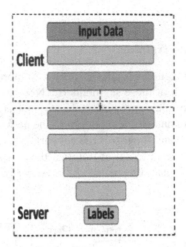

Fig. 2. Simple vanilla split learning configuration (Source: https://arxiv.org/abs/1812.00564)

3.2 Federated Training

The method of federated learning starts with a base data model which may be trained on public data. This model is now sent by the server to the participating clients. The number of clients can vary depending on the nature of the application from a few hundreds to millions. The clients start downloading the model from the server at a suitable time, such as when they are connected to a wi-fi network and connected to a power outlet. These clients generate local data, which it uses for training the model without sharing the data outside. The model now gets better with time. The clients now send their learnings to the server, which aggregates these learnings and updates the model. This updated model is again sent to the clients and this cycle continues until the model reaches an optimum level of accuracy.

A typical one communication round of distributed SGD is illustrated in Fig. 3. In (a), the Clients communicate with the server for participation in the training round. The server sends the initial model parameters to the clients. Based on the local data available with them, the clients compute a weight update independently (b). Finally, as in (c), clients send their locally computed weight to the server. The server then computes the average of the weights received from all the clients to produce the new master model [20].

Data Distribution in IID Manner

In this research, the federated learning studied with NIST datasets (MNIST and EMNIST) is used for performance comparison with SNNs. For the experimentation purpose, the dataset has been split with multiple clients in the IID (independent and identically distributed) manner. Here, the data distribution among clients is done using data shards. The training data is split randomly into equally sized shards and each client is assigned with one data shard. Informally, this Identically Distributed means that there are no fluctuations in the distribution and all items in the sample follow the same probability distribution.

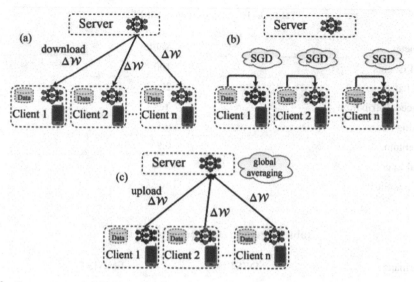

Fig. 3. One communication round of Federated Learning. (Source: https://arxiv.org/pdf/1903. 02891.pdf)

4 Experimental Results and Analysis

4.1 Model and Implementation of Federated Learning

As discussed in the previous sections, the MNIST and EMNIST datasets are used for the evaluation of the performance of federated and split learning models. The federated learning has been done using a method of implementation in Pytorch (PySyft for federated data). Table 2 gives the datasets followed by hyper-parameters in Table 3.

Table 2. Datasets for FL

Split	MNIST		EMNIST	
	No. of records	Class	No. of records	Class
Training	60000	10	240000	10
Testing	10000	10	40000	10

The performance metrics derived for the above mentioned experimental setup for federated learning is given in Table 4.

4.2 Model and Implementation of Split Neural Networks

The mode performance is tested by using LeNet architecture for the implementation using MNIST dataset and VGG16 for the EMNIST dataset. The training is carried out

Table 3. Hyper-parameters for FL

Parameter	Value
No. of Clients	100
Local batch size	20
Balanced distribution	Yes
Learning rate	0.1
Momentum	0.9
Global Epoch	200
Class per client	10

Table 4. Performance comparison for FL

Performance	MNIST	EMNIST
Train accuracy	97.98%	97.1%
Test accuracy	97.49%	96.8%
Train loss	0.06	0.10
Test loss	0.07	0.10

for 100 epochs. SNNs are implemented for multiple agents from Client-1 to Client-5. The comparison results of the single model CNN and SplitNN with 5 clients are tabulated in Table 5.

Table 5. Performance comparison of SNN

Dataset	Single model	Split model
MNIST	97.60%	97.83%
EMNIST	82.01%	88.05%

4.3 Result Analysis

The research objectives set in this study are given in Sect. 2.4. The first objective is to validate the applicability of the EMNIST dataset as a more challenging dataset for the task of image classification. From the results achieved through the experiments carried out stated in this section, from Table 4 and 5, both the federated learning and split NN models have achieved less accuracy for the EMNIST dataset compared to MNIST. This shows that the EMNIST dataset poses more challenges for the classification problem and can be used to validate similar image classification models in future. The second and third objectives focus on the performance of the SplitNN models in comparison with the single CNN models for the chosen datasets of MNIST and EMNIST. These results are addressed in Table 5, where the SNNs provide more classification accuracy compared to a single deep learning model. Higher classification accuracy is achieved for MNIST compared to the more challenging EMNIST datasets.

5   Conclusion and Future Research

In this research work, the performance of Split Neural Networks is studied with a more challenging dataset namely EMNIST. EMNIST is an extended version of the MNIST dataset which has a balanced combination of the handwritten characters. This study concludes that in addition to popularly used datasets such as CIFAR10, MNIST datasets, the EMNIST dataset is worth applying. The results show that both the learning methods, namely Federated Learning and SplitNNs were able to achieve a less accuracy with EMNIST dataset in comparison to MNIST dataset. This shows that the EMNIST dataset can be used to evaluate the performance of the classifiers in a more challenging way. Split Neural Networks is proposed to overcome the drawbacks of Federated Learning. This study evaluates the classification accuracy of SNNs for both MNIST and EMNIST datasets. In future, Split Neural Networks can be used to solve the machine learning problems with better accuracy, efficient resource usage and preserving the privacy of the user data and thus edge intelligence can be realized in a much more effective way.

References

1. Adhikari, A., Choudhuri, A.R., Ghosh, D., Chattopadhyay, N., Chakraborty, R.: Breast cancer histopathological image classification using convolutional neural networks. In: Mandal, J.K., Mukhopadhyay, S., Unal, A., Sen, S.K. (eds.) Proceedings of International Conference on Innovations in Software Architecture and Computational Systems. SADIC, pp. 183–195. Springer, Singapore (2021). https://doi.org/10.1007/978-981-16-4301-9_14
2. Kangkana, B., Manish, C., Lipi, B.M., Malay, K.K,, Anup, K.D.: Pap smear image classification using convolutional neural network. In: Proceedings of the Tenth Indian Conference on Computer Vision, Graphics and Image Processing (ICVGIP'16). Association for Computing Machinery, pp. 1–8, Article 55. New York, NY, USA (2016)
3. Patil, A.M., Patil, M.D., Birajdar, G.K.: White blood cells image classification using deep learning with canonical correlation analysis. IRBM **42**(5), 378–389 (2021)
4. Rostami, B., Anisuzzaman, D.M., Wang, C., Gopalakrishnan, S., Niezgoda, J., Yu, Z.: Multiclass wound image classification using an ensemble deep CNN-based classifier. Comput. Biol. Med. **134**, 104536 (2021)
5. Diakite, A., Jiangsheng, G., Xiaping, F.: Hyperspectral image classification using 3D 2D CNN. IET Image Process. **15**(5), 1083–1092 (2020). https://doi.org/10.1049/ipr2.12087
6. Pin, W., En, F., Peng, W.: Comparative analysis of image classification algorithms based on traditional machine learning and deep learning. Pattern Recogn. Lett. **141**, 61–67 (2021)
7. Gupta, O., Raskar, R.: Distributed learning of deep neural network over multiple agents. J. Netw. Comput. Appl. **116**, 1–8 (2018). https://doi.org/10.1016/j.jnca.2018.05.003
8. Dong, Y., et al.: Federated semi- supervised learning for COVID region segmentation in chest CT using multi-national data from China, Italy, Japan. Med. Image Anal. **70**, 101992 (2021)

9. Pradip Kumar, S., Jong, H.P., Kyungeun, C.: Blockchain and federated learning-based distributed computing defence framework for sustainable society. Sustainable Cities Soc. **59**, 102220 (2020)
10. Brendan McMahan, H., Moore, E., Ramage, D., Hampson, S., Blaise, A., Arcas: Communication-efficient learning of deep networks from decentralized data. In: Proceedings of the 20th International Conference on Artificial Intelligence and Statistics (AISTATS), vol. 54. JMLR: W&CP, Florida, USA (2017)
11. Bonawitz, K.A., et al.: Towards federated learning at scale: system design. https://arxiv.org/abs/1902.01046 (2019)
12. Song, M., et al.: Analyzing user-level privacy attack against federated learning. IEEE J. Selected Areas Commun. **38**(10), 2430–2444 (2020)
13. Nguyen, H.T., Sehwag, V., Hosseinalipour, S., Brinton, C.G., Chiang, M., Vincent Poor, H.: Fast-convergent federated learning. IEEE J. Select. Areas Commun. **39**(1), 201–218 (2021). https://doi.org/10.1109/JSAC.2020.3036952
14. Poirot, M., Vepakomma, P., Chang, K., Kalpathy-Cramer, J., Gupta, R., Raskar, R.: Split learning for collaborative deep learning in healthcare. In: 33rd Conference on Neural Information Processing Systems (NeurIPS 2019), Vancouver, Canada (2019)
15. Praneeth, V., Otkrist, G., Tristan, S., Ramesh, R.: Split learning for health: Distributed deep learning without sharing raw patient data. In: 32nd Conference on Neural Information Processing Systems (NIPS 2018), Montreal, Canada (2018)
16. Thapa, C., Chamikara, M.A.P., Camtepe, S.: SplitFed: When Federated Learning Meets Split Learning (2020)
17. Abhishek, S., Praneeth, V., Otkrist, G., Ramesh, R.: Detailed comparison of communication efficiency of split learning and federated learning. arXiv:1909.09145 [cs.LG]. (2019)
18. NIST Homepage: https://www.nist.gov/srd/nist-special-database-19. Last accessed 2022/03/13
19. Gregory, C., Saeed, A., Jonathan, T., van Andre, S.: EMNIST: an extension of MNIST to handwritten letters. arXiv:1702.05373v2 [cs.CV] (2017)
20. Sattler, F., Wiedemann, S., Müller, K.-R., Samek, W.: Robust and communication-efficient federated learning from non-i.i.d. Data. IEEE Trans Neural Netw. Learn. Syst. **31**(9), 3400–3413 (2020)

The Security Algorithm BR22-01 Used to Secure the COVID'19 Health Data

C. Bagath Basha[1]([✉])(iD), S. Rajaprakash[2], M. Nithya[3], C. Sunitha[4], and K. Karthik[2]

[1] CSE, Kommuri Pratap Reddy Institute of Technology, Ghanpur Village, Ghatkesar (M), Malkajigirl Dist., Hyderabad, Telangana, India
chan.bagath@gmail.com

[2] CSE, Aarupadai Veedu Institute of Technology, Chennai, Tamil Nadu, India
karthik@avit.ac.in

[3] CSE, Vinayaka Missions Kirupananda Variyar Engineering College, Salem, Tamil Nadu, India
nithyam@vmkvec.edu.in

[4] CSE, Sri Chandrasekerandra Saraswathi Viswa Maha Vidyalaya, Kanchipuram, Tamil Nadu, India
csunitharam@kanchiuniv.ac.in

Abstract. The current generation data is most valuable in people's life, because data only decided people's health affected in COVID'19 or not, and not only COVID'19 all related to health issues data. To analyze and predict the health issue data by using Machine Learning Algorithm. This prediction issues data has most confidential data and need more security. So, applying the previous method is ChaCha method. This method focusing only performance not fully security. The new method is BR22-01. This method has five stages. The 1st stage is finding the secret key x & y value. The 2nd stage is applying key in Eq. (1). The 3rd stage is merge all values into single row then pair from left and swap the values in the HS matrix. The 4th stage is applying key in Eq. (2). The 5th stage is merge all values into single line then pair from left and swap the values in the HC matrix but reverse. The new method has provide good security as well as performance while compared to ChaCha method.

Keywords: BR22-01 · ChaCha · COVID'19 · Health · HS · HC · Key

1 Introduction

The current generation, people's heath issue data increased day by day especially COVID'19 data. To analyze the COVID'19 data and predict the data by using machine learning algorithm. From Fig. 1, the classification prediction process is Yes or No. Random forest prediction process is Mean Square Error. Naive bayes prediction process is probability. Support vector machine prediction process is regression and Yes or No. Decision tree prediction process is tree. Artificial neural network prediction process is back propagation.

These prediction data is most confidential data and must be secure that data but security level is low level, so apply the existing method ChaCha. This method is four

© The Author(s), under exclusive license to Springer Nature Switzerland AG 2023
K. Kottursamy et al. (Eds.): IconDeepCom 2022, CCIS 1719, pp. 345–354, 2023.
https://doi.org/10.1007/978-3-031-27622-4_26

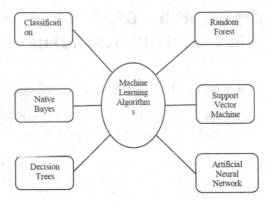

Fig. 1. Machine learning algorithms [1]

round process and "all diagonal values move to the first column". The encryption time of ChaCha method is very fast but security level is very low. So, the new method BagathRaj (BR) 22-01.

2 Related Work

The analyzing data with machine learning algorithms and get the performance result for many algorithms are compared with them. These algorithms performance showed and very easy and understand algorithm is classification algorithm [1]. The CBB21 algorithm is compared with Salsa20/4 algorithm and mainly compared the running time [2]. They analyzed data with machine learning algorithm and also analyzed data applied the CBB20 algorithm, and compared the running time with Salsa20/4 [3]. They studied the analyzed twitter data with machine learning algorithm, and also applied SRB21 security algorithm for that data, then compared the speed time with Salsa [4]. They discuss first twitter data then analyzed with predicted that data by machine learning algorithm, and applied SRB18 security algorithm to that data, then compared the running time with Salsa for encryption [5]. They proposed the RBJ25 cryptography algorithm for general data and compared the performance with AES and ChaCha for encryption [6]. They studied the AES and Salsa algorithm for encryption security and compared the performance of the proposed security algorithm is RB20 for encryption time [7]. The CBB22 algorithm is proposed and provide the security of generalized data. "This algorithm is compared the performance of the both encryption and decryption time with Salsa and AES" [8]. They studied the encryption speed time for Salsa and compared to the proposed SRB21 phase 1 algorithm [9]. The mainly analysis the feedback of movies through sentiment analysis by classification and SVM algorithms [10]. They analyzed the big data and store that data with protection process applied for RBJ20 algorithm. This algorithm has four stages used to protect the data [11–14].

3 Methodology

To analyze the health related data and predict the issues by using Machine Learning Algorithm. The predicted analyzed data used to apply the new method BR22-01. This method has five stages. The 1st stage is finding the secret key x & y value. The 2nd stage is applying key in Eq. (1). The 3rd stage is merge all values into single row then pair from left and swap the values in the HS matrix. The 4th stage is applying key in Eq. (2). The 5th stage is merge all values into single line then pair from left and swap the values in the HC matrix but assign 0th value as 25th cell value, 1st value as 24th cell value and similarly remaining cell values.

Encryption Method

(A) Take predicted health issues data and convert into matrix structure.
(B) Secret key value X & Y from the matrix structure.
(C)

$$H_S = \sin(x+y) = \sin(x)\cos(y) + \cos(x)\sin(y)$$
$$\textit{where H is health operations and S is } \sin \textit{ operations} \tag{1}$$

$$H_C = \cos(x+y) = \cos(x)\cos(y) + \sin(x)\sin(y)$$
$$\textit{where H is health operations and C is } \cos \textit{ operations} \tag{2}$$

(D) To merge all the H_S and H_C in the single row and make it pair from left.
(E) To swap the values in the matrix structure and H_C values swap by bottom to top.

Encryption Method Working Process

$$H_S = \begin{bmatrix} 101/22 & 102/22 & 103/22 & 104/22 & 105/22 \\ 106/22 & 107/22 & 108/22 & 109/22 & 110/22 \\ 111/22 & 112/22 & 113/22 & 114/22 & 115/22 \\ 116/22 & 117/22 & 118/22 & 119/22 & 120/22 \\ 121/22 & 122/22 & 123/22 & 124/22 & 125/22 \end{bmatrix}$$

By Applying the Eq. (1) Operations are

$$\sin(x+y) = \sin(x)\cos(y) + \cos(x)\sin(y)$$
$$\textit{where } x = 5, y = 7$$

• $\sin(5+7) = \sin(5)\cos(7) + \cos(5)\sin(7)$
  $\sin(12) = 0.087 * 0.992 + 0.996 * 0.121$

$$H_S = 0087099209960121$$

- Pairs are (0,0), (8,7), (0,9), (9,2), (0,9), (9,6), (0,1), (2,1)

Pair 1 (0, 0)

$$H_S = \begin{bmatrix} 101/22 & 102/22 & 103/22 & 104/22 & 105/22 \\ 106/22 & 107/22 & 108/22 & 109/22 & 110/22 \\ 111/22 & 112/22 & 113/22 & 114/22 & 115/22 \\ 116/22 & 117/22 & 118/22 & 119/22 & 120/22 \\ 121/22 & 122/22 & 123/22 & 124/22 & 125/22 \end{bmatrix}$$

Pair 2 (8, 7)

$$H_S = \begin{bmatrix} 101/22 & 102/22 & 103/22 & 104/22 & 105/22 \\ 106/22 & 107/22 & 109/22 & 108/22 & 110/22 \\ 111/22 & 112/22 & 113/22 & 114/22 & 115/22 \\ 116/22 & 117/22 & 118/22 & 119/22 & 120/22 \\ 121/22 & 122/22 & 123/22 & 124/22 & 125/22 \end{bmatrix}$$

Pair 3 (0, 9)

$$H_S = \begin{bmatrix} 110/22 & 102/22 & 103/22 & 104/22 & 105/22 \\ 106/22 & 107/22 & 109/22 & 108/22 & 101/22 \\ 111/22 & 112/22 & 113/22 & 114/22 & 115/22 \\ 116/22 & 117/22 & 118/22 & 119/22 & 120/22 \\ 121/22 & 122/22 & 123/22 & 124/22 & 125/22 \end{bmatrix}$$

Pair 4 (9, 2)

$$H_S = \begin{bmatrix} 110/22 & 102/22 & 101/22 & 104/22 & 105/22 \\ 106/22 & 107/22 & 109/22 & 108/22 & 103/22 \\ 111/22 & 112/22 & 113/22 & 114/22 & 115/22 \\ 116/22 & 117/22 & 118/22 & 119/22 & 120/22 \\ 121/22 & 122/22 & 123/22 & 124/22 & 125/22 \end{bmatrix}$$

Pair 5 (0, 9)

$$H_S = \begin{bmatrix} 103/22 & 102/22 & 101/22 & 104/22 & 105/22 \\ 106/22 & 107/22 & 109/22 & 108/22 & 110/22 \\ 111/22 & 112/22 & 113/22 & 114/22 & 115/22 \\ 116/22 & 117/22 & 118/22 & 119/22 & 120/22 \\ 121/22 & 122/22 & 123/22 & 124/22 & 125/22 \end{bmatrix}$$

Pair 6 (9, 6)

$$H_S = \begin{bmatrix} 103/22 & 102/22 & 101/22 & 104/22 & 105/22 \\ 106/22 & 110/22 & 109/22 & 108/22 & 107/22 \\ 111/22 & 112/22 & 113/22 & 114/22 & 115/22 \\ 116/22 & 117/22 & 118/22 & 119/22 & 120/22 \\ 121/22 & 122/22 & 123/22 & 124/22 & 125/22 \end{bmatrix}$$

Pair 7 (0, 1)

$$H_S = \begin{bmatrix} 102/22 & 103/22 & 101/22 & 104/22 & 105/22 \\ 106/22 & 110/22 & 109/22 & 108/22 & 107/22 \\ 111/22 & 112/22 & 113/22 & 114/22 & 115/22 \\ 116/22 & 117/22 & 118/22 & 119/22 & 120/22 \\ 121/22 & 122/22 & 123/22 & 124/22 & 125/22 \end{bmatrix}$$

Pair 8 (2, 1)

$$H_S = \begin{bmatrix} 102/22 & 101/22 & 103/22 & 104/22 & 105/22 \\ 106/22 & 110/22 & 109/22 & 108/22 & 107/22 \\ 111/22 & 112/22 & 113/22 & 114/22 & 115/22 \\ 116/22 & 117/22 & 118/22 & 119/22 & 120/22 \\ 121/22 & 122/22 & 123/22 & 124/22 & 125/22 \end{bmatrix}$$

<u>By Applying the Eq. (2) Operations are</u>

$\cos(x + y) = \cos(x)\cos(y) + \sin(x)\sin(y)$
$where\ x = 3,\ y = 6$

- $\cos(3 + 6) = \cos(3)\cos(6) + \sin(3)\sin(6)$
  $\cos(12) = 0.998 * 0.994 + 0.052 * 0.104$

$H_C = 0998099400520104$
- Pairs are (0,9), (9,8), (0,9), (9,4), (0,0), (5,2), (0,1), (0,4).

Pair 9 (0, 9)

$$H_C = \begin{bmatrix} 102/22 & 101/22 & 103/22 & 104/22 & 105/22 \\ 106/22 & 110/22 & 109/22 & 108/22 & 107/22 \\ 111/22 & 112/22 & 113/22 & 114/22 & 115/22 \\ 125/22 & 117/22 & 118/22 & 119/22 & 120/22 \\ 121/22 & 122/22 & 123/22 & 124/22 & 116/22 \end{bmatrix}$$

Pair 10 (9, 8)

$$H_C = \begin{bmatrix} 102/22 & 101/22 & 103/22 & 104/22 & 105/22 \\ 106/22 & 110/22 & 109/22 & 108/22 & 107/22 \\ 111/22 & 112/22 & 113/22 & 114/22 & 115/22 \\ 117/22 & 125/22 & 118/22 & 119/22 & 120/22 \\ 121/22 & 122/22 & 123/22 & 124/22 & 116/22 \end{bmatrix}$$

Pair 11 (0, 9)

$$H_C = \begin{bmatrix} 102/22 & 101/22 & 103/22 & 104/22 & 105/22 \\ 106/22 & 110/22 & 109/22 & 108/22 & 107/22 \\ 111/22 & 112/22 & 113/22 & 114/22 & 115/22 \\ 116/22 & 125/22 & 118/22 & 119/22 & 120/22 \\ 121/22 & 122/22 & 123/22 & 124/22 & 117/22 \end{bmatrix}$$

Pair 12 (9, 4)

$$H_C = \begin{bmatrix} 102/22 & 101/22 & 103/22 & 104/22 & 105/22 \\ 106/22 & 110/22 & 109/22 & 108/22 & 107/22 \\ 111/22 & 112/22 & 113/22 & 114/22 & 115/22 \\ 121/22 & 125/22 & 118/22 & 119/22 & 120/22 \\ 116/22 & 122/22 & 123/22 & 124/22 & 117/22 \end{bmatrix}$$

Pair 13 (0, 0)

$$H_C = \begin{bmatrix} 102/22 & 101/22 & 103/22 & 104/22 & 105/22 \\ 106/22 & 110/22 & 109/22 & 108/22 & 107/22 \\ 111/22 & 112/22 & 113/22 & 114/22 & 115/22 \\ 121/22 & 125/22 & 118/22 & 119/22 & 120/22 \\ 116/22 & 122/22 & 123/22 & 124/22 & 117/22 \end{bmatrix}$$

Pair 14 (5, 2)

$$H_C = \begin{bmatrix} 102/22 & 101/22 & 103/22 & 104/22 & 105/22 \\ 106/22 & 110/22 & 109/22 & 108/22 & 107/22 \\ 111/22 & 112/22 & 113/22 & 114/22 & 115/22 \\ 121/22 & 125/22 & 118/22 & 119/22 & 123/22 \\ 116/22 & 122/22 & 120/22 & 124/22 & 117/22 \end{bmatrix}$$

Pair 15 (0, 1)

$$H_C = \begin{bmatrix} 102/22 & 101/22 & 103/22 & 104/22 & 105/22 \\ 106/22 & 110/22 & 109/22 & 108/22 & 107/22 \\ 111/22 & 112/22 & 113/22 & 114/22 & 115/22 \\ 121/22 & 125/22 & 118/22 & 119/22 & 123/22 \\ 116/22 & 122/22 & 120/22 & 117/22 & 124/22 \end{bmatrix}$$

Pair 16 (0, 4)

$$H_C = \begin{bmatrix} 102/22 & 101/22 & 103/22 & 104/22 & 105/22 \\ 106/22 & 110/22 & 109/22 & 108/22 & 107/22 \\ 111/22 & 112/22 & 113/22 & 114/22 & 115/22 \\ 121/22 & 125/22 & 118/22 & 119/22 & 123/22 \\ 124/22 & 122/22 & 120/22 & 117/22 & 116/22 \end{bmatrix}$$

4 Result and Discussion

The proposed algorithm BR22-01 "encryption performance compared with ChaCha. ChaCha concept is the all diagonal values move to the 1st column". The three by three matrix has "24 bytes of fie size; the six by six matrix has 76 bytes of file size; the ten by ten matrix has 312 bytes of file size; the fifteen by fifteen matrix has 812 bytes of file size; the twenty by twenty matrix has 1531 bytes of file size; and the forty by forty matrix has 6580 bytes of file size" as shown in the Table 1.

Table 1. BR22-01 encryption performance

File size	ChaCha	BR22-01
24	1.69	2.01
76	1.29	2.51
312	2.73	3.11
822	2.64	3.55
1531	3.4	3.9
6580	2.27	4.1

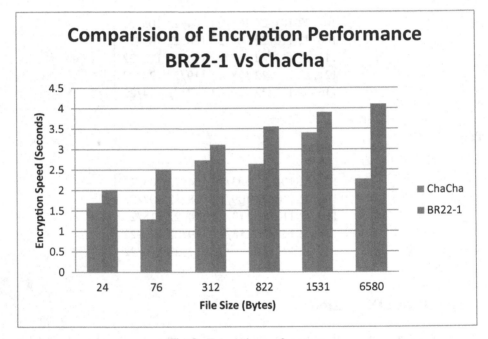

Fig. 2. Encryption performance

From Fig. 2, the BR22-01 method speed is 2.01 (s), 2.51 (s), 3.11 (s), 3.55 (s), 3.9 (s) and 4.1 (s) for the BR22-01. The BR22-01 gives "more protection of the data; when compared to existing techniques".

5 Conclusion

In today world generation data is much more important in public life, because people's health data only decided whether COVID'19 affected or not, and also related to all health issues data. These data used to analyzed and predict the health issues data by Machine Learning Algorithm, and then predicted data need more security. So, we applied the existing method ChaCha method and that method focused only "encryption performance" so security is less. In this paper, to apply the new BR22-01 method and this method has stages. The 1st stage is finding the "secret key value". The 2nd stage is applying key in Eq. (1). The 3rd stage is merge all values and make it pair in the HS matrix. The 4th stage is applying key in Eq. (2). The 5th stage is merge all values and make it pair in the HC matrix but reverse. The new BR22-01 method has provide security and performance are good while compared to ChaCha method.

References

1. Bagath Basha, C., Somasundaram, K.: A comparative study of twitter sentiment analysis using machine learning algorithms in big data. Int. J. Recent Technol. Eng. **8**, 591–599 (2019)
2. Bagath Basha, C., Rajaprakash, S.: Applying the CBB21 phase 2 method for securing Twitter analyzed data. Adv. Math. Sci. J. **9**, 1085–1091 (2020)
3. Bagath Basha, C., Rajaprakash, S., Muthuselvan, S., Saisatishsunder, P., Alekhya Rani, S.V.L.: Applying the CBB20 algorithm for twitter analyzed data. In: Proceedings of First International Conference on Advances in Physical Sciences and Materials, Coimbatore, Tamil Nadu, India (2020)
4. Bagath Basha, C., Rajaprakash, S.: Applying the SRB21 phase ii methodology for securing Twitter analyzed data. In: Proceedings of the International Confererence on Mechanical Electronics and Computer Engineering (2020)
5. Bagath Basha, C., Rajapraksh, S.: Enhancing the security using SRB18 method of embedding computing. Microprocess. Microsyst. **77**, 103125 (2020)
6. Rajaprakash, S., Bagath Basha, C., Muthuselvan, S., Jaisankar, N., Singh, R.P.: RBJ25 cryptography algorithm for securing big data. In: Proceedings of First International Conference on Advances in Physical Sciences and Materials, Coimbatore, Tamil Nadu, India (2020)
7. Karthik, K., Bagath Basha, C., Bhaswanth Thilak, U., Sai Kiran, T., Raj, J.: Securing social media analyzed data using RB20 method. Adv. Math. Sci. J. **9**(3), 1157–1163 (2020)
8. Bagath Basha, C., Rajaprakash, S., Harish, V.V.A., Krishna, M.S., Prabhas, K.: Securing Twitter analysed data using CBB22 algorithm. Adv. Math. Sci. J. **9**, 1093–1100 (2020)
9. Bagath Basha, C., Rajaprakash, S.: Securing Twitter data using SRB21 phase I methodology. Int. J. Sci. Technol. Res. **8**, 1952–1955 (2019)
10. Jaichandran, R., Bagath Basha, C., Shunmuganathan, K.L., Rajaprakash, S., Kanagasuba Raja, S.: Sentiment analysis of movies on social media using R studio. Int. J. Eng. Adv. Technol. **8** (2019)
11. Rajaprakash, S., Jaishanker, N., Basha, C.B., Muthuselvan, S., Aswathi, A.B., Jayan, A., Sebastian, G.: RBJ20 cryptography algorithm for securing big data communication using wireless networks. In: Nagar, A.K., Jat, D.S., Marín-Raventós, G., Mishra, D.K. (eds.) Intelligent Sustainable Systems. LNNS, vol. 334, pp. 499–507. Springer, Singapore (2022). https://doi.org/10.1007/978-981-16-6369-7_46 ISSN 237-3370
12. Polap, D., Srivastava, G., Yu, K.: Agent architecture of an intelligent medical system based on federated learning and blockchain technology. J. Inf. Secur. Appl. **58**(102748), 1–8 (2021)

13. Huang, J., Tan, L., Li, W., Yu, K.: RON-enhanced blockchain propagation mechanism for edge-enabled smart cities. J. Inf. Secur. Appl. **61**(102936), 1–10 (2021)
14. Tan, L., Yu, K., Shi, N., Yang, C., Wei, W., Lu, H.: Towards secure and privacy-preserving data sharing for COVID-19 medical records: a blockchain-empowered approach. IEEE Trans. Netw. Sci. Eng. **9**, 271–281 (2021)

Modelling Air Pollution and Traffic Congestion Problem Through Mobile Application

S. Amudha[1]([✉]) [ID], J. Shobana[2] [ID], M. Satheesh Kumar[3] [ID], and P. Chitra[4] [ID]

[1] Department of Computational Intelligence, SRM Institute of Science and Technology, Kattankulathur, Tamil Nadu 603 203, India
amudhas@srmist.edu.in

[2] Department of Data Science and Business Systems, SRM Institute of Science and Technology, Kattankulathur, Tamil Nadu 603 203, India

[3] Department of Information Technology, K.L.N. College of Engineering, Madurai, Tamil Nadu, India

[4] Department of Electrical and Electronics, Sathyabama Institute of Science and Technology, Chennai, Tamil Nadu, India

Abstract. As we know, air pollution is one of the major problems in the metropolis. Due to this a lot of consequences have to be faced by all people. One of the main reasons for this are the vehicles. Most of the time people use their vehicles unnecessarily without any certain reasons. Due to the same reason another problem of traffic congestion arises. And this can be reduced if people become a bit more serious about it. They should prefer using public transport rather than personal vehicles for travelling large distances. By this the number of vehicles on the road will be turned down and it might solve the above two problems directly. So, the main approach is based on this theory itself to reduce the number of transports on the road. The solution is an application which runs on phone and keep track of the fuel used by the vehicle. A certain fuel limit shall be set based on vehicle type, its fuel consumption and other constraints. Once the limit got exceeded, fuel price shall differ and automated calculation would get you actual fuel amount. This aims at reducing the unnecessary usage of vehicles. There is a CO_2 emission model in an application which can predict the amount of CO_2 produced by the vehicle. The objective of the proposed work is to control the usage of vehicles based on the fuel used by a particular vehicle for a period of time. As the module has been tested with ML model for mileage prediction and CO_2 emission with different algorithms and got the best accuracy of around 85%. There will be no hardware in this work, if any hardware implemented all over India then that prototype model will produce good impact in the vehicle fuel usage prediction and CO_2 emissions. Hardware based projects using IOT devices, VTRS etc. is something which is very hard to implement in India as CCTV are still not installed and used properly.

Keywords: Air pollution · Traffic congestion · Mobile application · Neural networks · SVM · Deep learning · Machine learning models · Random forest regressor · Application programming interface

© The Author(s), under exclusive license to Springer Nature Switzerland AG 2023
K. Kottursamy et al. (Eds.): IconDeepCom 2022, CCIS 1719, pp. 355–365, 2023.
https://doi.org/10.1007/978-3-031-27622-4_27

1 Introduction

Recent technological development in smart city made several improvements in their daily activities. There are several challenges existing in current scenarios. One of the important problem in metropolis has a common problem of air pollution which is increasing day by day. Vehicles are the ultimate reason for this and also the cause of traffic congestion. Many times, people use their vehicles unnecessarily and without any certain reasons [1]. This research work objectives are Controlling the usage of vehicles is a strenuous task in a metropolis. The enhancement of electric vehicles and IOT appliances would be financially heavy and practically may take several years. Turning down the no. of vehicles can strike two main problems at the same time – pollution as well as traffic congestion [2].

Our solution is simple and requires zero custom hardware. An application which runs on your phone and keeps track of the fuel used by your vehicle. A certain fuel limit shall be set based on vehicle type and other constraints. This aims at reducing the unnecessary usage of vehicles [3]. The fuel limit can be extended by certain ways like online payment, offers and vouchers. More involvement of digital payment which will be a step towards cashless society.

The application shall keep track of fuel used with the fuel limit of the vehicle. Once the limit got exceeded, prices shall differ and automated calculation would get you actual fuel amount. Let the customers have some benefits as well. They can extend the limit by various offers and in app payment.

2 State of the Art of Existing Work

The following chapter gives a detailed description about state of the art of existing research work in this field. A through literature survey was conducted with existing models for the past four years research papers in this survey. Based on that survey content, we can analysis various challenges happened with real-time application improvements.

An author Muvuna proposed a model for Air pollution removal using green infrastructure through smart routing system [4]. By using Sensor technology, they analyzed the air quality in different paths. An author Abdel Jamal proposed an agent based traffic regulation system for the Road Air Quality Control in the year 2021. The main logic is they are calculating real time air quality index on different paths and producing recommended result which contains least polluted route in the entire area [5].

The drawback of this system is hardware based implementation not done. The author shaik proposed a model for modelling traffic congestion based on air quality. Based on air quality index the consider alternative path with less distance [6].

An author Thiboult proposed real-time air pollution and vehicle emissions estimation using IOT, GNSS and Web based simulation models. The created vehicle IOT device gives feedback on vehicle emission and exposure using various sensor [12]. Martha proposed implementation model for evaluating air quality on public transport routes using IOT Sensors. But we need an optimal solution to control all this IOT connected sensors in smart way [13].

An agent based traffic regulation system for road air quality control was proposed by Fazziki Jamal [15]. They are calculating real-time air quality index on different route

Table 1. Comparative table for Existing work for traffic congestion prediction

S. No	Paper Title	Publication	Work Done	Work not done
1	A Case Study on Air Pollution Removal by Green infrastructure through a Smart Routing System [7].	J. Muvuna Slobodan B, Mickovski, Tuleen Boutaleb, MDBI 2020	This work the author is keeping track of vehicle and fuel used and providing suggestion accordingly.	The suggestion might not be properly followed by people. So certain fuel limit should be set.
2	A brief survey on Smart Community and Transportation [8].	Mo Jamshidi, Hamid Azgomi IEEE 2018	This article the authors are tracking fuel usage and using IoT based filter for detecting foul combustion.	IoT based implementation are expensive and difficult to setup in large scale. So a software-based solution would be better.
3	Modelling Traffic Congestion Based on Air Quality: an Empirical Study [9].	Shaik Anjum, Nasrin Aghamohammadi, Rafidha Noor, IEEE 2021	Here they suggest alternative path for vehicles based on Air-Quality index.	The suggestions are not followed as people do consider the path of less distance.
4	Real-Time Air Pollution and Vehicle Emissions Estimation using IoT,GNSS and Web-Based Simulation Models [10].	L. Thiboult, P. Degeilh, K. Thanabalasingam, G. Sabiron, PognantGros, IEEE 2018	In this they create a in vehicle IoT device which gives feedback on vehicle emission and exposure using various sensors.	It may be financially high for a person to install such system in the vehicle.
5	Implementation of an evaluation system to measure air quality on public transport routes using IoT [11].	Martha Medina DelaCruz, Martin. Soto-Cordova,Anderson Mariano IEEE 2018.	In this they evaluate air quality in different paths using various sensors.	There should be some solution or action to be taken to control it.
6	An agent based traffic regulation system for the Road air quality Control [14].	Abdelaziz Fazziki, Jamal Ouarzazi, Djamal Benslemane, AbderSadique IEEE 2021	They are tracking real time and Calculated Air Quality index on different routes and also producing recommendation for least polluted route in the area.	The recommendation system is not that effective in reducing pollution as people don't follow them and also costly.

and recommend a least polluted route in traffic areas. This process is time consuming and costly also.

Comparative analysis of survey content is represented in Table 1.

3 Requirement Gathering

3.1 Prototyping

Specifications for prototype consists of preparing and then creating a model that can be provided for consumers to "play," check and change.

3.2 Interactions

Interviews are the primary means of gathering information where the program manager can meet face-to-face with specific clients or subject matter specialists Interviews are the primary means of gathering information where the program is located.

3.3 Focus Groups

A synergistic conversation is taking place between individuals who are representations of consumers or buyers in relation to the requirements of the company.

4 Requirement Analysis

4.1 Functional Requirements

4.1.1 Collecting Data

Collecting data for the training of the models is the primary task. Data should be collected manually in the form of vehicle number while registering in the application.

4.1.2 Pre-Processing

Through this data other information shall be collected like vehicle model and year of purchase. These data can be used to train the model.

4.1.3 Training Models

Based on the data we collected our model will generate fuel limit for each vehicle.

4.1.4 Tracking Limit

Our model will keep track of the fuel used within certain time period and calculate the exceeded amount.

4.1.5 Payment Portal

As there is feature of online payment in our system, so a payment portal should be integrated in it.

5 Overall Framework for Proposed Model

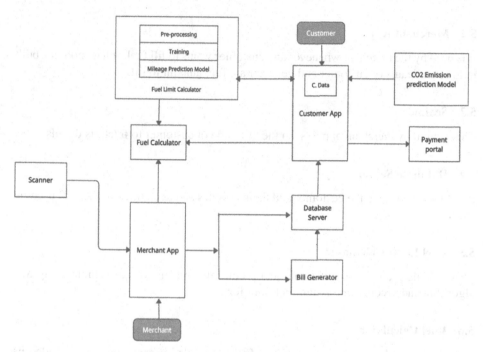

Fig. 1. Proposed system architecture

The above Fig. 1, depicts the proposed system architecture. For the control of air pollution our system would function in the following way such as, this application must be used by each and every person who owns a vehicle in the smart city. Customer should register by providing details of their vehicle mainly vehicle number. Through this vehicle number, information like vehicle model and year of purchase can be collected. Based on this our model would find the fuel limit for the vehicle.

Whenever any customer wants to fill fuel in the vehicle, merchant should scan the QR code on customer's app. Then merchant would be able to see customer details. Then customer mention the amount (in Rs) to fill fuel. And merchant checks for the actual amount to fill the fuel according the current limit or exceeded limit of the customer.

Customer can pay the amount through the app itself and at the same time merchant generates the bill. Both the bill and SMS notification would send to the customer. This model keeps track of the limit of each vehicle and when the limit exceeds, it informs the same to the user. Once limit exceeded customer can also check the actual amount of fuel to be filled.

Proposed system modules are described below.

5.1 Customer App

It is used by each customer who owns a vehicle. It keeps track of the fuel used and notify when limit exceeded. Various other modules are integrated in it.

5.2 Merchant App

It is used by the merchant whenever any customer wants to fill fuel. It has modules built in to fetch details of customer and get accurate fuel amount to fill.

5.3 Scanner

This is used by merchant app to scan the QR code of customer to fetch its details.

5.4 Database Server

It hold the data of all the customer and their vehicles and keep track of the fuel used by them.

5.5 Fuel Limit Calculator

This module pre-processes the data and predict the mileage of the vehicle using ML algorithm and accordingly assign fuel limit for it.

5.6 Fuel Calculator

It helps to calculate the exact amount of fuel to be filled if customer has exceeded its limit.

5.7 CO_2 Emission Prediction Model

This model is based on ML algorithm to predict the CO_2 emission from the vehicle based on certain parameter.

5.8 Payment Portal

It is used to make online payment through various mode.

5.9 Bill Generator

Once the payment done it generates invoice and at the same time SMS is sent to the customer. This will ensure good performance on unseen data, thus giving a more real time performance.

6   Implementation Modules

The App can be developed using Flutter API, for data base storage and retrieval Firebase backend server is used. The software module was implemented using Python packages in Spyder integrated development environment (IDE). From the python libraries Pandas, Matplotlib, Scihitlearn, Numpy are used for code implementations.

6.1   MC CALl's Quality Factors

Product Operation Factors

6.1.1   Correctness

The project aims at predicting the current mileage and CO_2 emission of vehicle with a high accuracy level.

6.1.2   Reliability

The degree to which the result of the prediction of mileage and CO_2 is very reliable.

6.1.3   Efficiency

The results of the prediction normally are having an efficiency of more than 82%.

6.1.4   Integrity

It is a virtue which deals with proper utilization of software at every level and its association with the modules of the system.

6.1.5   Usability

The project is made in such a way that it can be easily accessible and can be utilized by people of different strata of education and socio-economic status. It has a simple UI and can be easily understandable.

6.2   Product Revision Factors

6.2.1   Maintainability

The system aims to be up-to-date with time-to-time updates in software, database and interface according to the needs and usage.

6.2.2   Flexibility

The project aims for easy yet accurate results for various scenarios and situations like different vehicle type and its specifications.

6.2.3 Testability

The system is easily testable by-passing varying types of data to detect accuracy and mistakes.

6.3 Product Transition Factors

6.3.1 Portability

The system is very portable.

6.3.2 Reusability

The project holds a base strong enough for further improvement during its use and also act as a reference for other projects making use of its features.

6.3.3 Interoperability

This project does not focus on creating interfaces with other software systems or with other equipment firmware.

7 Results and Discussions

The proposed model in compared with existing model and achieve good performance improvement. The Mean Square Error (MSE) and Accuracy for Mileage prediction model is 89% and 86%. The MSE, R2-score, variance for CO_2 prediction model is achieved 94%, 85% and 86%. For the given test id ET01 the test action is to check the fuel limit assigned for the vehicle, for the expected output 18.5 L the system achieved 18.41 L as a result which will pass the test cases.

In second iteration for the given test id ET02 the test action is to check the fuel limit assigned for the vehicle, for the expected output 25.5 L the system achieved 25.36 L as a result which will pass the test cases. Sample dataset and corresponding result achievement is represented in Table 2.

Table 2. Sample user test data with expected output values

TestID	Test Action	Steps	Input	Expected Output	Actual Output	Pass/ Fail
ET01	Check the fuel limit assigned for the vehicle	-Save the coding file and provide input -Execute the coding file	Maruti Baleno 2017	18.5 L	18.41 L	PASS
ET02	Check the fuel limit assigned for the vehicle	-Save the coding file and provide input -Execute the coding file	Hyundai Creta 2015	25.5 L	25.36 L	PASS
ET03	Check the fuel limit assigned for the vehicle	-Save the coding file and provide input -Executethe coding file	Tata Altroz 2021	19.42 L	19.39 L	PASS

The below Fig. 2 depicts the comparative analysis of chart for the actual mileage value with the predicted mileage values.

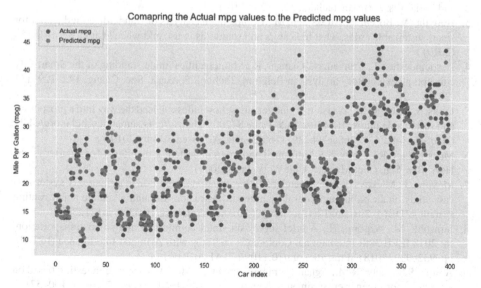

Fig. 2. Comparative analysis chart

8   Conclusion and Future Enhancement

We have made our application to run on some sample vehicle data as of now. Later on, this can be used in large scale for all the vehicles present in the smart cities of India. There would be the need of large capacity database and heavy computational processors. As we have tested ML model for mileage prediction and CO_2 emission with different algorithms and got the best accuracy of around 85%, this accuracy can be further improved later on by testing on more efficient algorithms. Various payment portal can be included in the application to make the payment process smoother. Another section of "Offers" can be included in the app so that customers can be benefited from the app as well.

In future enhancement we can include NLP concept for analyzing the human mood based on that we can predict which place the person what to move further.

Acknowledgements. I thank all the authors for their support and motivation to complete this work. I thank all our institutions for their environmental support and guidance.

Author Contributions. Writing—original draft preparation, S. Amudha; writing—review and editing, M. Satheesh Kumar; funding acquisition and Testing and Debugging: Shobana Devi and Chithra, All authors have read and agreed to the published version of the manuscript.

References

1. Nations: World Urbanization Prospects: The 2014 Revision—Google Scholar. https://scholar.google.com/scholar_lookup?title=World%20urbanization%20prospects%202014&author=United%20Nations&publication_year=2014. Accessed 30 July 2019
2. Albino, V., Berardi, U., Dangelico, R.M.: Smart cities: definitions, dimensions, performance, and initiatives. J. Urban Technol. **22**, 3–21 (2015)
3. Huovila, A., Bosch, P., Airaksinen, M.: Comparative analysis of standardized indicators for smart sustainable cities: what indicators and standards to use and when? Cities **89**, 141–153 (2019)
4. Desdemoustier, J., Crutzen, N., Gianger, R.: Municipalities' understanding of the Smart City concept: an exploratory analysis in Belgium. Technol. Forecast. Soc. Chang. **142**, 129–141 (2019)
5. Dirks, S., Keeling, M.: A vision of smarter cities: how cities can lead the way into a prosperous and sustainable future. IBM Inst. Bus. Value **8** (2009). https://pdfs.semanticscholar.org/e46b/641d546a348df63762b8ce79b23911568f36.pdf. Accessed 30 July 2019
6. Moss Kanter, R., Litow, S.S.: Informed and interconnected: a manifesto for smarter cities. Harv. Bus. Sch. Gen. Manage. Unit Work. Pap. (2009)
7. Muvuna, J., Mickovski, S.B., Boutaleb, T.: Information integration in a smart city system—a case study on air pollution removal by green infrastructure through a vehicle smart routing system. MDBI J. Sustain. **12**(12), 5099 (2020). https://doi.org/10.3390/su12125099
8. Jamshidi, M., Azgomi, H.: A brief survey on smart community and smart transportation. In: 2018 IEEE 30th International Conference on Tools with Artificial Intelligence (ICTAI), pp. 932–939 (2018). https://doi.org/10.1109/ICTAI.2018.00144
9. Anjum, S.S., Noor, R.M., Aghamohammadi, N., et al.: Modeling traffic congestion based on air quality for greener environment: an empirical study. IEEE Access **7**(99), 57100–57119 (2019). https://doi.org/10.1109/ACCESS.2019.2914672

10. Thibault, L., Pognant-Gros, P., Dégeilh, P., Voise, L.: Real-time air pollution exposure and vehicle emissions estimation using Iot, GNSS measurements and web-based simulation models. In: 2018 IEEE 88th Vehicular Technology Conference. pp. 1–5, August 2018. https://doi.org/10.1109/VTCFall.2018.8690622
11. Medina-De-La-Cruz, M., Mujaico-Mariano, A., Soto-Cordova, M.M.: Implementation of an evaluation system to measure air quality on public transport routes using the Internet of Things. In: 2018 Congreso Argentino de Ciencias de la Informática y Desarrollos de Investigación (CACIDI). pp. 1–4, IEEE Access, 2018. https://doi.org/10.1109/CACIDI.2018.8584346
12. Appio, F.P., Lima, M., Paroutis, S.: Understanding smart cities: innovation ecosystems, technological advancements, and societal challenges. Technol. Forecast. Soc. Change (2018)
13. Abhijith, K.V., Kumar, P.: Field investigations for evaluating green infrastructure effects on air quality in open-road conditions. Atmos. Environ. **201**, 132–147 (2019)
14. El Fazziki, A., Benslimane, D., Sadiq, A., Ouarzazi, J., Sadgal, M.: An agent based traffic regulation system for the roadside air quality control. IEEE Access **5**, 13192–13201 (2017). https://doi.org/10.1109/ACCESS.2017.2725984
15. Boriboonsomsin, K., Barth, M.J., Zhu, W., Vu, A.: Eco-routing navigation system based on multisource historical and real-time traffic information. IEEE Trans. Intell. Transp. Syst. **13**, 1694–1704 (2012)

Author Index

K. Kottursamy et al. (Eds.): IconDeepCom 2022, CCIS 1719, pp. 367–368, 2023.
https://doi.org/10.1007/978-3-031-27622-4

Printed in the United States
by Baker & Taylor Publisher Services